PUBLIC MANAGEMENT REFORM

Public Management Reform

A Comparative Analysis

Christopher Pollitt
and
Geert Bouckaert

OXFORD
UNIVERSITY PRESS

OXFORD

UNIVERSITY PRESS

Great Clarendon Street, Oxford OX2 6DP

Oxford University Press is a department of the University of Oxford.
It furthers the University's objective of excellence in research, scholarship,
and education by publishing worldwide in

Oxford New York

Athens Auckland Bangkok Bogotá Buenos Aires Calcutta
Cape Town Chennai Dar es Salaam Delhi Florence Hong Kong Istanbul
Karachi Kuala Lumpur Madrid Melbourne Mexico City Mumbai
Nairobi Paris São Paulo Singapore Taipei Tokyo Toronto Warsaw

with associated companies in Berlin Ibadan

Oxford is a registered trade mark of Oxford University Press
in the UK and in certain other countries

Published in the United States
by Oxford University Press Inc., New York

British Library Cataloguing in Publication Data

Data available

Library of Congress Cataloging-in-Publication Data

Pollitt, Christopher.
Public management reform: a comparative analysis/Christopher
Pollitt and Geert Bouckaert.
p. cm.
Includes bibliographical references and index.
1. Public administration. 2. Comparative government.
3. Organizational change. I. Bouckaert, Geert. II. Title.
JF1351.P665 2000 351—dc21 99–37269
ISBN 0 19 829596 0
ISBN 0 19 829722 X (pbk)

1 3 5 7 9 10 8 6 4 2

Typeset in Ehrhardt
by Cambrian Typesetters, Frimley, Surrey
Printed in Great Britain
on acid-free paper by
Biddles Ltd
Guildford & King's Lynn

For our parents,
Freda, John, Leen and Michel

Acknowledgements

Unsurprisingly, for a book of this scope, our debts are too numerous and go too far back in time for us adequately to acknowledge them all in a small space here. Thus we are, uncomfortably, obliged to be somewhat selective in our expressions of gratitude.

A first acknowledgement must go to our sheltering institutions, Brunel University in West London and the Katholieke Universiteit Leuven. Over the years they have supported our research efforts and, more specifically, enabled us to spend the 1997/98 academic year together at Leuven in order to accomplish the work that has led to this book. More recently, Erasmus University, Rotterdam, has become the new home of one of us, and has continued to encourage and facilitate this project.

A second acknowledgement is due to our network of colleagues and friends who share an interest in comparative public administration. Our citations make clear how extensively we have drawn on the work of others, but, in addition to the normal processes of benefiting from each other's publications, we have received a generous portion of informal assistance and comment from a number of individuals during the preparation of this text. We particularly wish to acknowledge Jonathan Breul, Maurice Demers, Jan-Eric Furubo, John Halligan, Sigurdur Helgasson, Jan-Coen Hellendoorn, Annie Hondeghem, Patricia Ingraham, Walter Kickert, Elke Löffler, Rudolf Maes, John Mayne, Nicole de Montricher, Guy B. Peters, Jon Pierre, Rune Premfors, Luc Rouban, Donald Savoie, David Shand, Hilkka Summa, Colin Talbot, Petri Uusikylä and Christel Vandeurzen.

Finally, we would like to acknowledge those organizations which have contributed—indirectly but significantly—to this book by being willing to fund serious empirical research into public management reform. In the age of the 'sound bite' and the 'packaged' management consultancy solution it takes some institutional courage to invest in the kind of time-consuming research which almost always reveals variety and complexity. As this book makes clear, however, if politicians' hopes, public money and civil servants' time are not to be wasted, such research is desperately needed. We therefore gratefully acknowledge the support we have at various times received from the Canadian Centre for Management Development, the Finnish Ministry of Finance, the Public Management Institute and the Research Council of the Katholieke Universiteit Leuven and the UK Economic and Social Research Council.

Christopher Pollitt
Geert Bouckaert

Contents

List of Tables

List of Figures

Abbreviations

APS	Australian Public Service
BPR	Business Process Re-engineering
CCT	Compulsory Competitive Tendering
DG	Directorate General (the main organizational division within the EU Commission and in a number of other continental European administrations)
The three 'E's'	Economy, Efficiency and Effectiveness
EFQM	European Foundation for Quality Management
EMS	Expenditure Management System (Canada)
EU	European Union
GAO	General Accounting Office (USA)
GDP	Gross Domestic Product
GPRA	Government Performance and Results Act (USA)
HRM	Human Resource Management
IMF	International Monetary Fund
KRA	Key Results Area (New Zealand)
MAP2000	Modernizing Administrative and Personnel Policy 2000 (EU Commission)
MbO	Management by Objectives
MP	Member of Parliament (UK)
MTM	Market-type Mechanism
NAO	National Audit Office (UK)
NHS	National Health Service (UK)
NPM	New Public Management
NPR	National Performance Review (USA)
OECD	Organization for Economic Co-operation and Development
PAR	Programme Analysis and Review (UK)
PEMS	Policy and Expenditure Management System (Canada)
PI	Performance Indicator
PPBS	Planning, Programming and Budgeting System (USA)
PUMA	Public Management Service of the OECD
Quango	Quasi Non-governmental Organization
RCB	Rationalisation des Choix Budgetaires (France)
SAI	Supreme Audit Institution (national audit office—their association is called the International Organization of Supreme Audit Institutions, or INTOSAI)
SEM2000	Sound and Efficient Management 2000 (EU Commission)
SES	Senior Executive Service
SIGMA	Support for Improvement in Governance and Management in

	Central and Eastern European Countries (a joint initiative of the OECD and the EU)
SOA	Special Operating Agency (Canada)
SRA	Strategic Results Area (New Zealand)
TQM	Total Quality Management
ZBB	Zero-based Budgeting (USA)
ZBO	Zelfstandige Bestuursorganen ('autonomous public bodies'—Netherlands)

Introduction

This is an ambitious book, aimed at remedying some perceived weaknesses in the current literature on public management reform. It is ambitious in several respects, most obviously in taking such a broad perspective (ten countries across three continents) and in attempting to compare such very different state apparatuses as those of Finland, France, New Zealand and the United States. However, we believe that a broad, comparative perspective is highly appropriate to our subject matter. The period since 1980 has witnessed a pandemic of public management reforms, which has swept across much of the OECD world. The working lives of millions of public officials have been substantially altered (and, in some tens of thousands of cases, prematurely terminated). The ways and means of managing vast public budgets have been reshaped. Large claims have been made for 'savings' and 'efficiency gains' (the inverted commas are deployed here to indicate that such concepts are seldom straightforward and uncontestable). In some countries huge quantities of previously publically owned assets have been sold to the private sector. The standards attained or aspired to by many service-providing agencies have come under unprecedented scrutiny. Millions of citizens in several countries have been offered 'charters', promising them improvements in the quality of the day-to-day services upon which they depend. The President of the most economically and militarily powerful nation state has announced that 'The era of big government is over' (Clinton, quoted in Gore, 1996, p. 1).

Changes—and claims—of this magnitude deserve close study and reflection. And there has, of course, been a considerable outpouring of reports, articles and books on public management. Many of these texts have been clarifying and enlightening. Some have also been theoretically creative, or methodologically ingenious (as our citations acknowledge). Yet much of the flow of management material displays fairly serious limitations. Some is openly envangelical, or energetically prescriptive, and could not be said to offer a detached or balanced analysis. Much is accurate and analytical but focused on one organization, or programme, or sector, or country. The number of genuinely comparative, multi-country studies is surprisingly modest and the whole field of comparative public administration and management has been seen by some well-informed commentators as being in the doldrums:

we need to ask more basic questions about administrative systems and the knowledge we need of them. Many of those questions are relational . . . we need to understand better how administration fits with the remainder of the political system and how it 'interfaces' with the social system (Peters, 1996a, p. 20).

Despite great surface similarity in civil service reform policy ideas and terms, there is little rigorous comparison of actual policy content (Ingraham, 1996, p. 262).

We would note one further limitation: much of the English literature has concentrated heavily on the Anglophone countries—those which have tended to 'to make the biggest noise' about the reforms they are undertaking. The Anglophone reader will tend to know considerably less about what has been happening recently in such countries as Germany and France, despite the prominent historical contribution which these states made to the development of modern public administration.

Taking these considerations into account, the present book aspires to contribute to the public management reform literature in a number of ways:

- By strengthening the field of comparative texts. There are rather few systematic comparisons of more than two countries. Those which exist tend to be edited collections rather than single, integrated works (though the edited *genre* includes some well-planned and highly informative works, especially Flynn and Strehl, 1996; Kickert, 1997; Lane, 1997). We have attempted to compare ten countries, and to say something about the EU Commission. Our selected countries are Australia, Canada, Finland, France, Germany, the Netherlands, New Zealand, Sweden, the UK and the USA.
- More particularly, by giving full attention to countries such as Germany and France, which have not participated so enthusiastically in the vogue for the 'New Public Management' (NPM) which has swept the Anglophone world.
- By integrating the study of management change with an analysis of political systems and contexts. We share the view put forward by Peters (1996a) and others that management changes in the public sector cannot be satisfactorily understood as some set of free-floating, generic phenomena. Instead they require to be interpreted as one element in a broader shift in the pattern of political problems and responses. In short, public management is always a part of the broader agenda of public governance.
- By developing explicit models and taxonomies of management reform and thus (we hope) enhancing a literature that is frequently untheoretical and primarily descriptive.
- By assessing the available evidence as to the *results* of the reforms in each country. What do we reliably know about the consequences of the huge administrative upheavals of the last two decades?
- By reflecting more generally upon what can reasonably be *expected* of management reform—its potential but also its in-built limitations as a means for improving democratic governance.

The book has been structured in such a way as closely to reflect the above aspirations. Chapter 1 sets out our basic understanding of the nature of public management reform. It asks what kinds of activities are involved, who is affected, what the main concepts in play appear to be and where the boundaries can be drawn between management reforms and other kinds of changes. In setting out our position on these matters we refer to some of the more problematic aspects of the subject, noting the existence of significant controversies as to the scope and nature of public management.

Chapter 2 then presents a model of management reform. It begins by identifying the stimuli which appear to have provoked the wave of management changes referred to above. What are the problems which have prompted politicians and civil servants to reach for the instruments of administrative modernization and change? How have these perceived problems interacted with the main flows of ideas, the play of political interest and power, and movements of popular opinion to generate specific agendas for reform? What constraints and distortions may have influenced the extent to which these agendas have been implemented? Our basic argument is that the construction of a broad model or menu of the chief ingredients is both useful and possible, even though countries may have combined and cooked these ingredients in very different ways.

While chapter 2 establishes a common conceptual vocabulary for the discussion of management reform, chapter 3 is more concerned with *differences* between our ten countries, and also with the unique character of the EU Commission. It develops a taxonomy of regime types and locates each state within this scheme. In some cases the very possibility of management change may be less than in others—at least in the short-term—because of constitutional, political or institutional features specific to the country or sector concerned. As Peters opined in the quotation above, many of the basic issues for public administration turn out to be *relational*. For example, in the 1980s a British prime minister abolished the local authority responsible for governing the capital city, whereas in Finland or Sweden, constitutionally and polit-ically, a prime minister simply could not make a change of that kind. Or again, rela-tions between the political elite and the civil service elite—which are crucial for management reform—vary significantly between countries. In France the two elites are thoroughly inter-penetrating ('mandarins' frequently become ministers, for example) while in Canada or the UK the two groups are largely separate.

Chapter 4 uses the concept of a 'trajectory' to describe the varying combinations of ideas, actions and inactions which particular states have adopted. As chapter 3 will have established, there is a sense in which each country begins its trajectory in a different place and therefore travels across a somewhat different terrain, even if two or more countries are ultimately aiming at roughly similar objectives. For each trajectory, however, it is possible to apply some general tests, for example, how coherent is the trajectory? Are reforms in the areas of, say, finance, personnel, and organizational structure mutually consistent and reinforcing? Are some areas or sectors left outside the reform process altogether? Are there strong guiding ideas and rhetorics or is there a more fragmented, *ad hoc* approach?

Having described the main trajectories in chapter 4, chapter 5 moves on to look for evidence of the results of reform. First, it is necessary to give some considera-tion to what we are going to count as a 'result' and how different kinds of impact may be conceptualized. When this ground has been cleared we move to ask what we know about what has been achieved, and how secure our knowledge is. Here we draw on various different types of data. The OECD and other international bodies provide some macro-comparative data, such as trends in public expenditure and changes in the size of the civil service in different countries. By itself, however, this kind of data poses almost as many questions as it answers, and so it is necessary to go deeper, to examine particular countries, to take into account specific evaluations and to interpret changing rhetorics. In some ways there is a remarkable absence of 'hard', 'scientific' data (Pollitt, 1995). In other ways one *can* begin to construct a picture, though only by carefully weighing and combining different types of evidence generated by different investigators pursuing different purposes. This is what chapter 5 seeks to accomplish.

Chapters 4 and 5 particularly (though also other parts of the book) are supported by tabulated factual and chronological material on each country, and on the European Commission, presented in Appendix A. Readers are invited to refer to this *corpus* of material as they go through the book. We have done our best to make it accurate and up-to-date, but, equally, we recognize that any such selection is bound to leave out some items that others will consider to be of importance (as well as unwittingly including errors or challengeable interpretations). As we hope to revise the book from time to time, we would welcome readers' correspondence on such issues—or, indeed, on anything else between these covers.

After chapter 5 we turn to a different kind of activity. Instead of modelling, identifying and categorizing public management reforms, we move to a more reflective interpretation of the record of the past two decades. Chapter 6 considers the implications of management reform for politicians and political roles. Some versions of the NPM, for instance, appear to envisage the politicians of the future principally as strategy-makers and definers of guiding values, who will leave operational matters to cadres of performance-oriented professional managers. But are most politicians—or political systems—attuned to such a role? Are they well-equipped as strategists? Do they even *want* to stay on the high ground and deny themselves the pleasures of delving into detail? In an era in which the scope for launching grand new programmes appears to have diminished, and during a time when many indicators seem to show a decline in the public's confidence in governments—and when media pressures are more intense than ever—what advantages and disadvantages do politicians see in involving themselves in management reform?

If chapter 6 partly takes the perspective of the politician, looking at public administrative organizations from 'above' or 'outside', chapter 7 examines some of the same issue from 'inside' or 'below'. It raises the issue of the limits of administration (Hood, 1976; Pressman and Wildavsky, 1973)—what can we reasonably expect from management improvements: 'citizen empowerment' (as some would have it) or merely shorter queues? There may be logical, categorical and/or economic reasons why management improvements are often bound to have the character of a trade-off or a marginal rebalancing of awkward alternatives rather than a 'great leap forward'. Furthermore, our state of knowledge about effective institutional design is probably less scientific and more proverb-like than we usually care to admit (Goodin, 1996; Hood and Jackson, 1991; Simon, 1946). There is at least some evidence to suggest that certain types of reform contain the seeds of their own decay. Consider the setting-up of decentralized, single-purpose delivery agencies—a popular reform in a number of countries, including Canada, the Netherlands, New Zealand and the UK. These new organizations were created in the name of debureaucratization, increased productivity and greater user-responsiveness. However, after a few years, concern grew about the 'flip side' of these virtues, namely loss of co-ordination, overconcentration on output targets rather than overall effectiveness and reduced accountability to ministers and/or Parliaments. Another example would be the efforts to strengthen the individual incentives for better performance by civil servants and to promote entrepreneur-ialism, which in some cases have led to concerns about the divisiveness of perfor-mance-related pay schemes and claims that there is a need to enhance trust and re-establish certain ethical standards among the same civil servants (e.g. Boston *et al.*, 1996, pp. 327–32; Chapman, 1998; Kernaghan, 1997). Is it possible that some public management initiatives end up, in practice, in circling round administrative dilemmas rather than solving administrative problems?

In the final chapter (8) we briefly return to the 'big questions' about the role of public management within the evolving framework of democratic governance. Has the international experience of the last twenty years generated reliable knowledge from which to draw 'lessons for the future'? This is a suitably speculative note on which to conclude.

1

The Nature of Public Management Reform

1.1 Why public management reform?

Public management reform is usually thought of as a means to an end, not an end in itself. To be more precise we should perhaps say that it is potentially a means to *multiple* ends. These include making *savings* (economies) in public expenditure, improving the *quality* of public services, making the operations of government more *efficient* and increasing the chances that the policies which are chosen and implemented will be *effective*. On the way to achieving these important objectives, public management reform may also serve a number of *intermediate* ends, including those of strengthening the control of politicians over the bureaucracy, freeing public officials from bureaucratic constraints which inhibit their opportunities to manage and enhancing the government's accountability to the legislature and the citizenry for its policies and programmes. Last, but not least, one should mention the *symbolic and legitimacy benefits* of management reform. For politicians these benefits consist partly of being seen to be doing something. Announcing reforms, criticizing bureaucracy, praising new management techniques, promising improved services for the future, restructuring ministries and agencies—all these activities help to attract favourable attention to the politicians who espouse them. A cynic might observe that, in these days when the power of individual governments to act independently is increasingly called into question by a complex interplay of local, national and international constraints, the one thing that ministers usually *can* do—with the appearance of dynamism but at little immediate cost—is to announce changes in their own machinery of governance. There are also legitimacy benefits for those senior officials who, almost invariably, play important parts in shaping and implementing such initiatives. They may gain in reputation by association with 'modernizing' and 'streamlining' activities.

If management reform really does produce cheaper, more efficient government, with higher-quality services and more effective programmes, and if it will simultaneously enhance political control, free managers to manage, make government more transparent and boost the images of those ministers and mandarins most involved, then it is little wonder that it has been widely trumpeted. Unfortunately, however, matters are not so simple. There is a good deal of evidence to show that management reforms can go wrong. They may fail to produce the claimed benefits. They may even generate perverse effects that render the relevant administrative processes worse (in some important senses) than they were previously. When a local authority 'home help' (domestic care) service for elderly and disabled people is reshaped along quasi-market lines, with a split between the authority purchasing the service and the staff providing it, we may consider this a typical 'reform'. When, however, we discover that the contract drawn up for the service is 700 pages long, and that the actual service provided seems to have changed very little in either quality or quantity, then doubt sets in. We wonder if more *trust* between the parties concerned might not be a more efficient option, enabling a much shorter contract (or no contract at all) and radically reduced monitoring costs.

Furthermore, even if a particular reform clearly 'succeeds' in respect of one or two of the objectives mentioned above (savings, say, and an improvement in quality) it is unlikely that it will succeed in all. Indeed, we shall argue later that certain trade-offs and dilemmas are exceedingly common in administrative change, so that the achievement of one or two particular ends might well be 'paid for' by a lowered performance in other respects: 'rule over specialised decision-makers in a bureaucracy is maintained by selective crackdowns on one goal at a time, steering the equilibrium—without ever acknowledging that tightening up on one criterion implies slackening off on another' (Dunsire, 1993, p. 29). For example, if we subject public servants to more effective political supervision and control, can we simultaneously gift them greater freedom and flexibility to manage? The optimists will say yes, by laying down a clearer, simpler framework of rules within which managers can 'get creative'. The sceptic will say no, pointing to survey evidence that the managers themselves think that political 'interference' has *increased* and arguing that it is unrealistic to expect politicians to 'leave well alone' in politically sensitive operations such as social security, health care, education or the prison service.

In any case, public management reform is only one way to achieve most of the desirable ends identified in the first paragraph. To be adequate, any account of its nature will need to take into account that governmental performance can be improved by a variety of routes and that management reform is frequently undertaken in conjunction with other types of policy initiative. Comparing administrative developments in a number of countries one academic observed recently: 'Administrative reform . . . is a subset of *all* policy performance, not a separable set of technical efforts' (Ingraham, 1997, p. 326, original emphasis).

Other routes to improved government performance include *political reforms* (such as changes in electoral systems or legislative procedures) and substantive *changes in key policies* (such as new macroeconomic management policies, labour market reforms or fundamental changes in social policy). The example of New Zealand—which combined management reforms with fundamental changes in both macroeconomic policies and, later, the electoral system—was alluded to in our introduction.

To make matters more complicated still, there is, as many commentators have noticed, a delay which affects a good deal of public management reform. The full benefits of major changes in the processes and structures of public agencies normally cannot be harvested until three, four, five or even more years after a reform programme has been launched. To begin with, new legislation might well be needed. Then it will be necessary to analyze the status quo, and subsequently to design, formulate and refine new operating procedures, train staff how to work with them, define new roles and the appropriate reward and appraisal systems, set new measurement systems in place, inform service users and other stakeholders, and work hard to reduce the anxiety all these novelties have probably caused, both among users and among staff. But this is not the kind of timescale that most senior politicians are comfortable with. Their focus is more intensely short-term: on the next election, the next government reshuffle, or even today's television news. The searchlight of political attention moves about from one issue to another much more quickly than complex organizational change can be accomplished. This has always been the case (Pollitt, 1984, pp. 148–9) but the discrepancy between the politician's need for 'something to show now' and the organization reformer's need for time, commitment and continuity has probably grown as a result of the general intensification and acceleration of the political process in many western democracies.

1.2 What is public management reform?

But what *is* public management reform? As with all definitional questions, this can be answered in a number of different ways. As a first approximation we could say that *public management reform consists of deliberate changes to the structures and processes of public sector organizations with the objective of getting them (in some sense) to run better.* Structural change may include merging or splitting public sector organizations (creating a smaller number of big departments to improve co-ordination or a larger number of smaller departments to sharpen focus and encourage specialization). Process change may include the redesign of the systems by which applications for licences or grants or passports are handled, the setting of quality standards for health care or educational services to citizens or the introduction of new budgeting procedures which encourage public servants to be more cost conscious and/or to monitor more closely the results their expenditures generate. Management reform frequently also embraces changes to the systems by which public servants themselves are recruited, trained, appraised, promoted, disciplined and declared redundant—these would be another kind of process change.

This way of describing what public management reform is is helpful, if not very sophisticated. Chapters 3, 4 and 5 will discuss the specifics of structures and processes in a range of countries and in the European Commission. However, it is not the only way of approaching the question of definition. The relevant literature offers a number of more analytical or synoptic definitions, and it is worth exploring some of these, if only to get a feel for the breadth of current thinking on this issue. There are at least two components to our definitional enquiry, namely 'public management' and 'reform'. We will deal first with public management:

1. 'Public management is a merger of the normative orientation of traditional public administration and the instrumental orientation of general management' (Perry and Kraemer, 1983, p. x).
2. 'The field of public management is better defined analytically than institutionally. No

clear institutional dictinction can be drawn . . . The critical area of public management is the management of organizational interdependence, for example, in the delivery of services or in the management of the budgetary process. Public management is concerned with the effective functioning of whole systems of organizations . . . What distinguishes public management is the explicit acknowledgement of the responsibility for dealing with structural problems at the level of the system as a whole' (Metcalfe and Richards, 1987, pp. 73–5).

3. 'We conceive public administration as the key output linkage of the state towards civil society. However, the interface between public administration and civil society is a two-way street, including public policy implementation as well as policy demands from private actors towards policy-makers' (Pierre, 1995, p. ix).

4. 'We talk about the *managerial* state because we want to locate managerialism as a cultural formation and a distinctive set of ideologies and practices which form one of the underpinnings of an emergent political settlement' (Clarke and Newman, 1997, p. ix).

5. 'Public administration may be interpreted as a social system existing and functioning in accordance with its own order but, on the other hand, it also depends on environ-mental conditions in a complex and changing society'. Also: 'In the light of the modern society's functional differentiation, state and market are notable for their own character-istic strategies to control the supply of goods. The type, scope and distribution of private goods are decided on by harmonising the individual preferences within the market mechanism; decisions on the production of public goods, on the other hand, result from a collective, i.e. politico-administrative, development of objectives' (König, 1996, pp. 4, 59).

The above quotations reflect a range of views not only on the extent of the field of public management, but on its nature and on the most appropriate strategy for conceiving and defining that nature. All five are broad, but in different ways. The first, from a pair of American scholars, relates the nature of public management to certain specific developments in the organization of the field as an academic subject. During the 1970s and 1980s the teaching of public management in the USA (and to some extent in the UK—Pollitt, 1996a) tended to migrate from university departments of political science to business schools or other business-related units where 'management' was regarded as a generic subject (how to manage anything). Generic management studies tend to be fairly functional/ instrumental in orientation: management is about getting things done as quickly, cheaply and effectively as possible—and usually about getting things done through other people ('staff', 'the work force', 'personnel', 'human resources'). The study of public administration, by contrast, although sharing a concern with effective-ness, was typically also focused on 'public sector values' such as democracy, accountability, equity and probity. Hence the proposed purpose for the field of public management studies, as being 'to develop an understanding of how public, primarily governmental, organizations may accomplish the missions charged to them' (Perry and Kraemer, 1983, p. xi). Note that the field of public management is seen here as being relatively new. There does not seem to be much use of the term before the 1970s, and 'public administration' is still preferred as the title for the leading academic journals in the UK and the USA. Interestingly, both journals accommodated the new trend by acquiring fresh section headings: 'Public Management Forum' for the American *Public Administration Review* and 'Public Management' as a part of the British *Public Administration*. Significantly, the leading French journal, *Revue Française de l'Administration Publique*, did not go down this road, and, more generally, in France, Germany and the Nordic countries, scholars continue to translate the title of their field of study as 'public administration' or 'administrative science' far more frequently than as 'public management' (e.g. Ahonen and Salminen, 1997; Derlien, 1998; König, 1996; Premfors, 1998; Trosa, 1995).

To return to the Perry and Kraemer account, here public management consists, in effect, of a benign merger between generic (overwhelmingly commercial, private sector) management and the more traditional concerns of public administration. The concern for democratic values is fully retained but the enterprise is given a sharper cutting edge in terms of risk-taking, flexibility, performance measurement and goal achievement. Thus construed, public management sounds unobjectionable, indeed 'bland' (Gunn, 1987, p. 35). Much depends, however, on just how compatible the different components which have been integrated to produce this middle-of-the-road vehicle actually are. Hood (1991), for one, has questioned whether the values of the 'new public management' (hereafter NPM) are easily combined with those of traditional public administration. He argues that *in practice* NPM has meant great stress being placed on 'sigma-type values' (efficiency, matching resources to clear goals) but points out that, even if it were to be proved beyond reasonable doubt that such values had been realized in practice, 'it remains to be fully investigated whether such successes are bought at the expense of honesty and fair dealing ['theta' values] and/or of security and resilience [lambda values]' (Hood, 1991, p. 16; see also Hood and Jackson, 1991).

The definition offered by Metcalfe and Richards (definition 2) is very different from that of Perry and Kraemer. It deals not so much in values as in processes. It is, in effect, an argument that there are certain processes which are unique to the public sector, and that these constitute the core of public management. The processes in question are those of managing whole sets of organizations, rather than a single organization, and of attempting to adjust the structure of the entire system of public governance. In a later paper Metcalfe expands on this theme, writing: 'The innovative task of public management as a macro process is to develop new and quite distinctive *macro-organizational* capacities to deal with structural change at the interorganizational level' (Metcalfe, 1993, p. 183).

By contrast, the task of public management at lower levels is seen as 'imitative'—that of adapting business or other management ideas to improve the micro-organizational abilities of governments. This is in many ways an ingenious line of argument. It draws attention to the limits of generic management ideas and the existence of unique, 'higher order' functions which, if they are to be tackled at all, must be tackled by the public sector. These functions have also attracted the neologism 'governance' , although that term is sometimes used in a loose way and is made to cover many issues that Metcalfe and Richards would probably deem 'micro-organizational'. Goodin (1996, p. 13) indicates the breadth of scope that some of those using the term lay claim to: 'Governance . . . is nothing less than the steering of society by officials in control of what are organizationally the "commanding heights" of society'. Indeed, 'steering' or 'guidance' are the preferred terms across much of continental Europe (see, e.g., Kaufmann, Majone and Ostrom, 1985; König, 1996). In these 'systems' approaches the boundaries between individual institutions become less significant than the question of how the whole ensemble dances (or fails to dance) together. It is a perspective within which the conventional boundaries between politics and administration are perhaps less significant, and which enables large social questions to be approached more directly than from within the narrower perspective of traditional public administration. The main boundaries are not so much institutional as between larger systems which operate according to different principles of guidance, such as the market economy, civil society and—of immense importance within the continental European approach but much less so within the Anglo-American world—the state.

Unfortunately, the Metcalfe and Richards definition of public management also has some significant drawbacks. In this book we are committed to try to integrate theory and empirical evidence. Empirically, a huge amount of the change that has taken place under the banner of 'public management reform' has been, in Metcalfe's terms, micro-organizational. Most public managers do not spend their time designing 'macro-organizational capacities to deal with structural change at the interorganizational level'—the latter is a task which usually falls to a relatively small number of elite *hauts fonctionnaires*. Therefore wholeheartedly to adopt the Metcalfe and Richards approach would be to exclude a large slice of our intended subject matter—and to use the term 'public management' in a much more restrictive and specialized sense than do most public servants and politicians. This is not to deny the claim that there are certain high level, structural adjustment functions that fall mainly to governments and have no close parallel in the world of commerce. It is simply to say that much of the discourse of public management reform treats with less elevated problems, and that we wish to include this more mundane territory within our scope too. Indeed, we would go further and suggest that the nature of the high level, 'macro' functions have an influence on micro-level operations (one might remark that it would be strange if they did not) and therefore micro-level operations also often have a degree of distinctiveness in the public sector.

There are also issues of interpretation around Metcalfe and Richard's use of the terms *structural, system* and *responsibility*. What does it mean to take responsibility for structural problems across a system? Systems are often collections of organizations with differing bases of power and legitimacy (European Union institutions for example). Is it possible for any person, group or even institution to 'take responsibility' for such an entity? And, if it is not, how is democratic accountability for steering the system supposed to be articulated? Furthermore, how are we to distinguish between 'structural' problems and other kinds of problem?

The third definition clearly denotes a field of much greater scope than high level 'macro-organizational capacities'. Pierre employs a conventional political science division of society into two spheres—the state and civil society. Public administration (not 'management', note) is then the buckle that joins these two. It is an 'output linkage' (i.e., it serves to transmit information and resources from the state to civil society), but it is also an 'input linkage' (because it delivers demands from actors in civil society back to the state). Again, this is a definition which makes a useful point, reminding the reader that public administration is a 'two-way street', and that, far from being just a technical exercise in achieving the best value for money, it is an instrument of state power. Indeed, Pierre goes on to identify the type of relationship which obtains between political career patterns and administrative careers as one of the key variables in determining the character of public administration (Pierre, 1995, p. 208).

By describing public administration as an 'output linkage' Pierre is also invoking the input/process/output/outcome model that is very widely used in both the study and practice of public management. Indeed, its usage has become so ingrained that it is worth making a short detour at this point in order properly to establish the model and explicate the sense in which we intend to deploy its key terms.

Our own usage will be fairly mainstream. We propose that the input/output model can be applied at various different levels. Pierre uses it at a very high level of generality, taking the entire apparatus of public administration as his unit of analysis—the 'thing' that produces the output. More commonly the input/output model is applied to programmes (e.g., health care, job creation, road construction) or to individual institutions or organizations (the Inland Revenue, the Driver and Vehicle Testing Agency). It assumes that institutions and/or programmes are set up to address some specific socio-economic need(s). They establish *objectives* concerned with these needs, and acquire *inputs* (staff, buildings, resources) with which to conduct activities in pursuit of those objectives. *Processes* are then those activities which take place inside institutions, in order to generate outputs. Processes would thus include, for example, teaching in a school or recording and labelling within a warehouse. The *outputs* are the products of these processes— what the institution 'delivers' to the outside world (academic qualifications, school reports or, in the warehouse case, issued stock). These outputs then interact with the environment (especially with those individuals and groups at whom they are specifically aimed) leading to 'results' and, in the longer term, more fundamental 'impacts' (students getting jobs and achieving competence within them, or stock items being used by their purchasers). Both results and impacts may be termed *outcomes* (results are sometimes called 'intermediate outcomes' and impacts 'final outcomes'). Ultimately the *value* of both the processes and the outputs rest on the outcomes. The relationships between these key terms are summarized in Figure 1.1.

To return to Pierre's definition, he does not use the term 'management' at all, though it is clear that many of the developments he is describing and analysing are

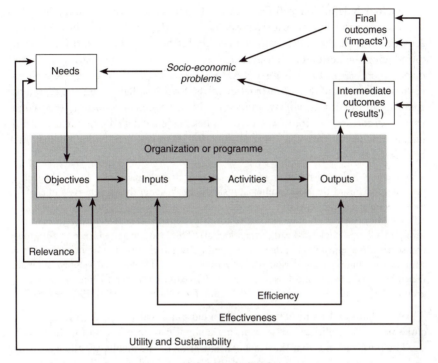

FIG. 1.1. The input/output model

what other writers have referred to as 'managerialism' (Pollitt, 1993) or the 'NPM' (Hood, 1991 and many subsequent publications). 'Management' can be seen as a new way of conducting the business of the state, occupying much of the same territory as traditional 'administration' but differing in style and emphasis (Dunleavy and Hood, 1994). This progressive replacement of 'administration' by 'management' was noted and described as early as 1972 by the English civil servant Desmond Keeling. He characterized the differences between the two as follows:

Administration: 'the review, in an area of public life, of law, its enforcement and revision; and decision-making on cases in that area submitted to the public service.'

Management: 'the search for the best use of resources in pursuit of objectives subject to change' (Keeling, 1972).

Of course, not all activity by public servants—not the whole of the 'output linkage'—becomes wholly 'managerialized'. Nor are Keeling's two types absolutely pure—administrators need to keep an eye on efficiency and policy objectives, just as managers cannot ignore the law in their pursuit of optimal resource use. But Keeling captured a real and enduring difference of emphasis, and one that we will need to revisit later in the book, particularly when we examine the *Rechtsstaat* regime in Germany and the French system of administrative law and control.

The fourth definition is different again. In one sense it is closer to the first than the second or third, in that it stresses ideas and values rather than institutions or activities. Yet Clarke and Newman go much further than Perry and Kraemer by introducing the notion of managerialism as an *ideology* and by relating the rise of management ideas to a distinct *political settlement* (in their case, the political realignments around the reconstruction of the British welfare state). To regard the concepts and values which have guided public management reform in many countries as an ideology is not new. One of us has made a detailed case for the usefulness of this perspective elsewhere (Pollitt, 1993). In this context an ideology may be defined as follows:

The essential characteristics of an ideology are, first, that it consists of values and beliefs or ideas about states of the world and what it should be. Second, these cognitive and affective elements form a framework. In other words, ideology is not simply a summation of a set of attitudes, but consists of some kind of relatively systematic structuring (though the structuring may be psychological rather than logical). Third, ideologies concern social groups and social arrangements—in other words, politics in its widest sense of being concerned with the distribution and ordering of resources. Fourth, an ideology is developed and maintained by social groups, and thus is a socially-derived link between the individual and the group . . . Fifth, ideology provides a justification for behaviour (Hartley, 1983, pp. 26–7).

The fact that Clarke and Newman make a close link between ideologies, practices and a particular political 'settlement' has a significant implication for their analysis. The implication is that the exact configuration of the ideology—the weightings and emphases as between its particular themes and values—will vary somewhat from one country (and even from one organization) to another. This is because the 'penetration' of the ideology will be influenced by whatever are the prevailing local political forces—the kind of political 'starting point' from which the spread of new ideas and practices begins. In fact this is precisely what we shall be arguing at greater length later in the book.

The fifth and final definition comes from a distinguished German scholar. We should note that he envisages 'public administration' as a system which works according to a distinctive set of principles ('its own order') but yet is influenced by developments in the society in which it is embedded. Its distinctiveness is the result of a more general process of 'functional differentiation' which is universally characteristic of modern societies. The particular quality which defines this state system is that its outputs (decisions, services, goods) are produced according to priorities set by the politico-administrative system rather than by the impersonal forces of the economic market, or by the relational affinities and obligations of civil society. Furthermore, these priorities can ultimately be backed up by the state's monopoly of the legitimate use of force and coercion. This approach therefore stresses the *distinctiveness* of public administration and the uniqueness of the state as a separate sphere of institutional activity, albeit one that is influenced by developments in civil society and economic markets.

We can now look back over the five definitions and draw out some general points. Our aim in doing this is not to arrive at a single, stipulative definition of what public management *really* is. That kind of semantic imperialism is very much out of fashion after the 'linguistic' or 'argumentative' 'turn' in so many social science disciplines (Fischer and Forester, 1993). However, what a comparison of definitions can achieve is a better appreciation of the varying meanings and the multiple dimensions of the concept in question. In short one can grasp *how* the terms 'public management' and 'public administration' are currently used, and what basic assumptions lie behind particular usages.

First, it is clear that the term 'public management' may be used in at least three main senses. It may denote the *activity* of public servants and politicians. Or it may be used to refer to the *structures and processes* of executive government (e.g., to the use of a technique such as Total Quality Management or results-oriented budgeting). Or, finally, it may mean the *systematic study* of either activities or structures and processes. The older term 'public administration' was also used in each of these three ways (Pollitt, 1996b). In this book we will be concentrating on the first two meanings for 'public management' and making only tangential references to its status as a field of systematic academic and professional study.

Second, it is equally clear that public *management* is often seen as a new kind of activity, and is contrasted with the older form, public *administration*. It is regarded as a symptom of modernization—a dynamic force for change. Thus it can act as a legitimizing label for those politicians and public officials who wish to identify themselves with the 'forces of progress'. Here is the American Vice President, Al Gore:

President Clinton and I are just as proud of making government work better as we are of making it smaller. It isn't good enough yet, or small enough yet, but we sure have things headed in the right direction (Gore, 1996, p. 4).

Our stance towards these aspects of public management could be described as 'sceptically open-minded'. In other words we doubt whether most of the ideas behind (for example) the NPM are quite as new as some of their more enthusiastic proponents claim (see also Hood and Jackson, 1991; Hood, 1998). Furthermore, we regard the matter of 'making government work better' (or even smaller) as quite a complicated one, requiring some discussion of whose values and perspectives are being adopted and what kind of evidence is on offer. While we are perfectly well convinced that real benefits have been secured in certain specific circumstances we doubt whether this can validly be enlarged into more sweeping claims of 'better government' on a large and unqualified scale. This is hardly the first time that the strength of the case for the benefits of managerialism has been questioned (Foster and Plowden, 1996; Hood, 1991; König, 1996; Pollitt, 1995; Wright, 1997).

Third, the relationship between *public* management and *generic* management is a contested one. Almost all writers about public management reform (including ourselves) acknowledge that, in many countries, the last twenty years have witnessed extensive borrowing by public sectors of management ideas and techniques which originated in the commercial sector. However, how far this has been 'a good thing', and how far it should go, are much debated. Some think it should go further, others that it has already gone too far (of course, both views could be valid if commercial techniques 'fit' some parts of the public sector but not others). The positions taken by commentators range from the proposition that public administration is a unique and separate field and that it should not be sullied by 'the methods of commerce' to the diametric opposite, that is, that business methods and a business culture are the solution to a wide range of pathologies which are said to be endemic in traditional public administration (Gunn, 1987). The Metcalfe and Richards definition fell somewhere between these two extremes, suggesting that at a micro level public administration might have much to imitate from the world of business, but that at the macro level it was *sui generis.* Our own position is also 'in between', but not in exactly the same sense. We argue that the applicability and appropriateness of business-derived approaches vary not only with the *level* (macro/micro) but also with the technical and political characteristics of the activity in question (Clarke and Newman, 1997, pp. 99–101; Lane, 1997, p. 307; Pollitt, 1998a; Stewart, 1992). (There is also, of course, a skill factor: even if political and technical characteristics are favourable to the introduction of a technique of business origin, the implementor may lack the necessary skills and 'make a mess of it'.)

Fourth, all five of the definitions remind us, in different ways, that management is not some neutral, technical process, but rather an activity which is intimately and indissolubly enmeshed with politics, law and the wider civil society. It is suffused with value-laden choices and influenced by broader ideologies.

Having dealt with 'public management' we can now turn to the other term in our title—'reform'.

In English we are conscious that 'reform' is only one among a congeries of alternative and competitor terms (including, significantly, several from the business world, such as 'transformation' and 'reinvention', as well as others with a longer public sector history, such as 'modernization' and 'improvement'). Like all these other words, 'reform' is a 'loaded' term, in the sense that it strongly implies not just change but *beneficial* change—a deliberate move from a less desirable (past) state to a more desirable (future) state. We accept this as an appropriate characterization of the intentions of many of those who pushed for management improvements, while always holding open the possibility that the actual effects of change could be experienced as less rather than more desirable by any or all of the main 'players'. Thus our use of the term should not be interpreted as a sign that we are believers in inevitable improvement, progress or 'evolutionism'.

In addition we are aware that 'reform' is a term with deep roots in the politics of improvement. English schoolboys have for many decades been required to study the 'great reform acts' of the nineteenth century (acts which successively extended the Parliamentary franchise). However, nowadays 'reform' does not carry the sense of rapid, across-the-board change which is conveyed by the American 'transformation' or, possibly to a slightly lesser extent, by 'reinvention'. Nor does it seem to convey quite the dynamism which continental European states have invested in the term 'modernization' (König, 1996, pp. 75–6.). In short, it has become a more sober, yet still explicitly political term. It refers not to total innovation, but to the reshaping of something which is already there (*re*form). We find this particularly appropriate because, as will become apparent in later chapters, it seems to us that the outcomes of many management reforms have very much depended upon the nature of the administrative–political systems in which they have taken place. It is also useful to bear in mind that reforms may be classified as more or less fundamental in character: 'At the most basic level we find adaptation and fine-tuning of accepted practices. The second order extends to the adoption of techniques. The third is concerned with sets of ideas which comprise the overall goals, the framework guiding action' (Halligan, 1997, p. 19).

Certain prominent contemporary sociologists see continuous 'reform' as a central feature of modern life, contrasting with the pre-modern emphasis on holding fast to (largely unexamined) traditions: 'The reflexivity of modern social life consists in the fact that social practices are constantly re-examined and reformed in the light of incoming information about those very practices, thus constitutively altering their character' (Giddens, 1990, p. 38).

Thus one might say that the structures and processes of public administration are constantly being revised in the light of fresh information about how things are going. Yet, put as baldly as this, the proposition sounds too straightforwardly empirical and far too crudely functional. We share the view expressed by many commentators to the effect that the 'incoming information' is not necessarily at all straightforward, and neither is the way in which it is interpreted and acted upon:

Policy reforms are . . . symbolically mediated change processes which can be understood only if we uncover the action-motivating reasons that guide efforts to alleviate practical problems . . . Claims about policy reforms are products of frames of reference; that is, they are systematically related assumptions that provide standards for appraising knowledge claims (Dunn, 1993, pp. 259, 270).

Thus it would be inadequate to conceive of reforms as simply a string of connected actions. If they are to be understood then they must also be considered as processes of debate to which different participants may bring, first, different objectives (including the achievement of symbolic purposes) and, second, different frameworks and standards for identifying and accepting relevant 'evidence'.

To conclude, if we return to our original, working definition of public management reform, we can see that, with some important qualifications and elaborations, it will still serve our present purposes. We proposed that public management reform had to do with *deliberate changes to the structures and processes of public sector organizations with the objective of getting them (in some sense) to perform better.* To this we now need to add that:

- Such deliberate changes are informed by specific sets of ideas, some of which have the characteristics of ideologies, and which merit study in their own right.
- Such ideas may be more or less well-specified, more or less adequate for their purposes. Success at getting things to run better should be tested rather than assumed.
- Changes are likely to be influenced by the actors at both ends of the 'output linkage'

between the state and civil society, that is, by politicians and civil servants at one end and by private actors (citizens), but also those with an economic interest such as management consultants and big corporations, at the other. (It is remarkable how the powerful corporate players that in practice dominate so many Washington lobbies have disappeared almost entirely from the account of government–citizen relations conveyed by the American bestseller on public management reform, *Reinventing government* (Osborne and Gaebler, 1992)).

- Thus the management reforms in any particular country will almost certainly be shaped by the local preoccupations and priorities of the politicians and private actors most concerned. These local frames of reference are likely to vary a good deal. The successful application of a single template for reform right across the globe (or even across the liberal democracies of Western Europe, North America and Australasia) is therefore inherently improbable.

- Reforms occur at different levels and may be of broader or lesser scope. A useful distinction is made by Halligan (1997, p. 19). He classifies reforms as *first order*—the adaptation and tuning of accepted practices—*second order*—the adoption of new techniques—and *third order*—changes in the sets of ideas which comprise overall goals and the frameworks which guide action. This book will be mainly concerned with second and third order reforms.

- 'To run better' may mean different things to different individuals and groups, and improving performance on one dimension or against one objective may lead (intentionally or unintentionally) to a lower performance in other dimensions.

- As well as seeking evidence about substantive performance improvement, we need to pay attention to the legitimation aspects of management reforms. Simply announcing, discussing and beginning to implement reforms may bring benefits to some politicians and public servants, even if the later, more 'substantive' effects are elusive or counterproductive.

- The very language of change—'reform', 'transformation', 're-engineering', 'modernization'—is suffused with assumptions about the speed, nature and value of what is being described or represented. In analysing management texts there is a need carefully to identify who is speaking and who is the intended audience, and to remember that frames of reference shift over time and that the meanings of words are slippery and variable. This is obviously true when moving from one language to another. For example, Finnish has no exact equivalent for the English 'public management', and even the French *gestion publique* carries somewhat different connotations. However, these linguistic slippages also occur *within the same language* as words are transferred from one context and group to another.

- Furthermore, once the rhetoric of managerial improvement has gained hold it can become, like other reform movements, a 'community of discourse', with its own logic, vocabulary and internal momentum. The way in which this can occur will be discussed further in subsequent chapters.

1.3 *Who* is public management reform?

To complement the preceding ideas about *why* reforms are proposed and *what* is meant by public management we now turn to the question of *who* is involved in these activities. To begin, it should be acknowledged that, in a sense, almost *all* public officials have been 'involved', because in many countries almost every public sector organization has been influenced, to some extent, by the reforms of the last two decades. Similarly, one might argue that almost every citizen has been involved too—affected especially by changes in public service delivery. These have included, for example, the publication of citizens' charters in Belgium, France, Italy, Portugal and the UK and the privatization of major public utilities such as airlines, telecommunications companies, water companies or the postal service in a considerable number of countries, including Australia, France, the Netherlands, New Zealand and the UK.

However, while it is important to bear in mind that the ripples from management changes can thus spread out to touch almost the entire population, the main focus of this section is on the key animators—those groups or individuals which supplied the power, the ideas or the skills that drove or enabled the process of reform.

In all the ten countries we examine in this book significant public management reform required the acquiescence, and more usually the active support of, leading politicians, particularly presidents, prime ministers and ministers of finance. In our eleventh 'governmental entity', the European Commission, management reform also required senior political support, in that case from the *collegium* of European Commissioners. The record shows that, since the early or mid-1980s, restructurings and 'reprocessings' have been popular with these powerful figures in Australia, Canada, Denmark, Finland, France, the Netherlands, New Zealand, Sweden, the UK and the USA. The European Commission has launched a programme entitled 'Sound and Efficient Management 2000' (SEM 2000), quickly followed by another, under the acronym of 'MAP 2000' (Modernizing Administration and Personnel 2000). However, the record also shows that some countries have proceeded with management change much more slowly, or on a much narrower front, than others. In the next chapter we will offer a preliminary model of the reform process which will identify the sources of such diversity between states.

Alongside executive politicians, senior civil servants have in almost every case themselves been crucial actors in the reform programmes. Indeed, in some countries they have been the prime moving force. This may seem strange—there is a stereotype abroad in many countries which depicts senior civil servants—'mandarins'—as instinctively conservative and opposed to change. However, the record shows that this is not the case. In countries as diverse as New Zealand, Finland and France, 'mandarins' have been active in generating reform ideas and pushing for their implementation. Meanwhile, in the academic world, new theories have been developed to explain this phenomenon. For example, Dunleavy (1991) has elaborated a model of 'bureau-shaping', in which senior officials actually gain from reorganizing their subordinates, both by distancing themselves from certain kinds of operational problems (through decentralization) and by casting themselves more and more in a high-status and intellectually more interesting role of institutional design and regulation. Of course, junior and middle level officials may not feel so positive about reform: for them it may mean heightened job insecurity, the need to learn new skills, more intense workload pressures and so on. As Wright (1997, p. 10) expresses it: '[C]urrent evidence suggests that top bureaucrats are not at all allergic to reform programmes, which, on the whole, impact most acutely on the lower ranks and which often open up more exciting opportunities of policy-oriented managerialism.'

Beyond the politicians and their senior official advisers certain groups of 'outsiders' have played prominent parts in the reform process—at least in some countries. Three such groups deserve specific mention: management consultants, independent 'think tanks' and academics (some individuals are active in more than one of these categories). In the USA, Australasia and the UK management consultants have been used on a vast scale. In the UK, for example, the civil service reforms of the 1960s were carried out largely as an internal matter, whereas almost every reform in the 1980s and 1990s included participation by one or more of the big management consultancies—PricewaterhouseCoopers, Andersen, Ernst and Young, Deloitte and Touche, KPMG and so on. In the USA Presidents Reagan, Bush and Clinton, whatever their other differences, all made continuous use of advice from the business world (so much so, indeed, that in 1997 we find the US Vice President proudly issuing a booklet entitled *Businesslike government: lessons learned from America's best companies* (Gore, 1997)). In both countries the influence of generic models of management, derived from private sector theory and practice, has been enormous (Pollitt, 1993).

In some countries political 'think tanks' have been influential. Mrs Thatcher's interest in the ideas generated by right-wing think tanks such as the Adam Smith Institute, the Centre for Policy Studies and the Institute for Economic Affairs has been well-documented (Denham and Garnett, 1998; Stone, 1996). These ideas frequently included specific proposals for the reform of institutions such as the National Health Service (NHS) or the state schooling system. Similarly, in the USA bodies like the American Enterprise Institute, the Heritage Foundation and the Hoover Institution found many sympathetic ears among the conservative administrations of Reagan and Bush (Weiss, 1992). In Germany the Bertelsmann Foundation sees itself as a workshop of reform, dedicated to removing the social, political and bureaucratic inflexibilities which may obstruct democratic development.

Finally, the academic world has not been without its influence. Quite commonly individual professors have made contributions to the work of the think tanks discussed above. Others have been hired as consultants, either by individual governments, or the European Commission, or by the OECD's Public Management Service, PUMA (Halligan, 1996). PUMA has been one of the nodal points in an international network, bringing together civil servants, management consultants and academics (and occasionally politicians themselves) who are interested in public management. It has helped to shape what has now become an international 'community of discourse' about public management reform (Premfors, 1998, offers a sharp critique of the PUMA 'line'). The World Bank, the IMF and the Commonwealth Institute have also been international disseminators of management reform ideas. Less influential, but not without significance, have been the more academically oriented networks of the International Institute for Administrative Sciences (IIAS) and its European Group for Public Administration (EGPA). Within particular countries specific university centres have been important—such as the Speyer Post Graduate School of Administrative Sciences in Germany (Schröter and Wollmann, 1997, p. 197). Finally, some professors have attempted to exert their influence by staying in their offices and writing books and tracts. As the authors of this book are only too painfully aware, the academic literature on public management reform has become enormous. The number of public management journals has increased. The list of references at the end of this book is long enough, yet represents only a modest selection of what is currently available.

1.4 Our approach

The present text is a work of synthesis. It represents a bringing-together of many previous, comparative studies with which, jointly and severally, the two of us have been engaged (e.g., Pollitt and Bouckaert, 1995; Halachmi and Bouckaert, 1995; OECD, 1997a; Pollitt, 1993; Pollitt and Summa, 1997a; Pollitt *et al.*, 1997; Pollitt *et al.*, 1999). This corpus of previous work was itself in need of systematization and revision, and, during that process, we have been able both to refine our underlying models of change and collect additional empirical data, especially in respect of countries which we had not included in our previous research.

In this labour of synthesis we have worked in stages. First, a broad model of public management reform was constructed, mainly on an inductive basis, in the light of a review of previous research by ourselves and many others (see chapter 2). This model is intended to provide a framework within which the main forces for and against management change can be identified and placed in relation to one another. It is also a comparative model in the sense that it permitted country-by-country differences in the pattern of these forces to be mapped and subsequently incorporated into interpretations and explanations. It was therefore the vehicle for what comparative methodologists would term a 'small—N analysis'—a systematic comparison of a limited number of cases (King *et al.*, 1994). This approach permits the testing of theories and the construction of generalized statements, but as *analytic* rather than statistical generalizations (Yin, 1994, p. 10).

Incidentally, our decision to move fairly swiftly to the presentation of a model of management reform has meant that we have not had space for a conventional 'literature review' chapter. Instead we have reviewed the most relevant literature as and when we have needed to, in terms of the logic of the book's own sequence rather than as a separate exercise.

Our second step, working initially with countries we knew well, was to test the model to see if it made reasonable sense, both as a way of structuring descriptions of developments in the countries concerned and, beyond that, as a vehicle for explanation. Several refinements to the model were made during this stage.

In the third stage the revised model was then used to guide a process of collecting further comparative data from additional countries. Comparativists will not be surprised to learn that this was, in part, a frustrating process, because, despite the heroic efforts of organizations such as the OECD, there are still many issues for which relevant data are either non-existent, of doubtful reliability or of doubtful comparability. We would agree with the American expert, Allen Schick, who wrote that:

The nature of management reform is such that an assessment cannot be grounded solely on hard evidence of what succeeded or failed. One's own judgement must be brought to bear, as well as that of others—participants and observers—who have seen the reforms in operation and have thought much about how the system is operating (Schick, 1996, p. 9).

Finally, following the thinking expressed by Schick in the above quotation, we attempted to validate the descriptive generalizations, interpretations and explanations which application of the model to the experiences of ten countries had yielded by placing them before selected academic and practitioner experts in the countries concerned. The question for these experts was basically one of 'Is our interpretation/explanation of what has happened in your country accurate, and does it make sense?' We remain profoundly grateful for the generous assistance we were given at this final stage.

1.5 Concluding remarks: the perspective of this book

There is a growing fashion for the authors of academic texts to 'confess' their own perspectives and likely biases. On the whole, we agree that this is a useful convention, although perhaps prone to 'Californian' excesses of lengthy introspection. We will therefore keep this last section brief. In any case, we suspect that the discerning reader will already have deduced some of the main features of our *point de vue*.

We are an Englishman and a Flemishman, formally educated with degrees in modern history, philosophy, engineering and government. We share several values and beliefs: for example, that the public sector *is* distinctive, that public sector (collective) approaches to many social problems are desirable/necessary/ultimately unavoidable; that the dull stuff of administrative implementation is actually crucial to the final effects of reforms; that the eventual impacts on citizens is usually the most powerful (though often fiendishly difficult to execute) test of the 'success' or 'failure' of a management 'improvement'. Further, we recognize that language is both rich and treacherous, and that the rhetorical dimension of public management reforms is substantial, in most countries. That is *not* to say that such reforms are mainly 'blather' but, on the contrary, that some understanding of rhetoric is crucial to the identification of the character and dynamism of reforms. Anyone who tries to read Osborne and Gaebler's *Reinventing government* under the illusion that it is a neutral, scientific text will find themselves in considerable difficulty. Reform language is very frequently deployed with an overtly persuasive purpose, and much may hang upon implied or claimed associations between—on the one hand—the (often boring) details of managerial change and—on the other—values that at least some sections of the potential audience hold dear ('fairness', 'efficiency', 'responsiveness', 'integrity', etc.).

We do not think that we are the slaves of any single theory or approach. On the other hand, it would be absurd to claim that we are somehow 'totally objective' or 'theory-free'. Our general stance is probably what some social scientists have come to call 'critical modernist'. In other words, we still hold to the importance of the empirical testing of theories and hypotheses, although accepting that this is only one kind of test, and that arguments concerning whether the appropriate conditions for falsification have been met will never cease. In brief, we are more sympathetic to the perspective of radical modernity than to a wholesale postmodernity (finding, for example, Giddens, 1990, more illuminating than Boje *et al.*, 1996 or Burrell, 1997). Reality is socially constructed, but not all constructions have equal claim to our credulity and certainly some constructions prove more durable than others. One important test is correspondence with such empirical evidence as may be available. Another is the extent to which the theory or hypothesis concerned resonates with the articulated experiences of those who have been directly affected by the phenomenon under discussion. A third is the extent to which a theory or model is internally clear and consistent, in a logical sense. The simultaneous application of all three of these tests may not steer us towards some ultimate and immaculate 'truth', but it should at least help us discriminate between more—and less—adequate descriptions and explanations.

Although fairly catholic in our approach to theory, it will become obvious that, in the sense of a general emphasis rather than adherence to a very specific set of propositions, we find that *institutionalist* explanations carry considerable power. This is *not* to deny the importance of politics or global economic forces or, sometimes, local contextual factors (Pollitt and Summa, 1997a—see also chapter 2). Neither is it to confess an unwavering addiction to some particular school of 'new institutionalism' (Lowndes, 1996). Rather it is simply to recognize that—at least in the field of public management reform—the broader forces of economics and politics are almost always mediated through networks of *institutions*. The specific characteristics of these networks, and of the individual institutions which compose them, frequently have a profound shaping effect upon what actually happens during the course of reform, and therefore upon the final results and outcomes of the change process. Of course the networks themselves can and do change, though often not nearly as swiftly as reform rhetoric would lead one to believe. Sometimes quite distant historical compromises are found still inscribed upon the face of our constitutional and institutional order. In this, limited sense, we are probably closer to a mildly constructivist historical institutionalism than to either rational choice or the more strongly constructivist sociological institutionalism (Premfors, 1998).

So it is at a middle level of analysis that most of this book is pitched—between, on the one hand, big political ideas and global economic pressures and, on the other, the 'micro-flow' of interactions between specific individuals, units and departments which makes up so much of the everyday life of public servants. This is a level of generality that reveals both interesting patterns and striking variations. In the following chapters we deal with convergences and divergences alike.

2

Problems and Responses: A Model of Public Management Reform

'Reform means change in a direction advocated by some groups or individuals. It does not necessarily mean improvement.'

Rubin, 1992, p. 20

2.1 Why has there been so much reform?

Over the last two decades there appears to have been a huge amount of public management reform. It is difficult to be certain—there are no readily available, common and commensurable units in which we can count and compare what has been happening. Yet the present authors share, with many other commentators, an impression of a wave of reforms across many countries. Of course, there was also reform in earlier periods (see, e.g., Hood, 1998; König, 1996, pp. 44–5; Pollitt, 1984; Savoie, 1994). However, the changes since 1980 have—in many countries—been distinguished by an international character and a degree of political salience which marks them out from the more parochial or technical changes of the preceeding quarter-century. In some countries there have been deliberate attempts to remodel the state. In many countries reform has been accompanied by large claims from politicians to the effect that wholesale change, with sharp improvements in performance, was both desirable and achievable. To put it more colloquially, there has been more 'hype' about administrative change, in more countries, more-or-less simultaneously, than ever before.

If this impression is even approximately correct, then one question must be 'why?' What are the forces driving the reformers? Is this just a policy fashion, or are there deeper influences at work? Why is it that, on the one hand, many countries have participated in the stampede to remodel their public sectors while, on the other, some have been much more cautious? How can we explain both the similarities and the differences between what has happened in this country as compared with that? The development of answers to these questions will occupy a good part of the remainder of this book. A useful first step, however, is to develop a general model of management reform, and that is the task we address in this chapter.

2.2 A model of public management reform

The model we will propose is intended as a first approximation. Its purpose is to provide a framework for subsequent discussion by depicting the broad forces which have been at work in both driving and restraining change. A model such as this is both a conceptual map and a diagram of forces. From it and within it we will develop more detailed sets of typologies and more specific theories which will classify and explain specific patterns and trends, both within individual countries and across groups of countries. Thus, later in the book, sections of the model presented below will be elaborated and modified, as evidence is introduced and our arguments are developed. The model is therefore also a heuristic device, a vehicle for learning—as anyone attempting to draw even a simple diagram of the influences on reform will quickly discover for themselves.

Figure 2.1 shows our general model. It represents a synthesis of what we have learned about the process of reform in many countries. It is as simple as we could make it without doing injustice to the real complexity of the processes we are endeavouring to identify and assess. Even so, it is complex enough to require some explication.

2.3 The forces at work

Let us first consider the broad architecture of the model, since this embodies a number of our own key assumptions and concepts. At the centre of the figure lies the process of elite decision making. That is no accident, since one of our implicit theories is that most of the changes we are concerned with have been predominantly 'top-down', in the sense of having been conceived and executed by executive politicians and/or senior civil servants. Of course (as the diagram explicitly acknowledges) these elites may be heavily influenced by ideas and pressures from elsewhere, and, furthermore, their plans may be blown off-course. Nevertheless, public management reform—certainly in central governments—is a process that tends to begin in the upper, rather than the lower reaches of governance. Notice (boxes I, J) that we distinguish between elite perceptions of what reforms are *desirable* and elite perceptions of what reforms are *feasible* (the elites are the same in both cases). This distinction reflects the commonplace of political life that, as Mick Jagger once put it, 'you can't always get what you want' (even if you are a president or prime minister). There are obstacles—economic and ergonomic—and there are conservative forces which resist change. Reformers are frequently in the position of desiring something more than what they actually propose, but 'censoring' their own aspirations in the interests of framing a lesser package that stands a better chance of being accepted. Notice, also, that perceptions of what is desirable are not merely identifications of what is technically optimal. They are very much *cultural* as well as technical, as, equally, they are perceptions of what is feasible.

There are two other general points to be made about the centrality of elite decision making in the model. First, it is the exception rather than the rule for reform schemes to be comprehensive, even in intent. Reformers try to improve this or that institution or programme, or sometimes a whole sector (health, education), but they seldom attempt to remodel the entire sweep of public sector institutions in one go. Goodin (1996, p. 28) expresses this point well: 'Typically there is no single

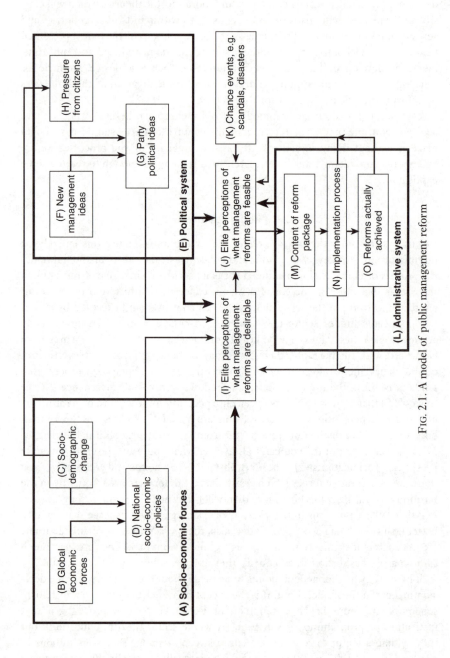

FIG. 2.1. A model of public management reform

design or designer. There are just lots of localized attempts at partial design cutting across one another, and any sensible scheme for institutional design has to take account of that fact.' Even the reforms in New Zealand, which were unusual for the extent to which they formed a coherent whole and were (initially at least) driven by one small group, evolved over time and were significantly affected by a host of practical considerations which blunted the purity of the theories which lay behind them (Boston *et al.*, 1996, pp. 81–6).

The second general point is that it is easy to exaggerate the *degree of intentionality* in many reforms. The final results of reform efforts (box O) in the diagram may bear only a loose relationship to the intentions embodied in the elite's original manifesto for change (box M). Again, Goodin makes the point: 'Institutions are often the product of intentional activities gone wrong—unintended by-products, the products of various intentional actions cutting across one another, misdirected intentions or just plain mistakes' (Goodin, 1996, p. 28). Thus, although we locate elite decision making at the centre of the process of reform, and although we would maintain that intentional acts of institutional redesign have been crucial to the story we have to tell, this should not be read as an elevation of organizational elites into God-like designers who are routinely able to realize bold and broad schemes of improvement. On the contrary, we envisage their schemes as frequently vulnerable to cognitive limitations, cross-cutting actions, politico-administrative roadblocks and unforeseen developments of a wide variety of kinds (see March and Olsen, 1996, chapter 6, for an extended account of the pitfalls, both cognitive and motivational). The most prominent of these complicating factors are discussed further later in this chapter, and subsequently.

Beyond the elite decision making at the heart of Figure 2.1 there are three large groups of elements. In the top left there is a group of economic and socio-demographic factors (A, including B, C, D). In the top right there is a group of political and intellectual factors (E, including F, G, H). In the bottom half of the figure there are a group of administrative factors (L, including M, N, O). It is from the interplay between these principal elements that management changes emerge. A leading German scholar expressed the matter thus: 'Extensive welfare state tasks, reduced financial latitude, economic structural crises, and the internationalization of public matters have put state administrations under reform pressure' (König, 1996, p. 31).

We will now proceed to examine each of these influences in rather more detail, beginning with the socio-economic factors (box A). Box A itself represents the general set of these factors, which is both broad and diverse. Some such factors can be thought of as *structural*, in the sense that they are deep-rooted and long-lasting. The population structure would be one example. Others may be more ephemeral, such as short-term economic cycles of upturn and downturn. Certain of these are likely to have a definite and discernable impact on state administrations, and it is these which are identified in boxes B, C and D.

Box B represents the influence of global economic forces. Some commentators ascribe a large and dominating influence to these (for a good introduction see

McGrew, 1997). It is said that the globalization of capital markets and the growth of multinational corporations and international trade have weakened the control national governments are able to exert over 'their' economic policies. It is therefore no longer possible for a government to sustain for very long a level of public spending that global money markets deem to be imprudent (hence König's reference to 'reduced financial latitude'). The intensification of international competition has also obliged governments to give greater attention than ever before to the competitiveness of 'their' firms. Firms are unlikely to compete effectively if they are weighed down by either high taxes (to finance high public spending) or by tedious and heavy bureaucracy. What is more, national and local governments are more restricted than they used to be in their ability to address costly and painful social problems such as unemployment:

As a consequence of increased capital mobility and tax competition, the power of all national governments to tax capital assets and capital incomes has been greatly reduced. By the same token national monetary policy can no longer reduce interest rates below the international level in order to stimulate productive investment, and higher rates of tax mean that running fiscal deficits to expand aggregate demand has become more expensive. National governments have thus largely lost their ability to avert rising unemployment through the strategies of macro-economic management that were still effective in the 1960s and 1970s. Hence, the more social policy systems were implicitly premised on continuing full employment, the more they have come under stress (OECD, 1997c, p. 211).

Hence one set of reasons for widespread public sector reforms—to restrain public spending, lighten the bureaucratic burden and reshape social policies that can no longer be afforded (see also Appendix A).

These are powerful arguments. They are widely rehearsed and believed. However, for our purposes it is important not to exaggerate their explanatory power. Whilst it seems entirely probable that global economic forces have been a vital background factor in prompting consideration of administrative reform, they do not determine the precise form or timing or degree of that reform. Some of the detail necessary to support this contention will be presented later, but it can immediately be pointed out that the pattern of management change has differed considerably from country to country, suggesting that the effects of global markets are not uniform. Furthermore, the timing of particular reforms in particular countries frequently do not correlate closely to economic crises. It is also noteworthy that some of the countries which were most successful economically during the 1980s (notably, Germany and Japan) were also the least active in the field of management reform. Finally, it should be noted that economic pressures do not themselves translate directly into some particular type of management reform. Reformers need ideas—models or patterns or plans or visions of how the public sector could be better organized. Markets may provide the pressure but they do not supply the ideas.

In practice, a further problem with those commentators who present 'globalization' as a dominant and determining influence on institutional changes is that the concept itself is frequently deployed in a vague or even contradictory manner. For a satisfactory analysis one would need, at a minimum, to distinguish the different mechanisms and modalities involved in the increasing interconnectedness of world financial markets, extensions to free trade, technological standardization and internationalization (e.g., the global spread of certain brands of computer software or hardware) and what one might term cultural globalization (McDonalds, certain films, fashions, sporting events, etc.). Too often these rather different processes are all lumped together in a single, utopian or dystopian fashion.

In short, *economic* forms of globalization do seem to have been a major influence on institutional change, but one which has acted through a number of other, intervening variables. These other variables have been crucial in determining the precise shape and timing of the reforms in particular countries.

Socio-demographic change (box C) is a second background pressure of considerable importance. By this we refer to the pressures arising from changes in the pattern of life for millions of citizens in each of our countries. They are too numerous to list in their entirety here, but include, most notably, increased life expectancy, changes in the patterns of family life (especially higher rates of divorce and family break-up) and a considerable rise in the average level of unemployment as compared with the boom years of 1950–73. Some data on these trends are given in Appendix A. The basic effect of many of these social changes has been to increase the demand falling upon state-provided or state-financed services— particularly health care, social care and social security. For example, in the early 1990s estimates of the average amount of health care resources consumed by the average British or American person over the age of 75 ranged between six and ten times the amount consumed by a middle-aged person. Thus to have an increasing proportion of elderly people in a population implies a considerable growth in welfare expenditure. In most modern states social security (pensions, unemployment benefits and other benefits in cash and kind) is the largest single item in the state budget, and health care is frequently the second largest. Broad changes in the levels of demand for these services therefore translate into significant public expenditure increases—just as global economic pressures are pushing in the other direction. In some countries commentators have painted frightening scenarios of state finances collapsing under unsupportable welfare burdens, with millions of citizens being deprived of their expected rights and benefits (for a flavour of the American debates, see Marmor *et al.*, 1990).

How does all this affect public management reform? Again, as with the globalization of capital and trade flows, the impacts are indirect. An increase in the number of pensioners or of the unemployed does not by itself produce a particular type of organizational change. But what it does do is provide powerful incentives for politicians and civil servants to look for ways of easing the strain on the system. These may include lowering the rates of increase in benefits (e.g., by de-indexing them from wages and salaries), narrowing the categories of eligibility (so as to concentrate on the 'most needy'), or increasing charges and co-payments by the beneficiaries. But they have also tended to include changes which have more obvious impacts on the ways in which such services are organized and managed.

For example, streamlining may be implemented with a view to reducing administrative overheads; commercial and voluntary sector participation in the process of provision may be encouraged and/or there may be wholesale restructurings of the relevant departments and agencies in an attempt to build in stronger incentives to economy and efficiency (see, e.g., Harrison *et al.*, 1992).

These background pressures therefore reflect themselves in foreground socio-economic policies which may oscillate quite rapidly over time (box D). For example, in pursuit of social security savings, some European governments have raised the minimum age for entitlement to a state pension. Or, in the economic field in the mid and late 1990s, EU member states struggled to meet the Maastricht 'convergence criteria' which would qualify them to join the European single currency. This put downward pressure on public spending and public debt, and may well have somewhat increased the numbers of unemployed, at least in the short-term. It was therefore a policy with considerable and diverse effects on the administrative apparatuses of those states concerned. It was of particular interest as a *supranational* initiative. At the time of writing the public affairs media are full of the need for an even wider (wider than the EU alone) international initiative to address volatility in the global money markets. If national governments can co-operate sufficiently to establish credible policies, it is conceivable that some of the control over economic policy lost by individual states could be regained at an international level—but this is a subject for another book, by other authors.

We can now move to the second cluster of influential factors—those concerned with the political system. To begin with we need to take into account the general, structural features of this system, which are represented in Figure 2.1 by box E. These features may make management reform more or less straightforward. For example, in Germany a strict constitutional law makes it difficult, if not impossible for major restructurings to take place at the federal level, whereas in the UK the process of changing the machinery of government has long been remarkably easy (Pollitt, 1984). Or again, in countries such as Finland, which are characterized by consensual political systems and coalition governments, the process of management reform is likely to be less harsh and combative than in countries such as Australia, New Zealand or the UK, where the political systems are more adversarial. A final example would be the high degree of protection which the constitutions of Germany and the Nordic countries afford to regional/local/municipal government. This usually means that central governments in these countries find it relatively difficult to extend the reforming process to the local level—unless and until there is a reasonable coalition of political support for reform at that level itself. Contrast this with Mrs Thatcher's ability, in the UK during the 1980s, actually to *abolish* the Greater London Council and the six Metropolitan County authorities when she found herself in disagreement with their politics and policies (Stoker, 1988, pp. 142–4).

In contrast with the constraints and restraints which are often manifested by the deep structures of political systems, there are also, within those systems, dynamic elements. One such that is of particular importance for our theme is the influx of new management ideas into the public sector (box F). Over the last two decades this has generated a rich flux of ideas about how to manage almost anything, from a corner shop to 'Great Britain, plc'. These ideas have echoed around business schools, corporate boardrooms, government seminars and even airport bookstands (for a brief analysis, see Pollitt, 1993, chapter 1). There has been considerable inter-country borrowing, facilitated by international bodies such as PUMA/OECD and the World Bank. Savoie (1994) details several important instances of mutual borrowing between the conservative regimes of Thatcher in the UK (1979–90), Reagan in the USA (1980–88) and Mulroney in Canada (1984–93). There can be no doubt that the selling of management ideas has been one of the growth industries of the 1980s and 1990s. Equally there can be little doubt that the writings of the gurus and the presentations of the management consultants have influenced political and civil service leaders in a number of the countries examined in this book. Perhaps the most celebrated case was the intellectual line of descent which ran from generic management writers such as Peter Drucker and Tom Peters through the authors of the American best-seller *Reinventing government* (Osborne and Gaebler, 1992) to the major US federal government report *Creating a government that works better and costs less: report of the National Performance Review* (Gore, 1993).

Of course, management ideas, however fashionable, very seldom get translated in a pure form directly into specific reforms. Rather they flow into a larger pool of ideas, drawn from a variety of sources, which are made use of by political and administrative elites (boxes I, J). Nevertheless, generic management ideas have been prominent on the face of public sector reforms, perhaps especially in Australasia, North America and the UK. In these countries (and, to a lesser extent, others) generic approaches and techniques such as Management by Objectives (MbO), Total Quality Management (TQM), benchmarking and Business Process Re-engineering (BPR) have been widely adopted within the public sector (National Performance Review, 1997b; Pollitt and Bouckaert, 1995; Trosa, 1996). Alongside these management ideas, and often interwoven with them, organizational design principles based on micro-economic theories have also been extensively used. In New Zealand, for example, public choice theory, agency theory and transaction cost economics were all influential (Boston *et al.*, 1996, chapter 2).

In the quotation we used near the beginning of this section (p. 27), König referred to the 'internationalization of public matters'. Certainly this has become increasingly true of management ideas, both those generated by gurus and business schools and those which derive from micro-economic theory. Departments and units charged with administrative reform have their own international networks, both bilateral and multilateral. The Public Management Service (PUMA) of the OECD was an influential nodal point in these networks from the late 1980s onwards (see, e.g., OECD 1993b, 1995, 1997a; Halligan, 1996a and—for a critique of the 'PUMA line'—Premfors, 1998).

Box G identifies party political ideas as a further influence on public management change. Political parties acquire ideas about how they would like to govern, and these include issues of structure, style and process. For example, a party may decide that it wishes to 'reduce bureaucracy' or to 'decentralize and put power closer to the people'. Or it may adopt more specific proposals such as creating a special ministry or agency for the environment, the regions, the family, sport or any other topic which happens to be prominent or fashionable. Party political ideas may be more or less ideologically charged. One doctrine that was influential in a number of countries during the 1980s and 1990s was that of privatization. When construed as a consistent preference for private over public provision, this doctrine had a very obvious and immediate impact on the public sector—it reduced its size. Australia, New Zealand and the UK all pursued vigorous privatization programmes of this type, and the doctrine was also applied, albeit in a less unremitting way, in Canada, France, the Netherlands and the USA.

Party political ideas are sometimes internally generated and derived from a specifically political agenda that party activists are developing. On other occasions the ideas may come from outside, from popular movements among the electorate (box H) or from the worlds of business or academia (box F). It is clear, for example, that in relation to public management issues, the ideas of the 1980s Conservative governments in the UK, and of the 1984–90 Labour governments in New Zealand, were extensively influenced by the theories of public choice-school economists (Boston *et al.*, 1996; Pollitt, 1993). Equally, the Republican administration of President Reagan was heavily populated with business advisers, while its Democratic successors during the mid-1990s also made deliberate use of what it called 'Lessons learned from America's best companies' (Gore, 1997).

Summing up the play of ideas, one scholar recently expressed himself as follows:

Public sector reform is in fashion and no self-respecting government can afford to ignore it. How a fashion is established is one of the most intriguing questions of public policy. Part of the answer lies in *policy diffusion* brought about by the activities of international officials (whose zeal for administrative reform mysteriously stops short at the door of their own organisations), by meetings of public administrators, academics and the so-called policy entrepreneurs (Wright, 1997, p. 8).

Box H in Figure 2.1 represents pressure from citizens. It should immediately be acknowledged that management reform is not usually at the top of the citizenry's list of priorities. Neither is it a topic upon which most men and women in the street have very specific suggestions to offer. However, although lay citizens are unlikely to be brimming with concrete proposals for better management, they can and, on occasion, do exert pressure for change. If, for example, citizens become used to very rapid and customer-friendly transactions in banks, building societies and shops they may become progressively more and more discontented with post offices or benefits payment agencies which are slow, inflexible and inhospitable. Such discontent with low standards of service in state institutions may then be expressed to political representatives (to the occupants of boxes I and J) or to the mass media. More dramatically, if it is widely believed that civil servants are corrupt, or that a particular service is being delivered in a seriously inequitable way, then public opinion may mobilize to create pressure for reform. Thus, while the views of citizens seldom seem to be the driving or shaping force for particular reforms, there can be circumstances in which they constitute an important background influence.

There is one influence which operates outside the main groupings of socio-economic forces, political system factors and elements of the administrative system. Box K represents the effect of chance events such as scandals, natural or man-made disasters, accidents and unpredictable tragedies such as shootings or epidemics. Whilst these can clearly partake of socio-economic or political factors (trains can collide because of lack of public investment in maintenance or signalling equipment; a crazed gunman may bear a grudge against the government), their most obvious features are their newsworthiness and their unpredictability. The effect of such events on reform programmes may not be obvious, but occasionally it is significant. For example, the Cave Creek disaster in New Zealand (when an observation platform collapsed in a public reservation) sharply focused media attention on the issue of public accountability in a newly decentralized system (Gregory, 1998). Similarly, failures in the UK National Health Service's breast cancer screening programmes were interpreted by the new Labour government of 1997 as evidence that the market-type mechanisms the previous (Conservative) government had introduced were inappropriate and required reform (Laurance, 1997). In the USA the disaster that destroyed the 'Challenger' space shuttle led to a major overhaul of the National Aeronautics and Space Administration (NASA), one of the largest federal agencies. At a more personal level, senior ministers are prone to a variety of 'accidents' and occasionally individuals with strong reforming ideas may arrive or depart for reasons quite unconnected with their management priorities. During the 1980s Nielsen in Canada and Heseltine in the UK were both examples of sudden departures of reforming ministers (Savoie, 1994, p. 130).

Taking a broad view, therefore, the upsurge of reforms in the last twenty years or so can be attributed to an intensification of a number of factors, but perhaps particularly global economic forces, socio-economic change and the supply of new management ideas (B, C and F). However, these pressures do not enjoy free play over a smooth surface. On the contrary, they soon wash up against countervailing forces—not only the recalcitrance of those groups with a vested interest in the status quo but also less animated sources of resistance. Existing ways of doing things may be entrenched in laws or regulations which take time or political majorities (or both) to change. At the extreme, a particular kind of management change requires an adjustment to a country's constitution—or, in the case of EU institutions—to the founding treaties. Furthermore, even if the majority are agreed that the existing administrative structures or procedures are inadequate, it may be hard to agree on what to do instead (especially if, as is often the case, reform in one direction raises risks in another). Or it may simply be that to manage in a new and desired way may require a considerable investment in new information technology, new accounting systems and/or new training programmes for the staff concerned before it can be put into practice. All these factors represent the *costs of change*. Often reformers underestimate the extent of these until they get close to them (as they approach or get into implementation—box N).

Many of the costs of change can be thought of as being associated with the dismantling of existing political and administrative systems in order to 'make room' for the new. In every country, much history and many political bargains— and therefore some wisdom—is built into existing systems. Such systems are archaeological maps of past struggles and settlements (March and Simon, 1996, p. 205). With management reform, staff have to relinquish old ways and learn new. Well-oiled networks of information and influence are disturbed and new, less certain ones put in their place. Politicians who were used to one configuration of authority within those state agencies that most interested them now have to get used to a new pattern, and possibly one which will be more difficult for them to influence or communicate through. And so on. We have already discussed the restraining effects of political structures (box E) and we will now move on to look at the corresponding structures of *administrative* systems. The two act jointly to temper the ardour of the reformers with the sober difficulties of shifting the status quo. Thus we depict them as enclosing and surrounding the more specific and dynamic pressures of the moment.

Administrative systems (box L) are often difficult to change in more-than-incremental ways. For example, the UK civil service is built around a core of generalists whereas many continental civil services, including the French and German, consist mainly of staff trained in law. A cultural and disciplinary differ-ence of this type cannot be eliminated overnight—it influences the way in which officials conceptualize and approach a wide variety of issues. Structural differences can also be significant: in Sweden and Finland central government for long consisted of a group of modest-sized ministries surrounded by a circle of relatively independent administrative agencies which had responsibility for most operational issues. This was a more decentralized system than that which obtained (until recently, at least) in France or the UK. Many of the issues for which local or municipal authorities in the UK would deal directly with a central ministry, would be taken care of by agencies in Finland or Sweden (although during the early 1990s the Finns launched a fundamental downsizing of their agency system). For the Nordic countries to change required new legislation and a reconsideration of the highly political issue of relations between central government and municipalities. It could be done (and to some extent has been), but not quickly or lightly. A third example would be personnel regulations. These are clearly necessary to ensure that public servants behave with propriety and consistency. Yet they tend to develop a momentum of their own. Over the years huge manuals are built up, with each unusual occurrence leading to more paragraphs or pages being added to the *magnum opus*. It can be very difficult fundamentally to reduce or revise this tangle of interlocking rules and regulations. When, in 1993, the American Vice President launched the National Performance Review, the federal personnel manual was ceremonially burned on the lawn of the White House. The reality was less impres-sive than this publicity stunt—a huge civil service could not really throw away all its internal rules, and most agencies seem to have continued to apply most of the rules as before. As one American colleague put it to us, 'the copy that was burned cannot have been the only one'. Personnel regulations have become notable constraints on reform in a number of countries—perhaps especially France—and also for the European Commission.

At a more pedestrian level, administrative systems can still be hard to budge. Consider a straightforward benefits-claiming system. Claimants come to a social security office and fill in a form. The form is then checked by counter staff who, if the claim is in order, make the appropriate payment. Let us suppose that a decision is made to reform this system by introducing computerized technology. In theory the new procedures will be quicker and less staff-intensive. Large efficiency gains are predicted. In practice even this simple-sounding reform can involve extensive complications. Hundreds, if not thousands of staff will need training to use the new computer technology. The educational qualifications needed for counter staff may need to be increased. Public service unions are likely to be concerned about any such changes, and are even more likely to resist attempts to reap efficiency gains which take the form of staff reductions. The purchase of the necessary computer software may be less than straightforward (Bellamy and Taylor, 1998, pp. 41–51; Hudson, 1998; Margetts, 1998). Questions about linking the data held on the new system to other computerized government data banks and about the security of personal details held on file may also arise, and these are likely to have legal implications. And so on. To manage the change well will take considerable forethought, planning and time. To announce the reform is the easy part, to carry it through requires patience and resolve.

Despite these potentially formidable obstacles to radical or rapid change, reform programmes *are* launched, and frequently make an impact. In Figure 2.1 boxes M, N and O represent this more dynamic aspect of the administrative system. These activities—announcing reform packages, implementing changes and achieving results—are the main focus of the remainder of our book, and their treatment here will be correspondingly brief.

The *content* of reform packages (M) are the product of the interaction between the desirable and the feasible, mentioned above. When announced, such packages frequently display a considerable rhetorical dimension, playing harmonies on the styles and ideas of the moment. They attempt to establish, or reinforce, discourses which support the particular institutional changes under consideration. Here is an example from the USA:

If somebody had said in 1993 that within 10 years the federal government would be smaller, customer-driven, worker-friendly, and run like America's best companies, they would have drawn . . . jeers.

But that was the challenge that President Clinton handed down four years ago when he asked me to reinvent the federal government—to put the wheels back on. We agreed right then that we needed to bring a revolution to the federal government: we call it reinventing government (Vice President Gore, 1997, p. 1).

More generally:

A discourse is a framework for apprehending the world embedded in language, enabling its adherents to put together diverse sensory information into coherent wholes. These adherents therefore share assumptions and capabilities, which they will typically take for granted ... No institution can operate without an associated and supportive discourse (or discourses) (Dryzek, 1996, pp. 103–4).

Reform announcements are therefore as much texts to be interpreted as they are blueprints for administrative action. Some reform announcements come to rather little, so it is always advisable to check how far the initial promises have been realized in the medium term. In this they are no different from most other political manifestos. March and Olsen (1995, p. 195) put it like this:

most democracies undertake comprehensive reforms of administration from time to time. They create special commissions or parliamentary initiatives to overhaul the administrative machinery of government. Those efforts regularly have their beginnings hailed, their aspirations praised, and their recommendations ignored.

In our view this is somewhat of an overstatement—*comprehensive* reforms are actually fairly rare, and it is quite common for at least some recommendations from some of the reviews to be implemented. Nevertheless, March and Olsen suggest an important idea, namely that *announcing* reforms and *making recommendations* may become activities in their own right, without any necessary follow-through. Politicians, consultants and academics can make quite decent livings out of producing statements and reports, even if little else happens in the longer run. For example, retrospective analysis shows that many of Canadian Prime Minister Mulroney's management reform initiatives came to not very much in the end (Savoie, 1994). Most countries can show at least some examples of political rhetoric outrunning measured achievement.

The process of *implementation* is a particularly important stage of the reform process. The 'science' of administration is hardly exact. Much is learned during the attempt to put reform ideas into practice, and some of that learning frequently translates into departures from the original design. During the 1970s an Anglo-American academic literature focusing on this stage appeared, and much of it was fairly pessimistic about the chances of reform packages actually unfolding according to plan. One particularly influential work was subtitled 'How great expectations in Washington are dashed in Oakland' (Pressman and Wildavsky, 1973). It explained how top-down reforms were implemented through long chains of decisions and many levels of administration, and the chances of success were no better than the strength of the weakest link. Although subsequent scholarship has suggested that this mainly linear model of the implementation process is too simple, the basic point about the complexity of reform stands firm.

Indeed, the complexity of implementation processes may well be on the increase. More and more programmes are delivered through complex networks of organizations rather than by a single implementor (Kickert *et al.*, 1997; Lowndes and Skelcher, 1998). These networks may include different levels of government, independent public corporations, public/private hybrid bodies, commercial firms and voluntary, non-profit associations. Increasingly, implementation networks need to be international—most obviously for policies in fields such as telecommunications, transport, the environment or communicable diseases. Some have advocated that the EU Commission, which sits at the centre of many such international webs, should transform itself into a 'network organisation' (Metcalfe, 1996). The implications of all this for management reform are complex. If such reforms are to be effective it seems they will often have to take the whole of a network as their 'unit of analysis', rather than just a single organization. However, both the available theories and the available authority could easily be inadequate for such a task. Ideas about how to design or redesign networks of different types of organization are in short supply. And the authority to carry through integrated reform of a whole network may not exist—each member of the network being its own master in the matter of management change.

Another problem that can arise during implementation is that individual reforms, though they may make good sense in themselves, may contradict or detract from other reforms which are being carried through at the same time. For example, the Assistant Auditor General of Canada, commenting on the slow progress made by various public service quality improvement initiatives during the early 1990s, observed:

Our review of relevant documents and our discussions with service managers indicated that they had many reasons for not having made more progress toward the government's repeated commitments. The reasons included the public service strike of 1991, government reorganisation in 1992, the change of government in 1993 and the subsequent Program Review and associated cutbacks, as well as re-engineering exercises carried out by individual departments (Auditor General of Canada, 1997, para 14.65).

Implementation is also a crucial stage in the sense that it can directly feed back to the elite decision makers ideas about what to do next—whether to continue along a given path or change tack. For example, in New Zealand a particularly elaborate and sophisticated performance management system was put in place from the mid-1980s onwards. By the mid-1990s, as this system matured, it was recognized that there were dangers in too tight a focus on measurable outputs. The ultimate objectives of programmes (to educate children, lower unemployment, etc.) could be displaced by an intense concentration on how well lessons were delivered, how many unemployment training courses had been held and a host of other measures of process and output. With this concern in mind the New Zealand Senior Public Managers Conference for 1997 had the title and theme 'Raising our game: from outputs to outcomes'.

Finally we come to the end of this long and complicated road—the achievements that eventually accrue from the process of reform (box O). These might, or might not, bear a close resemblance to the original aspirations of the politico-administrative elite. Whether they do or not, like the implementation phase, these 'results' are likely to feed back into earlier stages of the process—particularly to elite perceptions of what types of change are desirable and feasible (I, J). In practice—as we

shall see in chapter 5—the 'final results' of reform are frequently difficult to identify with any confidence. Rhetoric and reality can be very hard to disentangle.
Indeed, ultimately 'the final reality' *cannot* be wholly separated out, because it is so
thoroughly impregnated with the competing discourses through which it is constituted. Furthermore, although new administrative structures and processes may
unmistakably exist, it is often a problem to know just how far they can be attributed
to some preceeding reform (Pollitt, 1995). In interviews practitioners very often
trace specific impacts back to a variety of influences, of which a particular reform
is only one.

2.4 Concluding remarks

We have now presented our model of public management reform. It depicts the
process as multifaceted and liable to modification at a number of different stages.
It embodies interactions between background socio-economic influences, political
pressures and features of the administrative system itself. It identifies both pressures *for* change and sources of resistance *against* change. It reserves a role for the
unintentional and the accidental. It already hints at, and allows for, considerable
variation between countries, not least because they enter into the process of change
from different starting points, in the sense that each country has its own distinctive
political and administrative system (E and L). It incorporates several important
feedback loops, as reformers learn from the process of implementation (and with
the internationalization of the 'market' in management ideas governments
frequently look for lessons from the experiences of other countries, not just their
own).

   Nevertheless, there is still a lot to be 'filled in'. In particular, to breath life into
the model we need more detailed typologies of what goes on inside some of the key
boxes—particularly typologies of different types of political (E) and administrative
(L) regime. Once we have those in place it should be possible further to develop the
dynamic features of the model, by relating specific regime types to specific trends
in reforms. These are all tasks we shall take up in subsequent chapters.

3

Many Houses: Types of Politico-Administrative Regime

'Every house has many builders, and is never finished.'
Paavo Haavikko, in Lomas, 1991,
preliminary page

3.1 The starting point for management reforms

The model of public management reform developed in the previous chapter laid considerable stress on the characteristics of the existing political and administrative systems as shaping influences over processes of management change. These systems provide, as it were, the existing terrain—the topography over which reformers must travel. To continue the analogy, it is obvious that different countries display different topographical features, and therefore different challenges to those who wish to carry through reform. In this chapter we will offer relevant classifications for such differences, and will then use these to examine and locate the ten countries which fall within our scope. We will also attempt to use the strategy on the eleventh entity in our study—the European Commission—although its application in that unique case is less straightforward (Section 3.8).

Some accounts of public management reform say little or nothing of contextual differences of the kind to which the discussion of this chapter is devoted. They concentrate entirely on the characteristics of the reform instruments themselves—Total Quality Management, results-oriented budgeting, performance contracts or whatever. In our view such accounts are incomplete and inadequate. Their attention is, in effect, confined to the intervention alone, with minimal analysis of variations in the contexts in which the intervention takes place. Yet there is ample evidence from the study of public administration that 'implementation habitats' can make a huge difference to the effects yielded by a particular piece of management change (Pollitt, Birchall and Putman, 1998; Pressman and Wildavsky, 1973; Stewart, 1992; Schröter and Wollman, 1997). We are convinced that a conceptually identical, or at least very similar, reform develops differently in one national (or sectoral or local) context as compared with another.

On the other hand, we should remember that it would be misleading to think of politico-administrative systems as some kind of unchanging bedrock, to which every reform must adapt itself or fail. This is not a position we would wish to adopt. In our model (Figure 2.1) *every* element is subject to change, though at different speeds. Thus even the fundamentals of political systems (e.g., constitutions) and administrative systems (e.g., the educational and cultural characteristics of the higher civil service) may change over time. The phrase from Paavo Haaviko's poem which introduced this chapter well sums up the situation. However, these kinds of systemic feature usually tend to change only gradually—or infrequently—and may therefore be regarded as much more stable/less dynamic features of the reformer's environment than, say, the play of economic forces or the changing fashions in management ideas.

Towards the end of the chapter (Section 3.9) we comment on another type of regime—the *ancien régime*, or 'traditional bureaucracy', which recent reforms are often said to be departures—or escapes—from. We raise some questions about the accuracy of this picture of the past, and about the value shifts which are both explicit and implicit in the contemporary debate over 'bureaucracy'.

3.2 Politico-administrative systems: the key features

From the very beginning, comparative approaches to the study of politics and public administration have been intimately concerned with the question of what features to select as the most sensible and illuminating basis for comparing one state, or subnational jurisdiction, with another. In the fourth century BC Aristotle was already suggesting what the most important dimensions might be:

Of good constitutions there are three: Monarchy, Aristocracy, and Polity. Of bad there are also three: Tyranny, Oligarchy, Extreme Democracy (Aristotle, 1963, p. 12).

Whilst it is not feasible for us to replay all the twists and turns in the story of comparative methodology during the intervening 2300 years we will at least attempt to explain and justify our own selection.

It makes sense to concentrate on features which, prima facie, seem likely to affect the process of management reform. Fortunately, in the relevant academic literature, there is no shortage of suggestions as to what these might be. We have borrowed heavily from this corpus of comparative work. Typically, the key features identified by leading authors include *structural, cultural* and *functional* elements. Those we have chosen are as follows:

1. The state structure (including the constitution)—this is clearly a structural feature.
2. The nature of executive government at the central level—this is a mixture of structural and functional elements.
3. The way relationships work between political executives (ministers) and top civil servants ('mandarins')—a functional element, with strong cultural overtones.
4. The dominant administrative culture (conventionally divided between those cultures founded on the principles of a *Rechtsstaat* and those more oriented to a 'public interest' model)—this is a cultural element. We here take administrative culture to refer to the expectations the staff of an organization have about what is 'normal' and 'acceptable' in that organization. Such beliefs and attitudes manifest themselves in numerous different ways, including the symbols and rituals of the organization, and its stories, jokes and myths (Geertz, 1973; Handy, 1993). Cultures will vary from country to country and, indeed, from one organization to another.

5. The degree of diversity among the main channels through which the ideas come that fuel public management reform—this reflects both cultural and functional elements.

These five key features are depicted in tabular form in Table 3.1. In the following sections we discuss each feature in turn.

3.3 The basic structure of the state

Here there are two basic dimensions. The first refers to the degree of *vertical* dispersion of authority—that is, how far authority is shared between different levels of government. Along this dimension we recognize three broad types: unitary and centralized states, unitary but decentralized states and federal states (these will be explained in a moment). The second dimension concerns the degree of *horizontal* co-ordination at central government level—that is, how far central executives are able to 'get their acts together' by ensuring that all ministries pull together in the same direction. This dimension ranges from the pole of 'highly co-ordinated' to 'highly fragmented'.

In terms of the first dimension, the vertical dispersion of authority tends to be greatest within federal constitutions and least within the constitutions of unitary and centralized states. In a unitary state there is no *constitutionally entrenched* division of state power. Central government retains ultimate sovereignty, even if particular authority is delegated to subnational tiers of government. In a federal state the constitution itself prescribes some division of sovereignty between different bodies—in the USA between the federal government and the state governments for example, or, in Germany, between the federal government and the *Länder*. Of the countries included in this study Australia, Canada, Germany and the USA are federal states.

However, we wish to distinguish further within the category of 'unitary' states. Some of these may be highly centralized (e.g., France, at least until the 1980s decentralization reforms; New Zealand; the UK), whilst others are extensively decentralized (e.g., the Nordic states, where many powers have been delegated from ministries to agencies, and where local governments (counties, municipalities, etc.) have statutorily well-protected independence from central government). Indeed, in such circumstances the degree of *de facto* decentralization in a unified state can equal or even exceed the decentralization of a federal state:

It should be emphasized that the distinction between the two modes of territorial autonomy—decentralization within a unitary state and the extent of federalism in political systems comprising states—is a technical one in legal terminology. In reality the similarities must be underlined as the demand for territorial autonomy may be the same but take on different expressions due to the legal framework of the nation (Lane and Ersson, 1991, p. 207).

What are the consequences of these distinctions for public management reform? All other things being equal, reforms in federal states or highly decentralized unitary states are likely to be less broad in scope and less uniform in practice than in unitary, centralized states. In federal states different federal entities are likely to

TABLE 3.1. *Types of politico–administrative regime:*
five key features of public administration systems

	1. State Structure	2. Executive Government	3. Minister/ Mandarin Relations	4. Administrative Culture	5. Diversity of Policy Advice
Australia	Federal; Co-ordinated	Majoritarian	Separate Mildly politicized	Public interest	Mainly civil service until 1980s
Canada	Federal	Majoritarian	Separate	Public interest	Mainly civil service
Finland	Unitary; Decentralized; Fairly fragmented	Consensual	Separate Fairly politicized	Tending to *Rechtsstaat*	Mainly civil service
France	Unitary; Formerly centralized; Co-ordinated	Intermediate	Integrated Fairly politicized	Predominantly *Rechtsstaat*	Mainly civil service
Germany	Federal; Co-ordinated	Intermediate	Separate Fairly politicized	*Rechtsstaat*	Mainly civil service (plus a few academics)
Netherlands	Unitary; Decentralized; Fairly fragmented	Consensual	Separate Fairly politicized	Originally very legalistic, but has changed to pluralistic/ consensual	A broad mixture: Civil servants, academics, other experts
New Zealand	Unitary; Centralized; Mildly fragmented	Majoritarian (until 1996)	Separate Not politicized	Public interest	Mainly civil service
Sweden	Unitary; Decentralized	Intermediate	Separate Increasingly politicized	Originally legalistic, but has changed to corporatist	A broad mixture: Corporatist processes bring in academic experts and trade unions
UK	Unitary; Centralized; Co-ordinated	Majoritarian	Separate Not politicized	Public interest	Mainly civil service until 1980s Recently think tanks, consultants
USA	Federal; Fragmented	Intermediate	Separate Very politicized	Public interest	Very diverse: Political appointees, corporations, think tanks, consultants

want and to be able to go in different directions, or at least not all in the same direction at the same time. The federal government in Washington DC or in Canberra simply *cannot* order the state governments to reform themselves in particular ways. In Germany the *Länder* have tended to grow in strength (even aspiring to separate representation at European Community level) and different *Länder* have adopted varying stances towards administrative reform (Schröter and Wollmann, 1997). Indeed, it is often argued that federal states have the advantage that they form 'natural laboratories', where one approach can be tried in one state or at one level, while another is tried elsewhere. Even if external pressures are similar, states within a federation may adopt quite widely varying trajectories for management reform (an excellent account of this happening in Australia may be found in Halligan and Power, 1992). By contrast, one may once more refer to the actions of Mrs Thatcher's administration in the unitary UK when, in 1986, irritated with certain local authorities for a mixture of doctrinal and administrative reasons, central government simply abolished the Greater London Council and the six largest metropolitan county councils (Cochrane, 1993, pp. 28–47).

Another possible contrast between a unified, centralized state and a federal or a unified but highly decentralized state concerns the *focus* of management reforms. Central governments in unified, centralized states tend to be more heavily involved in the business of service delivery (education, health care, etc.) than do the central governments of federal or decentralized states (where these functions tend to be taken care of by lower tiers of government). It has been suggested that this may lead reformers in such centralized states towards a narrower focus on service-specific outputs and results (as in New Zealand during the late 1980s and early 1990s) rather than towards a more strategic concern with policy impacts and over-all outcomes (as in Australia during the same period—see Holmes and Shand, 1995). Behind this concern one may often detect budgetary preoccupations—if central government is responsible for running major welfare state services such as social security, health care or education, these are likely to dominate its overall spending profile. When pressures to restrain public spending mount it is to these services that ministries of finance are obliged to turn their attention.

The effects of extensive decentralization within unitary states tend to be similar to that of federalism, that is, the chances of the *scope* of management reforms being very wide or their application being very *uniform* is reduced. Piecemeal reform becomes a more probable scenario. Among our unitary states, Finland and Sweden have been highly decentralized throughout the period under consideration. New Zealand and the UK have remained highly centralized throughout the same period. These latter two are also the countries which have carried through the most vigorous, broad scope management reforms among the ten states under consideration (which therefore fits with our analysis). France is an interesting case because, having been famously highly centralized until the early 1980s, it then embarked upon a series of structural decentralizations, the full effects of which have been profound (and which are still working themselves out). The impacts of these changes appear to have included a modest decline in central government's share of both total public expenditure and total taxation (Steunenberg and Mol, 1997, pp. 238–9).

Thus, various indicators of decentralization can be constructed. Central government shares in total public spending, and in total taxation are two possibilities. A third is to examine the percentages of public servants who work for central governments, as compared with the proportion working for subcentral governments—states, regions, counties, municipalities and so on. Mapping our ten countries like this (Table 3.2) reveals some large differences.

Clearly some countries are much more 'centre-heavy' than others. New Zealand shows nearly 90 per cent of its public servants as working for the centre. France and the UK are also quite high scorers on this indicator, with 49 per cent and 48 per cent respectively. Germany, however, employs only 12 per cent of its public servants at the centre, and the Nordic countries are quite low too (Finland = 25 per cent and Sweden = 17 per cent, 1994 figures).

Comparativist political scientists have developed other relevant indicators. In particular, Lane and Ersson (1991) display two indices, one of institutional autonomy (p. 224) and the other of regional and local financial autonomy (p. 225). Roughly, the first purports to summarize aspects of federalism, regional and local government discretion and functional autonomy from central government control, while the second measures the proportion of total (general) government spending taken up by central government (therefore the lower this percentage the more regional and local autonomy is assumed to exist). These two indices are combined in Table 3.3.

TABLE 3.2 *Percentage shares of public employment by level of government*

Country	Central government			Other levels of government (1994 only)
	1985	1990	1994	
Australia	—	15.0	14.6	State 73.3 Local 12.1
Canada	—	17.9	17.1	Provincial 44.1 Local 38.9
Finland	33.3	24.3	25.2	Municipalities 74.8
France	56.3	55.0	48.7	Subnational 30.7 Health 20.6
Germany	22.1	21.6	11.9	*Länder* 51.0 Municipalities 37.1
Netherlands	—	—	—	—
New Zealand	—	—	89.7	Local 10.3
Sweden	27.2	26.7	17.3	Regional 24.6 Municipalities 58.1
UK	48.0	47.7	47.7	Local 52.3
USA	17.9	16.7	15.2	State 22.6 Local 61.1

Adapted from: OECD, 1997c, p. 36

TABLE 3.3. *Two indices of decentralization*

Country	1. Federalism	2. Special territorial autonomy (0–1)	3. Regional and local government direction (0–2)	4. Functional autonomy	5. Institutional autonomy (summary score of columns 1–4)	6. Central government final consumption as a % of final consumption of general government
Australia	—	—	—	—		(European countries only)
Canada	—	—	—	—		(European countries only)
Finland	0	1	1	0	= 2	33
France	0	0	1	—	= 1	72
Germany (FRG)	2	0	2	0	= 4	19
Netherlands	0	0	1	2	= 3	45
New Zealand	—	—	—	—		(European countries only)
Sweden	0	0	2	0	= 2	30
UK	0	1	1	—	= 2	59
USA	—	—	—	—		(European countries only)

Adapted from: Lane and Ersson, 1991, pp. 224, 225

We now turn to the second dimension of structure—the degree of horizontal co-ordination within central government. How far are one or two central ministries able to ensure that all the others take the same approach to matters of particular interest? This is a difficult variable to estimate, because it tends to be more a matter of convention and less clearly written down in constitutional or statutory provision than are questions of the distribution of powers between different levels of government. One is obliged to rely more on the impressions of knowledgeable observers and participants. Allowing for this, there appear to be some significant differences between countries.

In some countries there is a tradition that one, or sometimes two, ministries 'call the shots' as far as administrative reform is concerned. Other ministries have to fall in line. In New Zealand, for example, the Ministry of Finance and the State Services Commission were able to drive through the huge changes of the ten-year period after 1984 (Boston *et al.*, 1996). In the UK the Treasury is usually able to get its way, especially when it is in agreement with the Office of Public Service (based in the Cabinet Office). Other countries, however, are more fragmented in this regard. In the Netherlands no ministry enjoys the degree of pre-eminence held by the New Zealand Ministry of Finance or the UK Treasury. In Finland the Ministry of Finance is certainly powerful, but in matters of administrative change, shares responsibility with the Ministry of the Interior. In the USA the picture is complicated by the unusual strength of the legislature, its strong direct links with individual departments and agencies, and its ability to 'micro-manage' federal organizations, sometimes cutting across the intentions of the President and the executive leadership (see Appendix A: USA, country file, and Peters, 1995). In France, although the *grands corps* form a strong 'glue' at the top of the system, the state as a whole is a 'fragmented machine' and 'Ministerial structures are always in turmoil' (Rouban, 1995, pp. 42, 45). Germany is more fragmented still: 'Instead of having one single powerful actor or agency, possibly at the national level, that would take the lead, and have the say in public sector reform issues, the German politico–administrative system has a multitude of such arenas and actors' (Schröter and Wollmann, 1997, p. 187).

3.4 The nature of executive government

Whatever the *scope* of central government might be, what goes on within that scope will be shaped by the working habits and conventions of that particular executive. Comparativist scholars have developed a useful typology of these conventions, the basic features of which are as follows:

Single party or mimimal-winning or bare majority: where one party holds more than 50 per cent of the seats in the legislature;

Minimal-winning coalitions: where two or more parties hold more than 50 per cent of the legislative seats;

Minority cabinets: where the party or parties composing the executive hold less than 50 per cent of the legislative seats;

Oversized executives or grand coalitions: where additional parties are included in the executive beyond the number required for a minimal winning coalition (Lijphart, 1984).

The importance of these types is that each tends to generate a different set of governing conventions. Of course, following elections the executive of a given country can change from one of these types to another, but in practice such shifts are comparatively rare. In most countries the electoral system produces fairly stable results and thus executives tend to build up quite well-entrenched habits of government. In very general terms these habits tend to become more consultative and consensus-oriented/less adversarial the further one moves down the above list (i.e., single party majorities tend to go along with fairly adversarial styles of governance while minority cabinets and grand coalitions tend to behave in a more consensual fashion). The implication of this for public management reform is that the sweeping changes—which are highly likely to be those which will disturb the widest range of interests—are less and less feasible the further one moves away from the first category of executive government—single party or minimal-winning or bare majority governments. This is not necessarily a very strong or precise correlation—we do not wish to suggest that the pattern of reform can simply be 'read off' from the type of executive—but it is a background influence which shapes the boundaries of what is politically feasible (in terms of Figure 2.1 this is the political system—box E—influencing elite perceptions of what is feasible— box I).

The 'track records' of our ten countries would appear to lend general support to this line of reasoning. If we examine the clearly majoritarian governments (Australia, Canada, New Zealand until 1996 and the UK) and compare them with the clearly consensual regimes (Finland and the Netherlands) there can be little doubt that the scope and intensity of management reforms were greater in the former group than in the latter. However, there is also a large intermediate category where the application of this 'rule of thumb' does not work out so well.

There is an interesting relationship between the first of our features—state structure—and this second feature—the nature of executive government. In a complex statistical analysis Lijphart classified twenty-one countries along two dimensions; the first (Factor 1) being largely determined by the type of executive and the number of parties and the second (Factor 2) by the presence of federalism and the degree of decentralization. This approach gives the pattern depicted in Table 3.4.

Whilst this kind of analysis rests on a whole set of definitions and approximations, its value in relation to public management reform can be straightforwardly stated. Deep structural reforms to the public administrative apparatus tend to be less difficult in majoritarian regimes than in consensual ones. The general reason for this is that such changes usually create 'winners' and 'losers', and the more consensual the regime the more likely it is that the losing interests will be directly represented in the executive, and will seek to prevent, delay or dilute the envisaged changes. Thus consensual regimes are less inclined to, and, in terms of political

TABLE 3.4. *Types of democratic regime:*
state structure and the nature of executive government

		Factor 2		
		Majoritarian	Intermediate	Consensual
Factor 1	Majoritarian	New Zealand UK		Australia Canada Germany USA
	Intermediate		France Sweden	
	Consensual		Finland Netherlands	(Switzerland)

Adapted from: Lijphart, 1984, p. 219

feasibility, less capable of dramatic, radical reforms than are strongly majoritarian executives. The latter can force through their own schemes even against opposition from a range of other interests. In case this sounds like a 'plug' for majoritarian regimes, let it also be said that these same qualities mean that majoritarian governments may be more prone to disruptive policy reversals. In the UK, for example, the alternation between Labour and Conservative executives between 1945 and 1989 led to the nationalization, denationalization, renationalization and, under Mrs Thatcher, reprivatization of the steel industry.

The form of the political executive can thus affect change at several stages in the process of reform. First, it influences the degree of leverage that can be created to launch a programme of reform. Second, it may affect the stability of reforms, once carried through (consensually based innovations having a higher life-expectancy than single-party-based innovations which may be overturned when a rival party gets back into power). Third, there may also be an impact on the sense of 'ownership' of reform measures. In so far as these are seen to have emerged from a broadly based consensus of political opinion, they may assume a legitimacy among the public servants who have to carry them out. If, however, specific reforms are perceived as the doctrinaire instruments of a single party or group, then public servants may resist taking any 'ownership', regarding them with resentment, as alien impositions which may be delayed or diluted as much as possible. In terms of Figure 2.1 the nature of executive government (E) may thus affect not only perceptions of desirability and feasibility (I, J) but also the contents of reform packages (M), the implementation process (N) and the extent of reform eventually achieved (O).

When we test these hypothesized connections against the evidence there does seem to be at least some correspondence. The two most 'pure' majoritarian countries in our set (high on both Factor 1 and Factor 2) are New Zealand and the UK.

These are also the countries which are generally acknowledged to have carried through the most radical and far-reaching management reforms. France, on the other hand, is in an intermediate position—it has a multi-party system, but possesses a very strong executive figure in the shape of the President. When the President is of a party which is also a major party in the government, France has quite a majoritarian 'tinge'. During these periods (e.g., 1982–84 and 1988–92) extensive public management reforms have been carried out (see entry for France in Appendix A). However, at other times, the President has had to work with a Prime Minister who is not of the same party (*cohabitation*) and during these interludes policy making is likely to be more cautious. Overall, France may be said to have an intermediate regime, and to be a 'middling' player in terms of the extent and intensiveness of its management reforms. Thus the hypothesized connection still stands.

A third case would be Finland, again an intermediate case, but inclining more towards the consensual end of the spectrum than France. Here oversized coalitions are common, and the political culture is one of consensual caution and mutual accommodation. Inter-party disputes certainly occur, but their tone is seldom as fierce as is common in France or the UK. In the Finnish case we find a history of substantial but non-doctrinaire reforms which have been implemented calmly and continuously over a period of more than ten years and which have traversed the periods of office of three coalition governments of widely varying mixtures of parties (see Appendix A and Pollitt *et al.*, 1997).

The 'consensual/consensual' box in the bottom right corner of Table 3.4 is empty because none of the ten countries in our set is classified by Lijphart as falling within it. Interestingly, though, Lijphart does find at least one other country which he assigns to this category, namely Switzerland. And Switzerland is notorious for the difficulty its governments have in carrying through major policy reforms (Immergut, 1992).

Before concluding this section it is worth examining two further cases, Germany and the USA. In the German case the *structure* of the state is federal and extensively decentralized (the 'subsidiarity principle'), while the form of executive government has usually been that of a minimal-winning coalition (social democratic-liberal before 1982, conservative-liberal from 1982 to 1998). The effects of the first, structural feature (Lijphart's Factor 2) have been profound:

Lacking a single, possibly centrally-located powerful protagonist and trend-setter in public sector reform matters and, instead, disposing of a multitude of such arenas and actors each interacting in its own right, it almost follows from the 'logic' of the German federal system that public sector reform activities are bound to proceed in a disjointed and incrementalist rather than a comprehensive and 'whole-sale' manner' (Schröter and Wollmann, 1997, p. 188).

The effect of the nature of the central executive (Factor 1) has been less clear. In theory the minimum winning coalition provides a strong Chancellor with good possibilities for carrying through reforms. In the specific case of public administration, however, this possibility tends to be outweighed by the structural factors referred to above. Most public servants are not employed by, and most public programmes are not administered at the federal level. Also, the federal government's freedom of manoeuvre is restricted by the Federal Civil Service Framework Law. Considerable change has taken place at the level of the *Länder* and of cities such as Berlin, Dortmund, Duisberg, Hanover, Heidelberg, Cologne, Munich, Nuremberg, Offenbach and Saarbrucken. However: 'Compared to these developments the federal government has not yet put forward any strategic approach towards modernizing its administrative apparatus in a managerial fashion' (Schröter and Wollmann, 1997, p. 198).

Finally, the USA is another fascinating example of an executive with mixed characteristics. On the one hand, in relation to the nature of executive government (Lijphart's Factor 1) it is quite strongly majoritarian. It has a small number of parties, and executives normally consist of one party only (Democrats or Republicans). This would lead one to hypothesize the possibility of vigorous, broad scope management reforms—at least during those periods when the President is of the same party as holds the majority in Congress (at other times there may be an American parallel with the French *cohabitation*, although one in which the legislature is relatively much more powerful than it is in France). However, state structure (Factor 2) pushes in quite a different direction. The USA is a decentralized, federal state, with a somewhat rigid constitution. One further element needs to be taken into account. The US legislature (House of Representatives plus Senate) is unusually strong relative to the executive, and, furthermore, the executive does not wield the same control over same-party members in the legislature as is enjoyed by, say, the British cabinet. These factors further qualify the picture of majoritarian strength, and change the hypothesis in the direction of a more cautious assessment of the executive's reform capacity. When one comes to examine the track record of reform, it is in itself a mixture. From time to time Presidents have loudly proclaimed their intentions fundamentally to reform the management of federal departments and agencies, but actual achievements have lagged far behind (Ingraham, 1997; Pollitt, 1993). This 'more mouth than muscle' picture closely corresponds with the tensions between Factor 1 elements and Factors 2 elements already described.

Of course, although regime type does seem to be an important determinant of change, as a variable it usually acts in combination with other factors. It permits, but does not, of itself, 'drive'. That requires the intervention of some dynamic agency. Rhodes (1997, p. 44) expresses this clearly as he reviews the UK experience:

[W]hy was the pace of change in Britain greater than elsewhere in Western Europe? Three factors were of overriding importance. First, Margaret Thatcher pushed through reform of the civil service. The phrase *political will* is commonly used to explain the government's determination. *Strong, directive and above all persistent, executive leadership* is longer but more accurate.

Second, there are few constitutional constraints on that leadership, especially when the government has a majority in Parliament . . . Central administrative reform in Britain does not require a statute, only the exercise of Crown Prerogative, or executive powers.

Finally, the government evolved a clear ideological strategy to justify and sell its various reform packages. It attacked big government and waste, used markets to create more individual choice and campaigned for the consumer.

3.5 Mandarin/minister relations

In all countries, major public management reforms usually involve both executive politicians and senior public servants (as described in the previous chapter). However, the relationships between these two elite groups vary considerably from one country to another. We identify two principal dimensions to this variation. First, there is the question of whether political careers are separate from, or are integrated with, the careers of 'mandarins' (Pierre, 1995). Second, there is the extent to which senior civil service positions are themselves politicized, in the sense that most of their occupants are known to have (and have been chosen partly because they have) specific party political sympathies. Mandarins can still be politicized in this sense even if their careers are separate from those of politicians.

The effects of these features on management reforms may be quite subtle. They concern, in particular, 'ownership' of reforms, at different levels within the administrative system. Thus, where ministerial and mandarin careers are integrated, one might imagine that the ownership of reforms at the highest levels would be more easily achieved than in systems where the two career paths are entirely distinct. So in a system such as that of the *grands corps* in France, where many ministers would share closely intertwined careers with the senior civil servants, the shaping of reform packages can rely upon shared perspectives and a common professional socialization to an extent that would not usually be the case in, say, Canada or the UK. However, in a French-type system of integrated careers the problem of ownership may reappear lower down the hierarchy, where rank-and-file public officials feel little kinship or identification with the politicized high-flyers of the *grands corps*. In terms of Figure 2.1 the French problem may be with the implementation process (box N) more than with the original shaping of the 'package' (box M)—as does indeed seem to have been the case.

The second dimension—that of the politicization of top posts—adds its influence in roughly the same direction. It creates a bigger gap between the mandarins and the rank and file than would otherwise exist, and may lower the legitimacy of the former in the eyes of the latter. However, in its extreme form—where the occupancy of top civil service positions changes on a large scale following the election of a new political executive—the effect may be one of creating instability in the reform process. This would particularly dog administrative reform because reshaping organizations and standard operating procedures tends to take at least several years to carry through. We can illustrate this with several examples. Germany (Götz, 1997) and Finland (Tiihonen, 1996) offer cases of moderate politicization where the party political affiliations of senior officials are important but where a change of government does not result in the wholesale 'slaughter' and replacement of the mandarinate. In the Finnish case, the governments are usually coalitions and the style is consensual, and these factors have enabled considerable continuity and stability to be achieved in public management reform (Pollitt *et al.*, 1997). In the German case, the effects were masked by the long tenure of the Kohl-led conservative–liberal coalition, and, in any case, when German governments change there are opportunities for mandarins who are unsympathetic towards the new regime to take study leave or be moved to a variety of less politically sensitive roles (Götz, 1997). The American example is more extreme. The 'spoils system' results in an incoming President rapidly replacing a large number of senior officials in Washington, producing an odd situation which one American academic has memorably described as a 'government of strangers' (Heclo, 1977). The number of political appointees grew from 451 in 1960 to 2,393 in 1992 (Kettl *et al.*, 1996, p. 82). Change on this scale certainly disturbs continuity, requires a great deal of policy relearning and may well result in much reinventing of management wheels. As one group of critics put it:

It is one thing to rely on political appointees to set basic agency policy. It is quite another to appoint so many political appointees that they extend deeply into an agency's middle management. These extra layers increase the distance from the government's top to its bottom and can frustrate the ability of top leaders to give voice to their policies. The layers complicate the flow of information in both directions. They hinder the always difficult job of translating broad goals into specific goals and manageable objectives. They create an artificially low ceiling on the career paths for the bureaucracy's long term officials and, therefore, impose additional frustrations on the federal government's career work force (Kettl *et al.*, 1996, p. 83).

This state of affairs may be contrasted with what passes for normalcy in Canada, New Zealand or the UK. In these countries few overtly party political appointments are made to the upper reaches of the public service, and 'mandarins' can normally expect to serve out all or most of their working lives within the upper reaches of the state machine. This brings, in equal measure, the benefits of continuity and accumulated knowledge and the drawbacks of conservatism ('seen it all before') and limited breadth of experience. In these countries the career patterns of ministers and mandarins are largely separate.

3.6 The philosophy and culture of governance: *Rechtsstaat* or public interest?

Having considered the 'normal habits' of government (consensualism, majoritarianism and their variants) and the relations between ministers and mandarins, we can now begin to examine the 'normal beliefs' of administration. Can distinctive administrative cultures be identified, each with its own characteristic pattern of values and assumptions and, if so, how do these affect the process of administrative reform? Fortunately this is an area which has attracted a good deal of academic study and commentary, so we are once more in the happy position of being able to stand on the shoulders of other scholars. A number of these writers have argued for the existence of two particularly strong models: 'Most public administrative systems seem to be guided either by the *Rechtsstaat* model or by the Anglo Saxon notion of the 'public interest'; very few systems fall between these two models which appear to be inherently inconsistent and irreconcilable' (Pierre, 1995, p. 8).

From the *Rechtsstaat* perspective, the state is a central integrating force within society, and its focal concerns are with the preparation, promulgation and enforcement of laws. It follows from this that most senior civil servants will be trained in the law and, indeed, that a large and separate body of specifically *administrative* law will have been created. In such a culture the instinctive bureaucratic stance will be one of rule-following and precedent, and the actions of both individual public servant and individual citizen will be set in this context of correctness and legal control. The oversight of such a system will require a hierarchy of administrative courts, such as the *Conseil d'Etat* in France or the *Bundesverwaltungsgericht* in Germany. The typical values of this approach will include respect for the authority of the law as a socially necessary and integrating force, attention to precedent and a concern with equity, at least in the sense of equality before the law. All in all:

[I]t has become sufficiently clear now that, in countries like France and Germany, the issue of New Public Management in the civil service meets with cultural premises that differ from those in Anglo-Saxon countries (König, 1997, p. 222).

By contrast, the 'public interest' model accords the state a less extensive or dominant role within society (indeed, use of the phrase 'the state' is rare within, originally 'Anglo-Saxon' states such as Australia, New Zealand and the UK). 'Government' (rather than 'the state') is regarded as something of a necessary evil, whose powers are to be no more than are absolutely necessary, and whose ministers and officials must constantly be held to public account by elected Parliaments and through other means. Of course, the law is an essential component of governance, but its particular perspectives and procedures are not as dominant as within the *Rechtsstaat* model. All citizens are under the law, but law is usually in the background rather than the foreground, and many senior civil servants have no special training in its mysteries (as in the UK case, where the vast majority of senior officials are 'generalists'). Civil servants are regarded as simply citizens who work for government organizations, not some kind of special caste or cadre with a higher mission to represent 'the state'. The process of government is seen as one of seeking to obtain the public's consent (or, at least, acquiescence) for measures devised in the public (general, national) interest. It is recognized that different social interests groups compete with one another, sometimes in fiercely adversarial ways. In this context, government's job is to play the part of a fair and trusted referee, and not to get drawn in on one side or another. Fairness and independence of the play of sectional interests are therefore key values, with pragmatism and flexibility as qualities which may be prized above technical expertise (or even above strict legality).

What are the implications of each of these approaches for public management reform? In general terms we might expect that *Rechtsstaat* systems would be 'stickier' and slower to reform than public interest regimes. This is because management change would always require changes in the law and, culturally, because senior civil servants who are highly trained in administrative law may find it more difficult than generalists to shift to a 'managerial' or 'performance-oriented' perspective. There is at least some circumstantial evidence to support this interpretation. For example, French and German civil servants often find it surprising that the UK executive agency programme can, within a decade, have transferred more than two thirds of non-industrial civil servants out of ministerial departments and into a new form of organization without a single new statute being required (see Appendix: UK, country file). By contrast, the small amount of restructuring that has taken place in the federal German government has sometimes been explained as partly a result of the constraining nature of the basic framework laws in that country (Schröter and Wollmann, 1997).

Finally, though, one may question whether the bipolar categorization of administrative cultures as either 'public interest' or *Rechtsstaat* is really adequate. In a number of the countries under consideration there has been a considerable shift away from a highly legalistic state form, but towards something other than a straightforward public interest model. The Netherlands, Finland and Sweden all fall into this third category. The Netherlands went through a period of 'dejuridification' after the Second World War, and its administrative culture now appears as a complex mixture, with a rather open attitude that brings a range of experts and groups into the policy-making process. There are also remnants of the old 'pillarization' mind-set, in so far as it can still be considered important to ensure that the administrative decision-making process balances representation from each of the major social groups. It is therefore an essentially consensual approach, very different from the more closed and juridical purity of a full *Rechtsstaat* philosophy. In both Finland and Sweden a training in law has in the past been normal for higher public officials, but, as with the Netherlands, this lawyerly dominance has been considerably diluted over the past forty or fifty years. In both countries civil servants now come from a wide variety of disciplinary backgrounds, and the culture of upper civil service could be said to have as much to do with satisfying the demands of meso-corporatist intermediation practices as with a strict application of law. In both countries, also, there is a sense of the weight, centrality and continuity of the state—senior public servants are not quite the anxious, harassed breed one finds in Washington DC or sometimes in Whitehall.

3.7 Sources of policy advice

The final aspect of the administrative system which we wish to suggest is of significance is the diversity of the key sources of advice to ministers on reform issues. (We are here referring exclusively to advice on management reform issues. Advice on other types of policy innovation, such as defence policy or economic policy, may be taken from different networks.) In principle, political executives could take management advice from a wide range of sources—from their own political parties, from their mandarins, from management consultants, from academic specialists, from business corporations or from political or policy think tanks. The basic proposition here is that the wider the range of customary sources of advice, the more likely it is that new ideas—especially those from outside the public sector—will reach ministers' ears in persuasive and influential forms. Thus, for example, new management ideas (box F in Figure 2.1) will have an earlier and better chance of getting a sympathetic hearing from executive politicians.

Beyond this, the source of a particular reform idea may influence its perceived legitimacy and 'ownership' (a point already made in the section on minister/mandarin relations). Rank-and-file civil servants may be more suspicious of innovations that are believed to come from one particular political party or from 'whizz kids' in a fashionable think tank. Achieving 'ownership' of reform right down the hierarchy may be less difficult if it is perceived as having a significant 'home-grown' element, that is, if the innovation is seen to be based on accumulated experience within the civil service itself, rather than being a forced 'import' from Rank Xerox or Motorola. Of course, these reactions will themselves be influenced by the administrative culture. Ideas from big business may be accorded greater face legitimacy in a pro-business, anti-government culture such as prevails in the USA, than in a strong, proud state culture such as has existed for some time in France.

Contrasts are not hard to find. Consider the differences between France and the UK during the 1980s. In France reform policies emerged from within the 'usual networks' of members of the *grands corps*—mandarins and politicians with shared ENA backgrounds and intertwined careers. In the UK Mrs Thatcher was well known for her suspicions of the civil service and went out to right-wing think tanks for many of her reform ideas. Or again, we may note a similar contrast between Germany and the USA. In Germany most reform projects have been hatched within the public service itself, sometimes helped by advice from specialist academics at the Speyer Institute of Administrative Sciences (Schröter and Wollmann, 1997). In the USA President Reagan called in teams of businessmen to propose changes in the federal administration, most infamously the Grace Commission and its 2,000 businessmen (Pollitt, 1993, pp. 91–5). In 1984 Grace delivered 2,478 recommendations for improving efficiency and cutting 'waste', but the implementation of many of these ideas seems to have been lost track of within a fragmented, sceptical and probably resentful federal bureaucracy. In Canada, too, Prime Minister Mulroney exhibited considerable suspicions of the career bureaucrats and made a virtue of seeking business advice (Savoie, 1994).

Finland, the Netherlands and Sweden are each different again. The Finnish public management reforms of the decade from 1987 owed most to the thinking of senior public servants. External participation from business people or consultants was the exception rather than the rule (though one or two of the civil servants themselves had some business experience). By contrast Dutch reforms emerged from a procession of committees and enquiries which featured not only civil servants but also academics, auditors and individuals from the business world— there was a fairly open market place of advice and ideas. Sweden probably fell some way between Finland and the Netherlands—there was some 'external' debate and participation, but senior public servants kept a firm grip on the helm, and were never in the position of US or British or Canadian civil servants in being obliged to implement a reform agenda that had been substantially set by business advisers to the government, external think tanks or management consultants.

3.8 The European Commission: a special case

The European Commission is obviously a special case, because it is not a sovereign nation state. Furthermore, as a supranational authority, much of its business is conducted *with* nation states, and thus cannot be considered in the same breath as relations between a national government and its own subnational tiers of government. However, despite these *sui generis* aspects, much of the analysis which we have applied above to the eleven countries in our set can also be applied to the Commission. In fact we would argue that the third, fourth and fifth features of our general analysis can be related to the Commission without too much difficulty, and that the main differences arise with the first and second—state structure and the style of executive government. To begin with we will tackle these two more problematic features.

In terms of the vertical dispersion of authority we cannot neatly label the Commission as either federal or unitary. Certainly it is not federal in the sense of having inferior tiers of authority below it, sharing powers in a way that is defined by a single constitution. Yet there are some resemblances: the Commission very much operates within the framework of treaties (Rome, Maastricht) and these define the relationships which are supposed to obtain between the Commission, other EU institutions, and members states themselves. In this sense one might speak of the Commission working within a quasi-federal, treaty-framed environment, although one in which the other 'levels' are not 'inferior' in the usual sense. One obvious difference, for example, has been that, whereas the national level in most federal states retains responsibility for foreign and defence policies, within the EU member states have fiercely guarded their independence in these respects, and moves towards developing common approaches in these areas, though significant, have also been limited, hesitant and slow.

On the other hand the definition of 'unified' does not seem to fit very well either, because, although the Commission is itself a unified body, so much of its work depends on arriving at co-operative agreements with member states, each of which is an independent sovereign power in its own right. In this sense, therefore, only the most extreme Europhobes would liken the Commission to a powerful unitary state on the model of France or the UK.

Moving onto the question of horizontal co-ordination, we may immediately observe that the Commission has strong vertical divisions and is often difficult to co-ordinate (Middlemass, 1995; Page, 1997). Each Directorate General (DG) is to a significant extent a law unto itself, and the horizontally co-ordinating DGs (IX—personnel, XIX—budget and XX—audit and control) have to struggle hard to exert influence over the 'operational' DGs which run EU programmes. In short, the Commission is quite a fragmented body.

Given these structural characteristics, what might one deduce about management reform? Perhaps simply that broad-scope, radical reform of the kind carried through in unified, centralized states such as New Zealand and the UK would be difficult. The historical record would seem to bear this out—although there has been a tortuous history of partial, incremental reforms (and failed reforms— Spierenberg, 1979) there has been no general restructuring or reorientation towards performance or output/outcome-based styles of management. On the contrary, the Commission remains, for the most part, an old-fashioned bureaucracy.

The second 'key feature' in our analysis is the nature of executive government—the habits or style of governance. In the Commission's case this is much more consensual than majoritarian, although political parties play only a very subdued role. The Commission itself (i.e., the body of Commissioners) is an expressly collegial body, where it is vital for proposers of reform to gain common assent, or at least reluctant acquiescence. It is composed of people with executive political experience (typically ex-ministers from the member states) but they must deal with what is, in effect, a rival political executive in the shape of the Council of Ministers. The Commission is also accountable to the European Parliament. The latter is not usually a particularly strong political force, although in 1999 pressure from the Parliament obliged the Commissioners, unprecedentedly, to resign.

Moving on to what in Table 3.1 is termed 'minister/mandarin relations' we may say that the Commission is unique—for a mixture of reasons. To begin with, it has what in terms of most nation states would be regarded as an 'extra' political layer. The 'mandarins' are the Directors General, the permanent heads of the Commission's services. Above them floats the first political layer—the Commissioners, who, although appointed, are generally politicians by background (see previous paragraph). However, beyond the Commissioners lies another powerful body of executive politicians, the Council of Ministers from the member states. Just to make matters more complicated still, each Commisioner has a sizeable *cabinet* of personally appointed officials, who offer policy advice and (not infrequently) clash with the Directors General. Finally, we may note that, while *cabinet* positions are temporary (they do not last beyond the tenure of the individual Commissioner) even the career Director Generals, and the two grades immediately below them, are politically influenced appointments (Page, 1997). The upshot of all this is a very complex set of relations between senior career officials and 'their' Commissioners. Their careers are not usually intertwined after the French fashion, but the mandarin ranks are certainly politicized, and there is a large group of even more politicized temporary officials in the shape of the *cabinets*.

As for the administrative culture of the Commission, it would probably be fair to say that it still bears strong traces of the predominant French influence during its formative years. Many French practices and titles continue, including the existence of strong separate hierarchies (in the DGs), the financial control system, and the predominantly regulatory and legalistic cast of mind. It is more *Rechtsstaat* than public interest, although it must also be acknowledged that there is also considerable internal diversity, and that reforms and wider recruitment of staff from the newer member states are gradually changing the climate.

With respect to policy advice, that which reaches Commissioners may be said to be fairly diverse. In addition to advice from the DGs, Commissioners take the views of their own *cabinets*, and, not unusually, may tap sources within the administration of their own member state. They are also bombarded with evidence and demands from the multiplicity of pressure groups which have set up in Brussels. Whilst this is an exceedingly complex system it is not a closed one.

In sum, therefore, one could say that, within the Commission, the feasibility threshhold over which management reforms must pass is particularly high. The Commission is a collegial, consensual body and its operative Directorates General are vertically highly fragmented. No single source of power and authority is therefore strong enough to drive through across-the-board changes against significant resistance. The pressure of public opinion is weak and indirect: this is because of the intervening 'layer' of member states, because of the relative feebleness of the European Parliament and because the Commission anyway does not itself provide the kinds of public services which would bring it into direct contact with the public. Other 'difficult to change' factors should also be mentioned. The Commission mandarins have separate and generally extremely secure careers—they do not need constantly to 'show results' in order to keep their jobs (Page, 1997, p. 87). The top three grades in the hierarchy are fairly politicized, but in a way which tends to focus the occupants on sexy political topics and on what can be achieved within the four-year term of a Commission rather than on longer-term structural change. The administrative culture carries significant elements of *Rechtsstaat*, and the resort to legal rules and standard procedures is if anything intensified by the difficulties of running such a multi-lingual, multi-cultural organization. All these features combine to make the life of the would-be management reformer difficult.

Yet, despite all this, broader economic pressures and external currents of management ideas have at least placed large-scale administrative modernization once more upon the Commission's agenda. When the new Commission took office in 1995 it launched a Sound and Efficient Management Initiative (SEM 2000). This was quickly followed by MAP 2000 (Modernizing Administrative and Personnel Policy) which focused on internal reforms to the Commission's own machinery. It remains to be seen how much headway such initiatives can make against the strong constraints embedded in the politico-administrative regime. Early assessments seem to indicate that some progress had been made, but that very substantial obstacles to any attempt at coherent, co-ordinated and thoroughgoing reform remain (European Commission, 1998, and interviews).

3.9 Traditional bureaucracy: the *ancien régime*?

A good deal of the rhetoric associated with public management reform vividly contrasts the new (= good) with the old (= bad). The name given to the old—that against which the modern, reformed public sector organization stands out as superior—is usually something like 'traditional bureaucracy' (e.g., Hughes, 1998, chapter 2). Before concluding this review of regime types it is therefore necessary to explore this *ancien régime*—to understand what was supposed to be wrong with it and to clarify its relationships with the various dimensions of the politico-administrative world which have been discussed in Sections 3.2 to 3.8 above.

Osborne and Gaebler (1992, pp. 11–12) are fairly typical of at least the Anglo-American-Australasian critique of traditional bureaucracy:

Our thesis is simple. The kind of governments that developed during the industrial era, with their sluggish, centralised bureaucracies, their preoccupation with rules and regulations, and their hierarchical chains of command, no longer work very well. They accomplished great things in their time, but somewhere along the line they got away from us. They became bloated, wasteful, ineffective. And when the world began to change, they failed to change with it. Hierarchical, centralised bureaucracies designed in the 1930s or 1940s simply do not function well in the rapidly-changing, information-rich, knowledge-intensive society and economy of the 1990s.

An Australian commentator, Hughes (1998, pp. 38–9) takes a similar line:

The traditional model was rigid and bureaucratic, narrowly-focused and preoccupied with structure and process. It was, however, much better than what existed before . . . However, despite its years of worthy service, there are major criticisms of the traditional model . . . It was a good model for a long time, but its time has passed.

Hughes is one of many who links the traditional model with the ideal-type rational/legal bureaucracy in the writings of Max Weber (Weber, 1947). This type of organization was characterized by:

* fixed spheres of competence;
* a defined hierarchy of offices;
* a clear distinction between the public and private roles (and property) of the officials;
* specialization and expertise as the basis for action;
* full-time, career appointments for officials;
* management by the application of a developing set of rules, knowledge of which was the special technical competence of the officials concerned.

This, then is the type of regime which is said to be in need of replacement by more flexible, fast-moving, performance-oriented forms of modern organization. Of the various types of administrative culture which have been discussed earlier in this chapter, it is fairly clear which one is closest to the traditional model—it is the *Rechtsstaat*. This line of interpretation therefore leads towards the conclusion that countries like Germany are 'behind' and need to take up 'reinvention' or the 'New Public Management' more vigorously—to follow the 'leaders' such as New Zealand or the United States' National Performance Review.

Unfortunately, however, what one might term the 'Osborne and Gaebler story' is misleadingly neat and over-simple. There are many detailed criticisms which could be made of it, but here we will confine ourselves to just three general points. First, as is dazzlingly clear from the earlier sections of this chapter, for many years there has not been just one type of administrative regime in existence, but several. Second (by way of extension to the first) even if some parts of some public sectors 'fitted' the image of the traditional bureaucracy, others definitely did not. For example, in the UK (as in most other western European states) the most expensive and labour intensive sectors of state administration—health care and education— were never legalistic bureaucracies. On the contrary, they were heavily profession- alized organizations in which individual professions were able to exercise a great deal of discretion. Clarke and Newman (1997) call this 'bureau-professionalism', to distinguish it from pure bureaucracy. Third, the accounts of traditional bureau- cracy given by the Osborne and Gaebler 'school' tend to be rather one-sided. They emphasize the negatives ('rigidity', 'centralization', etc.) but ignore or underplay the positives, such as continuity, honesty and a high commitment to equity in deal- ing with the citizen-public. In his seminal article on the NPM, Hood terms these 'theta-type core values', and comments that, even if NPM reforms do increase frugality and efficiency, these gains could be 'bought at the expense of guarantees of honesty and fair dealing and of security and resilience' (Hood, 1991, p. 16).

Our conclusion is *not* that the negative features of the 'traditional model' are fantasies, with no basis in reality. Every reader can probably vouchsafe some personal experience testifying to the capacity of public (and private) bureaucracies to work in infuriatingly slow and inefficient ways. However, it is a long—and unjustified—leap from there to the idea that the governments of the industrialized world previously operated their public sectors as Weberian-style traditional bureaucracies, and are now able to move, without significant loss, to a new, modern type of organization which avoids all the problems of the past. As this book will continue to demonstrate, public sectors have not all come from the same place and are not all headed in the same direction. Modernization often involves losses as well as gains (chapter 7 is particularly concerned with this theme). Each country is different (though there are some groups and patterns) and within each public domain, individual sectors have distinctive organizational cultures of their own. The idea of a single, and now totally obsolete, *ancien régime* is as implausible as the suggestion that there is now a global recipe which will reliably deliver 'reinvented' governments.

3.10 Concluding remarks

The main points of this chapter can be straightforwardly summarized. Features of the existing politico-administrative regime are likely to exert a significant influence over both the choice of reforms to be adopted and the feasibility of implementing certain types of reform (desirability and feasibility—boxes I and J in Figure 2.1). State structures, the nature of central executive government, relationships between ministers and mandarins, the prevailing administrative culture and the diversity of channels of advise all have effects on which ideas get taken up, and how vigorously and widely these are subsequently implemented. Certain regimes look as though they are much more open to the 'performance-driven', market-favouring ideas of the NPM than others: particularly the 'Anglo-Saxon' countries, Australia, Canada, New Zealand, the UK and the USA. However, not every member of this group has an equal capacity to *implement* such ideas in a coherent, broad-scope way. For structural reasons, executive power is less centralized and focused in the USA than in New Zealand and the UK. Australia and Canada—both tinged with the 'Westminster system', but both federal by constitution—lie somewhere in between in this respect. Other countries, with a strong *Rechtsstaat* tradition, are more resistant to NPM ideas, although nonetheless interested in reform. Germany and France are the most prominent examples here. Each has tried to carve its own reform path. Of the two, France finds it less difficult to make broad changes, to the extent that it remains fairly centralized and is governed by a President with strong powers. In federal Germany some of the constraints on change are entrenched in constitutional law, so one might expect change to be difficult at the federal level, though possibly more in evidence at the lower levels of *Länder* and municipalities. Finally, there are the three north-western European states—Finland, the Netherlands and Sweden. These differ among themselves in a variety of ways, but share a general disposition towards consensual, often meso-corporatist styles of governance. This tends to blunt the sharper corners of the NPM, leading to less outright criticism of the state bureaucracy, a cautious rather than a wildly enthusiastic approach to MTMs and to privatization, and a less rapid (some would say less ruthless) style of implementation than prevailed in New Zealand and the UK.

The above remarks are a brief foretaste of what is to come. In the next chapter, and in Appendix A, there will be more detailed accounts of the reform trajectories in each of the ten countries. These will therefore provide a test for the predictive powers of the politico-administrative variables here identified and discussed.

4

Trajectories of Modernization and Reform

'Why are Anglo-American countries the centre of the reform universe? How
do the reforms fare when they are taken from that context and placed into
different political and administrative environments?'

(Peters, 1996a, p. 115)

4.1 From regimes to trajectories

In the previous chapters we examined the relatively enduring—yet slowly changing—politico-administrative regimes of ten countries, plus the European
Commission. Now we shift focus to more rapid and short-term forms of change:
the reforms themselves. Is it true that the Anglo-American countries are the centre
of the reform universe, or is that a perspective largely confined to Anglo-
Americans? How far can it be said that everyone has been following the same route,
albeit from different starting points in terms of their politico-administrative
regimes? Are there clear patterns, or is the story really one of ad hockery dressed
up as strategy?

These are questions we will address in this chapter, but continue to pursue
throughout the remainder of the book. There are, as always, too many 'facts' for
anyone to master them all, so any explanation is bound to be selective (and therefore interpretive). Our first step was to use the model of change advanced in chapter 2 to organize the elements of what seemed to be the 'basics' of each country's
experience into some sensible categories. The results of that exercise may be seen
in tabular form in Appendix A, where there is a summary for each country, and
chronological tables. Appendix A should be used as an adjunct to the whole book,
but especially to this chapter. In this chapter itself we adopt a broad comparative
perspective, looking for patterns of similarity and difference. We do this by
employing the concept of *trajectories* to help us sort out the data.

4.2 Trajectories and scenarios: a conceptual preliminary

A trajectory, as defined here, is more than a trend. A trend is simply some pattern
in the data (e.g., if the rainfall goes up every year for ten years, that is a trend). A
trajectory, by contrast, is an *intentional* pattern—a route that someone is trying to
take. It leads from a starting point (an alpha) to some desired place or state of
affairs in the future (an omega). Thus a *scenario* consists of three basic elements,
an initial state, a trajectory, and a future state (see Figure 4.1).

Scenarios may exist at various levels of specificity. They may amount to little

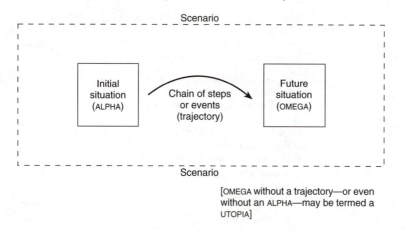

FIG. 4.1. The concept of a trajectory

more than a set of vague ideas and orientations. Or they may be developed into a strategic plan, with specified actions, timescales and objectives. Scenarios are not always complete, in the sense that one or more of the three basic elements may be missing. For example, if there is only an omega—a vision of the desired future— but no clear specification of alpha or of trajectory, then we speak of a *utopia*. Alternatively, there may exist a critique of the status quo (alpha) and a desire to move in a certain direction (trajectory) but no well-developed picture of the final state that is aimed for. This could be thought of as a kind of drifting with the tide, and there is certainly evidence of a good deal of that in the world of management reform ('everyone seems to be doing this so we had better try it too').

To anticipate, we are of the view that fully-worked out scenarios, with each of the three main elements clearly analysed and described, are definitely the exception rather than the rule in public management reform. The real world is usually more untidy, with poorly specified visions of the future, inadequate analyses of the status quo and partial and sometimes conflicting or oscillating trajectories for different aspects of the administrative apparatus.

4.3 The main components of reform

Table 4.1 sets out some of the main components of reform trajectories, and these headings will be used as a template for the following sections and subsections.

We have selected four main components for the substance (or 'what') of reform, plus three for the process (or 'how'). The divisions are fairly conventional: finance, personnel, organization and performance measurement constituting the 'what' and top down/bottom up, legal dimensions and organizational processes constituting the 'how'. These topics are reviewed in the following subsections, before a final overview is given in 4.10.

TABLE 4.1. *Aspects of trajectories: context (what) and process (how)*

Starting position: Alpha	*What trajectory: scope and components*	End position: Omega
	– Finance: budget, accounts, audits – Personnel: recruitment, posting, remuneration, security of employment, etc. – Organization: specialization, co-ordination, scale, (de)centralization – Performance Measurement Systems: content, organization, use	
	How trajectory: process of implementation	
	– Top down vs bottom up – Legal dimensions – Task allocation: (new) organizations	

4.4 Trajectories in financial management reform

Budget reforms have been widespread, and have been driven by two particular external pressures. The first has been to restrain the growth of public expenditure, for macro-economic reasons. Clearly, this need goes up and down with the economic cycle and the strength or weakness of the particular economy. The Norwegians, for example, with a small population and a huge revenue from offshore oil and gas, have experienced much less budgetary pressure than any of the ten countries covered by this book. The second pressure has been that for performance improvement within the public sector—for types of budgeting and financial management which will stimulate or even force greater efficiency or effect-iveness, or higher quality, or some mixture of the three.

Taken together, these pressures have led to what in effect has been an expansion in the scope or purpose of budgeting. Instead of a situation in which budgets were mainly a process by which annual financial allocations were incrementally adjusted, legalized and made accountable to legislatures, budgeting has become more inti-mately linked with other processes—planning, operational management and performance measurement. Greater integration of these different systems has been a common objective (Bouckaert and Van Reeth, 1998; Le Loup, 1988; Pollitt, 1998b). Caiden (1988) describes this broadening and complexifying of the budget agenda as the emergence of 'super budgeting'. Similarly, financial management, which often used to be the preserve of financial management specialists, has now become an element in the training and professional socialization of many, if not most, middle managers and professionals (see Zifcak, 1994 on initiatives in Australia and the UK). If one examines, for example, the Local Management of Schools Initiative in the UK in the late 1980s and early 1990s, one can see how delegation of budgets from local governments to individual schools turned most headteachers into financial managers, whether they liked it or not (Pollitt, Birchall and Putman, 1998, chapter 6).

The reforms which have served the *savings* objective have not always fitted well with the reforms that would be required to encourage performance improvement. For example, the first reaction of some governments to expenditure pressures was to 'cheese slice', that is, to strengthen the hand of central finance ministries to cut back programmes from the top down. This occurred in, *inter alia*, Canada and the Netherlands. In a study of budgetary behaviour in Australia, Canada, Germany, Japan, Mexico and the UK, the US General Accounting Office concluded that: '[A]ll six governments departed from previous budgeting approaches and imposed "top down" overall limits on government spending . . . Despite . . . variation, each represented a multi-year approach that sought to reduce overall real spending' (General Accounting Office, 1994, p. 6).

The depth and incidence of the cuts depended on the political opportunities (some targets are politically 'harder' than others—e.g., it may be easier to cut new weapons systems than to cut pensions) and on the severity of the macro-economic position (e.g., New Zealand in 1984 and Finland in 1992 were in more severe circumstances than either country was in 1998). In general, however, this kind of approach sits uneasily with performance improvement. This is because opportunistic cheese-slicing generates a highly unpredictable and negative environment for operational managers, in which they may suddenly find they have lost part of their budget for no good performance-related reason. Managers come to see themselves as the victims of particularistic interventions from seemingly all-powerful central finance departments.

A second route to savings was perhaps more compatible with performance improvement (though no programme manager enjoys budget reductions, however they are executed). It was to adopt or increase the use of frame- or block-budgeting, as was done by a number of countries, including Finland, Sweden and the USA. Here the central ministry sets and polices broad ceilings (frames) but within those delegates responsibility for allocation to particular services, programmes or projects to local politicians and/or managers. In Finland, for example, the introduction of frame budgeting in 1994 meant a change from a system in which central agencies had been heavily involved in regulating and controlling individual local services to a new relationship in which central government fixed a formula-determined total for each municipality and left local politicians to decide how to distribute that total between the various activities (see Appendix: Finland, country file). This approach does permit the local determination of priorities. However, as many commentators have pointed out, it also neatly delegates the unpopular business of making painful choices between competing priorities. Frame budgeting also required some redesign of budgetary procedures, in that there needed to be clear and separate phases to the budgetary discussion—first, the determination of aggregate financial frames (and therefore a debate about what the most appropriate formulae should be) and then, second, a detailed local discussion of what allocations there should be to specific programmes (and how the performance of those programmes should be measured).

Turning to those aspects of financial management reform which are more related to *performance* rather than savings, one finds a number of partial trajectories. A first step is sometimes simply to publish some performance information alongside the annual budget documents (though it may be difficult or impossible to relate specific 'performances' to specific financial allocations). A second step is to begin to change the format and contents of the budget itself, typically by moving away from line item budgeting towards some more performance-sensitive type of categorization, or by trying to link up budgeting with new processes of strategic planning. A third, and more ambitious step is to change the procedure of budgeting itself, for example, by altering the incentives to key budget actors or by fundamentally changing the structure or timing of the budget discussion, or even by attempting to alter the role of the legislature in the budget process.

Before moving to greater detail it should be emphasized that caution is required in the interpretation of the evidence of budgetary reform. Budgeting is an intensely political process, behaviours during which can be very difficult to change—even when formal procedures are modified. Furthermore, headline statements such as 'Country X adopted performance budgeting from 1995' seldom tell the whole story. Even when budgetary reform is implemented successfully, it may take years for all the various organizations concerned to become comfortable with and fully practice the new procedures. Finally, the process of budget reform is continuous, so it is inevitable that by the time this book is in print, further initiatives, not recorded here, will have been launched.

Bearing these caveats in mind, one can discern a broad pattern in budget reform. Major changes to enhance the performance focus of budgeting have been implemented in Australia, Finland, New Zealand, Sweden and the UK. Indeed, from the late 1970s, 'results-oriented budgeting' has formed a central plank of the management reform process in both Finland and Sweden (Pollitt and Summa, 1997a). All these countries therefore fall in the 'third step' category (see Table 4.2). We have also included Canada in this category because, although the links between performance information and budgetary allocations are as yet rather general and vague (President of the Treasury Board, 1997), the timing and periodicity of the budget have been altered, and efforts have been made to discover formats which will encourage members of the legislature to make more informed use of performance data.

Canada provides a good example of the difficulty of 'reading' budget reforms. In the early 1980s the federal government introduced a range of budget-modernizing measures—a Policy and Expenditure Management System (PEMS), a Multi-Year Operational Plan (MYOP) and an Operational Framework Plan (OFP). On paper this system sounded highly rational. In practice, however, under the Mulroney administrations from 1993, the PEMS system singularly failed to persuade or enable ministers to achieve their expenditure targets. It was partially replaced in 1989 and then in 1995 completely superseded by a new Expenditure Management System (EMS). EMS managed to deliver the first balanced budget for more than a decade, but even then the relationship between budget allocations and performance

TABLE 4.2. *Budget trajectories*

Budget status	Routes
Input oriented line item budget	0:Fr1/Germ1/EU1/Neth1/Can1/Sw1/ Finl1/Aus1/NZ1/US1/UK1
A: include some performance information	I: EU2
A+B: change format and content and add other documents	II: Neth2/US2
A+B+C: adapt procedures and timing	III: Can2/Sw2/Finl2/UK2/AUS2/NZ2

was debatable. Indeed, this is far from being just a technical issue. During almost half a century many countries have experienced considerable and persistent difficulties in trying to establish close links between the performance of programmes and their budget allocations (General Accounting Office, 1997; Pollitt, 1998b). There is no particular reason to believe that the latest generation of budget reforms will enjoy more than marginally greater success than previous efforts.

Other countries have not gone quite so far as those in the bottom row of Table 4.2. The Dutch and US governments have taken steps to change the format of budget documents, and to display much more performance information (either in the basic budget document or alongside it) than would have been usual twenty, or even ten, years ago. The German federal government and the EU Commission have also made changes, but of a yet more modest type (type one). At the time of writing there is much discussion within the Commission of the introduction of 'activity budgeting', but the first efforts seem to consist mainly of the construction of elaborate accounting 'cross walks', which display exisiting information in a new way, but which, by themselves, are likely to do little to encourage performance management.

If we move from budgetary reform to the modernization of accounting systems, we find a roughly similar pattern of country trajectories (Table 4.3). Again, Australia, New Zealand and the UK are among the countries which appear to have made the most far-reaching changes, with the USA and the Netherlands having moved, but not quite so far, and the least change being visible in Germany and the EU Commission. This is the pattern which seems to appear if one defines three broad positions, beginning with a traditional, cash-based accounting system, then a shift to double-entry book keeping, possibly with elements of cost analysis, modified cash or modified accrual and, finally, the development of accrual accounts with a focus on providing performance-related information.

This is not a place for a full exposition of the different bases for keeping public accounts. There is space only to point to the very basics of our three-fold classification. In pure cash accounting, a public sector entity is given a budget, calculated in cash terms, and proceeds to spend the money, keeping records of each cash

TABLE 4.3. *Accounting trajectories*

Accounting status	Routes
A: Cash based system	I: Neth1/Finl1/Sw1/Can1/Aus1/NZ1/US1/Fr1/Germ1/UK1/EU1
B: Double book-keeping	II: US2/Neth2/Finl2
C: Accrual accounting with extended cost calculation supported by performance measurement system	III: Sw2/NZ2/Aus2/UK2

disbursement so as to ensure neither an overspend (which may actually be illegal) or an underspend (which is likely to act as an invitation to the political level to arrive at the conclusion that not so much money is needed, and that the budget can therefore be cut in the following year). In the EU Commission, for example, an elaborate cash system operates in which each piece of expenditure has to be approved by three separate officials, as, first, legal, then, second, in accordance with the programme, then, third, as affordable (there is sufficient cash to pay it). This is a system which has been traditional in much of the Francophone world for some time. A problem with it is that, by itself, it gives few incentives for efficiency, or even economy. The name of the game easily becomes that of spending the money allocated, within the financial year. Large expenditures are rushed through in the last few weeks. EU officials, for example, seem to worry about 'absorption' (i.e., their ability to spend all the money allocated) at least as much as they do about efficiency and effectiveness of expenditure.

The shift to double-entry book-keeping marks a significant change from this position. It brings public accounts closer to the private sector model. Every transaction is entered on the accounts twice—once as a credit and once as a debit. If wages are paid, for example, the sum involved can be shown as a *credit* to the organization's central cash account and, simultaneously, a *debit* to the wages account. This approach is founded on the perspective that the organization is a separate business, in which its total assets must, by definition, remain equal to its capital plus its liabilities. It can be used to raise consciousness of a wider range of management issues than is usually provoked by cash-based accounting. In particular, if double-entry book-keeping includes capital assets (land, buildings) it can stimulate managers to make more efficient use of these resources, rather than treating them as a 'free good', as often occurs in cash-based systems. On the other hand, much depends on the *level* at which the books are balanced, and on the extent to which links to performance are made explicit. If double-entry systems are confined to a high level, and accounting itself is performed as a very centralized function, far from 'street level' management, then the impact on most managers may be limited.

Our third stage, accruals accounting, brings the public sector on to as near as possible a comparative basis to the private sector (lowering 'grid' in anthropological terms—Hood, 1998). It means that government organizations report commitments when they are incurred (rather than when the cash is actually disbursed), allow for the valuation and depreciation of all capital assets, and present annual 'balance sheet-type' financial statements (Likierman, 1998a and b). When coupled with a system of decentralized financial management it can form the basis for a close link between resource allocation and performance management at the level of individual agencies and programmes. At the time of writing, full accruals accounts for public sector entities were being produced by Australia, New Zealand and Sweden, soon to be joined by the UK (HM Treasury, 1998).

The significance of these shifts in accounting practices for management is considerable. So long as a cash-based system prevails, without double book-keeping or accruals accounting, it is hard to make either global or specific links between expenditure and cost, and between cost and performance. Managers are not faced with the full costs of their use of assets, and performance measurement, if it exists, tends to be a separate system from financial management. On the other hand, the application of accruals systems is not equally straightforward for all different types of service and circumstance, and reform can create perverse incentives as well as advantages (Gillibrand and Hilton, 1998; Pollitt, 1998b; Straw, 1998).

When reform takes place it has frequently been a step-by-step process, moving from pilot projects to larger scale roll-outs, or from one part of the public sector to others (which means that distortions can arise during the sometimes long transitional periods, when one part of the public sector is operating according to one set of accounting principles and another is following a different set). For example, in the UK, accruals accounting was introduced in the National Health Service before it was adopted for central government, and in the Netherlands double-entry book-keeping is required for some agencies but not for their parent ministries. Furthermore, our three broad 'stages' of accountancy are inevitably a somewhat over-neat classification of detailed practice. In the real world governments blur these categories considerably, by adding performance elements to basically cash-based systems or by introducing partial accruals accounting with lots of exceptions and special features (see HM Treasury, 1998, pp. 132–54). In the late 1990s, for example, the Finnish Ministry of Finance had a project aiming at introducing a full accruals system by the beginning of 1998. However, what was implemented was both later and less than the original proposals had suggested.

Completing the financial circle, we now turn briefly to reforms in public sector *auditing*. Again, we distinguish three stages (and again, these should be regarded as no more than rough approximations to the complexities of detailed practice within each country and sector). The first stage is that of traditional financial and compliance auditing. Here the basic concern of the auditor is with legality and procedural correctness. Has the money been spent on duly approved objects, through the correct procedures? Is there evidence of unauthorized expenditure or corruption? The second stage is to add investigations of some performance issues. For example, auditors may be empowered to search for waste—items which have been purchased at unnecessary expense, or items which have been perfectly legally purchased but which are not being used very much (the school purchases a computer but no teacher can use it, so it sits in the storeroom). Another extension of traditional audit is to extend it into a deeper questioning of data quality ('validation'). The figures presented to Parliament or Audit Office may add up, but how reliable are they? Have all transactions been recorded, and recorded accurately? This is, in effect, an audit of the performance of the organization's internal auditing system. The third stage is the development of full-blown performance auditing as a distinct activity, usually with a separate unit or section of the national audit office to develop performance auditing expertise. The development of performance auditing over the last fifteen years has been considerable, but it has been taken much further in some countries than others (Pollitt and Summa, 1997a; Pollitt *et al.*, 1999). Performance auditors claim to focus directly on the 'three Es', economy, efficiency and effectiveness (see Figure 1.1). These three stages are the basis for Table 4.4.

Performance auditing is fully established, with its own procedures and staff, in Australia, Canada, Finland, the Netherlands, New Zealand, Sweden, the UK and the USA. In some countries Supreme Audit Organizations (the imposing title which national audit offices give themselves) have gone further, and set up groups which concentrate specifically on evaluation (New Zealand, USA—though in the mid 1990s the USA dissolved the evaluation and methodology section which had existed within the General Accounting Office since the 1970s). In other countries the SAOs have taken an active interest in evaluation, and have examined the scope for borrowing techniques and concepts from evaluation, but have not created separate units to carry out evaluations *per se* (e.g., Sweden, UK). Elsewhere, however, the place of performance audit is not so developed or clear cut. In France there is no doubt that the magistrates of the *Cour des Comptes* can and often do analyse performance aspects, but the performance audit function has not been separated from more traditional, compliance-oriented forms of audit, and the general culture is still highly legalistic. In Germany the main emphasis of the *Bundesrechnungshof* has been on compliance and financial auditing, though some performance elements

TABLE 4.4. *Audit trajectories*

Audit status	Routes
A: Traditional financial and compliance audit	I: Neth1/Sw1/Finl1/Can1/Aus1/NZ1/US1/ Fr1/UK1/Germ1/EU1
B: Traditional audit enriched with some elements of performance and evaluation	II: Fr2/EU2/Germ2
C: Institutionalized financial, compliance and performance auditing	III: Neth2/Sw2/Finl2/Can2/UK2/US2/Aus2/ NZ2

are also covered. The same might be said of the European Court of Auditors, which has a definite capacity for performance audit but which, in practice, seems to find most of its staff resources drawn into the identification of fraud and the provision, since 1994, of an annual statement of assurance (DAS) to the European Parliament (National Audit Office, 1996; Pollitt *et al.*, 1999).

Thus far the discussion of audit has been exclusively in terms of external audit by independent audit offices. In practice the work of external audit organizations is made either much easier or much more time-consuming and difficult according to the state of sophistication of *internal* audit within public sector organizations. Thus, if the internal audit of a department concentrates solely upon compliance work it becomes that much more difficult for the external audit body to conduct performance audit (partly because necessary types of data will not exist). In short, reform of auditing usually entails more than just remandating, retraining and reskilling the national audit offices. It also requires matching changes in internal audit services. We are not aware of substantial comparative research in this area, but our own impressions (no more) are that the same rough pattern as emerges for SAOs in Table 4.4 also fits the development of internal audit.

4.5 Trajectories in personnel management/HRM

4.5.1 The volume and direction of reform

As chapter 3 made clear, different countries entered the 1980s with contrasting legal and cultural assumptions about the nature of public service (even the words are treacherous here—'public service' already suggests an Anglo-American-Australasian perspective, by contrast to continental countries in the *Rechtsstaat* tradition, which might rather regard civil servants as 'officers of the state', or some such term). Yet despite differences of 'starting line' most countries suffered similar pressures, and some recipes for personnel reform were adopted by a majority of our ten countries. Certainly there has been no shortage of activity (the following list is selective, not comprehensive):

- Australia: 1983 Amendent of the Public Service Act; 1987, 1993, 1995 Guidelines on Official Conduct of Commonwealth Public Servants; 1990 Guidelines on Appraisal of Performance of Senior Executive Service; 1997 Public Service Bill.
- Canada: 1989 new Personnel Management Manual; Public Service 2000 initiative; Public Service white paper; 1992 Public Service Reform Act.
- Finland: 1994 State Civil Servants Act.
- France: 1989 Prime Ministerial circular on public service renewal included some personnel reforms.
- Germany: 1989 law amending working provisions for civil servants; 1994 Public Service Reform Act; 1996 amendments to the law relating to federal civil servants.
- Netherlands: 1993 delegation of detailed negotiations on labour conditions from Ministry of Home Affairs to eight sectors (state, judiciary, municipalities, etc.).
- New Zealand: 1988 State Sector Act; 1991 Employment Contracts Act.

- Sweden: 1990 modification of Public Employment Act.
- UK: 1992 Civil Service (Management Functions) Act; 1993 Civil Service Management Code; white papers *The civil service: continuity and change* (1994) and *The civil service: taking forward continuity and change* (1995).
- USA: 1978 Civil Service Reform Act (including creation of a Senior Executive Service); 1994 Federal Personnel Manual abandoned (with ceremonial burning of a copy on the White House lawn, as part of NPR); 1994 Federal Workforce Restructuring Act.

Most of these measures were characterized by the same broad orientation (Farnham *et al.*, 1996). Politicians wanted civil services which were more flexible and responsive, more focused on getting results, more skilful and, if possible, less numerous (and therefore less expensive in total). Civil servants, meanwhile, while not averse to some of these demands, also sought to retain existing privileges and protections. They obviously did not want drastic downsizings with compulsory redundances, and neither did they want salary freezes or other arrangements which would further erode their material rewards in comparison with the private sector. In some places (France, the EU Commission) they had strongly entrenched unions and fought long and hard to stave off erosions of their basic conditions of service (Howard, 1998). Elsewhere constitutional protections were so formidable that it was almost impossible for governments to effect radical change (as for German federal civil servants). In other cases resistance was either less well organized or less effective, and fundamental changes were driven through. For example, security of tenure was significantly reduced in Australia, New Zealand and the UK. Substantial downsizings were carried through in Australia, Finland, New Zealand, the UK and the USA (though one has to be careful in interpreting the statistics because in some cases most of these staff were transferred to other parts of the public sector). One common feature was that personnel changes seldom, if ever, came first on the reform agenda. It was much more common for them to follow— sometimes at a considerable distance—innovations in financial management, organizational structures and management techniques. In this respect Australia was not unusual (at least not for the Anglo–Saxon countries):

Financial management dominated the reform programme of the 1980s. In the latter half of the decade, the limitations of this emphasis were increasingly acknowledged and pressures to broaden the directions being taken and to reduce the subservience of management processes to financial questions. Other forms of management were increasingly being advocated, human resource management assuming a prominence from the end of the 1980s (Halligan, 1996b, pp. 102–3).

It is perhaps easiest to describe the trajectories of change in respect to a 'base case'. This base case is very general, and applies to both the *Rechtsstaat* and the public interest countries (chapter 3, Section 6). In it a typical civil servant is assumed to be:

- A tenured, career appointment—not dependent on the whims of transient politicians or on one's civil service superior (although dimissable, with difficulty, in cases of extreme dereliction of duty or of criminal actions).

- Promoted principally in relation to qualifications and seniority.
- Part of a unified civil service, within a distinct and particular national framework of terms and conditions (including national pay scales).

These are all features which made being a civil servant different (and increasingly different during the 1970s and 1980s) from most private sector jobs. They are also features which, at least in the NPM countries, came to be seen as inhibiting the greater responsiveness and efficiency which it had become fashionable for politicians and public alike to demand. In Australia the Public Service Commissioner, explaining the main thrust of the 1997 Public Service Act, said:

As public servants we need to walk the same fields and gaze the same blue skies that inspire innovation in the private sector. Central to that is the need to bring our employment arrangements more into line with the wider Australian community. Does anyone really believe that, protected by a monopoly status and inadequate scrutiny, we can defend an approach to management that we now know is at least twice as expensive as best practice? (Shergold, 1997, p. 33)

Note the elements in this quotation—the setting up of the private sector as the standard to be attained, the emphasis on cost saving and the suggestion that the public service is over-protected and 'feather-bedded'. One should beware of accepting all this at face value. For example, it is easy to exaggerate the prevalence and influence of the three distinctive features mentioned above (e.g., many categories of civil servant in the UK never had particularly strong tenure, low pay was common, and there had long been many non-career and part-time appointments, especially in the clerical grades). Nevertheless, the popular stereotype of a tea-drinking, probably not very efficient, yet secure and well-pensioned civil servant was never far from media reporting and political characterization, especially by neo-conservatives. Even in France, a country with a proud tradition of a powerful and talented civil service, there was a period when '[F]rom a model of social success, the civil servant became an awful figure, the pure representation of waste and incompetence' (Rouban, 1997, p. 150). In the Netherlands, generally a more consensual and incremental politico-administrative system than Australia or New Zealand, the early 1990s saw steps being taken to 'normalize' the status of government employees, and in 1992 it was agreed that the general pension fund for public employees would be privatized.

The three indicated characteristics therefore became easy foci for reform. In each case the tendency in the NPM countries was to reduce the distinctiveness of a civil service job—to make it more like jobs elsewhere (in the terms used by Dunleavy and Hood, 1994 and Hood, 1998, this was a deliberate lowering of 'group'). We will now look at each of the three features in turn.

4.5.2 A tenured career

The directions of change here were to make careers less secure, and to encourage larger inflows and outflows of staff so that a smaller and smaller proportion of civil servants were 'lifers' and a larger and larger proportion had experience of other ways of doing things. A typical development in NPM countries was the appointment of top officials (especially agency chief executives, but also, in some cases, the heads of ministries) on two-, or three-, or five-year performance-related contracts. The most extreme case is again New Zealand. There all members of the Senior Executive Service (see 4.5.3) have to reapply for their own jobs after five years, except for the heads of ministries (called Chief Executives), who enjoy a provision which permits their contracts to be extended (Boston *et al.*, 1996, pp. 117–20). UK ministers expressed themselves thus:

[T]here is a belief in some quarters that civil servants have a job for life. That is not the case. In the case of senior staff, more than 50% of the individuals who have left the existing Senior Open Structure in the last seven years did so before the normal retirement age. 30 per cent of the departures were brought about by management through voluntary or compulsory early retirement. (Prime Minister *et al.*, 1994, p. 43—and the government in question was at that time just about to embark upon a programme of radical downsizing of a number of central ministries, which included reductions of, typically, 25 per cent of senior staff—see, e.g., HM Treasury, 1994.)

Elsewhere, however, there has been much less change. In Canada, Finland, France, Germany and Sweden most top civil servants are career 'mandarins' with long experience and well-established personal networks (see, e.g., Bourgault and Carroll, 1997). France is perhaps rather different from the other countries in this group, to the extent that the members of the *grands corps* frequently move in and out of jobs in the business world, and therefore could not be accused of being monkishly bureaucratic. Indeed, one problem is that, with falling civil service prestige, increasing numbers of these mandarins have been leaving for the better-paid positions in the private sector (Rouban, 1997, p. 147). The USA is different again: here members of the Senior Executive Service have tended to be narrowly specialist and, in any case, are obliged to work within a system where so many of their colleagues are short-term political appointees (Kettl *et al.*, 1996, p. 56; on the 'spoils system' see Appendix: USA, country file).

4.5.3 Promotion by seniority and qualifications

Here the shift was to link promotion more to results and responsiveness, often by embodying the required results in an annual agreement or quasi-contract, containing specified individual targets and priorities. Usually the change was only partial—seniority and qualifications were still elements in the overall calculation— but the intention of making civil servants more sharply focused on specific and usually short-term objectives was quite clear. This new emphasis was frequently reinforced by linking pay as well as promotion to 'track record' in achieving results (see 4.5.4).

A further important development in a number of countries was the creation of some form of senior executive service (Australia, Canada, New Zealand and the USA—see Ban and Ingraham, 1984; Boston *et al.*, 1996, pp. 117–20; Halligan,

1996b, pp. 86–7). In the UK the Conservative government favoured a 'senior management group' employed on the basis of written contracts (Prime Minister *et al.*, 1994). This kind of grouping was supposed to bring a variety of benefits ('supposed' because in every case there were significant difficulties in achieving the originally-proclaimed goals). Basically an SES was intended (with slightly different emphases in each country) to create a more mobile, flexible, responsive and managerially competent group at the top of the public service. The SES would be more mobile because provisions would allow the easier recruitment of competent executives from outside the normal career ladder of the civil service, and because the terms and conditions would explicitly include horizontal movement within the politico-administrative machine ('horses for courses'). It would be more responsive partly because the right (wo)man could be moved into the right place at the right time, but also because promotion was intended to be for the 'can do' individuals with track records of achievement, rather than by seniority and precedence. As the UK Conservative government put it:

Entry to the Senior Civil Service from within a department or agency would be marked for the individual concerned by leaving negotiated group pay arrangements and moving to individually-determined pay, and by acceptance of a written contract of service (Prime Minister *et al.*, 1994, p. 37).

This type of system was usually backed up by some form of performance related pay (in both Australia and the USA this was also intended to be a way of circumventing general civil service pay restrictions so as to be able to retain 'high flyers'). Experiments with performance pay have been implemented in most of our ten countries, and elsewhere, but often with mixed or downright disappointing results (Gaertner and Gaertner, 1985; OECD, 1993b; Perry and Pearce, 1985). Again, the pattern is of the widest use coming in the NPM countries (and, on this score, the USA) with more cautious and limited projects in the Nordic countries and France (Vallemont, 1998). Additionally, managerial competence can be increased by bringing in outsiders with managerial backgrounds as well as by the provision of intensive high-level management training programmes. The advantages of this trajectory are thus obvious, but it has potential disadvantages too. Concerns about the dangers of increasing the number of 'yes-men' (and 'yes-women'), and endangering the promotability and security of those who give 'frank and fearless' advice, have been expressed in several of the NPM countries.

4.5.4 Part of a unified national service

In this case the thrust in quite a few countries was towards decentralization of personnel authority, initially for the day-to-day management of individuals, but increasingly also in terms of a widening range of terms and conditions, so that, ultimately, line managers could hire and fire on terms they set according to local conditions, and the concept of a unified public service was for all practical purposes abandoned. This direction of change had many ramifications. Pay, hours of work, required qualifications, disciplinary and dismissal procedures—all these and more might cease to be a matters of national negotiation by management and union leaders and be decentralized by organization, region or occupational group. The new philosophy was succinctly enunciated in a UK white paper in 1994:

No two civil service organisations are identical, any more than two organisations elsewhere in the public or private sectors. It is right that pay and grading systems, like other management arrangements, should be attuned to individual circumstances and relevant labour markets (Prime Minister *et al.*, 1994, p. 26).

In Australia, as in the UK, the outline shell of a unified public service was retained but, with the 1997 Public Service Bill:

It is departmental secretaries and agency heads who will determine the remuneration, conditions and terms of employment. No longer will the legislation distinguish between public servants on the basis of whether they are permanent or fixed-term. It is secretaries who will decide how they will employ public servants and on what conditions of engagement. It is they who will assign duties and delegate responsibility (Shergold, 1997, p. 34).

In New Zealand the government moved away altogether from the concept of a single, unified service. The 1988 State Services Act established departments, under their Chief Executives, as the employers of their own staff. The Annual General Adjustment (of pay) and public service-wide negotiation of non-pay conditions of service were abolished (Boston *et al.*, 1996, chapter 10). The public sector came under the provisions of the Labour Relations Act, which had previously been meant for the private sector.

This kind of 'normalizing' trajectory, where the civil service is 'deprivileged' and increasingly treated on the same fragmented and locally-varying terms as private sector employment, has certainly not been followed by all countries. France, Germany and the European Commission are notable and weighty exceptions (if 'exception' is the word). The MAP 2000 initiative by the Commission, for example, was proclaimed as a major decentralization in personnel management, but by comparison with what had already been implemented by the NPM countries, it was quite timid and conventional (European Commission, 1997b). Within those jurisdictions the state servant remains a very distinct category—legally, culturally and politically. As we saw to be the case with financial management reforms, the Nordic states have followed a path somewhere between the NPM enthusiasts, and the more conservative *Rechtsstaat* regimes. Finland and Sweden have made provisions for performance-related pay, and for more decentralized and results-oriented styles of personnel management—for example in 1992 each Swedish agency became responsible for the training and development of its own staff. Yet these countries have not more than marginally dismantled the essential unity of the civil service, and in some cases agencies have in practice made only limited use of their supposed new 'freedoms'. The same could be said of the Canadian federal civil service (Bourgault and Carroll, 1997). In the Netherlands career management of top civil servants was actually *centralized* during the mid-1990s (Mazel, 1998).

The USA is once more a unique case. In theory a scrupulously fair and impersonal merit system provides a national framework for recruitment and job classification:

However, the federal government's uniform merit system today is neither uniform, merit-based, nor a system. It now covers barely more than half—56%—of the federal government's workers. Only 15% of the federal government's new career employees enter through the system's standard testing-and-placement process (Kettl *et al.*, 1996, p. 1).

Despite much debate during the 1980s and 1990s, no comprehensive reform was agreed or implemented (so in this respect the USA was unlike Australia and New Zealand). The problem, in the complex and fragmented US political system, is that:

Civil service reform is on everyone's list of jobs that must be done—but it is high on virtually no one's list. It has too little sex appeal to excite political interest; and though everyone agrees on the need for change, the consequences of *not* reforming the civil service never seem great enough to force it onto the policy agenda (Kettl *et al.*, 1996, p. 2).

In short, the USA, while far from the European *Rechtsstaat* model in political temperament and rhetoric, was nevertheless home to an often rigid and unreformed (or perhaps one should say partially and incoherently reformed) bureaucracy.

4.6 Organizational trajectories

The restructuring of organizations is a ubiquitous feature of public sector management reforms (OECD, 1994, 1995; for details on the ten countries, see Appendix: country files). Of the many different possible ways of classifying these restructurings we have chosen a four-fold scheme which is fairly 'mainstream' in terms of classical organization theory, namely:

• specialization (should institutions be single-purpose or multi-purpose?)
• co-ordination (by what means should co-ordination across different functions, levels and sectors be achieved?)
• centralization/decentralization (what functions should be centralized/decentralized, and to what degree?)
• scale (what is the optimal size for organizations?).

We will deal with each of these dimensions in turn, but first a brief overview may be useful. As a broad generalization it can be said that the main thrust of the Australian/New Zealand/UK reforms has been towards organizations which are more specialized; towards co-ordination by means of market mechanisms and contractual and quasi-contractual relationships instead of through hierarchies of authority; towards decentralization of authority from the centre towards the periphery (in both hierarchical and geographical terms) and towards decreasing the size of public organizations by breaking up and downsizing large bureaucratic organizations (Boston *et al.*, 1996; O'Toole and Jordan, 1995; Peters and Savoie,

1998). Trends towards specialization and fragmentation have also been discernible in Canada, France and the Netherlands (though to a lesser degree than in the NPM countries), but are much less marked in Finland, Germany, Sweden and the European Commission, each of which has retained its central ministerial or direct-orate structure with limited or no fragmentation, downsizing or 'hiving off'. The USA already possessed a fairly fragmented and specialized administrative system (see Appendix: USA, country file) and has been concerned to try to develop over-all systems which will permit greater coherence (e.g., common accounting proce-dures, common reporting procedures through the Government Performance and Review Act). As for decentralization, almost everyone seems to believe in it, though, as we shall see, it takes on a different personality in different contexts. The four dimensions will now be examined in sequence.

Specialization. Alternation between a preference for broad-scope, multi-purpose organizations and, by contrast, a predilection for tight-focus, specialized organizations has been one of the salient features of the history of administrative thought. The idea that specialization is the basis of good administration can trace its supporters back through Adam Smith and Jeremy Bentham. The opposite doctrine—that consolidation is good—has been advanced by, *inter alia*, Sir Edwin Chadwick and Karl Marx (Hood and Jackson, 1991, pp. 114–16). The pendulum may swing within a single generation, witness the shift in UK central government from a preference for large, omnibus central ministries (favoured by both Labour and Conservatives in the late 1960s and early 1970s) to the current model of down-sized and relatively focused ministries surrounded by shoals of specialized execu-tive agencies (Pollitt, 1984; O'Toole and Jordan, 1995).

During the 1980s the international swing was towards more specialization, most clearly in those countries which were the most influenced by the application of micro-economic reasoning to questions of institutional design. This took place at all levels—micro, meso and macro. Thus in New Zealand 'the preference for single-purpose organisations and the separation of potentially conflicting func-tions has led in some cases to a plethora of functionally distinct, but nonetheless quite interdependent, organisations' (Boston *et al.*, 1996, p. 88). By the time this book was being written there were signs that the pendulum had reached its furthest point and was beginning to return: there was much discussion in New Zealand government circles of the drawbacks of having such a large number of ministries to deal with such a small population.

New Zealand is probably the clearest, but is not the only case. In the UK the Next Steps programme, launched in 1988, led within ten years to the creation of more than 140 specialized executive agencies (Chancellor of the Duchy of Lancaster, 1997). In France more than 200 *centres de responsabilité* have been set up since 1989. In the Netherlands many ZBOs were created during the 1980s, and since 1991 more than 20 specialized agencies have also appeared (Ministerie van Financiën, 1998; Roberts, 1997). The Canadians moved more cautiously, but there, too, some 'Special Operating Agencies' (SOAs) were carved out of the federal ministries (the first five appeared in 1989—see Appendix: Canada, country file).

If one moves away from central government to examine other public functions the trend is equally, if not even more clear. Most of our ten governments hastened to give distinctive organizational forms to commercial or potentially commercial activities within their public sectors. At the extreme, of course, there has been large-scale privatization, especially in New Zealand and the UK, and, to a lesser but still substantial extent, in France and the Netherlands. Most other countries had less to privatize in the first place, but selective privatization nevertheless occured in Finland, Germany, Sweden and the USA (for details see Appendix: country files, and Pollitt *et al.*, 1997). Short of full-blooded privatization, a number of countries have preferred to invent other specialized corporate forms—such as the state enterprises and state-owned companies in Finland, or the state-owned enterprises in New Zealand. Some of these have survived, while others have acted as brief staging posts on the route to full privatization.

In local governance, too, specialization has been in evidence. In the UK the setting-up of MTMs (quasi-markets) in health care, education and social care entailed a good deal of *de facto* specialization into separate purchaser and provider units (Pollitt, Birchall and Putman, 1998). The Conservative governments of 1979–97 also supported the creation of several types of specialized educational institution (e.g., City Technology Colleges) and infrastructural renewal organizations (e.g., Urban Development Corporations) plus diverse other quangos. Taken together, these constituted a rather crowded new environment of specialized entities with which traditional local authorities had to try to deal (Painter *et al.*, 1996). Furthermore the process of compulsory competitive tendering (CCT) for local authority and health services meant that, even where an 'in house' bid won the contract, it usually had to recreate itself as a distinct, specialized organization (e.g., for refuse collection or laundry or building maintenance—see Ascher, 1987; HM Treasury, 1991).

In sum, one might say that the use of specialized administrative and managerial bodies appears to have grown almost everywhere. This trend has given rise to criticism in some countries, focused on the sometimes uncertain legal and political status of these new creations. As a recent comparative article put it:

Indeed, the growth in, and use of, quasi-autonomous non governmental organisations (quangos) is evident at all levels of society from local quangos to regional and central government agencies and also at the European level where new bodies have been created which reflect similar problems of accountability and legitimacy, the European Monetary Institute, for example (Greve, Flinders and van Thiel, 1999).

Assessments of the problems associated with increased specialization and decentralization is not, however, the job of this chapter. This task will be taken up later, especially in chapters 6 and 7.

Co-ordination. In a traditional hierarchy, co-ordination is ensured by the exercise of authority from the top. Coherent and consistent orders are passed down the line. Central staff units, supporting the top administrators, check lower-level proposals to ensure that they all fit the strategy, that precedents are observed, that division X does not set out along a line that contradicts what is being done at division Y. Regulations are issued from the centre which all must observe. When new situations occur, new regulations are formulated to deal with them, and these are fitted in to the existing body of law and procedure which guides every part of the organization. Such exercise of hierarchical authority is, however, not the only way of achieving co-ordination. Co-ordination can also be achieved less formally, by voluntary co-operation within a network. This form of 'solidarity' tends to be more easily achieved where objectives are widely shared among all network members, communications are easy and full, and the scale of operations is modest. A third mode of co-ordination is the market mechanism. The miracle of the market is that a price mechanism enables the activities of many producers/sellers and consumers/buyers to be co-ordinated without any central authority ordering it so. The 'hidden hand' of supply and demand does the work, and with the assistance of modern communications and information technologies, that work can be accomplished with great speed.

Thus co-ordination may be achieved by hierarchy, network or market (Kaufmann, Majone and Ostrom, 1986; Thompson, Frances, Levacic and Mitchell, 1991). The main thrust of NPM reforms has been, *de facto*, that market and network forms of co-ordination—especially market forms—should wherever possible be substituted for hierarchical co-ordination. Although it is conceded that under certain conditions—most influentially specified in theoretical terms by Williamson, 1975—hierarchies may be preferable to markets, the main weight of argument has been that there are many hitherto unseen opportunities to 'marketize' relationships within the public sector. Indeed, just as certain words such as 'decentralization' and 'empowerment' have become unassailably positive in their connotations, 'hierarchy' and 'hierarchical' have become invariably negative—at least within the NPM discourse. Even where an indisputably hierarchical relationship remains there may be an attempt to package it into a quasi-contract, where the 'agent' ('subordinate', in old-fashioned hierarchical terms) agrees to supply the 'principal' (superior, boss) with a defined set of outputs within a fixed time period and at a predetermined cost. In the countries which have been most enthusiastic about NPM there has therefore been a wide-scale substitution of market and quasi-market co-ordination and contractualization for hierarchical co-ordination. In New Zealand, for example, the chief executives who run ministries agree an annual quasi-contract with their minister, promising to deliver specified outputs which are then supposed to lead to the outcomes at which the minister and his/her government are aiming. In most countries contractualization has not infiltrated so high up the chain of minister/mandarin command. Slightly lower down, however, contractualization and marketization have spread widely in Australia, New Zealand and the UK, and to a lesser extent in Canada, Sweden and the USA. It has gone hand-in-hand with many of the measures of specialization referred to in the previous subsection. Thus, for example, where a pre-1991 District Health Authority in the UK might have given an instruction to a local hospital, in the post 1991 'provider market' it contracted for defined services with a legally independent corporation—the NHS trust which the previously 'directly managed' hospital had become. The two parts of the previously hierarchical National Health Service had specialized into a purchaser and a provider, joined by contract. The example of the Canadian Special Operating Agencies provides a further illustration of the general logic:

The SOA is based on the same theoretical models as organisational forms being adopted by other governments and large corporations. The models are more contractual than hierarchical; provide greater autonomy to individual units of the whole; and rely more on market mechanisms then central decisions to allocate resources (Auditor General of Canada, 1994, p. 2).

This spread of contractual and quasi-contractual relationships has provoked a certain amount of academic concern, both by legal theorists worried about the inadequacies of the relevant areas of administrative law (Harden, 1992) and by public administrationists who have pointed to the difficulties of writing 'complete' contracts in conditions where the providers of services have much more information than the purchasers and/or users (Le Grand and Bartlett, 1993).

Not all countries have been as enthusiastic about the potential of MTMs and contractualism as New Zealand and the UK. Such devices have been used much more sparingly in Germany, France and even the Nordic countries. Here limited local experiments have been more characteristic than sweeping marketizations of entire sectors.

The connection between specialization (dealt with in the previous subsection) and co-ordination is important. All other things being equal, increasing specialization implies a need for *greater* efforts at co-ordination, at least if the level of overall coherence of policy and services is to be maintained. Otherwise the danger is that newly specialized agencies, many of which also enjoy decentralized authority, will go their own ways. No country has been content to rely entirely on MTMs to address this problem. Even those states which have favoured MTMs have also added new hierarchical devices to try to ensure that co-ordination is preserved or enhanced.

At a local, micro-level, 'one-stop' or 'one window' service delivery arrangements have proved popular. Quite a number of local authorities have tried them in the UK. In 1994 France adopted a programme of integrated Rural Service Outlets in country areas, which necessitated co-operation between different services (Ministère de la Fonction Publique, 1994). One-stop ideas have also been implemented in Finland and Sweden, where the arrangement of having one integrated outlet in remote and thinly populated areas has an obvious logic.

At higher levels a variety of new co-ordinating mechanisms have been created. In Germany there is some evidence of greater co-ordination between the *Länder*: 'What increased during the 1980s was, perhaps, less the scope for regional policy makers to develop and implement independent initiatives than their determination to make use of the hitherto neglected potential for subcentral policy making' (Benz and Götz, 1996, p. 7). In France a simpler and more co-ordinated arrangement for the central states' regional and provincial services has been developed. The *sous-préfet* now has a major role in directing and co-ordinating deconcentrated service delivery (*Comité pour la réorganisation et la déconcentration de l'administration*, 1995). In the UK, too, the 1980s saw central government implementing stronger regional co-ordination of the work of the various ministries. In Finland provincial units of central administration have been merged and reduced in number. In both the Netherlands and New Zealand the numbers of local government jurisdictions has been reduced—an interesting case of a different organizational logic being applied at local level from that being simultaneously implemented for the central state.

Within central governments themselves the signs of attempts at improved co-ordination are clear to see (although in some cases they have appeared as rather late responses to the fragmentation caused by earlier enthusiasms for specialization and decentralization). One popular initiative has been to develop some form of strategic planning. This has been tried (in different ways) by Australia, Canada, Finland, New Zealand and the UK. The New Zealand system of Strategic Results Areas (SRAs) and Key Results Areas (KRAs) is probably the best known (Boston *et al.*, 1996, pp. 282–3; Matheson, Scanlan and Tanner, 1997). In Canada the 1994 Program Review exercise was intended to put an end to the fragmented and volatile policy making which was seen as a characteristic of the preceeding Mulroney administrations (Aucoin and Savoie, 1998). In Finland there has been a more recent attempt to develop a 'Strategy Portfolio' and a strategic overview of government organization (*High quality services, good governance and a responsible civic society*, 1998a, especially pp. 19–22). In the UK, following a period of distaste for central planning and co-ordination under Mrs Thatcher, the Blair Labour government has committed itself to better 'joined-up', horizontally co-ordinated policy making. It has set up cross-departmental reviews in areas such as criminal justice, services for young children and the countryside, and conducted a comprehensive review of all government spending (Chancellor of the Exchequer, 1998, especially pp. 33–41). A brief assessment of strategic planning is made in the next chapter, which questions the results of these activities.

Merging departments has for long been one way of improving co-ordination. Of course, this route rather contradicts the trend to specialization, noted above, but it is a device that has been used by some countries. While New Zealand was allowing the number of its ministries to proliferate, its neighbour, Australia, was reducing its population of departments from 28 to 18 (1987—see appendix A). In 1993 Canada followed suit, reducing the number of federal departments from 32 to 24 (see Appendix: Canada, country file). These initiatives were reminiscent of much earlier (1960s and early 1970s) attempts by UK governments to rationalize the pattern of ministries by creating large, 'strategic' departments (Pollitt, 1984).

Another feature in a number of central governments has been an attempt by politicians themselves to exert greater control over the bureaucracy. This phenomenon will be discussed in more detail in chapter 6, but it should be noted here as, in effect, another species of co-ordination effort. It has been particularly noticeable in Australia, New Zealand, the UK and the USA, but softer echoes have also been heard in Finland, the Netherlands and Sweden. Australia offers perhaps the clearest case. As Halligan puts it (1996b, p. 82): 'Reform programs [during the Labor governments of 1983–93] were driven by a foremost concern of Labor—political control—which had come to be regarded both as an end in itself and a means to implementing party policy. To achieve this required a redistribution of power between the bureaucracy and the politicians.' To achieve this the capacity of the Prime Minister's office and cabinet were enhanced, the pattern of ministries was radically altered (1987), ministers made more active use than hitherto of their right to influence senior bureaucratic appointments and much greater use was made of specially recruited ministerial advisers.

To conclude this review of co-ordination, it should be remarked that, even where traditional hierarchies remained in place, the instruments of hierarchical co-ordination tended to change. In particular there was a shift from control and co-ordination by rationing inputs and regulating procedures to a greater emphasis on co-ordination by targets and output standards (this was already referred to in the subsection on financial management, and will be further explored in subsection 4.7, below). The majority of the ten countries became active in developing indicator sets for the performance of almost every imaginable public service (for Australia see Department of Finance, 1996; Department of Finance and Administration, 1998a and b; Development Team, 1998; for Canada see Mayne, 1996; Treasury Board of Canada, 1996; for the Netherlands see Leeuw, 1995; Mol, 1995; for the UK see Carter *et al.*, 1992; Chancellor of the Duchy of Lancaster, 1997; Likierman, 1995; Pollitt, 1986, 1990; for the USA see Radin, 1998).

Decentralization. Decentralization, ministers and mandarins have said, makes possible more responsive and speedy public services, better attuned to local and/or individual needs. It facilitates 'downsizing' by leading to the elimination of unnecessary layers of middle management. It even produces more contented and stimulated staff, whose jobs have been 'enriched' by taking on devolved responsibilities for financial and personnel management, and by escaping from the overburden of centralized regulation. Given all these benefits it is little wonder that almost everyone in every country (and in the European Commission) seems to be officially in favour of decentralization. Like virtue, however, decentralization is differently construed by different parties, and is far easier to preach and praise than to practise. If we are to describe the actual trajectories in a way that carries some real meaning then we have to distinguish between different aspects of decentralization, and to some extent between rhetoric and reality.

One way of deconstructing the concept of decentralization is to recognize that it is a process which contains at least three strategic choices. These are depicted in Table 4.5.

The first choice is therefore between *political* decentralization, where the decentralized authority is transferred to elected political representatives (e.g., when central government decentralizes a power to local government) and *administrative* decentralization, where authority is passed to an appointed body such as a UK

TABLE 4.5. *Strategic choices in decentralization*

Either	Or
Political decentralization	Administrative decentralization
Competitive decentralization	Non-competitive decentralization
Internal decentralization	External decentralization (devolution)

Urban Development Corporation or a Swedish agency. The second choice is between transferring authority to another body which is selected by *competitive* means (e.g., through competitive tendering for a local authority refuse collection service) and transferring authority by *non-competitive* means (e.g., where a District Health Authority transfers some of its authority to an NHS trust). A third choice is between *internal* decentralization (where the act of transfer takes place 'within the walls' of an existing organization) and *external* decentralization, where the authority is transferred to an independent external body (which might be an existing one or a new, specially created one). When authority to spend up to $X without seeking permission is (was) delegated from the Principal Finance Officer to senior line managers, that is internal decentralization. When authority was transferred from a UK Local Education Authority to a Grant-Maintained School under Mr Major's Conservative government, that is (was) external delegation (Pollitt, Birchall and Putman, 1998).

The balance between these different forms of decentralization has been rather different in different countries. Once more, different countries have *started* from very different positions. Thus, for example, in each of France, Sweden, Finland and the UK central governments have praised the virtues of decentralization, but in the early 1980s France and the UK were relatively centralized countries while the two Nordic states were both already extensively decentralized (see chapter 3 and the respective country files in the Appendix). Germany had been very decentralized since the Second World War, at least by Franco-British standards (Schröter and Wollman, 1997). Taking this into account, we can say that administrative decentralization has been the preferred form in New Zealand and the UK, while political decentralization has been the dominant type in Finland, France and Sweden. Few new powers have been given to local governments in New Zealand and the UK. In each case decentralization has transferred authority to a range of specialized administrative bodies (such as Grant-Maintained Schools and NHS trusts in the UK—see Pollitt, Birchall and Putman, 1998). In France, by contrast, probably the most significant single reform of the last three decades was the decentralization to local and regional *elected* authorities carried out by the Mitterand Presidency and the socialist government from 1982 (see Appendix: France, country file, and de Montricher, 1996). In Finland and Sweden there has been both political and administrative decentralization, but the transfer of responsibilities to the municipalities and counties has been a central plank of their respective reform programmes (Pollitt and Summa, 1997a). Thus the UK has been the 'odd one out' in the EU, because it has done so little to transfer responsibilities to elected subnational authorities. Under the Labour government since 1997, however, this has begun to change, in that, at the time of writing, plans are well advanced for the creation of elected legislatures for Scotland and Wales. It is too early to say how much real authority will be devolved to these new democratic assemblies.

Turning to the distinction between competitive and non-competitive decentralization, we see a roughly similar pattern. The competitive approach was prominent in Australia, New Zealand and the UK, but much less so in France and the Nordic countries. The USA was fairly enthusiastic about contracting out (but in a sense had less to commercialize, at least at the federal level) and Canada (again at the federal level) was generally more cautious. This, of course, follows from the pattern of enthusiasm and caution over the use of MTMs, as discussed above.

As for the internal/external distinction, it is safe to say that all countries practised both types to some extent, but that the NPM countries have probably undertaken more *external* decentralization, because they have been the ones who have been keenest to create new, autonomous and specialized bodies, and then devolve powers to them. France has also been fertile in setting up new subnational authorities, in line with the government's wider strategy of political and administrative decentralization. The picture in the Netherlands is complicated. The creation of ZBOs and departmental agencies can be taken as evidence of external decentralization by central departments. On the other hand, during the 1980s and 1990s, '[S]pending departments often held out resolutely (and with success) against the transfer of powers to provinces and municipalities' (Derksen and Korsten, 1995, p. 83). Other countries (e.g., the Nordics) have also practised devolution, but have tended to rely more on existing local governments as the recipients of new responsibilities. There has been some divergence between Finland and Sweden, however, with respect to central agencies. Whereas, during the mid-1990s, the Finns downsized the numbers and functions of their central agencies, the Swedish agencies remain extremely powerful and, in some cases, have received even greater devolved power from their ministries than hitherto (OECD, 1998).

This raises the point that it would be quite misleading to suggest that there was a global rush towards decentralization, with the only differences between countries being which types of decentralization they prefer and how far they have gone. Centralization is also part of the picture: as some authority has been decentralized, simultaneously there have been significant instances of a tightening of central control and oversight. One fairly prominent case has been the way in which pressures on public spending have strengthened the hands of treasuries and central finance ministries in a number of countries. For example, there is a general perception among officials that economic constraints have reinforced the dominance over other ministries of the Finnish Ministry of Finance and the New Zealand and UK Treasuries. Furthermore, centralization has certainly not been exclusively a matter of finance. There are countless instances, especially perhaps in the NPM countries, of central authorities using performance indicator systems or standard setting, to reassert control over lower tiers or local units. In the UK central government forced national 'league tables' on every school and hospital, and from 1988 for the first time imposed a national educational curriculum on all state schools (Pollitt, Birchall and Putman, 1998). In the EU there have been many examples where the 'harmonization' of some product or rule or procedure across Europe has resulted in a *de facto* centralization on the Commission in Brussels. Thus the idea that everything is travelling in the direction of decentralization is, to say the least, over-simple.

Scale. Obviously, scale is intimately connected with some of the other dimensions of organization discussed immediately above. In addition to the general pressure for 'downsizing' which arrives from the savings objective, the trends towards specialization and decentralization also indicate reductions in the average size of many public sector organizations. The ideal public sector agency, as envisaged by the enthusiasts and visionaries of the NPM and reinventing government movements, will be 'flat', flexible, specialized ('focused') and decentralized, and therefore very probably quite *small*. These approaches to reform include a deep doctrinal suspicion of large central bureaucracies. Such organizations represent (as we will see in subsequent chapters) the 'old world' from which the reformers are determined to escape. The US Vice President put it like this: 'Big headquarters and big rule books never have kept the government from making big mistakes. In fact, they often kept front-line workers from doing things right. So we asked agencies to cut layers of supervisors, headquarters staff, and other management control jobs by 50%' (Gore, 1996, p. 16).

However, the 'small-is-beautiful' vision is evidently not universally shared. For example, while central ministries have been considerably reduced in size in New Zealand and the UK (Boston *et al.*, 1996; HM Treasury, 1994) in Finland the reforms of the 1990s actually led to slight growth in the size of central ministries, as they absorbed some of the functions previously performed by central agencies (Ministry of Finance, 1997). In general the continental European countries have been less enthusiastic about 'downsizing' as an overall goal. The EU Commission itself has grown considerably. Between 1977 and 1997 the number of Commission staff grew by 104 per cent, with an increase of 150 per cent in the policymaking 'A' grades. However, it should be noted that the EU budget grew by 206 per cent in real terms over the same period, and, since it is widely acknowledged that the tasks of the Commission expanded rapidly during the 1980s, it can be argued that the extra staff were needed to cope with new responsibilities. Nevertheless, the organizational development of the Commission has certainly not followed the NPM trend: it has specialized only to a limited extent, created only weak forms of horizontal co-ordination, did not begin to decentralize in any significant way until right at the end of the 1990s, and has grown in size.

4.7 The measurement of performance

It is clear from the previous subsections that increased measurement of performance has been a central feature of public management reform in many countries.

In a sense, these accounts of financial and personnel management, and organizational restructuring, have already partly dealt with performance measurement, so this section can be correspondingly brief. There are, however, some generic measurement issues which it makes sense to address under this separate heading.

Performance measurement certainly is not new (Bouckaert, 1994). Indeed, it is as old as public administration itself. In the latter part of the nineteenth century there were already schemes in place in the UK and the USA for measuring the performance of teachers in state schools. Woodrow Wilson was writing about the need to design an administrative system that would perform well against efficiency criteria, and F. W. Taylor was advocating a generic approach towards measuring the efficiency of workers (Dunsire, 1973). Acknowledging all this, however, does not prevent one from recognizing that interest in measuring public sector activities has blossomed over the last quarter century. It has developed along several dimensions:

Measurement is becoming more *extensive*. More levels . . . and more fields . . . are included. Performance measurement is becoming more *intensive* because more management functions are included (not just monitoring but also decision-making, controlling and even providing accountability).

Finally, performance measurement becomes more *external*. Its use is not just internal, but also for the members of legislative bodies, and even for the public (Bouckaert, 1996, p. 234).

It may be useful to look at each of these dimensions in turn. The growing *extent* of performance measurement was best exemplified in the NPM countries, although significant measurement initiatives were also to be found in Canada, France, the Netherlands, the Nordic states and the USA. We therefore turn to the UK for an assessment of the full extent of the trajectory:

No public sector employee has escaped the ever-extending reach of performance evaluation schemes. The pressure to meet targets or performance standards, whether hospital waiting lists, school exam results, crime clear-up rates or university research ratings—has introduced profound changes in public organisations. As PIs [performance indicators] have become increasingly linked to resource allocation and individual financial rewards, so organisational cultures and individual behaviours have been transformed (Carter, 1998, p. 177).

Examples of the spread of performance measurement to new fields can be found in many countries. Often they have been tied in with developments in information technology (e.g., Bellamy and Taylor, 1998, pp. 68–70). In the USA the 1993 Government Performance and Results Act effectively mandated PIs for every federal agency (Radin, 1998). In Australia performance measures were widely introduced during the 1980s and the systems were still being tightened and toughened by the neo-conservative Howard government at the time of writing (Department of Finance and Administration, 1998a and b). In New Zealand the system of Strategic Results Areas and Key Results Areas (mentioned above) required wide-scope PI systems. In the Netherlands during the 1990s a strategy of progressively integrating performance measurement with the budget process has been pursued (Sorber, 1996). In several countries initiatives to raise the quality of public services have led directly to a wider scope for performance measurement (e.g. the UK Citizen's Charter from 1991; the French Public Service Charter from 1993; the 1994 Declaration of Service Quality and 1995 Quality of Service Intitiative in Canada).

One might suppose that the extension of PI systems would proceed in a rational fashion, with relatively straightforward, tangible services (e.g., refuse collection, the mail) being measured first and then more individually variable, less concrete services such as health care and education, and finally, perhaps, non-tangible, non-routine services with a high subjective content such as the provision of policy advice or the co-ordination of different agencies in the pursuit of some general policy goal (Bouckaert and Ulens, 1998). In practice, however, any such logic is hard to find. In the UK, for example, one of the earliest national PI schemes (from 1983) was for the National Health Service (Pollitt, 1986; Carter, Klein and Day, 1992). What is perhaps a clearer pattern is that the powerful have been better able to postpone or deflect the tide of measurement than other groups. Thus, within health services, the activities of nurses and receptionists have been measured far more intensively than the quality of clinical decision making by doctors. In the NPM countries, at least, the public can read plenty of reports containing measures of the performance of teachers, police, social workers, social security clerks and specialist agencies, but few, if any, measuring the performance of MPs or ministers (the USA may offer one of the rare exceptions to this generalization, at least in respect of the voting and attendance habits of members of Congress and Senate).

Extending PI systems is not only a matter of finding hitherto unmeasured sectors or organizations and subjecting them to 'the treatment'. It is also a question of broadening the scope of measurement in a more analytical sense—of beginning to measure efficiency and effectiveness, not just inputs, processes and compliance. As noted elsewhere in this book, for example, many national audit offices have extended their work beyond questions of regularity and legality, beyond even the hunting-down of waste, to embrace more sophisticated concepts of efficiency, effectiveness and service quality. These are the focus of the field of performance audit, which has developed rapidly since the mid-1980s (Pollitt *et al.*, 1999). This shift of measurement systems beyond the relatively mundane issues of input and process towards the more politically sensitive and methodologically challenging problems of assessing effectiveness has proved both difficult and controversial—in several countries and in many contexts. For example, consider the words of a New Zealand minister, reflecting upon the way in which, with one of the world's most sophisticated performance measurement systems, New Zealand public servants have nevertheless tended to over-concentrate on outputs (e.g., cases completed) at the expense of the final *outcomes* (e.g. satisfied clients) that their efforts are supposed to lead towards:

One [danger is that] risky, unattractive, but nevertheless important functions might start to fall between the cracks, or that absurd demarcation disputes might arise, of the kind that used to be endemic in the cloth-cap trade unions of old. If 'output fixation' distracts departments from outcomes, and 'contract fixation' encourages them to ignore everything that isn't actually specified, aren't these things very likely to happen? (East, 1997).

These more ambitious uses of PIs—to assess impacts, guide programmes or help decide the fate of policies—are perhaps less difficult for the public service cultures of the 'public interest' administrative systems to absorb than for the *Rechtsstaat* systems. The latter are more used to trying to guide administrative behaviour by the formulation of precise laws and regulations, than by giving more discretion and then measuring results (Bouckaert, 1996, pp. 228–9).

The NPM countries have also been at the forefront of the more *intensive* use of PIs. Over the last twenty years one may discern a trajectory which runs from the use of PIs principally as supplementary or background information towards their use for a variety of management purposes—to inform specific decisions, to compare different organizations or functions (benchmarking), to determine budget allocations and even as a major input to decisions concerning the career development and promotion of individuals. An example would be the research quality ratings given to UK university departments on the basis of their published output, research grants and honours won, PhDs awarded, and other factors. This elaborate national exercise, which is conducted roughly every four years, now directly and formulaically produces each department's allocation of baseline research funding. Planning to achieve a 'high score' in this assessment has become a core component of the management of most university departments. In short, the use of PIs, having once been an 'extra' or novelty, has been progressively integrated with other aspects of management (Carter, 1998). This can significantly sharpen the management of public services and the orientation of those services to their users. On the other hand it can also lead to various pathologies where the activity of measurement itself distorts the administrative process in undesirable ways (Bouckaert, 1995; Pollitt, 1990).

Finally, we turn to the *external* use of performance measurement—not exclusively for internal management purposes, but to inform legislatures, taxpayers, service users and a variety of other stakeholders. For those who know where to look (and, more importantly, for those who are interested in looking) the official publications of the late 1990s contain far more performance information than was available in 1980. Publications such as the annual Next Steps agencies review or various National Health Service performance indicators booklets (UK) or the GPRA reports (USA) or the Swedish Ministry of Finance reports on public sector productivity contain a great deal of potentially useful data (see Chancellor of the Duchy of Lancaster, 1997; Swedish Ministry of Finance, 1997). Gradually these data sets are being refined so as to reduce the weaknesses and poor presentation of some of their early versions. In the case of the NHS, for example, the first national sets of PIs were unwieldy and unwelcoming, and overwhelmingly concerned process issues such as average lengths of hospital stay. Over the years, however, the presentation and explanation of this information has improved enormously, and, if there are still many possible improvements that can be discussed, at least some indicators or proxies for clinical outcomes are now included in the package. In some cases performance information is given considerable publicity by the mass media (the 'league tables' of English state schools for example) although in others the 'take-up' of such data by politicians has been disappointing (Carter, Klein and Day, 1992, p. 182). Some governments and parliaments have begun to take special steps to improve the relevance and accessibility of PI data for politicians (e.g., in the Canadian case, Duhamel, 1996).

4.8 Modes of implementation

In this subsection we move from the 'what' of reform to the 'how'. This poses an immediate problem. It is usually harder for academics to obtain systematic information about how reforms are being put into practice than about what the reforms are. Governments are frequently keen to announce what they are going to do but are understandably less energetic in offering a blow-by-blow account of how things are going. Some aspects of implementation are particularly hard to research and write about: it is only rarely that we get scientific accounts of the strengths and weaknesses of individual leaders and managers, of the resentments and conflicts which reforms so easily stimulate, of the compromises and threats by which these are often settled, and so on (though journalistic treatments are more common). There is plenty of circumstantial evidence to indicate that such factors can be influential in determining the success or failure of some innovations, but these things can rarely be subject to rigorous testing.

What can be seen from the outside is the broad direction and energy of implementation that seems to be characteristic of a particular government during a particular period. Even this is partly impressionistic, but, pending more systematic comparative evidence, is worth recording nonetheless. Here we will quickly review three aspects:

- The extent to which reform has been a *top-down or bottom-up* exercise.
- The extent to which *new organizations and structures* have been created specifically to advance reform (the alternative being the pursuit of reform through existing structures).
- The *intensity* of reform, that is, have governments barged ahead, trampling opposition underfoot, or have they tiptoed delicately, consulting and co-operating with the other stakeholders (such as public service unions) as they go?

The distinction between top-down and bottom-up reforms has itself to be used with some caution. These are not two separate categories but poles on a spectrum which passes through 'top-down-guided bottom-up'. So there are more intermediate cases than pure polar examples. Furthermore, since our focus is principally on central governments, it must be acknowledged that what constitutes the 'bottom' of central government may be far from immediately clear.

Bearing these caveats in mind, we can go straight to a major generalization about implementation. It is that *all three aspects have in practice gone hand in hand*, that is, those countries which have employed more top-down strategies also tend to have created more new institutions *and* to have pushed on with reform at a more intense pace. Furthermore *the Anglo-Saxon NPM countries again stand out as a separate group*—it is they, more than Germany and France, more than the consensual Dutch and the Nordics, more even than the voluable Americans or the somewhat quieter Canadians, who have driven reforms from the top, with relentless speed, throwing up all manner of new organizations—and new *types* of organization—as they have rushed onward. The range of implementation styles therefore matches very well the characteristics of politico-administrative regimes which were identified in the previous chapter.

There is space here only to offer brief illustrations of these generalizations, although evidence for them continues to accumulate throughout the remainder of the book. One way of doing this would be to compare the reform process in, say, Finland, Germany, the UK and the USA (i.e., an active modernizer, a country that has been conservative with respect to management reform, an 'NPM-enthusiast' and, in the case of the USA, a country where reform rhetoric has been loud, but reform achievements not necessarily commensurately impressive).

In Finland, considerable reforms have been implemented, and the numbers of civil servants has been markedly reduced, but this has been done in a low-key way and at a relatively leisurely pace. Furthermore, high levels of continuity have been maintained despite the existence of three different coalition governments over the relevant period. The reform programme that was launched in 1987/88 was still being 'rolled out' ten years later. It was conceived and co-ordinated mainly by the Ministry of Finance and, in that sense, was fairly 'top down'. It was of broad scope, affecting all or most of the central government, but could not directly apply to the municipalities, which enjoyed the constitutional autonomy which allowed them to decide on their own reforms. A good example of a central government reform would be results-oriented budgeting, one key element of the broader programme. It began with a small number of voluntary pilot projects from 1988, and then developed into a government decision to extend the system to all ministries and their agencies. The target was to have the system fully in place by the beginning of 1995—seven years after the launch. On the organizational dimension, new forms of state-owned company were a significant innovation, and the system of central agencies was extensively remodelled during the mid-1990s, but the ministries themselves remained largely undisturbed. Personnel reforms were placed on the statute book, but came into use only slowly and on a limited scale. The Finns paid close attention to reforms throughout the OECD world, and were active members of PUMA and other international bodies, but they imported reform ideas cautiously and selectively, adapting them to fit the Finnish politico-administrative system. Privatization and quasi-market mechanisms were elements of the NPM package that the Finns treated with considerable reserve. There was no 'rush to the market', and no large political constituency for the idea that the market was automatically superior to the 'nanny state' (Ministry of Finance, 1997; Pollitt *et al.*, 1997).

The federal German government was more conservative than its Finnish counterpart. There was no broad programme of management reform at the federal level (though there was considerable activity in a number of municipalities—see

Appendix: Germany, country file). The main laws governing the civil service were not changed. No flocks of new organizations were created. There was no drastic downsizing. German activity at PUMA and in other international fora was modest in terms of active participation in the global debate about management reform. Most of the leading German academics appeared to be lukewarm or actively hostile to NPM thinking (König, 1996; Derlien, 1998). When faced with the huge administrative challenge of reunification, the government decided not to innovate, but to transplant virtually the whole of the existing system in West Germany to the former East Germany.

The implementation process in the UK was more hectic, harsh and sweeping than in either Finland or Germany (and it began in 1979, almost a decade earlier than in Finland). Wave after wave of broad-scope reform followed each other for more than fifteen years, often to the accompaniment of assertively doctrinaire statements by ministers. Most change was decidedly top-down. In central government Rayner Scrutinies (1979) were followed by the Financial Management Initiative (1982), the Next Steps Programme (1988), the Citizen's Charter (1991), the Private Finance Initiative, the downsizing of a number of ministries (1994–97), the introduction of accruals accounting right across central government and various other new systems. Extensive personnel reforms led to wider application of individual contracts for senior public officials, extensive use of performance-related pay and the decentralization of most personnel authorities to individual ministries and agencies. Central government also drove radical reforms in subnational and local government, often in a directive manner that would have been impossible in either Finland or Germany. MTMs were imposed on the National Health Service, education and community care. Many new types of organization were created, including Urban Development Corporations, City Technology Colleges, Grant-Maintained Schools, an Audit Commission, NHS trusts, various types of public housing agency, and so on (see Painter *et al.*, 1996).

The USA offers our last, and contrasting, illustration. Here there has been the surface appearance of top-down reform, with many Presidentially sponsored commissions and councils during the 1980s, and then the National Performance Review (NPR) in the 1990s (see Appendix: USA, country file). Behind this façade, however, it becomes apparent that the fragmented American politico-administrative system seldom allows reforms to be implemented via a concerted drive from the top (Peters, 1995). The follow-through on a number of these reforms has been weak or uncertain (President Reagan's Grace Commission providing one example of this). The central executive does not have the untrammelled implementation ability of its counterparts in New Zealand or the UK. Some of the most interesting parts of the NPR have been the 'reinvention laboratories', and these show large variations from one agency to another (Ingraham, 1997). New organizations have certainly been created, but not on the scale of the UK's Next Steps agencies. The pattern of departments has not changed that much, and certainly has not changed in line with any centrally-determined strategic plan. Personnel management, as was noted above, has included a good deal of innovation, but there have been significant problems with the SES and performance related pay, and more than half the federal workforce still falls within the somewhat rigid merit system (Kettl *et al.*, 1996). Thus it could be said that reform *debate* has been quite intense—and sometimes highly doctrinaire—but reform implementation has been quite 'patchy'—energetic here but slow there.

4. 9 Summary: multiple omegas, multiple trajectories and unforeseen developments?

At the beginning of this chapter questions were posed as to whether all ten states were following one, basically similar route (first mapped out by the Anglo-American countries) or whether, at the other extreme, there was no discernable pattern to the multiplicity of reforms—just a national and international game of reform ad hockery. On the basis of the evidence developed above—and in Appendix A—what can now be said in response to these propositions?

A first observation might be that trajectories would be much more likely to converge if every government in every country shared the same omega—the same vision of the desired future arrangements that the reforms were intended to propel that jurisdiction towards. However, it does not seem that there *is* such a universally shared vision. Although the question of visions of future states remains to be explored in greater depth in subsequent chapters (especially 5 and 8) it can already be suggested that there are different emphases as between our ten countries. Some seem to have the relatively modest ambition of 'lightening' the existing bureaucracy, through deregulation and streamlining, and simultaneously saving money by tightening up on budgets and financial management. Germany appears to fall into this category—at least at the federal level—as does the European Commission. One might think of this as an essentially conservative strategy of *maintaining* as much as possible of the status quo by taking steps to make current structures and practices work better.

A second group are more adventurous *modernizers*: they still believe in a large role for the state but acknowledge the need for fairly fundamental changes in the way the administrative system is organized. Such changes typically include budget reforms which move towards some form of results or performance budgeting, an emphasis on the importance of evaluation, some loosening of personnel rigidities (but not the abandonment of the concept of a unified career public service) and extensive decentralization and devolution of authority from central ministries and agencies. A greater emphasis on strategic planning is a further characteristic of such a trajectory. Among the modernizers there are different emphases as between managerial modernization (concentrating on management systems, tools and techniques) and participatory modernization (giving greater salience to devolution of authority to subnational governments, and to developing user-responsive, high-quality services). Despite considerable differences in these and other respects, Canada, Finland, France, the Netherlands and Sweden belong to this group.

A third group also want to modernize, but hold a particular view of what the most successful kind of modernization is likely to be, namely the introduction of more competition and MTMs *within* the public sector. They are therefore *market-izers*. These countries favour quasi-markets, large-scale contracting out and market-testing, corporatized forms of organization, contractual appointments and performance pay for civil servants, more people brought in from outside the traditional career pattern and a general reduction of the distinctiveness of the public sector *vis-à-vis* the private. Australia, New Zealand and the UK all fit this category, at least for parts of the period under scrutiny. Occasionally Finland and Sweden have ventured into this territory, but only selectively and cautiously, remaining more usually among the modernizers of the previous group.

Finally there is the omega of a *minimal state*, where everything that could possibly be privatized is privatized, leaving only a 'nightwatchman' administrative apparatus, performing core functions that the private sector is quite unable or unwilling to perform. Massive privatization and wholesale downsizing of public sector organizations would be key features of this approach. None of our ten countries has consistently adopted this minimizing position, which exists in full-blown form only in the tracts of right-wing politicians and theorists. However, it has been at least flirted with under certain, usually right-wing, governments: during the late Thatcher period in the UK and under the 1990 National Party government in New Zealand and Howard's 1996 Liberal (neo-conservative) government in Australia. Rhetorical empathy for such minimalism was also to be found on the lips of President Reagan, but there the gap between practice and vision was particularly wide. More generally, the USA remains difficult to classify: there have been strong elements of modernization, but also a considerable thrust towards marketization.

Thus there *is*, in our view, a pattern. However, its precision must not be exaggerated. As we said at the beginning of the chapter, scenarios are frequently vague or incomplete or both. So the pattern is very rough and approximate, for both political and organizational reasons. Politically, governments change and may hold different visions of the future, so that, following elections, certain types of reform are de-emphasized and other types given greater salience. The arrival of Mr Blair's Labour government in power in the UK in 1997 did not by any means completely alter the trajectory of UK reforms, but it did shift the emphasis. The automatic preference for private sector solutions was replaced with talk of partnerships. Some MTMs were partially dismantled (e.g., in the NHS), though others were retained. Greater emphasis was laid on horizontal co-ordination or 'joined-up' government. In general it might be said that the change of administration shifted the UK from the 'minimalist' end of the 'marketizing' group towards the 'modernizing' end. Similarly, in the US the replacement of the Bush Republican Presidency with the Clinton Democrats resulted in an end to the neglect and sometimes scorn which the federal civil service had suffered between 1980 and 1992. In rhetorical terms it shifted reform away from a mixture of minimalism (especially under Reagan) and marketization and towards modernization as the dominant *motif*.

A second set of political reasons for 'untidiness' is to be found among the pressures represented by external socio-economic forces (Figure 2.1, box A) and by political demands (box E). These might demand urgent responses which then blow chosen trajectories off course. Consider, for example, the balance between three basic types of reform objective. First there is the objective of reducing public expenditure, or, at least, restraining its rate of growth. Second, there is the laudable desire to design better-performing public services—higher quality, greater efficiency and so on. Third, there is the aim of sharpening accountability and therefore—hopefully—enhancing the legitimacy of the administration in the eyes of the public. These three objectives—all of them widely held and proclaimed among our ten countries—exist in some tension with each other. The nature and extent of that tension will be analysed in greater detail in chapter 7, but for the moment the point to note is that trouble for governments may blow up on any of these three fronts at quite short notice. An economic downturn may heighten the need for economies and cuts. Revelations of low standards in, say, nursing homes or public transport, may lead to strident and popular calls for something to be done. The discovery of cases of corruption or gross waste or concealment of important decisions may fuel calls for greater transparency and stricter accountability procedures. (A good example of this occurred at the beginning of 1999, when a huge political fuss was caused by the European Parliament's challenge to the European Commission, expressed through a motion of no confidence in the Commissioners which eventually led to their collective resignation. Intense media attention was focused on allegations of corruption, but one consequence of the storm was to divert interest from the arguably even bigger issue of the inefficiency and ineffectiveness of some EU programmes.) When one or more such events occurs political leaders and their senior officials have, temporarily at least, to alter the balance of their efforts. 'Firefighting' may lead to some neglect of longer term tasks of forest management. Progress along a particular trajectory wobbles or halts. A small-scale example might be when the needs of the national economy seem to require a budget cut, and the impact on particular public service organizations is that they abandon their plans for service improvement, which can no longer be afforded. Alternatively, attempts to decentralize authority and increase managerial discretion and flexibility may be halted if a particular 'decentralized' manager is discovered to have acted corruptly, so that calls for tighter centralized control cannot be resisted.

Organizational factors also intrude to spoil the possibility of any truly neat pattern. There are frequently implementation difficulties, and these can persuade governments to change instruments, or to 'soft pedal' on types of reform about which they were previously very enthusiastic. Mr Major's UK Conservative government soon retreated from the rhetoric of vigorous competition with respect to the NHS provider market, and took steps to see that it was closely managed, in an effort to avoid volatility (Pollitt, Birchall and Putman, 1998). Following criticism, the Dutch government of the mid 1990s became more cautious about creating highly autonomous ZBOs and tended to favour more controllable departmental agencies instead (Roberts, 1997).

More fundamentally, different governments have different *capacities for reform,* according to regime type (as explained in chapter 3). During the 1980s, for example, the gap between rhetoric and actual implementation was perhaps particularly wide in Canada and the USA (see their country files in the Appendix). During the 1990s one may question the extent of actual reform achievements within the European Commission, despite the impressive-sounding rhetoric of SEM 2000 and MAP 2000. SEM 2000 was introduced in 1995, but by the beginning of 1999 no fundamental reform of budgets or personnel regulations or organizational structures had yet taken place, despite much debate and many schemes on paper. There were plans and promises for the future, but all those would depend on the new Commission that was to succeed the old Commission, which had resigned before the end of its tenure.

Overall, therefore, our interpretation is that, whilst there has undoubtedly been great diversity, and while many trajectories turn out to be partial or interrupted, there is a rough but discernible longer-term pattern beneath the welter of detail. Whilst this pattern certainly does not mean that each individual reform instrument (performance budgets, contracting out, etc.) can be ascribed exclusively to one single trajectory (still less to one group of countries and not to others) it *does* suggest that there are some usually-continuing broad differences between different groups of countries. It also suggests that these differences are indeed related to the types of politico-administrative regimes which were analysed in the previous chapter. In terms of trajectories or strategies, not every country is playing the Anglo-Saxon game—not even all the Anglo-Saxon countries!

There is, of course, another, uncomfortably sharp question, which has been waiting in the wings throughout this chapter. It is whether any or all of these trajectories actually *work*? That is, what have been the *results* of the many efforts at reform? The next chapter wrestles with this by no means straightforward issue.

5

Results: Through a Glass Darkly

'One of the ideological outputs of organisations is *talk*. The political organ-isation sets great store by what it says, orally or in writing . . . Talk, decisions and products are mutually independent instruments used by the political organisation in winning legitimacy and support from the environment . . . hypocrisy is a fundamental type of behaviour in the political organisation: to talk in a way that satisfies one demand, to decide in a way that satisfies another, and to supply products in a way that satisfies a third.'

(Brunsson, 1989, pp. 26–7)

5.1 Results: a slippery concept

The question of what has resulted from all the many reforms is obviously an absolutely fundamental one. Yet it is not at all simple. The label 'result' can be applied to many different aspects, and may incorporate a variety of concepts. As Brunsson says, talk and decisions, as well as actual actions, may be considered as important types of outputs. Furthermore, much depends on who is evaluating, for whom and why. A full discussion of 'results' therefore embraces the wider ques-tions of 'results for whom, defined by whom, against what objectives?'

There is a utopian quality to some of the political rhetoric around the reforms—particularly in the UK and North America. In Paradise citizens will enjoy services which are high quality yet low cost, easily accessed and responsive. They will become more satisfied with their governments. Meanwhile civil servants will take on a new culture, infused with the values of economy, efficiency, effectiveness and customer service. Citizens will be empowered, civil servants will be trusted by politicians and citizens alike, politicians themselves will provide 'leadership' and strategic guidance. If only all this could be bottled! Yet perhaps it can—a number of governments have seemed to have ambitions to export their reform products: 'The Citizen's Charter is the most comprehensive programme ever to raise quality, increase choice, secure better value and extend accountability. We believe that it will set a pattern, not only for Britain, but for other countries in the world' (Prime Minister, 1991, p. 4). When expectations are pitched so high it becomes extremely hard for internal evaluations and reports to register anything less than good results. '*Tout est pour le mieux dans les meilleurs des mondes possibles*' (Voltaire, *Candide*). It was no surprise, two and a half years after the launch of the UK Citizen's Charter when the responsible Minister reported that performance had been impressive—the political price of saying anything less would have been considerable.

To form a more balanced picture is not easy. However, some materials are less gushing and more thoughtful than the 'headline' statements of ministers and other *parties pris*. There are reports from line departments, intended principally for internal consumption (Employment Service, 1994; Ministry of Finance, 1997). There are some attempts at academic assessments (e.g., Aucoin and Savoie, 1998; Peters, 1998a; Pollitt, 1995, 1998a). There are reports by relatively independent public commissions or experts (e.g., Schick, 1996; Task Force on Management Improvement, 1992). There are performance audits by national audit institutions (e.g., Auditor General of Canada, 1993, 1997; National Audit Office, 1995). Taking these together there are still many significant gaps, but there is enough to begin to sketch out a broad picture. The first message from this picture is that—unfortunately—there is no straightforward 'rational adaptation based upon a simple, complete cycle of learning from unambiguous experience' (Olsen and Peters, 1996a, p. 5). On the contrary, there is often contradictory information and an ambiguous and changing reality.

Whilst this state of affairs may seem frustrating to the rationalist (or to the rationalist elements within each of us) it may also, as Brunsson's book suggests, carry some positive benefits. From a political viewpoint it may enable a discourse of high (but somewhat conflicting) ideals to be maintained even in conditions where the possibilities for concrete actions are quite limited:

We seldom reflect high values in action, and because of their unreal elevation and their internal inconsistencies our best values cannot be adequately reflected in action. The maintenance of high values involves sin, i.e. a discrepancy between values and actions. And if norms, which are not or cannot be adapted to action are to be advocated, some hypocrisy is called for. Sin and hypocrisy are necessary to the creation and preservation of high morals. Those without sin or hypocrisy are those who pursue or advocate realizable goals, trading in their morality in exchange (Brunsson, 1989, pp. 233–4).

The remainder of the chapter is divided into seven main sections, each with a number of subsections. In the first main section (5.2) we distinguish between a number of different levels at which results can be defined and assessed. In the next four sections we look at some of the typical evidence which is available at each of these levels, and we also consider the (plentiful) problems of interpretation (5.3 to 5.6). Finally (5.7) we try to sum up what is known and what is not about the results of public management reform.

5.2 A brief taxonomy of results

It may be useful to distinguish between four levels of results, as follows:

First, operational results. This is perhaps the simplest and most concrete sense of 'result'. In principle, operational results are discrete and quantifiable. More outputs are obtained for the same inputs. Without additional expenditure a programme succeeds in reaching a higher percentage of its target population. The police crack down on car theft, and succeed in halving the number of vehicles which are broken into (and so on). Operational results may be found at the micro, meso and macro scales. Examples might be a local office which provides the same service with one fewer staff (micro) or a government which manages to reduce the overall rate of growth of public expenditure (macro).

Second, there could be improved *processes* of management or decision making. Related matters (such as health care and housing) are better co-ordinated. 'One-stop shops'/'single window' arrangements are examples of this—the particular decisions taken and the information given are not necessarily any different, but they are all conveniently available in one place. Processes are streamlined (e.g. planning applications are now processed in only 70 per cent of the average time which they used to take). Much 're-engineering' is about this kind of improvement. The assumption is that process improvements of this type will lead directly to improvements in operational results—that is, to better or more outputs and outcomes. Of course, in practice it is necessary to check that this assumption actually holds—public sector re-engineering projects, for example, do not always produce identifiable effects on final outcomes, or even on outputs (Packwood *et al.*, 1998).

Third, a 'result' may take the form of some broad change in the overall capacity of the political or administrative system. The pattern of institutions may be redesigned so as to be more flexible, with the intention that this will make the system more resilient in dealing with pressures which are expected to arise in the future. For example, it may be decided that all senior civil service appointments will be competitive and open to any applicant, rather than being confined to those already in the civil service and at the relevant level in the hierarchy.

Fourth, and finally, 'results' may be assessed relative to the degree to which the system has shifted towards some desired or ideal state. This is perhaps the most strategic sense of result. It is also the most obviously doctrinal or ideological. If the ideal is very small, 'light' state apparatus, with most activities undertaken within the private, market-oriented sector, then public management reforms may be judged in terms of how far they have moved the system in the direction of this vision.

It is immediately apparent that the first and second levels are more precise and concrete and—potentially at least—quantifiable, than the third and fourth. The third and fourth are both 'systems-level' kinds of results, and both involve somewhat abstract and intangible changes, including value shifts. In practice the borderline between these two is not always clear but, in principle, the third level is somewhat more specific and less explicitly normative than the fourth.

A moment's thought will also indicate that results—at any level—lead to further results. On level four the 'result' of a determined drive towards minimizing the state/maximizing the market may be a backlash of voters who wish to safeguard the welfare state and who succeed in electing a different government which then slows or reverses the original strategic direction. On level one a 20 per cent improvement in the productivity of a particular tax collection agency may lead top management in the taxation service to launch an investigation as to why the other collection agencies are not making similar efficiency gains.

5.3 Operational results

5.3.1 Operational results: inputs and 'savings'

In the simplest case the operational result will be expressed quantitatively, and will be compared with some pre-set standard. In practice, however, the standard is often inferred rather than explicit (for example, a licensing office may have cut costs by 5 per cent, but there may be no guidance on whether this is a great achievement, less than could reasonably be expected, or 'about right').

One of the commonest forms of operational 'result' can be seen in the traditional budget. The budget as made shows the resources appropriated for programme Z at $120M. At the end of the year to which the budget refers the accounts are audited and show that in fact $119M was spent. This result indicates that input control is probably good—the amount spent is close to, but within, the amount budgeted (which was, in effect, the standard set).

At a higher level of aggregation one can ask about the total mass of public expenditure. Even if a government is successful at achieving its budget forecasts for some programmes, there may be others which get out of control so that the overall total is wide of what had been planned. So 'hitting the target' for public expenditure as a whole is also an important result.

As we have seen in earlier chapters, saving money has been a salient objective for many countries, and a major influence on public management reform. Governments have certainly striven to achieve overall savings 'targets', which may have been represented as a reduction in the rate of growth of public expenditure, a levelling off of that expenditure as a proportion of GDP, or even an absolute reduction of that share. The Canadian Program Review of 1994, changes to the UK Public Expenditure Survey, reforms to budgetary procedures in the Nordic countries and New Zealand—all these and many more were designed with savings in mind. One should also remember the EU's Maastricht 'convergence criteria', which included the standard that public sector deficits must be held below 3 per cent of GDP.

Yet even with these apparently simple 'results' measures, ambiguity easily creeps in. As any experienced budget official knows, a 'saving' may mean any one or more of the following:

a) a reduction of the financial inputs compared with the previous year using the current price basis in each year (i.e., not allowing for inflation);

b) a reduction of the financial inputs compared with the previous year, using the same price base for both years (so that, for example, if the nominal/current cash spend in the previous year was 100 and the nominal/current cash spend this year is 105, but general inflation has been 10 per cent, then this will be counted as a saving, despite the fact that the nominal spend is higher);

c) a reduction in the financial input for year X compared with the previous *forecast* input for year X (such reductions may still leave the inputs higher than they were in the previous year);

d) a reduction in inputs with no reduction of the services provided/activities conducted (i.e., an efficiency gain in terms of Figure 1.1);

e) a reduction in inputs which leads to a reduction in the services provided/activities conducted (which may even mean an efficiency *loss*, depending what the relative proportions of the reductions in inputs and outputs turn out to be);

f) a reduction in unit costs (e.g., the cost per application processed). If activity volumes increase then perfectly genuine savings in unit costs may nevertheless be accompanied by an increase in the budget (because the latter is determined by unit cost x quantity, so the increase in quantity may outweigh the reduction in unit costs);

g) the transfer of an activity from one part of the state to another (e.g., from central government to local government) so that one jurisdiction can show what appears to be a 'saving', though the system as a whole has made no saving;

h) the transfer of an activity out of the state sector altogether (privatization). In this case the government 'saves' money (at least in terms of gross public spending) and also wins a one-off receipt in the form of the sale price. The citizen may or may not benefit. Taxes may go down, or not; the citizen may now have to buy the same service from the private sector at the same or even a higher price; or may benefit from lower prices and higher efficiency—these outcomes all depend on situationally specific factors of markets, regulatory regimes, management skills and other variables (Naschold and von Otter, 1996);

i) a purely hypothetical future event (as in 'if we make these changes to our working patterns now then in two years time we should be able to reduce our overheads by 15 per cent').

Claims that savings have been made should therefore always be subject to further questioning and scrutiny, in order to determine precisely what is meant and what the implications may be for outputs and outcomes. With that caveat in mind we will now look at some of the broad evidence concerning 'savings'.

Table 5.1 shows changes in the ratio of government spending to GDP in the ten countries between 1985 and an estimate for 1999. At first sight the GDP share appears to have fallen in eight countries and risen in two. It is also noticeable that there appears to be a particularly rapid fall in New Zealand, which is a country known to have conducted an especially vigorous reform programme. Before jumping to the conclusion that this means public management reforms have been successful in producing savings, however, several qualifications must be made.

First, the pattern between countries does not always fit what one might expect from the record of management reform. For example, the Netherlands—a consensual

TABLE 5.1. *Changes in government outlays, 1985–99* (% of nominal GDP)

| Country | General government | | |
	1985	1990	1999
Australia	36.5	34.8	33.8
Canada	46.0	46.7	41.0
Finland	43.8	45.4	50.9
France	52.2	49.8	53.4
Germany	47.0	45.1	46.7
Netherlands	57.1	54.1	46.9
New Zealand	—	57.5	44.9
Sweden	63.3	59.1	58.6
UK	44.0	39.9	39.0
US	32.9	32.8	31.6

Source: OECD

regime—achieved a large reduction while the UK—a self-styled 'world leader' in reform along with New Zealand—achieved something proportionately more modest. Meanwhile Finland, which implemented quite a substantial programme of reforms (Pollitt *et al.*, 1997), experienced a substantial *increase*.

Second, the figures tell us little about what kind of 'savings' may have been involved here. In particular they give no clue as to whether reductions in the share of GDP taken by public spending have been achieved with no losses in efficiency, effectiveness and quality, small losses or severe deterioration in the overall standards and scope of public services (i.e., the difference between savings of types d) and e) in the above list). Neither do they tell us to what extent the 'results' have been gained by transferring large sets of activities to the private sector, or what the consequences of this have been for the pockets of citizens—issue h) in the above list. In fact there are no good international, comparative data sets to show what in these senses has been the 'price that has been paid' for 'savings'. Indeed, the methodological problems in constructing such a data set would be enormous.

A third qualification is that much depends on the state of the economy at the time the measurement is taken. If the economy is depressed, various kinds of social protection expenditures rise and tax revenues fall. The public sector tends to remain large while the private sector contracts or ceases to grow so rapidly. For this reason the public-spending:GDP ratio can change quite rapidly because of general economic conditions, without this implying anything about the underlying state of management reform.

A fourth qualification is that *care must be taken not to attribute all savings to management reform, because the 'arrow of causation' may well be working in the opposite direction.* That is to say, it may be that hard-pressed governments have made relatively arbitrary cuts to public spending and that it is these which have pushed public sector organizations into serious reform, not the other way round. In Sweden, the country which, among the ten, has carried out the most comprehensive investigation of productivity changes within the public sector, it seems likely that cuts lead to reform or, at least, that reform is much more effective in raising productivity when it is carried out in a stringent fiscal climate. In a survey of productivity measures for the whole of the Swedish public sector from 1960 to the early 1990s, one expert concludes that: 'public management reforms are necessary but not sufficient to make the public administration produce more value for money ... it takes strict control of public budgets to realise the efficiency potential' (Murray, 1998, p. 16). However, this example takes us beyond input savings into the realm of productivity, a topic to which we will return in more detail in 5.3.3 below.

Table 5.2 gives us a second perspective on the question of 'savings'. It shows the net lending of the ten governments in 1980 and 1990, with an estimate for 1999. Net lending is sometimes used as an indicator of public sector deficit (the larger the minus sign the larger the deficit).

The picture on net lending is mixed, though the overall trend appears to be virtuous. Seven out of nine countries recorded negative figures in 1980 whereas only four

Table 5.2. *General government net lending* (% of nominal GDP)

	1980	1990	1999 (est.)
Australia	−1.8	0.6	0.2
Canada	−3.1	−4.5	1.8
Finland	2.8	5.4	0.6
France	0.0	−1.6	−3.5
Germany	−2.9	−2.1	−2.5
Netherlands	−4.2	−5.1	−1.7
New Zealand	—	−5.4	1.0
Sweden	−4.0	4.2	1.7
UK	−3.4	−1.2	−0.8
USA	−1.4	−2.7	0.4

(Net lending is often referred to as a measure of Government deficits (−) or surpluses (+))
Source: analytical databank, OECD

TABLE 5.3. *General government gross public debt* (% of nominal GDP)

	1990	1998 (est.)
Australia	21.2	36.5
Canada	71.5	89.2
Finland	14.5	53.4
France	40.2	65.7
Germany	45.5	64.5
Netherlands	78.8	69.5
New Zealand	—	—
Sweden	44.3	74.8
UK	39.3	59.1
USA	55.5	60.3

Source: analytical databank OECD

out of ten expect to in 1999 (although it should be observed that 1980 was the beginning of a world recession and 1999 was expected to be the continuance of a boom). Some individual countries show large changes. New Zealand swung from −5.4 in 1990 to plus 1.0 in 1999. France travelled in the other direction, from 0.0 in 1980 through −1.6 in 1990 to −3.5 in 1999. An NPM enthusiast might remark that the three leading NPM countries—Australia, New Zealand and the UK—each show a consistent movement 'upwards', while the two 'least NPM-ish' states—Germany and France—show, respectively, a level trajectory and a movement 'downwards'. However, the qualifications expressed above in respect of Table 5.1 also apply here.

Table 5.3 provides a third perspective on 'savings'. It records the OECD's estimates of gross public debt as a percentage of nominal GDP, in 1990 and in 1998. What is surprising here is that the debt percentage has *increased* in eight out of nine cases. This is hardly in line with the rhetorics of most governments during this period. We can see that the debt ratio climbed particularly fast in Finland and Sweden, and substantially in France and the UK. There seems little correlation here with any of the four strategies (maintaining, modernizing, marketizing, minimizing) that were identified at the end of chapter 4.

If we now turn to Table 5.4, we can see which countries have made the biggest reductions in their public service staffs (columns 2 to 4) and in their public service wage bills (columns 5 to 7). Unsurprisingly, the pattern is similar to that in Table 5.1: the Netherlands and New Zealand have made large reductions in staff as a percentage of total employment in their economies, whereas some other countries have actually experienced increases in this ratio (Finland, France). On this measure the performance of the UK is quite startling (a big reduction) probably mainly because of the large scale privatization of previously nationalized industries.

Equally startling, however, are the huge differences in the 1985 'starting points', ranging from Sweden, where a third of all employees were in the public sector, to the Netherlands and the USA where the corresponding percentage was 14–15 per cent.

5.3.2 Operational results: activities and outputs

Thus far we have discussed operational results mainly in terms of 'savings', where savings is a concept (in all its many forms) closely linked to financial *inputs*. Yet, as noted earlier, much of the management reform of the past two decades has been intended to produce a more *output-* and *outcome*-oriented approach to public administration. Increasingly, therefore, operational results have been conceived in terms of outputs (or sometimes activities believed to lead directly to outputs) or outcomes, or some mixture of the two. Popular slogans such as 'doing more with less', 'not working harder but working smarter' and 'more bang per buck' all draw attention to the output side of the equation, linking it with efforts (inputs). This is perfectly sensible—to maintain level outputs may not sound very exciting, but if this has been accomplished against the background of steadily falling inputs then it represents a significant productivity gain. Equally, for an agency to increase its activities under conditions of a static budget can be counted as a useful 'result'.

Information about changes in *activities* tends to be much more copious than information about productivity. Public sector organizations frequently keep detailed records of what they *do* even if they have much less information about what effects it has, or even how much each activity costs. There is a wealth of reports and studies showing how management reform has led to an intensification of activity (e.g., Carter, Klein and Day, 1992; Chancellor of the Duchy of Lancaster, 1997; Management Advisory Board, 1994; Swedish Ministry of Finance, 1997).

Activity has not only been intensified, it has also been transferred to a variety of alternative providers (i.e., the state still pays for a service but contracts out its

TABLE 5.4. *Public employment reduction*

Country	General government employment (% of total employment)			Compensation of general government employees (% of nominal GDP)		
	1985	1990	1996	1985	1990	1996
Australia	17.6	16.2	15.2 (1995)	12.7	11.6	11.4 (1997)
Canada	20.7	20.5	19.9 (1997)	12.7	12.8	11.7
Finland	19.2	20.9	23.6	14.1	14.6	15.1
France	22.8	22.6	24.7	14.6	13.2	14.4 (1997)
Germany	15.5	15.1	15.4 (1997)	10.6	9.7	10.0 (1997)
Netherlands	14.8	13.2	11.6	11.1	9.8	9.4
New Zealand	16.2	16.5	14.2	11.8	11.8	10.0 (1995)
Sweden	33.3	32.0	32.0	18.9	18.8	17.8
UK	21.7	19.5	13.8	12.1	11.6	8.4
US	15.3	15.4	15.2 (1997)	10.6	10.5	9.7 (1997)

Source: OECD

provision to external organizations). One rough indicator of this process, depending on accounting conventions, can be the proportion of total public spending which goes in direct consumption, as compared with transfer payments. Table 5.5 gives the picture for the ten countries at the beginning of our period (1980) and in 1996.

Clearly, the percentage of final consumption has fallen in every case. In six of the nine cases for which figures are available the percentage of transfers has risen. Interpretive caution is necessary, however, because most of this shift represents the continuing growth of welfare transfer programmes—particularly pensions and unemployment benefits—which have responded to demographic and employment trends (see Appendix A). Relative to this growth, contracting out is probably quite a minor influence. Nevertheless, the move away from direct service provision has been significant in a number of countries, and at both central and local government levels. For example, the Dutch Socio-Cultural Planning Office describes the trends for Dutch central government as shown in Table 5.6.

Of course, some countries started from a position of heavier involvement in direct service provision than others, and therefore had more scope for contracting out. Sweden and the UK, for example, were relatively heavy direct providers, Germany much less so. While there has been a good deal of intensification of activities, delegation of activities to lower levels of government and contracting out of activities, the fact remains that activity data or output and activity data *alone* is of limited value or meaning. Unless it is coupled with quality data and cost data it floats in a vacuum. To know that agency X now deals with 25 per cent more applicants is interesting, but this information needs to be married to other data about agency costs and the quality of service the applicants are receiving.

Finally, there is the issue of validation. This concerns all performance and cost data. The question is, 'how do we know that the data we see is accurate?'. This is a source of real concern, not least since there have been several cases where, upon inspection, performance data has turned out to be seriously inaccurate (e.g. Hencke, 1998 reports how a Jobcentre provided misleading figures for its success rate). A number of national audit offices have expressed concern over this, and those in Finland, Sweden and the UK have begun major attempts at validation (for a UK example, see the NAO report on the Meteorological Office—National Audit Office, 1995; more generally see Pollitt *et al.*, 1999). As the UK National Audit Office put it in its 1997 annual report: 'The National Audit Office are at the forefront of developing the methodology by which performance measures can be validated and we would like to see greater public reporting and auditing of performance data' (National Audit Office, 1997, p. 1).

5.3.3 *Operational results: productivity ratios*

A productivity increase is usually defined as an improvement in the ratio of inputs to outputs (see Figure 1.1). As such it may come about via a variety of quite different circumstances:

TABLE 5.5. *Final consumption, social security outlays, debt interest and investments, and other transfers and subsidies in 1980 and 1996* (% of total in each year)

Country	Final consumption		Social security		Debt interest and investments		Other transfers and subsidies	
	1980	1996	1980	1996	1980	1996	1980	1996
Australia	52.5	45.3	—	—	14.3	14.7	33.2	40.0
Canada	47.4	40.5	13.3	17.2	20.1	25.3	19.2	17.0
Finland	45.9	37.0	21.2	28.2	12.0	13.7	20.9	21.0
France	38.6	34.5	33.3	33.2	10.0	12.7	18.1	19.7
Germany	41.3	39.7	24.2	28.3	10.8	11.7	23.6	20.3
Netherlands	29.0	26.5	34.6	35.5	12.4	15.6	24.1	22.4
New Zealand	—	—	—	—	—	—	—	—
Sweden	47.0	40.1	22.2	25.5	13.5	15.1	17.3	19.3
UK	48.1	47.8	14.2	13.7	16.0	11.4	21.8	27.1
US	51.0	46.0	19.8	23.0	15.0	13.7	14.2	17.3

Source: OECD

TABLE 5.6. *Policy shifts: the case of the Netherlands*

Policy field in the Netherlands	Position of central government
Education	Careful withdrawal
Health	Partial expansion
Social Security	Careful withdrawal
Social Housing	Partial withdrawal
Environment	Clear expansion
Land use planning	Status quo but less detail
Emancipation/Minorities	Modest development

Source: SCP, The Netherlands, 1991

- where resources (inputs) decrease and outputs increase;
- where resources remain the same and outputs increase;
- where resources *increase* but outputs increase by an even larger amount;
- where outputs remains static but resources decrease;
- where outputs *decrease* but inputs decrease by an even larger amount.

Clearly it is important to know which of these situations one is dealing with. For example, in the 1970s and 1980s both British Steel and British Coal considerably increased their average productivity. This sounds fine until one realizes that both corporations were contracting fast—closing down plants and throwing many people out of work. Productivity rose as fewer and fewer steel plants/coal mines— the most modern and productive ones—were left. Such a contextual understanding affords a more sceptical perspective on statistics such as those portrayed in Table 5.7.

Comparative data on public service productivity (as distinct from the productivity of industries such as coal and steel) is rare. The most detailed figures come from single countries, especially Sweden and Finland (the USA also had a long-running statistical series, but it focused on labour productivity only). The Swedish data is shown in Table 5.8. The overall pattern appears to be a *decline* in productivity during the 1960s and 1970s, followed by a levelling-off in the 1980s, and an increase in the early 1990s. More detailed analysis indicates a strong correlation between bouts of spending cutbacks ('savings') and productivity increases (see Table 5.9).

A closer examination of specific cases suggests that public management reforms *could* help to increase productivity, especially when carried out in conjunction with budget cuts or increases in demand for a service which were not paralleled by any significant increase in resource inputs, but that management reforms in the absence of downward pressure on inputs were not necessarily terribly effective in improving productivity (Murray, 1998; Swedish Ministry of Finance, 1997).

Some figures for Finland are shown in Table 5.10. Like the Swedish statistics they convey a general picture of falling productivity in the 1970s and 1980s and then a reversal of this trend during the 1990s. In another study (Niemi, 1998) the

TABLE 5.7. *Changes in total factor productivity and ownership: six UK corporations*

Sector	Change in ownership	Total factor productivity	
		1979–83	1983–90
B Airport Authority	private in 7/87	−1.6	2.6
B Gas	private in 12/86	−1.0	2.2
B Coal	still public in 1990	−0.8	4.6
B Rail	still public in 1990	−2.9	3.7
B Steel	private in 12/88	4.6	7.5
B Post Office	still public in 1990	1.7	2.7

Source: As quoted in Naschold and von Otter, 1996, p. 24

TABLE 5.8. *Productivity in the Swedish public sector, by policy area, 1960–90*
(% of annual charge)

	1960–70	1965–70	1970–75	1975–80	1980–85	1985–90
Central government						
General administration	−0.2	−3.6	−5.1	4.3	0.3	1.3
Justice/Police	−4.7	−2.5	−6.2	2.8	−1.4	−1.3
Defence			−0.1	−0.6	−0.6	−5.0
Education	−2.1	−10.5	−2.1	0.7	2.5	2.0
Social insurance	−1.0	−2.6	−4.8	−0.2	2.8	1.2
Social welfare	9.0	−6.4	−4.7	−1.7	6.1	−2.3
Community planning	5.0	−0.6	6.6	1.9		
Culture, recreation, theatres					−8.8	0.6
Economic services	−2.2	1.6	3.5	1.1	3.7	0.0
Central Total	**−1.3**	**−2.2**	**−2.1**	**1.1**	**0.8**	**−1.2**
Central Total excl Defence	**−1.3**	**−2.2**	**−3.0**	**1.9**	**1.2**	**0.1**
Local government						
Education	−4.1	−6.1	0.5	−3.7	−0.5	−1.5
Health care	−3.8	−3.4	−1.4	−2.2	−0.2	−1.4
Social welfare			−2.0	−1.0	0.5	0.1
Community planning			0.0	−9.7		
Culture, recreation	−4.9	3.0	1.1	−1.8	−1.2	−3.7
Local Total	**−4.1**	**−4.9**	**−0.8**	**−2.6**	**−0.2**	**−1.1**
Public Sector Total	**−3.7**	**−4.3**	**−1.1**	**−1.6**	**0.0**	**−1.1**

Source: Swedish Ministry of Finance, 1997, pp. 25–6

weighted average total productivity growth, 1994–95, across 48 Finnish institutions, was 0.8 per cent. It may well be significant that the early 1990s were a period of severe economic crisis in Finland, and that there were sharp budgetary cutbacks, including cutbacks to municipal budgets, that were delivered through a new system of 'framework budgeting' in which central government set broad totals for each municipality and left them much more leeway than hitherto in deciding how to

TABLE 5.9. *Productivity trends of central government, excluding defence, and rate of change in public consumption, 1960–90* (% of annual change)

	1960–70	1970–80	1980–90
Productivity	–1.8	–0.6	0.6
Public consumption	3.7	1.8	0.6

Source: Swedish Ministry of Finance, 1997, p. 36

allocate these resources between services (see Appendix: Finland, country file). In other words, the Finnish data are consistent with the interpretation previously advanced for Sweden: that budget cuts are a sharp stimulus to productivity growth.

Generally it might be said that there appears to be a great deal of productivity data around, but close inspection reveals much of it to be of questionable validity and/or reliability. An interesting example of this may be found in Boyne's review of contracting out in US local government. Although it was widely believed that such contracting out would produce higher levels of productivity—and despite the fact that a number of previous studies pointed to precisely such an outcome—Boyne found numerous methodological and other weaknesses in the supporting evidence. He concluded that 'public choice hypotheses on contracting are not directly supported or undermined by the empirical evidence' (Boyne, 1998, p. 482).

Even the privatization of state-owned industries—the area in which, perhaps, one might expect productivity changes to be most transparent—has provoked a considerable debate. Changing to private ownership does not seem to have made much difference by itself. Large productivity gains have been more closely associated with intensification of competition, whether the corporation concerned had been privatized or was still in public ownership (Naschold and von Otter, 1996, chapter 3).

5.3.4 Operational results: outcomes and impacts ('effects')

As was seen in the previous subsection, there are often difficulties in *attributing* productivity growth to a single, definite cause, or proportionately to a limited number of causes. These difficulties grow still larger when the focus shifts to outcomes. New Zealand is a case in point. Certain outcomes—both positive and negative—were observable in the period of the great management reforms of 1986–92 (see Appendix: New Zealand, country file). Unemployment reached new heights and then, in the early 1990s, dropped. Inflation also rose and fell. Crime and youth suicides rose. And so on. Were these the results of *management* reforms, or policy changes, or changes in external circumstances (the continuing dynamic of the global economy), or some mixture of all three? As it happens, New Zealand was a country that built up an unusually sophisticated system of performance measures for its public services. Yet most of these measures were of outputs, not outcomes.

TABLE 5.10. *Productivity development in public services and government activities*

	Time period 1980s	Productivity change (%)	Time period 1990s	Productivity change (%)
Hospitals	80–85	–3.9	90–93	+5.2
	85–90	–4.1		
Health Centres	88–90	–2.9	90–94	+2.3
Senior Citizen's homes	86–91	–2.8	91–93	+0.5
Theatres	87–90	–3.3	90–95	+3.0
Land Survey offices			91–93	+10.4
Tax Offices			92–95	+0.9
Employment offices			92–93	+26.0

Main results of studies based on Malmquist-index approach in Finland
Source: Hjerppe and Luoma, 1997, p. 15

Attribution problems of this kind are present in almost every country. In Australia, for example, the 1992 evaluation of management reforms concluded that 'the new framework has strong support and is seen, overall, to have increased the cost effectiveness of the APS [Australian Public Service] including outcomes for clients' (Task Force on Management Improvement, 1992, p. 52). However, closer inspection shows that the causal link suggested here was far from proven, and, in another part of the very same report, a rather different emphasis is given:

since the reforms took place at a time of rapid social and economic change, there is no defin-itive way of separating the impact on cost, agency performance and clients (among other things) of these broader changes and the government changes which accompanied them (Task Force on Management Improvement, 1992, p. 8).

This is quite typical: the same could be said of the Thatcher management reforms in the UK, the great French decentralization measures of the early 1980s, the multiple Swedish efforts to decentralize and most other large-scale public sector restructurings. On the one hand, the conventional wisdom is that: 'Experience has shown that developing performance measurement systems that are outcome oriented is critical for using performance measures to improve programmes' (Mayne, 1996, p. 8). In practice, however, the availability of such outcome measures, confidently linked to programme interventions, is the exception rather than the rule. At the level of broad programmes of management reform we know of not a single study from our ten countries that convincingly links the actions taken with a set of positive and safely attributable final outcomes. This kind of rationality may occasionally be possible for very specific programmes in particular, well-understood contexts (e.g., an evaluation of traffic management measures—see Bureau of Transport and Communications Economics, 1995), but it is seldom, if ever, possible for broad strategies of reform such as those referred to above. Recent academic attempts to develop a 'theory of effective government' show what a wide range of information would be required—much wider than anything that is normally available, even in these electronically lubricated, data-rich times (Rainey and Steinbauer, 1999, see especially p. 3).

Nevertheless, the search for a rationally-defensible notion of 'results' continues—indeed, appears to have intensified. One technique in which much effort has recently been invested in several countries is that of 'benchmarking' (Department of Finance, 1996; Dahlberg and Isaksson, 1997; National Performance Review, 1997b; Next Steps Team, 1998). There are several different species (internal benchmarking; functional benchmarking, competitive benchmarking, generic benchmarking, etc.). Most of these rest on the fundamentally simple idea of finding an organization that is good at some process or activity, comparing one's own performance at that same process or activity with theirs, and then analysing in some detail how the superior performance is achieved, in order to be able to learn from it (Pollitt, Cave and Joss, 1994). However, the technique has been developed into a generic format which, it is claimed, can be used to compare virtually any organization, public or private sector, with any other. In Europe this has resulted in the 'Business Excellence' model of the European Foundation for Quality Management (European Foundation for Quality Management, 1996). Some of the UK's 'Next Steps' agencies have participated in a pilot exercise in which, using the EFQM model, their performances were compared with each other and with high-performing private sector companies. The conclusion was that:

In comparison with the private sector agencies scored well in the areas of customer satisfaction, business results, policy and strategy and the management of financial resources . . .

The agencies tended to score rather less well than the private sector in the areas of leadership, human resources, processes and employment protection (Chancellor of the Duchy of Lancaster, 1997, p. 10).

In Australia it is considered that:

[I]nternational benchmarking is considered a priority by most countries. An international focus is necessary to capture public service activities where the only possible benchmark comes from similar public services in other countries (Trosa, 1997, p. 6).

Like so many other techniques adopted by public sectors during the course of reform, benchmarking had its origins in US private sector practice (Camp, 1989). Its suitability for public sector applications is debated between optimists (Next Steps Team, 1998) and those who wish instead to stress either its limitations (Talbot, 1997) or the existence of preconditions which render its usefulness questionable in significant parts of the public sector (Pollitt, Cave and Joss, 1994).

Bearing in mind the contested status of benchmarking, we will now look more closely at the 'results' which some of its applications have yielded. First, Table 5.11 compares the results of 26 UK Next Steps agencies, which employ 200,000 staff, with a private sector average, using the EFQM 'Business Excellence' model.

In this model 50 per cent of the marks are awarded for 'results', weighted as 20 per cent customer satisfaction, 15 per cent business results, 'people satisfaction' (staff), 9 per cent and 'impact on society', 6 per cent. Perhaps the main point about

TABLE 5.11. *EFQM scores for benchmarked UK agencies*

Unweighted criterion	UK quality award standard	Private sector average	Agency average	Maximum agency score	Minimum agency score
Leadership	63	60	35	48	19
Policy and strategy	68	40	36	57	15
People management	66	50	36	50	18
Resources	68	60	41	52	17
Processes	75	50	35	53	14
Customer satisfaction	60	30	38	61	14
People satisfaction	66	40	22	45	7
Impact on society	55	30	17	30	0
Business results	86	50	46	63	23

Source: Next Steps Team, 1998; Cowper and Samuels, 1997

a table such as this is that in one way it looks so final, but, in another, the process of arriving at the figures in each cell is fraught with contestable assumptions and compromises. In particular, it should be noted that less than 50 per cent of the over-all score is attributable to outcomes as defined in chapter 1 (Figure 1.1). More than 50 per cent is placed on 'enablers', such as 'leadership' or 'people management'.

Another form of benchmarking is the comparison of different units delivering the same or similar services, within a single national organization. There has been a great deal of this in the UK, including published national 'league tables' for schools, hospitals, community health organizations and local authorities. A small extract from one of these is shown in Table 5.12.

These tables are published annually, and cover all National Health Service establishments in the country. Initially they contained very few direct measures of clinical outcomes (e.g., Table 5.12 shows us how long patients had to wait under various circumstances, but not whether the care they eventually received was ef-fective) but, over time, some clinical indicators have been added to the set. Benchmarking can also be applied to many other aspects of administration, for example, there has been considerable work on both internal and international rating of budgetary and financial management processes in Swedish agencies (Dahlberg and Isaksson, 1997).

Another way of conceiving 'results' or impacts is to use citizens as final arbiters, and to ask them to say how good or bad particular services are. In 1998 a mail survey of 2,900 Canadian citizens was commissioned, seeking comparative judge-ments as between selected public and private sector services. It produced the scores shown in Table 5.13 (although with a response rate of only 9.5 per cent).

Contrary to some popular beliefs, this piece of research shows that the public have quite differentiated views of the quality of services from public and private sectors—some public services (in bold) scoring high and others low, with the private sector services scattered though the top two-thirds of the same range, but not anywhere falling as low as the very poor score accorded to road maintenance.

TABLE 5.12. *NHS performance indicators* (excerpts)

Anglia and Oxford area	Average performance	East Berkshire Community Health NHS Trust	Ipswich Hospital NHS Trust
Accident and Emergency: Patients assessed within 5 minutes of arrival	93%	100% *****	99% *****
Patients seen for first appointment within 13 weeks of referral by GP	83%	81% ***	79% **
Patients seen for first appointment within 26 weeks of referral by GP	97%	99% ****	96% ***
Appointments where patient did not attend	11%	9% ****	7% *****
Patients seen within 30 minutes of appointment time	91%	95% ***** up	66% * down
Patients admitted within 3 months of decision to admit	72%	77% ****	72% ****
Patients admitted within 12 months of decision to admit	97%	100% *****	95% ****
Number of patients not admitted within a month of last-minute cancelled operation	11	1 ****	72 *

Source: NHS Performance National Guide 1996–97 (1997:10).
Note: Stars (*) are given depending upon performance. The better the performance against standards, the more stars. Significant change in performance is mentioned with 'up' or 'down' signs. Numbers refer to 1996–97 data.

TABLE 5.13. *Service quality scores of public (in bold) and private sectors: Canada*

Service	Score	Service	Score
Fire departments	**78**	**Canada Post**	**55**
Public libraries	**75**	**Public transit**	**55**
Supermarkets	74	Insurance agencies	55
Private mail carriers	68	**Municipal govt services**	**53**
Provincial parks, campgrounds	**64**	Banks	51
Police	**64**	**Revenue Canada**	**50**
Provincial electric utilities	**63**	**Federal govt services**	**47**
Telephone companies	63	**Public education system**	**47**
Private sector in general	60	**Provincial govt services**	**47**
Passport office	**60**	**Hospitals**	**46**
Taxis	57	**Road maintenance**	**35**

Source: Canadian Centre for Management Development (CCSN), 1998a

In principle such surveys could be undertaken before and after major reforms (this was not the design of the Canadian survey) and would provide one way of registering any shift in public satisfaction levels. In practice such before-and-after studies are not terribly common, although there are a few (e.g., concerning passenger satisfaction with rail journeys before and after improvements) where changes have definitely translated into higher scores. We will return to this particular survey in chapter 6, where we consider citizens' attitudes to public services in more depth.

5.4 Results as process improvements

5.4.1 *Process measures: an overview*

In the first chapter a working definition of management reform was adopted which focused on changes in the structures and processes of public sector organizations made with the aim of getting them to perform better. That suggested that improving *processes* was frequently an important step towards achieving improved outputs and outcomes. It is also the case that process improvements may have a value of their own in a democratic state, where *how* things are done may be as important as what the operational results are (engaging values such as 'due process', fairness, transparency and participation). For both these reasons, therefore, changes in processes merit attention.

Changes in process may also signal a shift in administrative cultures—indeed they are often made with a definite consciousness of their symbolic impact. A status report on the US NPR lists ten pieces of evidence that government is starting to work better:

- Over 90% of National Performance Review recommendations are underway;
- the President has signed 22 directives, as well as performance agreements with seven agency heads;
- over a hundred agencies are publishing customer service standards;

- nine agencies have started major streamlining initiatives;
- agencies are forming labor-management partnerships with their unions;
- agencies are slashing red tape;
- the government is buying fewer 'designer' products and doing more common sense commercial buying;
- throughout the federal government 135 're-invention laboratories' are fostering innovation;
- the government is shifting billions of dollars in benefits to electronic payments;
- the federal government is changing the way it interacts with state and local governments (National Performance Review, 1994, p. 5).

Clearly, the above items are *process* improvements, which are supposed to lead to improved final outcomes in due course. One crucial process in public administration is that of giving advice to the political leadership. If we take the Australian case:

[I]t can be argued that we should in fact be able to provide far better quality advice as a result of the reforms. Objectives are being clarified with participation of staff from both the regions and the centre, information systems are being linked to objectives and there is far better integration of policy development and implementation than was the case in the past (Keating, 1990, p. 392).

The main problem with process improvements of this kind is that the link with final outcomes is less than certain. If the administrative culture remains hostile to the spirit of the reform then the new process may be observed in a minimalist and ritual way, but no real change may follow. For example, Rouban suggests that German and French civil servants may sometimes resist changes in the professional culture if they seem likely to threaten their social values and/or personal status (Rouban, 1995, pp. 28–9).

A further difficulty in interpreting lists of process changes—such as that quoted above from the NPR—is that they may be the products of an acute form of selection bias. That is, good examples are chosen from the best-performing parts of the public sector, and both side effects and the other parts of the public sector (which may even be getting *worse*) are ignored:

It is interesting to note that new management practices have been more often successfully implemented in departments and agencies that were already reputed to be well managed . . . or in machine-like organisations that process large numbers of claims and forms, hence the boiler room part of government. Efforts have been less successful in departments that have many goals and activities and a medium-to-high policy content in their work. The reforms have thus served to fix departments that were operating well but have had limited impact on departments that needed more attention (Peters and Savoie, 1994, p. 423).

The next two subsections will be given over to an analysis of two of the most common and popular types of process improvement.

5.4.2 Increasing client orientation

The assumption here is that, by paying more attention to clients, public service organizations will learn to deliver better results, and that clients will notice the change and experience increased satisfaction.

The notion of putting clients, customers, users, patients, passengers (or whatever) first has been given tremendous rhetorical emphasis in many jurisdictions and in many countries. The NPR in the USA, the *Citizen's Charter* in the UK, the 1994 French programme *Année de l'accueil dans les services publiques*, the service charters being introduced in Finland at the time of writing, and more—all claim to increase client orientation. Furthermore, modern quality improvement techniques such as TQM are founded on the centrality of customer requirements, and have been introduced in parts of the Australian, Canadian, Dutch, Finnish, French, New Zealand, Swedish, UK and US public sectors, as well as being promoted by some parts of the European Commission. In 1987 the OECD jumped on a rhetorical bandwagon that was then gathering speed and posed a shrewd question: 'If the public service already exists to serve the public, then why are so many OECD governments embarking on campaigns to make it happen?' (OECD, 1987, p. 9).

However, achieving a client orientation is not straightforward. Consider the case of the reforms to the Australian Public Service (APS). A 1992 survey of Australian citizens indicated that 73 per cent of those who had had prior contact with a given agency thought its quality of service had remained the same, and 26 per cent thought it had changed (about three-quarters of whom thought it had changed for the better). At the same time members of the Australian Senior Executive Service (SES) were asked whether *they* thought that the reforms had led to an increased client focus, and 77 per cent said they thought it had. Only 51 per cent of lower grade staff were of the same view. This—and other evidence within the same report—shows a complicated picture in which perceptions of client emphasis and of quality improvements depend to some extent on where the respondent sits. The senior staff appear to be more optimistic than more junior staff, while only a minority of citizens notice much difference. Elsewhere we have suggested that the relevant variables are quite complex (Pollitt and Bouckaert, 1995). Much depends on the expectations of the various parties concerned, and satisfaction levels may go up and down as much because expectations vary as because the underlying 'producer quality' of the service changes. Indeed, one strategy for a cynical government that is determined to raise satisfaction scores might be to attempt to lower public expectations (which may almost have been the case with some governments in certain instances—for state pensions for example). Thus the measurement of perceived quality in public services is by no means just a technical issue. It has political and psychological elements, and these make 'satisfaction' a moving target, something which may jump to a new position as soon as or even before it is achieved.

5.4.3 *Increasing performance orientation*

A second common theme within the conception of results as improvements in process is that an increasing emphasis on processes which emphasize *performance* is a good thing. A performance orientation is frequently contrasted with a 'traditional' focus on inputs and procedural correctness (compliance). It is seen as a good in itself.

At different times and in different sectors every country in our set of ten has praised the (supposedly) new stress on 'performance', which has sometimes been seen as virtually synonymous with 'getting results' (see country files in the Appendix). In the mid-1990s even the EU Commission expressed an intention to move somewhat away from its elaborate *ex ante* controls on expenditure towards a greater concentration on the monitoring of results. The US General Accounting Office undertook a comparative study of Australia, Canada, New Zealand and the UK and came to the conclusion that strategic planning, operational planning, measurement, accountability for performance, resource flexibility and the presence of incentives for line management were all critical to the success of performance-oriented management (General Accounting Office, 1995).

Behind views such as this lies the assumption that performance-based budgets somehow provide better results than traditional line-item, incremental budgeting. Further, it is widely assumed that the integration of budgeting processes with performance measurement will be 'a good thing'. The problem for this general approach is to explain why attempts to make this kind of integration have seemingly so often failed to take root. It may be that economic logic and political logic do not lead to the same conclusions, and that, from a political perspective, application of strict economic rationality is not the final word (Pollitt, 1998b). Perhaps certain kinds of political deal can only be arrived at within contexts where objectives are left as somewhat ambiguous and results information is inconclusive. In other words, it may be that better information about the results to be expected from particular allocations of resources does not actually help very much when politicians come to the point of having to make those allocation decisions. Mayne (1996, pp. 13–14) concluded a survey of attempts to use performance information in the budgetary process as follows:

In general performance measures are not being used to make decisions about the level of resources that a program or organisation will receive. This is true even for those who have defined a specific objective to do so . . . Resource allocation decisions continue to be driven, for the most part, by traditional budget practices . . . Performance information *supports* internal management decisions on setting priorities, adjusting operations and resource levels, etc.

In the field of human resource management the introduction of 'performance logic' is even more controversial. In some jurisdictions revisions to regulations have made it easier to dismiss or discipline individuals who persistently fall below the required performance. Presumably this has been beneficial in enabling public organizations to get rid of a few cases of really serious incompetence or laziness. Performance-related pay systems have been applied to a far larger number of staff, but have not always been a huge success (OECD, 1993b; Gaertner and Gaertner, 1985; Perry and Pearce, 1985). The idea that current performance will become the only—or at least the dominant—criterion for tenure and advancement—carrying greater weight than seniority, loyalty, qualifications and other factors—is far from universally popular. Support for this tendency seems to come more from politicians and senior civil servants (those who have already 'made it') than from lower ranks (Bourgault, Dion and Lemay, 1993). Part of the problem is that merit pay systems can be divisive—it is very common for civil servants to feel that such arrangements are unfair, too crude to register real differences in performance, or are even open to a degree of manipulation. Another part is that the actual 'bonus' that is to be distributed frequently turns out to be either quite small per capita (and therefore likely to have little effect on motivation) or that it is larger but confined to a few outstanding individuals (in which case the majority feel disappointed that they haven't received anything). A system that distributed sizeable bonuses to a substantial proportion of the total work force would actually be rather expensive, if not downright unaffordable.

The development of strategic management can also be portrayed as a way of increasing the performance orientation of an organization. One or other variety of strategic approach has been much discussed and—to varying degrees—implemented in, *inter alia*, Australia, Canada, Finland, New Zealand and the UK. The basic link here is that a strategic approach will permit the organization to focus more clearly and consistently on its high priority goals, which will, in turn, lead to a more intensive pursuit of the results which are deemed to be of the greatest importance. New Zealand provides perhaps the best-known example. A system was developed which included an annual consideration of Strategic Results Areas (SRAs—broad, often cross-portfolio priorities set by the cabinet) and their linkage to a more detailed set of Key Results Areas (KRAs—a set of critical medium-term objectives which are written into the contracts of the chief executives who head departments). The articulation of this system was not without its problems, but nevertheless led to:

improved information flows, more substantial consultation with commercial interests and non-profit organisations, greater clarity about the Government's vision and priorities and a surprising synergy among agencies with a history of sometimes fractious relationships (Matheson, Scanlan and Tanner, 1997, p. 88; see also Boston *et al.*, 1996, pp. 282–3, 359).

In Australia, also, reforms meant that: 'ministers are now in a better position to set the strategic directions for their portfolios and to direct the efforts of their departments' (Management Advisory Board, 1993b, pp. 9–10). In Finland, the Lipponen coalition government (1995–99) developed a 'Strategy Portfolio' which contains the 'key results or strategic results areas of the government', and serves as one of the main platforms for overall steering and priority-making (*High quality services, good governance and a responsible civic society*, 1998a, pp. 19–22). In the UK the incoming Labour government of 1997 laid great emphasis on carrying out a 'Comprehensive Spending Review', which formed the basis for a 'new, strategic approach to public spending' (Chancellor of the Exchequer, 1998, Prime Minister's foreword). In the USA the GPRA was portrayed by some as an exercise in strategic planning, although many experts doubted whether its provisions could yield much in this regard (General Accounting Office, 1997).

The fundamental difficulties in assessing most, if not all, of these strategic initiatives are those of determining how far (if at all) the quality of top-level decision making is improved, and whether the new decision procedures ultimately lead to more efficiently produced outputs and/or substantively better outcomes. There is some testimony from insiders to indicate that the quality of decisions does benefit from more strategic approaches, but it is hard to be sure. Much is likely to depend on how receptive the broader civil service culture is to exercises of this kind. If the products of strategic exercises are placed in the public domain then one less disputable benefit is that public accountability is improved to the extent that the relevant documents give reasonably clear and concrete descriptions of political priorities and intentions (e.g., Chancellor of the Exchequer, 1998). It would be prudent, however, to remember Brunsson's point that political organizations frequently devote great energy to talk and to decision procedures without these necessarily having much effect on external actions—or even being intended to have such an effect (Brunsson, 1989).

5.5 Results as system improvement

5.5.1 The concept of systems improvement

In the previous section we briefly discussed strategic management initiatives as one type of process improvement. There is a sense in which the adoption of a more strategic approach shades upwards into the more general category of *systems improvements*. The achievement of such improvements may be counted as a kind of 'result', in so far as a systems improvement leaves the entire governmental system more flexible, more quickly responding, with a higher capacity to learn and adapt, and so on. Thus (for example) the transformation of a rigid bureaucratic hierarchy into a flexible, 'flat', multi-disciplinary organization could be said to have increased the capacity of that organization to cope with new developments in its environment. These could well include the kinds of global economic developments and new socio-demographic phenomena mentioned in chapter 2 and described in the first part of Appendix A.

A systems improvement is not a small thing, not a particular individual reform such as the introduction of performance indicators for the police force. Rather it is something broad, which is intended to influence the whole structure or character of government. The Clinton/Gore NPR is apparently of this type, as is the Finnish government's 1998 resolution *High quality services, good governance and a responsible civic society* (1998a and b). Such improvements are therefore virtually bound to have a number of different aspects and elements. For the sake of convenience they will here be divided into just two: structural improvements and cultural changes.

5.5.2 Structural change in systems

Major reorganizations alter the architectures of politico-administrative systems, and thus the pattern of interactions within them and across their boundaries. In the UK between 1988 and 1998 more than 70 per cent of the non-industrial civil servants found themselves working for a new type of organization—the 'Next Steps' executive agency. Also in the UK, Conservative ministers made claims to the effect that structural changes introducing greater autonomy plus a measure of competition into the health care and educational sectors would revitalize hospitals and schools, making them more efficient and user-responsive. In New Zealand almost every public sector body underwent substantial restructuring in the decade following 1984. In Finland, during the early and mid 1990s, the whole range of central agencies was streamlined and remodelled, producing a much less heavy regulatory layer between the central ministries and the municipalities. These are just some of many examples of efforts at widescale restructuring.

It is not unusual for politicians and senior civil servants to claim that such changes have significantly improved the system of government and, indeed, that is one of their central purposes. To assess these claims is, however, difficult. To begin with, organization structures are intermediate variables, and there is no tried and tested, widely accepted model showing exactly what structural change will lead to what shift in outputs or final outcomes. To take one small example of this uncertainty, when a French survey posed the question of whether privatization would lead to an improved performance by certain organizations, the results were as inconclusive as is shown in Table 5.14.

Furthermore, one may observe that the reformed structures themselves are frequently far from stable. Countries like New Zealand and the UK can be seen to have subjected some sectors to two or three waves of structural reform since 1980, and there is every sign that this process will continue. In France ministerial departments are frequently reshuffled, but few observers believe that this process fundamentally alters the nature of the system (Rouban, 1997). A longer-term view reveals shifting fashions for different types of structure—big departments, small departments, regional level organizations, local level organizations, and so on (e.g., Pollitt, 1984). All of which raises a doubt as to whether the process of securing systems improvements via structural change is a particularly stable or certain one. Detailed studies tend to reveal a complicated pattern of impacts, some of which could be counted as improvements (always depending on

TABLE 5.14. *Privatization would allow a better performance: France* (%)

	Yes	No	Without much effect	No opinion
Health insurance	25	30	27	18
Postal service	27	27	32	14
Education	29	32	24	15
Prisons	20	23	20	37
Hospitals	30	29	24	17

Source: Rouban, 1995, p. 33

one's values) and some of which would probably be regarded by many observers as problematic (e.g., Boston *et al.*, 1996; Halligan and Power, 1992; Pollitt, Birchall and Putman, 1998).

5.5.3 *Cultural change in systems*

The difficulties of evaluating cultural change are as great, if not greater, than those of assessing widescope structural change. While there can be little doubt that organizational cultures can have a significant influence on organizational performance, the tasks of actually *measuring* that influence, and knowing how to go about reshaping cultures in some desired direction, are fraught with pitfalls and problems.

In fact the empirical basis for conclusions about cultural change at the systems level is extremely slender. The number of studies where researchers have been able to measure broad shifts in attitudes and beliefs over time (essential to a full identification of cultural shifts) is small indeed. Most of the limited number of works that do exist measure at a single point in time and then hypothesize what the results imply for cultural change (Rouban, 1995; Talbot, 1994).

Nevertheless, such fragments as we have help to cast some light on the claims that management reform has produced cultural change. A survey of 3,800 UK public service managers, conducted at the end of 1993, indicated that 'managers' willingness to accept and implement change was remarkably high; it was clear that managers' attitudes to change are broadly in line with the actual changes taking place'. Yet at the same time 'over 40% of managers feel inadequately supported for dealing with political influences' and 'Almost a third of all respondents expect to have left the public sector within the next five years' (Talbot, 1994, pp. 5–6). The message here—among managers though not necessarily other categories of staff—seemed to be that a real change in attitudes was underway, but that some aspects of this change were negative. A survey of French civil servants, carried out in 1989, drew an interesting distinction between professional values and broader social values. It then concluded that:

Professional values depend closely on the nature of the job and the strategic position within ministerial circles. They can therefore evolve and can be improved with training. However, the transformation of these values cannot be so great as to modify the global conception that civil servants have of the relationship between public administration and political spheres, or the ranking of social values which determine their professional success. One cannot change civil servants' social values through administrative reform. Such a change requires extra-professional resources . . . (Rouban, 1995, p. 51).

This line of interpretation may help to explain why, in a number of jurisdictions, it has seemed possible to change—for example—civil servants' attitudes towards the 'customer', but much less so other attitudes, such as a distrust of politicians or a scepticism towards the benefits of MTMs within the public service. Rouban went on to argue that the perceived legitimacy of administrative reforms varied up and down the hierarchy, usually being highest with senior civil servants, but only so long as they could continue to control the process of change itself. This finding

of a variable adhesion to reforms, correlated with rank and position, has been repli-
cated in other countries also. A large survey of staff carried out in conjunction with
an Australian 1992 evaluation of the management reforms of the previous decade
found evidence that public servants at different levels exhibited significantly different degrees of belief in the usefulness and impact of the reforms (Task Force on
Management Improvement, 1992).

5.5.4 Trust the system?

One of the hoped-for outcomes of systems change is a reversal of falling levels of
citizen trust in government. This is clearly stated in, for example, the US 1995
budget documents, where one of the headings, referring to the NPR, was
Rebuilding public trust through results and service (Executive Office of the President
of the United States, 1995, p. 158). To put it crudely, do all the many reforms
described elsewhere in this book persuade publics to trust their governments more,
and to believe that public sector organizations are accessible, reliable, efficient and
sympathetic to their varied needs?

Once again, no clear and simple answer can be given. Some of the evidence on
citizens' attitudes to management reforms is reviewed in the following chapter, but
here it may be sufficient to say that there is, as yet, no indication that there is a widespread national or international shift of public opinion in favour of governments that
make public sector reform a central part of their programmes. As an example, we
may examine the findings of a 'European Values Survey', in so far as these concern
public confidence in institutions (see Listhaug and Wiberg, 1995, pp. 304–5).

Table 5.15 shows shifts in public confidence towards specific institutions (vertical axis) between 1981 and 1990—a decade which saw extensive public management reforms in France, the Netherlands, Sweden and the UK, and also, towards

TABLE 5.15. *Confidence in institutions in six West European countries, 1981 and 1990*

	Sweden		Finland	Germany		Netherlands		UK		France	
	1981	1990	1981	1981	1990	1981	1990	1981	1990	1981	1990
Church	39	38	49	44	40	40	32	47	43	54	50
Armed forces	61	49	71	53	40	43	32	82	81	55	56
Education system	62	70	83	43	54	73	65	60	47	57	66
Legal system	73	56	84	67	65	65	63	66	54	57	58
Press	27	33	34	31	34	28	36	29	14	33	38
Trade unions	49	40	56	38	36	39	53	25	26	40	32
Police	80	74	88	70	70	73	73	86	77	64	67
Parliament	47	47	65	52	51	45	54	40	46	56	48
Civil service	46	44	53	33	39	45	46	48	44	53	49
Major companies	42	53	45	34	38	35	49	50	48	49	67
N (unweighted min.)	1,115	949	983	1,292	2,093	1,173	996	1,173	1,436	1,031	902

Source: European Values Survey (1981, 1990) as quoted in Listhaug and Wiberg, 1995, pp. 304–5
Note: No data exist for Finland in 1990.

the end of the decade, in Finland. If one were naive enough to think that confidence in the civil service was determined by the volume of reform, one might expect to see the highest score for the civil service entered against the UK, with rises everywhere except in Germany. Unsurprisingly, the picture is nothing like this. Germany actually shows the largest *rise*, and the majority, including the UK, show a distinct *fall* in confidence in the civil service. It is also clear that different countries *start* from very different positions: in 1981 the civil service commanded the confidence of 53 per cent of respondents in France but only 35 per cent in the Netherlands.

Of course, much depends on exactly what questions are posed. Asking citizens about the civil service is not the same as asking them about their local fire service, or about whether they have noticed any improvement in the refuse collection service (again, we will have more to say about this in the next chapter). If, instead of asking about the civil service, the question is changed to one about the degree of satisfaction with the way democracy works, the responses are as shown in Table 5.16 (this time for three dates, 1980, 1990 and 1994).

This Eurobarometer survey shows some surprising trends. Here Germany, instead of being one of the few countries to show improvement (as in Table 5.15) becomes the only one to record a significant fall in satisfaction. France, by contrast, scores a remarkable increase, while the UK remains fairly steady.

Roughly similar survey questions have been put to the American public. Table 5.17 shows the findings since 1958—a history of considerable fluctuation, with no very strong pattern (the 1966 score looks like an outlier).

TABLE 5.16. *Trust in democracy: EU countries*

Country	Score	X–XI 1980	X–XI 1990	XII 1994
Germany	++/+	West G: 73	West G: 81	West G: 65
			East G: 49	East G: 41
			Total G: 75	Total G: 59
	–/—	West G: 21	West G: 15	West G: 34
			East G: 48	East G: 57
			Total G: 21	Total G: 39
France	++/+	36	42	58
	–/—	50	50	40
Netherlands	++/+	51	67	64
	–/—	45	29	34
UK	++/+	51	52	51
	–/—	43	44	46

++: very satisfied; +: fairly satisfied; –: not very satisfied; —: not at all satisfied
Question: On the whole, are you very satisfied, fairly satisfied, not very satisfied, or not at all satisfied with the way democracy works (in your country)?
Source: Eurobarometer

TABLE 5.17. *Trust in US government index* (all)

Selected years	Trust in government index (all)
1958	49
1966	61
1970	39
1974	29
1978	29
1982	31
1986	47
1990	29
1994	26

Source: The National Election Studies as quoted in Lawrence, 1997, p. 129

Interpretation of broad survey data such as this is extremely difficult. As already indicated, macro-level perceptions are not necessarily reflected at micro-levels (e.g., it is very common for American citizens to have a low opinion of Congress but quite a high opinion of their local Congressman/woman). The more general the question (and the questions in Tables 5.16 and 5.17 are very general indeed) the harder it is to be confident in attributing the 'result' to any specific influence or influences. It is extremely rare to be able to attribute a shift in general views to a specific set of changes in the politico-administrative system (indeed, most citizens have very little knowledge of the existence of administrative reform programmes).

Ultimately, therefore, the main difficulties in assessing systems improvements are twofold. First, there is a need to separate out the substance from the rhetoric, a distinction which is often far from straightforward. Many government documents and speeches, in several countries, have claimed a 'system transformation' of one kind or another, only for closer empirical study to show that there has actually been high continuity between the old and the new (e.g., Ingraham, 1997 on the US NPR; Pollitt, Birchall and Putman, 1998 on the British Conservative government's decentralization reforms of the late 1980s and early 1990s). These commonplace divergences between words and deeds are discussed further in chapters 7 and 8.

Second, there is a possibly even more stubborn difficulty in assessing the claim that a system has acquired greater flexibility, capacity, and so on. How are these claims to be tested? Presumably the counterfactual is the way that the old (previous) system would have tackled the new circumstances and pressures. But that is usually a very difficult criterion to apply: who can say exactly how the old system would have performed? Nor does it help that the most prominent voices saying that the new system is better/worse are frequently insiders with strong and obvious interests in conveying a picture of either progress or decline.

All in all, the category of systems improvement, while appealing in theory, is very hard to pin down in empirical practice. The dangers of hindsight are considerable, and the risks of perceptions being distorted by a few salient incidents or episodes are high. There is also a temptation to see change in an over-coherent way—to presume that all the changes one sees were intentional, rather than forced or accidental, and, further, to assume that they were related to each other within some overall 'systems approach'. These issues of coherence and intentionality are discussed further in the final chapter. It is also misleading to assume that there are singular entities called 'the public service culture', or 'public opinion about reform'. As indicated above, such research as has been carried out conveys a more fragmented and variegated picture. Organizational cultures seem to depend to some significant extent on role and rank, and they shift more quickly along some dimensions than others, with some basic elements of social values which may be beyond the power of reformers to change. Public opinion is also a complex issue, with no easy or straightforward link between the success of reforms and the perceived legitimacy of the politico-administrative system.

The most, perhaps, that one can say is that the politico-administrative system in some countries appears to have undergone deeper change than in others. As is clear from chapters 3 and 4, and from the Appendix, high-change countries (in management terms) would include New Zealand and the UK, and low-change countries would include Germany, with the other countries considered in this book stretched out somewhere in between. Whether the many innovations in the high-change countries are all to be considered as *improvements*, however, is another question altogether. Some commentators, for example, clearly believe that sticking with a strong existing system is better than playing around with flawed and ephemeral fashions in management reform (Derlien, 1998).

5.6 Results as the realization of a vision

Sometimes management reforms are *ad hoc* and functional. Sometimes they are emergency measures, designed to stave off a crisis, real or anticipated. But there are also occasions when management reforms are carried through with the aim of realizing some larger vision of how things should be in some imagined future world. These imagined futures may be framed in very general terms, or in more specific ways, but they serve a useful function as rallying points and guidance for the faithful and as siren calls to the as-yet agnostic. In terms of the trajectories discussed in chapter 4 they are highly normative omegas, which may or may not be accompanied by plans for how to get from here to there.

There was certainly something of this visionary element to Mrs Thatcher's reforms, encapsulated in the phrase from her 1979 election manifesto, 'Rolling back the state'. There was a similarly vivid (and almost certainly more coherent) vision informing the New Zealand reforms of 1984–94 (Boston *et al.*, 1996, pp. 3–6). No one could accuse Vice President Gore of being without a vision for the NPR—many publications elaborate on the theme of reinventing government so that it 'works better and costs less'.

In other countries the vision was perhaps less strongly enunciated, less combative towards the *status quo ante*, but there were nonetheless elements of idealism and futuristic imagery. The Finnish government recommitted itself to a combination of democracy and egalitarianism (*High quality services, good governance and a responsible civic society*, 1998a). The new 1994 'purple coalition' in the Netherlands committed itself to the 'primacy of politics', and the reining-in of unaccountable quangos (Roberts, 1997). In Germany one might say that there was a conscious rejection of 'fashions and fads' in favour of the virtues of the existing system (Derlien, 1998). Indeed, when East and West Germany were unified, the existing western system was proudly rolled out to replace the administrative institutions of the east.

Of course, academics adore ideal models and utopian visions. They (we) take an intense interest at the merest whiff of a new 'paradigm', and tend to react by polishing, systematizing and elaborating the fragmentary visions proclaimed by political leaders, so as to be able to analyse them—and subsequently often to damn or praise them. Politicians, on the other hand, usually have the street-wisdom to cast their references to the desired future in rather more vague, malleable and ambiguous terms. The purposes and skills of the two groups are different. Since we are academics rather than politicians it will come as no surprise when we say that the 'teasing out' of visions can be a useful and illuminating exercise. This is not the place to do justice to all the various schemata which have been offered (though we do develop our own brand in the final chapter) but it may be helpful to pause long enough to look at one example.

Peters (1996b) suggests that four main visions may be identified within the national and international rhetorics of public management reform:

- *The market model*, which holds out the prospect of extensive privatization and therefore of a much smaller public sector—and one that will itself be infused with market-type mechanisms. Citizens become consumers and taxpayers, the machinery of government shrinks to a policy making, lightly regulatory and contract-letting core. This corresponds to the omega of 'minimization/privatization' which we introduced in the concluding section of chapter 4.
- *The participatory state*, which lays great emphasis on the empowerment and participation of citizens in the running of 'their' administration. Like the market model, it envisages radical decentralization and a sharp move away from bureaucratic hierarchies. Unlike the market model it is suspicious of the divisive and inegalitarian features of competitive markets and confident of citizens' ability and willingness to play a more creative part in their own governance. This is, in effect, one version of the 'modernization' omega from chapter 4.
- *Flexible government*, which is opposed to the rigidities and conservatism attributed to permanent organizational structures and individuals with permanent, highly secure careers. The remedy is a 'temporary state', with shifting squadrons of adaptable and re-adaptable organizations, each purpose-built to address the most salient issues in the current, but rapidly-changing environment. Advanced information technology is frequently seen as a major force in this new state of affairs, which can be represented as less 'doctrinaire' or 'ideological' than either the market model or the vision of participatory government (Bellamy and Taylor, 1998; Hudson, 1998). This is one version of the 'marketization' vision of chapter 4, in that the state apparatus becomes more like the

rapidly-shifting world of business, even if organizations remain mainly state-owned and
state-run. The temporary state is likely to be an extensively contract-based phenomenon.

• *Deregulated government.* This vision is built on the assumption that the public service and
its organizations are full of creative ideas, relevant experience and well-motivated
people—if only they can be released from the heavy constraints of bureaucratic regulations. This vision is perhaps the least widespread of the four, being mainly confined to
those—such as public service unions and professional groups—who share its optimism
about the character and motivation of civil servants. It is essentially a version of the
modernized state, but a very different version from the participatory state described
above.

As Peters makes clear, each of these visions has aspects of silence or even incoher-
ence, lying quietly alongside its 'headline' messages. That none of the four has
been implemented in a pure way will come as no surprise, given the constraints on
radical change identified in chapters 2 and 3. Nevertheless, in certain countries the
'flavour' of one dominant model can be tasted in the key speeches and documents
of reform. Thus the New Zealand reforms clearly owed much to micro-economic
thinking that favoured a market model (see Appendix: New Zealand, country file).
The latest Finnish reform documents lean more towards the participatory model:
'earlier administrative reforms have been experienced to have increased the
bureaucracy of administration. The government wants to ensure the democratic
development of the policy of governance' (*High quality services, good governance
and a responsible civic society*, 1998a, p. 8).

To conclude this section, it might be said that, while visions play an important role in shaping the rhetorical dimension of reform, it is hard to use them as
a means of assessing the results of the reform process. For the zealots, the ever-
closer approximation of reality to the vision is the abiding concern, but the
zealots are usually few in number. Even the most powerful spokespersons for a
particular view are obliged to compromise and exercise patience. Mrs Thatcher
left the level of UK public spending only marginally different from that which
she had found in 1979. President Reagan bequeathed a huge public sector deficit
and a federal civil service little altered in size by his eight years at the helm. The
enthusiastic privatizers in the new Dutch government of 1982 and the new
Swedish government of 1991 found that they could not transfer to private
ownership anything like as much of their respective public sectors as they had at
first envisaged. For the reasons developed in chapter 3 (and to be elaborated in
chapter 7) purity of vision must almost always be tempered with an understanding of political, economic and functional constraints and trade-offs. Therefore
even those who are advocates of a particular vision, and who wish to assess
'results' in terms of that vision, must make allowances for the strength of the
forces of tradition, inertia and recalcitrance. Talk, decisions and actions
frequently diverge. Our argument has been that the strength of these forces
depends to a considerable extent on the nature of the politico-administrative
regime in question, and the extent to which the new vision which is proposed
cuts across, or goes along with its grain.

5.7 Conclusions: what do we know and what can we say?

5.7.1 *Different perspectives on results: what you look for is what you see*

This has been a long chapter and the conclusions may be briefly stated. First (Sections 5.1 and 5.2) 'results' may be looked for in different ways, in different places and on different levels. For some commentators the most significant evidence lies in the 'changed climate', the existence of new 'talk' and the promulgation of visions of privatization, marketization, participation, deregulation and flexibility. In short, the crucial evidence is the growth of a new community of discourse, with its main production centres located in the 'Anglo-Saxon' countries and certain international organizations such as PUMA/OECD, the IMF, the Commonwealth Secretariat and the World Bank. For others the focus is the record of decisions—the publication of white papers and national review documents, the enunciation of programmes such as citizens' charters or Public Service 2000, and the passing of laws decreeing administrative reform. Others, however, look for 'hard' evidence in the form of actions and impacts. This is itself a large domain, within which one may look for macro-level effects or local impacts, for concrete outputs or longer-term outcomes, and so on. One's judgements on the achievements of reform is likely to vary considerably according to which of these various types of evidence is given the greatest weight.

Where one looks is, in turn, influenced by where one sits. The three most obvious sitting positions tend to generate rather different 'vibrations' about management reform. The state apparatus itself, and particularly the political heads of department, tend to report steady progress—everything is in hand and remaining issues are being addressed (e.g., Chancellor of the Duchy of Lancaster, 1997; Commonwealth Secretariat, 1993; Gore, 1996). Management consultants tend to focus more on the future, on the potential of new techniques and systems to solve the perceived problems of today. They do issue warnings, but these are usually about the constraints which may inhibit progress rather than about the nature of that progress itself. This may be considered understandable for a group the existence of which depends partly on their being able to sell innovatory concepts and techniques. Significantly, management consultants usually address themselves privately (as it were) to their clients, and only occasionally to the public domain, whereas the other two groups are accustomed to delivering their conclusions to a wider audience. Academics are undoubtedly the least optimistic of the three groups, worrying about what may be lost as well as what is gained, expressing caution about long-term effects and generally hedging achievement claims with qualifications and critique (e.g., Derlien, 1998; Dunleavy and Hood, 1994; Ingraham, 1997; Radin, 1998).

There are also differences *within* each group. The differences within the state apparatus itself are perhaps the most interesting, since this is the group that one might suppose would be most likely to speak with one voice. One obvious divide is between legislatures and executives. Another is between executives and independent audit offices (Pollitt *et al.*, 1999 gives an extended treatment of audit offices' reactions to management reforms). A third is within the executive itself, between central finance departments (on the one hand) and operational departments (on the other). Two brief examples can illustrate these differences of perspective. In 1996 the President of the Canadian Treasury Board made an annual report to the legislature, entitled *Getting government right: improving results measurement and accountability* (Treasury Board of Canada, 1996). The minister claimed that: 'We have already achieved tangible results in this area. For example, modernizing the financial management system, better reporting to Parliament, improving how we use information technologies, and adopting alternative ways of delivering government services' (Foreword). However, when the Auditor General's Office reviewed these documents they made a number of strong criticisms, including:

[T]he President's report does not give an adequate picture of success in measuring effectiveness [. . .] The President's report does not distinguish evaluation from other forms of review [. . .] The President's report presents an overly optimistic picture of progress for an activity which is undergoing major change and dealing with many important challenges [. . .] The Treasury Board should ensure that its report to Parliament credibly represents the performance of review and includes specific measures on evaluation (Auditor General of Canada, 1997, sections 3.80, 3.83, 3.85 and 3.86).

At the same time a Parliamentary Working Group was considering the same documentation. In their own report they also expressed critical views:

One of the perceived shortcomings of these documents, as expressed by MPs, was the lack of objectivity in the reporting. Many respondents suggested that it was inappropriate for departments to be reporting on their own performance—the perceived result of which was 'feel good' documents that said little about the true performance of the department (Duhamel, 1996, p. 14).

To complete the circle, we might add that parliaments themselves—including the Canadian one—have been less than exemplary in making use of performance data, even when they have been supplied to them. There has perhaps been a tendency to succumb to the temptation of grabbing a few headlines by highlighting unusual or extreme statistics, but not to work through or try to understand the broad picture which is presented to them.

As for internal differences of perspective within executives, the European Commission offers many examples of tensions between different Directorates General, some of which involve management issues (e.g., Middlemas, 1995, pp. 247–55). The SEM 2000 and MAP 2000 initiatives, for example, were seen as coming mainly from the 'horizontal' parts of the Commission—DGIX (Personnel), DGXIX (budgets), DGXX (internal control) and the Secretariat General. As such, aspects of the reforms were regarded with suspicion and were slow-pedalled by certain 'operational' ('vertical') DGs, which regarded them as belonging to someone else's agenda, and potentially burdensome.

5.7.2 Data, criteria, attribution

The foregoing sections have been liberally peppered with references to the often-incomplete, or downright inadequate, state of the available data. There is no need to repeat that at length here. What is very clear is that data availability varies sharply according to how one defines 'results'. The records of reform *talk* are voluminous, and the analyst's problems are mainly to do with information overload. The records of reform *decisions* are also very extensive—even a list of the titles of major reform legislation in the ten countries runs to many pages. The situation with reform *actions and achievements* is more complex. The available information on inputs, savings, process improvements and outputs is vast. There can be little doubt that, in many public sector organizations in many countries, the work process has intensified; more measured outputs are being generated per pound spent or per member of staff employed. Not all of this information may be entirely reliable, but it would take a giant dose of cynicism to arrive at the conclusion that nothing had changed and that the productivity of specific organizations had remained static.

Where the information begins to get thin is at the two next stages. First, what have been the costs of the many measured improvements in productivity, in terms of other activities foregone, stress and reduced loyalty or commitment among the public sector workforce, loss (or gain) of trust by the public and so on. In most cases there are few answers here: these hidden costs could be very high or very low, and there could also be hidden benefits, which the bald statistics of productivity fail to capture.

More importantly, however, information about what may be regarded as the final stage—the ultimate outcomes of all the reform talk, decision making and action on society at large—is both sparse and ambiguous. This is partly because most governments do not seem to have looked very hard for this type of information, but partly also because such information is difficult and expensive to collect, and then hard to interpret.

There is therefore something of a paradox at the heart of the international movement in favour of performance-oriented management reform. The reformers insist that public sector organizations must reorient and reorganize themselves in order to focus more vigorously on their results. They must count costs, measure outputs, assess outcomes, and use all this information in a systematic process of feedback and continuous improvement. Yet this philosophy has clearly not been applied to many of the reforms themselves, which thus far have been evaluated relatively seldom, and usually in ways that have some serious methodological limitations (Pollitt, 1995; 1998c).

Finally, it may be observed that information itself means little until it is combined with some *criterion*. An increase of 5 per cent may be good if the criterion for success is an average increase elsewhere of 2 per cent, but poor if the average elsewhere is 8 per cent. Contracting out refuse collection may be deemed a success if the criterion to be applied is cost per bag collected but thought to be a problem if the criterion is promoting equal opportunity of employment. The main point to be made here is that there is often room for debate about which criteria are the most appropriate and, in any case, there seem to be fashions for particular criteria or measures, which come and go. Indeed, there is quite a persuasive theory that suggests that this kind of change over time is necessary, to prevent particular performance indicators getting 'worn out' and becoming the target for excessive gaming and manipulation (Meyer and Gupta, 1994). Even in the market sector, the dominant measures used to judge the performance of commercial firms have shifted several times:

a number of factors, especially the tendency of performance measures to run down or to lose the capacity to discriminate good from bad performance, trigger ongoing creation of new performance measures different from and therefore weakly correlated with existing measures (Meyer and Gupta, 1994, p. 309).

Perhaps this is why a number of studies have found that it is difficult to construct good time series of indicators for public organizations, because they seem to change rather frequently (Pollitt, Birchall and Putman, 1998; Talbot, 1996).

5.7.3 Who needs results?

One mildly controversial conclusion can be drawn from the foregoing. It is that, if 'results' are defined in a narrow way as scientifically tested data describing the final outcomes of changes, then *the international management reform movement has not needed results to fuel its onward march*. This will come as no surprise to analysts who stress the symbolic and rhetorical dimensions of politics and institutional life (Brunsson, 1989; Hood, 1998; March and Olsen, 1995; Meyer and Rowan, 1991; Power, 1997). Nevertheless it does represent what might politely be termed a discontinuity within some of the paradigms used by the proponents of reform themselves—particularly the hard-edged, performance-driven visions of those who would minimize or marketize the state apparatus.

Equally, 'results' of another kind *are* needed to maintain the momentum of reform. A continuing high level of production of talk and decision making is probably essential. Until now, the flow of white papers, charters and 'new initiatives' has been unceasing since the early 1980s. Every country has to have a reform programme of some sort, or at least to be seen to be discussing one (even Chancellor Kohl went into his ill-fated 1998 German election campaign talking about a slimmed-down state). To the knowledge of the authors of this book, there are many international conferences on public management reform every year, and even more national ones (the brochures arrive without the need for any special research!). One may ask whether this procession of talk and decision is now a permanent feature of governance, or whether it is conceivable that the flood tide may begin to ebb? If management reform *did* fall from fashion that would not imply that institutions would cease to change. It would simply mean that reforms were no longer so news-worthy—they would resume the status of technical adjustments, which is what they were mainly seen as during some periods in the past.

5.7.4 *Regimes, trajectories and results*

Finally, we should ask what are the connections between the politico-administrative regimes described in chapter 3, the reform trajectories chosen by different jurisdictions and commented upon in chapter 4 and the picture of 'results' put together above?

In an ideal world the regime types would influence the reform trajectories, and evidence would show that given trajectories led to specified but different mixtures of results. The connecting mechanisms or processes (what works and what doesn't) would also be clear, and the would-be reformer could thus inspect the local regime and then choose a reform trajectory which would generate the mix of benefits and costs which s/he most desired.

Unfortunately neither we nor anyone else can 'fill in' all the spaces in this ideal model. Chapter 4 did show that some broad connections could be established between types of politico-administrative regime and the choice of reform trajectories. Even those links were subject to exceptions and deviations, temporary or otherwise. However, there is a considerable 'disconnect' between trajectories and results. The record does not permit confident and specific statements to be made concerning the different mixtures of results that will be harvested from each main trajectory. On the contrary, there are conflicting claims, with advocates advancing the respective merits of the 'New Zealand model' (Boston *et al.*, 1996), the 'Canadian model' (Bourgon, 1998), German 'disjointed incrementalism' (Derlien, 1998), American 'reinvention' (National Performance Review, 1997a and b) and so on. These arguments are only occasionally backed up by results data, and, when they are, the attribution of effects is usually disputable.

On the other hand, it would be wholly mistaken to draw the conclusion that public management reform was a meaningless charade, played only by the cynical or the stupid. On the contrary, it is absolutely clear that many of the changes made have carried definite 'payoffs' for particular groups and individuals, even if longer-term outcomes remain comparatively obscure. It is also the case that some very broad consequences can be predicted on the basis of the different 'visions' or 'omegas' which reformers seem to have in mind. To explore these issues further requires, first, a disaggregation of the 'players', and in particular a further examination of the role of management reform at the interface between politics and management. This will be undertaken in the next chapter. It also requires the development of a closer analysis of some of the trade-offs and paradoxes which have come to light in chapters 4 and 5. They will be the subject of chapter 7. Finally, in chapter 8, it will be possible to return to the overarching question of the likely connections between different reform strategies and their consequences for relations between politicians, public servants and the rest of society.

6

Politics and Management

'on the one hand we see policy-makers using administrative reform to displace accountability for public policy; on the other hand we see the very same policy-makers trying to increase their control over bureaucracy. Whilst this appears to be two inconsistent developments, they may in fact reflect a general desire among elected politicians to increase their influence over bureaucracy while at the same time avoiding responsibility for the bureaucracy's actions.'

(Pierre, 1995, p. 3)

6.1 Forwards to the past?

At this point we shift gear. In chapters 2, 3, 4 and 5 we have been engaged in building a model of management reform, classifying key contextual features which differentiate one country's regime from another, identifying alternative trajectories for change and examining the evidence as to the results of this change. Each of these chapters has therefore been intended to help build up a general picture of what has been happening in the world of public management reform. In the remainder of the book, however, we stand back from this picture in order to reflect upon and interpret some of its broader features. We shift mood from construction towards deconstruction, from creating an accurate and convincing depiction towards exploring its contradictions and acknowledging its limitations. This exercise will carry us from the excitements of the ostensibly new ('reinventing', 're-engineering', 'revitalising', 'modernization') and take us back to some of the abiding, recurrent problems of governance in liberal democratic regimes.

From the outset we have argued that public management cannot be adequately comprehended without reference to the crucial relationships which exist between administration and politics, and between administrators and politicians. In this we are at one with the many authors who have made an identical or similar point (e.g., Flynn and Strehl, 1996; Götz, 1997, p. 753; Peters, 1996a, p. 20; Pierre, 1995, pp. 205–7).

While there is wide agreement that this frontier is an important one, there appear to be sharply varying opinions as to what is taking place along the borderlines. Some have seen 'management' (in the sense of modernized public administration plus privatization) invading politics and taking over slices of political territory (e.g., Clarke and Newman, 1997; Pollitt, 1993, chapter 1; Stewart, 1994). Others, in apparent contrast, suggest that management reform has been a vehicle by which executive politicians have gained a tighter grip of their officials (Halligan, 1997; Pierre, 1995). One recent comparativist goes so far as to assert that 'as far as most countries are concerned, the possible dominance of the civil service by political regimes seems to be of greater concern than the possible dominance of the political regime by the civil service' (Hojnacki, 1996, p. 144). Less speculatively, a large poll of public service managers in the UK found that: 'the largest single negative response in the whole survey was concerned with managers' ability to "resist political interference in operational management decisions" ' (Talbot, 1996, p. 38).

At this point it may be useful to examine more closely the concept of a 'frontier' between management and politics. It should immediately be emphasized that this frontier is related to, but by no means necessarily identical with, the boundary between civil servants and politicians. In terms of most contemporary definitions, 'politics' is not limited to certain persons (elected politicians) or to specialized arenas in which an action takes place (Parliament, ministerial offices, 'smoke-filled rooms', etc.). More commonly politics is defined by the *processes* involved. In particular political activity is that which involves the exercise of power, especially the mobilization of various kinds of resources in order to achieve a chosen set of ends in a situation where the interests of the various parties concerned potentially or actually conflict (Leftwich, 1984). Thus, even 'neutral' public servants in Westminster-type systems, though they may remain 'neutral' and scrupulously avoid 'party politics', nevertheless frequently engage in 'political' processes, in the sense that they bargain and negotiate and deploy resources of money, information and presentational skills in order to improve the chances of success for policies and programmes with which they are associated. For example, a senior civil servant charged with implementing his or her minister's policy of privatizing a public utility, will negotiate with the various parties involved and attempt, on the minister's behalf to make the policy work. Similarly, the chief executive of a hospital may negotiate with the local trade unions over redundancies or terms and conditions and the head of a government regional office will bargain with other powerful local figures (local government officers, local business leaders and so on) to try to promote regional development. In these senses, then, many public servants are involved in 'politics'. To the popular definition of politics as the process which determines 'who gets what, when and how' we would therefore add the thought that, albeit within legal frameworks and (possibly) under explicit guidance from elected politicians, the person making such determinations will often be an appointed official.

From such a perspective some interesting interpretive possibilities open up. The apparently contrasting views referred to above (between those who believe that the domain of management is increasing and those who argue that political scrutiny is increasing) become more understandable and—to a degree, if not entirely—mutually reconcilable. For example, it could be simultaneously true that politicians are intervening more in public administration *and* that the sphere of public management has begun to encompass more and more issues which used to be mainly the preserve of politicians. Equally, the quotation from Jon Pierre which heads this chapter could be understood as identifying a strategy by executive politicians to shift issues into the management domain precisely so as to be able to 'disown' them when things go badly and then intervene and claim credit when things go well.

These are, then, crucial, boundary issues for public management, and they deserve more detailed consideration here. We will focus on three key questions:

a) Has public management reform shifted the borderline between politics and administration, and, if so, in what way?
b) What are the main implications of the new trajectories and models of public management for elected politicians (in both executive and legislative roles)?
c) What is the relationship between public management reform and public attitudes towards politicians and civil servants?

Our answers to all three of these questions—perhaps particularly to the third—are tentative. The available evidence is patchy. One of the features of the rhetoric surrounding a good deal of management reform has been that it has drawn attention *away* from these overtly political issues—the emphasis has tended to be placed on saving money or improving the public services received by citizens rather than on the effects of all this upon basic political and constitutional relationships. The implication has seemed to be that management can be a professional and technical exercise, relatively free of 'politics'. Typical of this dominant emphasis was Vice President Gore's characterization of the US National Performance Review exercise as one aiming at a government which 'works better and costs less'. Typical also was Mrs Thatcher's bold assertion that moving 70 per cent of the civil service out of conventional departments and into a new type of executive agency had no constitutional significance:

The government does not envisage that setting up executive agencies within departments will result in changes to existing constitutional relationships (Prime Minister, 1988, p. 9).

However, after two decades of intensive change across many countries, we are far from alone in suggesting that the 'three Es' and improved 'customer service' are only one dimension of the picture: the relations between politics and administration have changed too, and these aspects have only recently begun to receive the systematic attention they deserve.

Having addressed the three questions listed above, the chapter concludes with some synthesizing comments on the extent to which 'politics' may represent a structural limit to the effectiveness and reach of management reform.

6.2 Has public management reform shifted the borderline between politics and administration?

There have, in any case, been significant changes in the nature of politics in many OECD countries, quite apart from the impacts of management reforms. Specifically, there has been an erosion of the perceived legitimacy of government and an increase in the volatility (decrease in the party loyalty) of most electorates. More sectors of politics—including management reform—have developed through international rather than purely national networks (Halligan, 1996a;

McGrew, 1997). Finally, economic pressures have meant that in most OECD coun-tries the era where ministers made their reputations by introducing big new programmes has long passed. We have moved into an era of largely 'technical poli-tics' rather than the welfare state construction of 1945–75. Executive politicians are now usually engaged in streamlining, repackaging, marginally modifying or actually downsizing ('decrementing') existing programmes, rather than any heroic new efforts (Appendix). Publics tend to be vigilant against reductions in popular and basic welfare state services (health care, education, pensions) yet more scepti-cal and more demanding (in terms of service standards) than in the past *and*, at the same time, more resistant to tax increases. Furthermore, in most countries the mass media have become more aggressive and sceptical, no longer accepting the 'official line' or deferring to the minister's authority or access to expertise. To put it bluntly, it is even more difficult being a minister than it used to be, partly because the kinds of things a minister gets to do in the 1990s are inherently less popular than those that were being done during the boom years of the 1950s and 1960s, and partly because the public audience out there are more sceptical, less deferential and less trusting. One should add that it is also more difficult being a 'mandarin'. Rouban (1997, p. 148) is referring specifically to developments in France, but his words apply to most of our other countries as well:

The time is over when civil servants, representing an all-mighty State, could steer most actors of the social life and could impose their choice without too much difficulty. Moreover, the classic political game has been changed. Controversies are no longer built along the lines of ideological frontiers but involve technical arguments that often cross the political parties boundaries.

Within this context, management reform ministers have been caught in the dilemma captured by the Pierre quotation at the beginning of this chapter: on the one hand they have sought greater control over the bureaucracy and its programmes but on the other they have seen advantages in decentralizing respon-sibility and trying to sit 'above' the dangerous cauldron of day-to-day operational failures and achievements. Generally speaking, it might be said that 1980s-style NPM on the Anglo-Australasian model contains contradictory ideas (or, at least, ideas which exist in some tension with each other). NPM doctrine holds that decentralization is good, and letting/making managers manage is good, but also that political control and accountability need to be strengthened *and* that consumer power should be strengthened. This conundrum—which will be explored in more detail in the next chapter—looks rather like an 'eternal triangle'. The grass in the other two corners is always greener. Nor have continental European states—which, as we have seen, have not embraced NPM to anything like the same extent—been able to avoid problems. In France:

Many civil servants have perceived modernisation as a means to put them in charge of polit-ical choice that had not been decided upstream, as a tricky game whose winners are always the politicians who can get rid of embarrassing responsibilities in a time of budget cuts and, simultaneously, of high defensive corporatism (Rouban, 1997, p. 155).

Decentralizing devices such as frame budgeting (Sweden, Finland) or delegation to provincial or regional tiers of government (Canada, USA) have clearly been
used partly in order to transfer the political pain of sharp prioritizations and downsizings from the national to subnational levels of government (from one set of
elected politicians to another—although within each jurisdictional level there may
also be some passing on of 'hot potatoes' to officials). However, at least in these
cases the arguments have taken place *within* the political sphere, between different
strata of elected representatives.

The precise ways in which these tensions play themselves out are therefore
shaped by the type of regime in which they occur (see chapter 3). In the 'Anglo-
Saxon' regimes (Australasia, UK, USA) where politics and government in general
tend to be held in lower esteem, it has been less difficult for politicians to retreat
from responsibility for the management of public services (indeed, easier for them
to pursue outright privatization). Thus many developments have seemed to signal
a shift of the borderline in favour of management, so that its empire (both private
and public) has grown while the empire of politics appears to have shrunk. This
has been done in the name of efficiency and consumer responsiveness. Yet executive politicians have also been cunning. They have, in effect, reasserted the distinction between politics and administration (though now calling the latter
'management'), making managers responsible for achieving targets, but at the same
time they have frequently retained powers of intervention so that, if things go
badly wrong in the public eye, then the politicians can appear to ride to the rescue
with inquiries, inspection teams, restructurings and all the other paraphernalia of
crisis management. This generalization would apply, for example, to UK executive
agencies, Grant-Maintained Schools and NHS trust hospitals (see, e.g., Rhodes,
1997, pp. 44–5).

Beneath the surface, the process of letting—or making—public sector
managers manage has not been so simple. There have been countervailing currents
and considerable centralization, partly through the establishment of evermore
sophisticated performance indicator and target regimes, underpinned by rapidly
advancing information technologies. As we have seen, executive politicians have
transferred their focus for control from inputs to outputs, via processes. This may
account for the somewhat ambiguous responses from public service managers
themselves—they have experienced greater freedom to deploy their inputs (e.g.,
switching money from staff to equipment, or vice versa) but at the same time they
have felt themselves under closer scrutiny than ever before as far as their results are
concerned. Even where an activity has been fully privatized—as with the UK
public utilities such as gas, water, electricity and telecommunications—politicians
have gradually been obliged to give more attention to arrangements for the public
regulation of the resultant private corporations (Foster, 1992).

What is clear is that, in the UK, but also in other Westminster-influenced
systems, the additional pressures which NPM reforms have put on traditional
concepts of public accountability have not been met with any clear and coherent
new doctrine to cope with the new circumstances. The problems are increasingly

widely recognized, but most politicians have shrunk from the task of articulating a 'new model' (Barberis, 1998; Stone, 1995).

In the more consensualist and decentralized regimes (Nordics, Netherlands) the 'anti-government' theme has not been so strong. Instead the rhetoric has stressed modernization, with the political elites largely holding to their usual role of directing a substantial state apparatus, and the mandarins continuing to play a strategic role with relatively little challenge to their status and competence. Considerable decentralization has taken place (Sweden, Finland) but this has been political decentralization (to subnational elected authorities) rather than predominantly managerial decentralization on the New Zealand/UK model. In the Netherlands the trajectory was slightly different, with a significant growth in appointed quangos (ZBOs) during the 1980s. However, this trend soon attracted political criticism (including some accusations that the ZBOs were being used to create well-paid jobs for sympathizers of the ruling Christian Democrat party) and in 1994 an incoming left-right 'purple coalition' made restoring 'the primacy of politics' one of its leading slogans (Roberts, in Ministry of Finance, 1997). Departmental agencies with more sharply defined accountability became the preferred vehicle for decentralization of central government tasks, rather than ZBOs.

In sum, neither in the Nordic states nor in the Netherlands has the borderline between management and politics moved much, one way or the other. On the other hand, these regimes have shared in the shift to systems of output rather than input controls, even if this move has not been as vigorously reinforced by personnel reforms (performance appraisals, annual results targets for individual public servants) as in the most pro-NPM countries.

In Germany and France the politics/administration frontier has not shifted very much either. Neither has significantly dismantled central civil service controls; neither has created flocks of powerful new quangos to take over functions formerly under direct political oversight (Germany already possessed a large and significant set of para-statal, corporatist organizations with responsibilties for carrying out public functions). France has implemented a significant privatization programme, but cautiously, and nowhere near as sweepingly as the UK or NZ. Germany was already extensively decentralized and France has carried through a major decentralization programme since 1982 but, as in the case of the Nordics, these have been primarily acts of political decentralization (to local and regional *elected* bodies) not pure managerial decentralization. In short, political and civil service elites (which, significantly, in both countries are intermingled rather than separate) have retained their grip, and the politically led state, even if leaking legitimacy, is still seen as a major, socially-integrating force to be reckoned with. There have been significant attempts to begin to shift large, rule-following bureaucracies towards a more performance-oriented approach, but this has been both patchy and a largely internal matter. It has not been accompanied (as in Australia/NZ/UK/USA) by general rhetoric about how 'political influences' have to be removed/minimized and professional management/business-like approaches substituted. On the contrary, while this book was being written a prominent German scholar expressed himself thus:

Not only would it be undesirable to once again in German history have senior civil servants conceal their functionally politicized role, it is also hardly imaginable how to turn them into a-political managers. Possibly, the formal neutrality of civil servants in the UK and the absence of the safety valve of temporary retirement could be reasons for the easy adoption [in the UK] of a managerialist role understanding (Derlien, 1998, pp. 23–4).

Nor have the German or French publics been copiously supplied with 'league tables' of 'results' as has been the fashion in the UK and, to a lesser extent, the USA and New Zealand. The Anglo-American-Canadian rhetoric of citizen 'empowerment' has been far more muted in *Rechtsstaat* regimes, where the dominant legal perspective and the distinctiveness of the state sphere make such concepts more difficult to conceive or fill with any sensible meaning. Citizen justice and citizen rights, *Conseil d'Etat* style is very different from consumer choice in the style of John Major's *Citizen's charter*.

6.3 What are the main implications of the new trajectories and models of public management for elected politicians?

We will deal with the executive roles—that is, ministers—first. According to the NPM model, the new role held out for ministers is as strategists and opinion-leaders. They will clarify and communicate visions and values, choose appropriate strategies and identify, allocate and commit resources at the macro-level. The managing/operations will then be done by professional managers, whose performance will subsequently be appraised against clear objectives and targets.

There seems little evidence that this is a credible vision of any likely reality. Most senior politicians, in most countries, have not been trained for such a role, and the pressures on them are not likely to encourage them to adopt it. They may learn the rhetoric—particularly if it enables them to shed responsibility for policy failures (the Prison Service and Child Support Agency cases in the UK)—but not much more. Politically, the incentives are still short term: to make popular announcements of new initiatives, to intervene dramatically when things appear to be going wrong, to follow popular opinion rather than try to educate it, to take up single issues (mirroring the media) rather than to develop integrated strategies, and so on. And there is evidence that this is exactly what happens (Talbot, 1996 for the UK; Zifcak, 1994, chapter 5, for Australia; Radin, 1998 for the USA). 'While the intellectual exercise involved in defining goals and measures of success has its own rigor, it does not fit comfortably into the fragmented decisionmaking process in both the White House and the Congress' (Radin, 1998, p. 313).

In consensualist political systems the attraction of the new NPM vision of ministers as strategists seems even less than in the majoritarian systems of Australia, Canada, New Zealand and the UK. In the Nordic states and the Netherlands ministers are not far-sighted strategists—their political success and survival depends upon their skills and creativity in putting together coalitions of support to steer through particular programmes. This is even more true for EU institutions. In these environments clear statements of strategies and priorities may actually prove counter-productive: the ability to be all things to all (wo)men is much more useful. Nothing in the NPM can change this political dynamic.

Again, as far as the substantive content of management reform is concerned, nothing has happened to alter the diagnosis made by many previous writers on public sector organizational reform, namely that such reforms have little interest for most ministers, as they are not 'vote-catchers' and because they yield results only over long periods of time, if at all. *Announcing* reforms may be mildly rewarding (e.g., Gore, Thatcher, Lange, Howard) but following them through and checking to see if they worked are not high-priority tasks for most politicians. Of course, when organizational boundaries are changed, politicians take an interest, either to protect their 'patch' or to try to gain 'territory', but this is hardly the perspective of the strategic figure implied in much of the NPM literature. At a supranational level one may cast one's mind back over the poor record of the Council of Ministers in respect of the attempts to reform EU institutions so as to make them more performance-oriented. The 'bottom line' has usually proven to be a national interest in holding on to a particular share of senior positions, or even a reluctance to aid the emergence of a more efficient and effective (and therefore potentially more powerful) Commission.

The analysis in the previous paragraph is even more true for the second group of politicians—those in the legislatures. Their careers are hardly ever shaped by organizational reforms, their constituents are seldom interested in them or knowledgeable about them, and there is little incentive to get involved in such matters, except in the most superficial ways, or as constituency advocates in particular cases when things go wrong ('crippled widow denied disability benefit', etc.). Legislatures have been very slow to make constructive use of the increase in performance information available to them (Carter, Klein and Day, 1992, pp. 182–3). Most MPs simply don't have the time or inclination to get involved in the details of management. Describing the US Congress' reaction to the National Performance Review Kettl (1994, p. 49) vividly crystallized the problem:

Congress, by practice and the Constitution, attacks problems by passing laws. The NPR seeks to solve problems by improving performance. Congress as an institution works on the input side. The NPR focusses on the output side. Congress has little incentive to worry about results and, in fact, has long indulged itself in a separation-of-powers fantasy that absolves it from any complicity in the executive branch's performance problems.

In the late 1990s this judgement was reinforced by Congress' treatment of the first set of reports that came out of the Government Performance and Results Act (GPRA). The more quotable aspects of their contents were treated to a brief burst of publicity, but there was little sign of any appetite or plan on Congress' behalf to make more sober or systematic use of these much-heralded performance reports.

On the other hand there is some evidence that management reforms have—at least marginally—reduced the access of some legislatures to certain types of information. For example, Finnish MPs can no longer debate the roads programme in great and local detail (as they used to) because it now comes within a block budget transfer from central government to the municipalities. UK MPs are no longer supposed to go to ministers with detailed questions about operational matters in civil service executive agencies (as they could when these activities were still part of ministerial departments). Now they are supposed to channel their queries to agency chief executives.

6.4 What is the relationship between public management reform and public attitudes towards politicians and civil servants?

On the face of it the question 'what do the citizens think about public management reform?' may seem both fundamental and straightforward. Surely, in a liberal democracy, this is the ultimate test of any government action or programme? Such assumptions are further supported by both political rhetoric around the issue of rebuilding citizens' trust in government and by academic discourse concerning the apparent loss of legitimacy by governments throughout the western (and Australasian) world. The academic fascination with this began a long time ago, and has embraced academics of very different theoretical persuasions (see, e.g., Habermas, 1976; Nevitte, 1996; Nye *et al.*, 1997). Some write of a loss of legitimacy, others of a decline in deference, others still of a loss of trust. There are interesting differences between these concepts (legitimacy/deference/trust) but from the point of view of management reform they all point towards a more critical and possibly recalcitrant audience for attempts to remodel at least those public sector organizations which deal directly with the citizenry.

Unfortunately, the question itself is packed with doubtful assumptions. For example, do most citizens know anything about the many reforms which have been proclaimed and implemented by OECD governments? They are seldom the stuff of TV news or newspaper headlines. Even if they may have encountered some references to reforms, are most citizens sufficiently interested to pay any attention? If we take one of the most extensively (and expensively) promoted reforms, the UK *Citizen's charter*, one survey indicated that 71 per cent of citizens had heard of it (ICM, 1993), but other research indicated that very few people possessed any accurate knowledge of what was in it (Beale and Pollitt, 1994). This ignorance of actual mechanisms and substance survived despite a government campaign that had mailed a glossy leaflet to every household in the land. One imagines that more technical reforms—such as the 'reinvention labs' in the US NPR, or results-oriented budgeting in Finland and Sweden—would remain completely unknown to the vast majority of the populations of the countries in question.

Lack of knowledge may not be the most serious barrier. Equally distorting can be the possession of *false* information or serious conceptual misconceptions. Take, for example, the average American's view of the efficiency of federal programmes. Surveys show that most Americans believe that more than 50 per cent of the expenditure in social security programmes goes in overheads. The true figure is less than 2 per cent (Bok, 1997, p. 56). Surveys in the UK in the 1960s were said simultaneously to reveal majorities against 'nationalization' but in favour of 'public ownership'.

However, let us set the (major) problems of citizen ignorance and indifference on one side for a moment, and concentrate on those issues where citizens do, it seems, hold definite opinions. After all, surveys in a number of countries have been carried out with questions such as 'How do you rate the overall performance of government?' or 'Do you have no confidence/some confidence/a great deal of confidence in politicians/civil servants/bank managers/doctors?' and there has been no difficulty in obtaining responses and adding them up to percentage 'answers'. It is on the basis of time series of surveys of this genre that political scientists have identified a problem of declining legitimacy and trust in many liberal democracies (for summaries, see Nye *et al.*, 1997; the Pew Research Centre, 1998). These are certainly interesting data, but the problems of interpretation are considerable. For example, two important questions are what are respondents thinking of when they declare their opinions on the overall performance of government? What they read in the newspaper last week? A recent TV appearance by the Prime Minister? The government's decision not to increase the state pension by the full rate of inflation? The poor service the respondent received in the post office that morning? Furthermore there is the question of the rationale behind the opinion. *Why* does the respondent think that state pension decisions/macro-economic policy/counter service at the post office is good or bad? What expectations did s/he bring to the question, and how were those expectations formed? Unfortunately, only a few surveys can offer any help with these sorts of questions—we may know *what* the average citizen thinks, but seldom *why* they think it (the 1993 ICM survey on the UK *Citizen's charter* being a case in point).

Nevertheless, some provocative, if inconclusive findings emerge from survey data. First, opinions as to overall governmental performance, or levels of trust, do not necessarily correlate closely with opinions on much more concrete and specific issues (e.g., how adequate is the postal service?). It seems quite possible for citizens to maintain a generalized cynicism or mistrust of 'government' whilst simultaneously being reasonably satisfied with many of the specific public services they actually make use of (Canadian Centre for Management Development, 1998a and b). The level of this generalized dissatisfaction with government is 'strongly connected to how people feel about the overall state of the nation' (Pew Research Centre, 1998, p. 1).

It also seems that the belief that private sector services are generally much better regarded than public services is questionable. In Canada at least:

many public sector services such as police, trash collection, weather services and fire services are rated more highly by the public than many private sector services such as banks, cable companies, and automobile dealers . . . In general they rate public and private sector services within much the same ranges (Canadian Centre for Management Development, 1998b, p. 5).

In the UK too, the 1993 ICM survey found that the public's perceptions of improvements in services by no means put private sector services consistently above those provided by the public sector—for example, NHS doctors and state postal services were placed somewhat above building societies and far above banks (ICM, 1993, p. 16).

Certainly, there is no firm ground for the assertion that the public would like the welfare state to be 'rolled back' and replaced by private modes of provision. For example, a 1993 attitudinal survey of New Zealanders showed:

strong endorsement for the notion of a universalist rather than a residualist welfare state, including support for more taxes (although not necessarily a willingness to pay more tax personally), as well as an underlying conviction that politicians are out of touch and unworthy of the government's trust (Vowles *et al.*, 1995, p. 97).

Even in the USA, supposedly the stronghold of anti-government, pro-private sector sentiments, it has been shown that: 'Fully 72% of Americans believe that government should see to it that no one is without food, shelter or clothing . . . as many as felt that way in the 1960s' (Pew Research Centre, 1998, p. 7). In the UK, before, during and after the apex of Thatcherism, polls frequently showed a majority of voters favouring more public money being spent on the public health care and educational services, and, in some cases, even a majority declaring itself willing to pay more taxes if they could be assured that the revenue thus raised would go to those causes.

Second, respondents are frequently able to distinguish between different groups of actors in the process of governance. Most commonly they extend a tolerable degree of trust towards civil servants, but a considerably lower (and falling) degree towards political leaders. For example:

surveys suggest that the public's frustration is directed more at politicians who lead government than at civil servants who administer it. By a margin of 67% to 16% the public has more trust in federal workers than in their elected officials to do the right thing. In that vein 69% now say that they have a favorable opinion of government workers—an improvement from the 55% that held that view in a 1981 *Los Angeles Times* national opinion survey (Pew Research Centre, 1998, p. 2).

Thus, if President Reagan was right in saying that the federal government was part of the problem rather than part of the solution, it was the politicians rather than the bureaucrats he should have been aiming to reform! Furthermore—for the USA at least—it is not so much failures in the *efficiency* of elected politicians that provokes public distrust, as the perception that such leaders are failing to uphold high moral standards (Pew Research Centre, 1998). This is extremely interesting material, as it carries the implication that public management reform is unlikely to contribute much to the enhancement of governmental legitimacy for two solid reasons. First, the public *do* distinguish between political leaders and civil servants, and the bulk of their distrust is directed at the former. Second, the deepest roots of discontent with the political leadership do not grow out of perceptions of their incapacity to manage affairs but rather from their (perceived) untrustworthiness or low moral standards.

Third, citizen responses can be highly context-specific, and need to be interpreted in the light of that. For example:

it appears that fire services are always rated highly by citizens while municipal planning services are rated much lower. This may reflect the nature of the services: one is an essential service; while the other is a regulatory function that may impact on some citizens negatively, in order to ensure fairness in protecting other citizens, such as in zoning regulations. *Thus a rating of 7.0 would be a poor score for a fire service, but an excellent score for a planning service* (Canadian Centre for Management Development, 1998b, p. 6, italics as in the original).

Fourth, a decline in deference may mean that more citizens are willing— actively or passively—to resist and criticize public authorities, making life more difficult for the latter. What it does not necessarily mean, however, is that those citizens want to play a much bigger part in the process of reaching decisions or running public programmes. The evidence here is mixed: many members of the public may want 'more say' but that is a far cry from full-blooded and time-consuming participation. Offering more places on citizens' panels or in focus groups may well appeal to some, but it would be an unwarranted leap of logic to presume that lots more 'participation' was the principal answer to problems of recalcitrance and low trust.

Thus, ideally, analysis of citizen opinion needs to be topic specific (some services are inherently more popular than others) and person specific (politicians are distrusted more than civil servants). One also needs to know something about the citizens' own experiences (are responses coming from those who have little knowledge and no experience to be counted as equally valid as those from other citizens who are regular, indeed, 'expert' users of the particular service in question?). The question of 'trust in government' turns out to be as complex as government itself, and it is by no means clear what significance or meaning should be attached to large sample surveys which come up with the answer that 61 per cent of the population think this or that about some very generalized question about trust or efficiency.

Indeed, the concept of legitimacy itself is far from simple (Held, 1987). To say that one accepts the current government, or the current system of public administration, as legitimate is a statement which may conceal a range of states of knowledge and a variety of attitudes. As already noted, respondents to questionnaires (or, indeed, voters) may be very knowledgeable or profoundly ignorant about the topics which they are being asked to assess. Equally, with respect to attitudes, these may range from reluctant acquiescence ('I suppose there isn't any alternative') through lukewarm acceptance to enthusiastic approbation ('American democracy/the British National Health Service/the French system of *grands corps* is the best in the world').

In sum, we may conclude that the public's attitude to management reform in particular, and to public administration in general, is both complex and as yet only lightly researched. Most of the evidence we have found comes from the Anglo-Saxon countries, and it would be extremely useful to be able to compare that with equally sophisticated surveys carried out in the Nordic countries or in Germany or France. Most of the public probably know little about most specific reforms. Most of them are also capable of simultaneously maintaining a spectrum of attitudes towards the state apparatus, distinguishing between different groups of actors, different services and questions of greater generality or specificity. Some of their attitudes may be deeply founded and hard to shift (for example, the widespread apparent support, in many countries, for the continuance of the basic fabric of the welfare state) while other opinions may be quite volatile, easily altered by new information or experiences. Thus sweeping assertions that the public have lost confidence in public services, or that they 'want' less bureaucracy, or that they are demanding higher quality, frequently turn out to be fragile—and therefore inadequate as platforms upon which to erect specific programmes of reform.

6.5 Politics and management: an overview

The relationship between politics, public management and public opinion is a contentious area, and one in which systematic data are at best patchy. Having made these caveats we will attempt to draw out a few broad propositions from the evidence advanced above.

First, public management reforms *have* altered the relationships between elected and appointed officials, in a number of countries and a number of ways. In this sense, at least, they are not 'neutral'. Second, there is an absence of evidence concerning the willingness or ability of executive politicians to become the 'strategic managers' of their portfolios. The kindest thing that could be said about reform models which cast politicians in such roles would be that they are unproven and seem to fly in the face of known incentives to behave in a more traditional 'political' fashion. Third, managers do appear to have gained extra authority in a number of ways but at the same time political control has been vigorously reasserted in many of the ten countries. There is no *necessary* contradiction between these two developments—the public sector is large and diverse enough for both to be happening at the same time. In specific cases, however, there may be a quite definite tension. Fourth, any suggestion that public management can be radically depoliticized (in the sense of 'political' outlined above) is either a misunderstanding or flies in the face of evidence from many countries. The allocation of, say, health care resources or decisions about educational standards or major public infrastructure projects are all inherently 'political' decisions, whether they are taken by powerful politicians or tough public managers (or, indeed, medical doctors or teachers). The public will often see the political authority as ultimately responsible—or, at least, sharing responsibility—however much ministers may protest that these are technical or professional decisions which have been taken by the appropriate officials. Fifth, there is a certain ambiguity in much of the rhetoric around strengthening accountability and increasing transparency, in so far as some executive politicians have used the new politics/administration split to redefine programmatic weaknesses as managerial failures. This enables political leaders to shuffle off direct responsibilities for things going wrong. Furthermore, it appears that legislatures have been slow to take up and use the increased flow of performance data which greater transparency and the contemporary emphasis on outputs and outcomes afford. With chapter 5 in mind, one might say that even when a 'real result' manages to climb over the conceptual, methodological and political barriers, and escape into the wider public world, it is often left wandering around looking for an audience. Sixth, few of the specific reforms appear to have been undertaken in direct response to 'public opinion'—although somesuch rationale has quite often been claimed. Privatization, the introduction of market mechanisms, downsizing and the promotion of performance indicator systems are the products of elite, not popular agendas (even if public opinion has subsequently accepted some of these innovations and begun to make use of them). The sector of greatest tension would appear to be the welfare state, the basic elements of which remain enduringly popular in most countries but the expense of which inevitably draws it into the line of fire of the cost-cutters and downsizers (see Appendix A). Seventh, any simple picture of public opinion as being 'for' or 'against' 'big government' is misleading. Such evidence as is available shows that, however limited the public's knowledge may be of the specifics of reform, popular attitudes towards government are multi-faceted and, in some respects, quite sophisticated.

One further conclusion that might be drawn is that there is a strong need for a more realistic model of the role politicians can and should play in the running of the state apparatus. Neither the representative democracy/public interest model of the Anglo-Saxon countries nor the continental *Rechtsstaat* model seems sufficient to cope with the new forms and practices which have emerged. It is not so much that these traditional models are wrong, more that they are, by themselves, inadequate to present-day circumstances. More controversially, one might suggest that any rethinking of these matters ought to focus at least as much on the induction and training of politicians, and on the framework of incentives and penalties surrounding them, as on reforming the public service or yet again reshuffling its organizations. Why is it usually assumed that it is the civil servants who are in need of reform but not ministers or the other politicians who may hope to become ministers in due course? This is *not* to advocate some modern version of Platonic guardians and neither, certainly, is it a plea for MPs to be forced to take MBAs. However, it *is* to suggest that the preparation of politicians for high office has, in many countries, been a 'no-go' area for reformers for too long. If it is in fact the *politicians themselves* who are most widely and deeply distrusted, then perhaps there are sound democratic reasons for bringing their readiness for the tasks they are confronted with to the fore as an item on the agenda for public debate?

[T]he time has come for elected officials to recall the biblical injunction: 'heal thyself'. It is crucial that they look to their own institutions. Every government is being affected by the information revolution and the global economy. Yet, parliament and cabinet still function much as they did twenty years ago (Bourgault and Savoie, 1998, p. 16).

7

Trade-Offs, Balances, Limits, Dilemmas and Paradoxes

'[T]he major paradoxes, with their unpalatable medium term and long term implications, appear to be general and permanent in character and seem to be rooted in misunderstanding, in the policy contradictions which characterise the reforms and in the naivete of the reformers themselves'.

(Wright, 1997, p. 12)

7.1 Reform optimism/memory loss

A prominent, but frequently unremarked feature of the public sector reforms of the last twenty years has been a large optimism about the *potential of management itself* (Pollitt, 1993, pp. 1–5). Few boundaries seem to be envisaged for the exercise of this set of dynamic and purportedly generic skills. At the beginning of the most intensive period of reform a British cabinet minister expressed himself thus: 'Efficient management is the key to the [national] revival . . . and the management ethos must run right through our national life—private and public companies, civil service, nationalized industries, local government, the National Health Service' (Heseltine, 1980). Such optimism stands in contrast to an older tradition of speaking and writing about the running of public sector organizations, one that sees these activities as subject to a number of widespread, 'built-in' and possibly inevitable limitations and trades-off. In traditional, permanent bureaucracies, cautionary wisdom about such administrative constraints was built up, case-by-case and over time, and used by seasoned career officials to warn politicians of the likely limitations of their proposed innovations (which, in administrative form, were seldom as novel as the politicians may have supposed). Since the 1970s, however, in the most radically reforming countries this kind of cautious mandarin has gone out of cultural fashion in favour of the 'can-do' chief executive. Furthermore, in these same countries, a combination of downsizing, the spread of term contracts for senior officials and higher rates of turnover of various categories of staff has operated to shorten institutional memories, so that fewer and fewer in the organization are likely to know of the precedents of ten or twenty years ago, or to wish to bring these inconveniences to the attention of their political masters. As one senior Canadian public servant put it recently: 'some of the grey matter of the public service has disappeared' (seminar discussion, November 1998).

The grip of the 'lessons of history' has been further weakened by the popularity of the notion that, catalysed by rapid economic and technological change, the business of management is constantly confronting *new* challenges, and therefore, by implication at least, rapidly leaving *old* concerns far behind. The best selling texts with titles such as *Thriving on chaos: a handbook for a management revolution* (Peters, 1987) or *Re-engineering the corporation* (Hammer and Champy, 1995) have encouraged the belief that the past is irrelevant. Consider the following advice from the founding fathers of re-engineering:

Re-engineering is about beginning again with a clean sheet of paper. It is about rejecting the conventional wisdom and received assumptions of the past. Re-engineering is about inventing new approaches to process structures that bear little or no resemblance to those of previous eras (Hammer and Champy, 1995, p. 49).

It might be objected that the cited sources are concerned with the private sector. In fact the management 'gurus' in question insist that their insights apply to *all* organizations (see, e.g., Hammer and Champy, 1995, pp. 218–19) and their work has certainly been taken up and noticed by governments in a number of countries. Furthermore there is a parallel stream of rhetoric specifically focused on government. Probably the most read and talked-about English language text on government reform of the last decade is replete with declarations such as the following:

. . . the bureaucratic model developed in very different conditions from those we experience today . . . Today all that has been swept away. We live in an era of breathtaking change . . . Today's environment demands institutions that are extremely flexible and adaptable . . . It demands institutions that *empower* citizens rather than simply *serving* them (Osborne and Gaebler, 1992, *Reinventing government*, p. 15).

Without wishing to deny the evident truth of changing conditions for government, we do wish to register a profound scepticism concerning what one might term the 'history is dead, everything is new' school of management thought. On the contrary, as governments have geared up to tackle the problems of the late twentieth century, the record (as we read it) shows many examples of old constraints and trades-off reappearing in new clothes. One might even observe that individuals who undergo extreme memory loss are usually referred to as suffering from dementia, and that at least some of the more frenetic reform pronouncements share that same, sad quality of a loss of touch with everyday, here-and-now reality.

In this chapter, therefore, we wish to take seriously the concept of there being intrinsic constraints and limits to administrative reform. This is hardly revolutionary. It has been espoused, in different ways, by a number of the most distinguished academic writers on public administration and management. For example, Charles Perrow envisaged bureaucratic processes as being inherently beset with dilemmas, in which to organize in one way was inevitably to pay a serious price in another (Perrow, 1972). Aaron Wildavsky and John Pressman argued that the implementation of public policies was a deeply chancy business in which the realization of the policymakers' vision depended upon the weakest link in what was usually a very long chain of intervening decisions and inter-organizational linkages (Pressman and Wildavsky, 1973). Christopher Hood developed an extended typology of 'limits' to administration, in which administrative dilemmas and non-linearities commonly conspired to distort the process of implementation in the direction of inefficiency, corruption or even counter-intentional effects (Hood, 1976). Hood and Jackson have also drawn attention to the way in which administrative 'principles' often come in matching pairs, with advantages and disadvantages trading off as one moves from one polar principle to its opposite (Hood and Jackson, 1991). More recently the same author has articulated an even more elaborate scheme of constraints, using grid/group cultural theory in an attempt to demonstrate that each administrative philosophy carries not only intrinsic limitations but, beyond that, the seeds of its own decay (Hood, 1998). In a more 'applied', specific work John Halligan, commenting on the deep and wide-ranging reforms carried through in Australia and New Zealand, observed that, even in these two cases: 'While management practice and discourse have been transformed, the perennial questions of public administration remain' (Halligan, 1997, p. 43).

Whilst we do not follow any of these authors exactly, we do believe that their shared perception that the administration of public programmes commonly exhibits deep-seated and recurring types of dilemma and contradiction is accurate, and deserves to be reiterated. The substitution in Anglophone environments of the magical word 'management' for the unfashionable 'administration' does little to change the types of limits with which these analysts were concerned (though it may lead to an increase in the proportion of certain types of problem in relation to other types). Obtaining reliable information about tax evasion behaviours or co-ordinating a variety of agencies which are all delivering services to the unemployed are activities which pose fundamentally similar organizational problems whether the public officials concerned deem themselves to be rule-following bureaucrats or performance-chasing managers. Neither do the wonders of information technology dissolve the need to balance, choose and recognize limits. Vastly improved capacities for data processing and rapid communication certainly make possible styles of governance, co-ordination and (not least) supervision which were difficult or unachievable previously. However, computers cannot resolve logical contradictions, bruised motivations, ergonomic constraints or problems of competing and divergent values (Hudson, 1998). They may, however, help decision makers to muster a clearer or more detailed picture of the options before them—whether this clarity is welcome or not.

In this chapter, as earlier in the book, a distinction is drawn between the more 'gung ho' reform rhetorics in some countries and the more cautious discourses of others. We concentrate mainly on the claims of the more radical reformers (or, at least, the more ambitious rhetoricians). It is hard to find an exact characterization of this group—sometimes they may be thought of as the 'NPM' countries and sometimes as the 'Anglo-Saxon' countries, but neither of these is an entirely satisfactory collective title. More specifically we mean Australia, New Zealand, the UK and the USA. Canada has sometimes also been a member of this 'community of discourse', and Finland, Sweden and the Netherlands have occasionally borrowed from the rhetoric, though only selectively and cautiously from the practice.

Germany has not been a member of the club (certainly not at the level of the federal government) and France has kept its distance, while articulating a rather distinctive reform rhetoric of its own. The EU Commission only began to dabble, rather unconvincingly, in the NPM brand of reform rhetoric in the mid-1990s. Our critique therefore concentrates on the 'radical reformers' (and would be radical reformers) with only occasional remarks about the others. A charitable preliminary interpretation might be that these other countries have been more sensible to balances, limits and the persistence of traditional problems from the outset. A less optimistic interpretation would be that they have yet to face up to some of the awkward choices involved in thoroughgoing modernization of their public sectors. Regrettably, we have neither the space nor the data to pursue these enquiries concerning 'the others' here.

7.2 The vocabulary of balance and contradiction

Thus far in this chapter we have referred to 'constraints', 'limits' 'trades-off' and 'problems'. In an attempt to be slightly more precise we will henceforth distinguish between:

Trade-offs: where having more of one desideratum, or lessening one problem, inevitably diminishes some other wished-for quality or increases a different problem. This is therefore a situation where decision makers are obliged to *balance* between different things which they want, but cannot feasibly have more of all at the same time—indeed, where to have more of one entails having less of another. An example that Hood (1976) gives is that of appointing long-serving local officials is likely to increase local knowledge and continuity but simultaneously to increase the number of instances where the local officials 'go native' or succumb to the temptations of corruption. On the other hand one can send in mobile officials whose allegiances are to the centre and who know they will soon be posted on elsewhere. Choosing this second route reduces corruption and the dangers of the official developing excessive sympathy for the percieved difficulties faced by the administered local population, but it also reduces the local knowledge available to the administering organization, and thereby increase the chances that the local population are managing to evade or pervert the intended system of controls.

Limits: we will use the dictionary definition of a limit as 'a point, degree or amount beyond which something does not or may not pass' (Harrap's *Chambers Encyclopedic English Dictionary*, 1994, p. 741).

Dilemmas: situations in which the manager is faced with a choice of two or more unsatisfactory alternatives, that is, in which the available decisions about a given problem cannot be made in such a way as to *solve* the problem, but only to substitute one set of undesirable features for another. A dilemma is thus the limiting case of a trade-off, in that it is a trade-off in which the situation remains negative whichever option is chosen. Sometimes rooting out public service corruption and/or incompetence may take on the characteristics of a dilemma. To publicize the problem lowers the standing of that part of the public service, undermines public trust and may even encourage increased citizen recalcitrance ('why should I pay my taxes if they are putting them in their own pockets?'). On the other hand, not to publicize the problem may allow it to continue and can prevent the formation of a sufficient coalition of support to ensure that real action is taken.

Another concept to which we will resort is the *paradox*. Paradoxes are *seeming* contradictions: statements which appear self-contradictory and false, and yet may contain a particular kind of truth. The dictionary example is often 'More haste, less speed'. Some commentators have found a whole string of paradoxes entwined in the rhetoric and practice of contemporary administrative reform (Wright, 1997). Some of these are pitched at the level of whole countries or systems, others at the level of specific institutions or practices. Wright begins his account with a striking example of a macro-paradox:

The first major policy paradox is that the most radical reform programmes appear to have been introduced in countries with the most efficient administrations, in other words, in those countries with the least need! (Wright, 1997, pp. 9–10).

Earlier chapters in this book have contained some possible reasons for this curious state of affairs. Perhaps (chapter 3) it has been the countries which are constitutionally and politically most *able* to make big changes to their administrative arrangements that have done so. Yet these are also probably the countries *which had already made significant modernizations of their public sector organizations in the past* (for the same reason). Thus the gap between radical reformers and those who are 'stuck' or can only change very slowly and incrementally may go on growing, at least until the stress is such that some kind of major fracture takes place in the legal and political systems of the slowly-changing states. Perhaps it should be underlined once more that these are propositions about the *volume* of change, and do not presuppose that change will be in the same direction or assume the same forms in every country.

Our own account will mainly address more specific propositions within the portfolio of current reform ideas. One might argue, for example, that the statements which have been made in a number of countries to the effect that public management reforms will make public servants more accountable to political leaders *and simultaneously more accountable to the citizens who use public services*, though appealing, are paradoxical. How can public officials serve two masters, masters who are quite unlikely to have identical needs or preferences? Further examples occur when policymakers say that they intend to empower middle managers in the public service whilst at the same time radically downsizing the numbers of that group who will continue in public employment. *Perhaps* these apparent dissonances can be harmoniously reconciled, but it is not immediately obvious how.

It must be allowed that sometimes what sounds to be an incompatibility *is* an incompatibility, which cannot be reconciled. In such cases we may speak of straightforward *contradictions*. Guy B. Peters is one comparativist who has suggested that, while the contemporary nostrums of public management reform appear to contain a number of contradictions, some at least of these can be resolved into a question of finding an appropriate *balance* rather than a question of choosing between wholly incompatible alternatives (Peters, 1998a). In effect he is saying that some contradictions are really trade-offs rather than absolute contradictions. Thus one may think of a contradiction as a case of a very steep-sided trade-off—that is, as a situation in which having more of one benefit immediately and sharply reduces another benefit. This is a notion we explore in more detail below.

7.3 Public management reform: some candidate contradictions

Many writers have noticed apparent contradictions or tensions within the body of contemporary management prescriptions, and each has offered a slightly different set (e.g., Hood, 1991, 1998; Peters, 1998a; Savoie, 1994; Wright, 1997). We will draw on these to compile our own shortlist of 'candidate contradictions'—sets of prescriptions which at first sight appear incompatible, or at least unstable, and which therefore merit further discussion and investigation.

Our focus is on the substance rather than the process of management reform—on the types of reform to be put in place rather than on how the implementation of the change is managed. This is an important restriction, and we would be the first to acknowledge that there may be significant contradictions and paradoxes in process as well as substance (indeed, the arguments provided by some commentators concentrate as much if not more on implementation strategies as on actual types of reform—e.g., Peters, 1998a). Obviously, implementation is important. A fundamentally sound reform can be 'messed up' through poor implementation and the worst effects of an unsound reform can be obscured, delayed or otherwise diluted by shrewd management. However, this is not principally a book on 'how to do it', and the 'comparative advantage' of an academic account probably lies with an analysis of the substantive content of reform rather than in attempting to second-guess the craft-skills of the implementors. At any event, it is with the limits, contradictions and paradoxes of *substantive* reforms that the remainder of this chapter will be concerned.

Our selection includes some (seemingly) incompatible paired statements and some more complicated/less obvious combinations. Each will be explained in the sections that follow. We will begin with four 'candidate contradictions' at the level of the whole system of public administration in a country, and then move on to a further six which are pitched more at the level of specific operations, giving ten in all. The shortlist is set out below:

1. Increase political control of the bureaucracy/free managers to manage/empower service consumers.
2. Promote flexibility and innovation/increase citizen trust and therefore governmental legitimacy.
3. Give priority to making savings/give priority to improving the performance of the public sector.
4. 'Responsibilize' government/reduce the range of tasks that government is involved with.

5. Motivate staff and promote cultural change/weaken tenure and downsize.
6. Reduce burden of internal scrutiny and associated paperwork/sharpen managerial accountability.
7. Create more single-purpose agencies/improve horizontal co-ordination ('joined-up government'; 'horizontality').
8. Decentralize management authority/improve programme co-ordination.
9. Increase effectiveness/sharpen managerial accountability.
10. Improve quality/cut costs.

7.4 Increase political control of the bureaucracy/free managers to manage/empower service consumers

Each of these three admonitions features regularly in the rhetoric of public management reform. There is no doubt that reform leaders such as (among others) Thatcher, Reagan and Mulroney wished to reassert (as they saw it) political control over the bureaucratic machine (Savoie, 1994). So did, for example, the French political leadership (Rouban, 1997) and at least some elements among Swedish politicians (Pierre, 1995) and the Australian Labor governments of the 1980s (Halligan, 1997). Equally, there is no doubt that increasing the freedom managers have to manage has been a recurrent theme in countless texts and speeches. For example, a key line in the report which led to the UK's creation of 130 plus executive agencies, employing more than two thirds of the non-industrial civil service, was: 'At present the freedom of an individual manager to manage effectively and responsibly in the civil service is extremely circumscribed' (Efficiency Unit, 1988, p. 5).

Finally, the empowerment of customers is a theme which has been repeatedly on the lips of politicians bent on reform, especially in the Anglo-Saxon countries. One US National Performance Review document puts it like this: 'Once President Clinton signed the Government Performance and Results Act in August 1993, strategic planning and listening to the "voice of the customer" was no longer just a good idea—it was the law' (National Performance Review, 1997b, p. 6).

The problem with these superficially attractive formulations can be encompassed in the question 'How is it possible to give managers greater freedom and yet at the same time place them more under the control of ministers *and* oblige them to be more responsive to newly-empowered consumers?' Is it conceivable that all three corners of this triangle can be strengthened simultaneously (minister power, manager power, consumer power), or is this simply a contradiction? As Hood (1998, p. 208) puts it: 'Since not everyone can be "empowered" at the same time, who exactly is to be empowered against whom, and how, is a key test of cultural bias in visions of modernization'.

If it is assumed that the appropriate concept of power and authority in this case is zero-sum (i.e., power is a fixed quantum, so that a gain here must be balanced by a loss somewhere else) then this particular NPM 'recipe' is a double contradiction. However, it is possible, on the basis of a different assumption, to interpret these guidelines in a more sympathetic, or paradoxical light. Such a defence might run along the following lines:

1. Managers can have greater freedom over the marshalling of their resources (combining inputs and processes in different and perhaps innovative ways) while at the same time ministers are offered a clearer picture of what is achieved—the outputs and outcomes of all the newly-unencumbered management activity. So both politicians and managers can increase their control—though of somewhat different things. The clearest expression of this philosophy has been the New Zealand system in which ministers are deemed responsible for objectives and outcomes, and they then contract with the heads of departments (chief executives) for packages of measured outputs that are calculated to produce the desired outcomes (Boston *et al.*, 1996; Halligan, 1997).

2. Similarly, empowered consumers may have access to better information about the performance of a service, and may enjoy improved means of complaint/more efficient redress if things are not to their liking, and may participate in planning and prioritizing the service through a variety of mechanisms (these empowerments manifesting themselves in the shape of charters, better complaints systems, user panels, etc.—though whether the majority of citizens actually want to spend more time doing these things is an open question, as we saw in the previous chapter). At the same time managers can gain new freedoms to arrange their resources in ways that are calculated to maximize consumer satisfaction. There is no contradiction between these two separate but complementary spheres of autonomy.

3. Thus, all three groups—politicians, public service managers and public service users—*can* gain greater control, each in their own corner. Power is not zero-sum but rather variable: everyone can be a winner.

Is this a convincing defence against the charge of contradiction? Perhaps, but only if certain fairly demanding conditions are met. Three deserve particular mention. First, politicians must refrain from interfering in the management sphere (the allocation, manipulation and combination of different kinds of resource, the motivation of staff, the establishment and maintenance of suitable organizational structures, systems and processes) and confine themselves to scrutinizing 'results' and taking action if the results are short of target. Second, the priorities and targets handed down by the political leaders must be both clear and reasonably congruent with the demands and expectations of consumers (otherwise managers will be being asked to dance simultaneously to two discordant tunes). Third, where there are different organizations and levels involved in service delivery (as there very frequently will be), all must work within the same, shared set of objectives, targets, and—to some extent at least—procedures. Otherwise there is the likelihood that managers will receive conflicting messages from above and consumers will encounter different priorities, standards and attitudes in different parts of the 'shop'. If one or more of these conditions is transgressed the likelihood of the triangle being squared (so to speak) will be swiftly reduced.

The question of how often the above conditions actually *are* met (and how often they are not) is an empirical one, and the rate may vary with regime type, organizational culture, political ideology and so on. What is clear is that there have been many occasions in many countries when the vision of mutual, three-cornered empowerment has been announced but not achieved. Some have been recounted earlier in this book. Particularly in welfare state services such as health care, education, personal social services and social security the figure of the empowered service user has in practice been hard to find (e.g., Clarke and Newman, 1997, chapter 6; Evers *et al.*, 1997; Flösser and Otto, 1998; Harrison and Pollitt, 1994, pp. 125–34). 'Shop front' public service staff may have had customer service training and been enjoined to deal more flexibly with individual service users, but meanwhile managers seem often to have extended their domain without conceding any substantial space for 'consumer power'.

Nor is the evidence on the second side of the triangle especially encouraging. As we saw in the previous chapter, politicians have not been spectacularly willing to relinquish their former habits of detailed intervention. In some surveys managers have recorded more political 'interference', not less (Talbot, 1994). Nor have ministers necessarily been prepared to spell out their values in a sufficiently precise manner to give managers a clear set of priorities to work to (and therefore, by derivation, a clear set of targets to aim at).

As for the achievement of co-ordination between different levels and types of organization (the third condition), there can be no doubt that 'partnership' and 'networking' have become extremely fashionable in most of our ten countries, and with the EU Commission (e.g., Chancellor of the Exchequer, 1998). Being in fashion and being well understood are, however, not at all the same thing. A rapidly burgeoning literature demonstrates that most governments are still on the steep part of the learning curve as far as these pluriform approaches to service delivery are concerned (e.g., Kickert *et al.*, 1997; Lowndes and Skelcher, 1998; Peters, 1998b). The available 'technologies' for ensuring 'seamless' service are therefore still experimental and uncertain, so it would be reasonable to conclude that the third condition cannot be satisfied regularly and with certainty.

To sum up: first, the reformers' claims to empower consumers, free managers and strengthen political control are not always and not necessarily contradictory. Unfortunately, however, the conditions for their simultaneous achievement are difficult to cultivate, so that, in practice, these three aims often do collide or, perhaps less dramatically, one or more of them is simply sidelined or forgotten. In a perfect world the three objectives might be compatible. In the real world public managers usually find themselves facing trade-offs or even downright contradictions.

7.5 Promote flexibility and innovation/promote citizen trust and increase legitimacy

The possible contradiction between these two appealing propositions is not necessarily obvious. The tension arises in those situations where continuity, trust and predictability are likely to be the qualities most sought after by the majority of service users. In such circumstances the excitements of constant change and innovation become counter-productive. Confusion and mistrust may grow. Take, for example, the issue of local post offices, which have been a focus for debate in a number of our countries, including Finland and the UK. Many small, (often rural) post offices are uneconomic to maintain. Therefore efficiency-promoting innovations are proposed (remote electronic means of conducting the same transactions; in Finland the relocation of the postal services in local shops rather than separate premises). However, the public reacts against these 'improvements'. At least one section of the public values the cultural and social aspects of the local post office—they want stability and continuity. In Finland it seems that some persons trust a post office with their personal business but do not wish to reveal details of the same to their local shopkeeper (an interesting example of the public servant being perceived as more trustworthy than the business person).

Part of the problem with innovation is that it frequently requires users as well as service providers to learn new tricks. This tends to be far more difficult for some sections of society than for others, and innovations thus, unintentionally, acquire inegalitarian aspects. One could see this in the post office example mentioned above: citizens in rural areas lose their post offices and may have to learn to use remote systems, citizens in big cities get to keep them. An even clearer example occurred in the 1990s in a London Borough which embarked upon a policy of installing automated electronic information kiosks for the public. The hope was that this innovation would extend service (through 24-hour availability) and enable the authority to economize on staff. Unfortunately, as subsequent research showed, matters were not so straightforward. Most of those who used the kiosks were male and under forty years of age—women and older residents seem to have suffered greater anxiety about using keyboard and screen. Furthermore, considerable difficulties were encountered in having all the (voluminous) information translated into all the ethnic languages represented in a very mixed-ethnicity area. Also, it emerged that some ethnic groups had a cultural norm that located trust in transactions only in face-to-face contacts with officials (needing to see a face). For all these reasons (and more) the actual effect of the automated kiosks tended to discriminate against the elderly, women and certain ethnic groups (at least at first—the experiment continues, and solutions to some of these problems may be found—at a cost).

A case which affects many millions of citizens in a number of countries is that of pensions. Governments have, in several instances, come to realize that their previous planning of pensions has been inadequate, and that they are unlikely to be able to afford all the demands that will fall on them in the future. Legislation is therefore introduced to change national pension systems—sometimes restricting eligibility, sometimes changing terms, sometimes incentivizing citizens to take up occupational or personal pension schemes rather than rely on the state pension. Many innovations in pension provision are attempted, some with very good intentions, some to save money. The outcomes are mixed. One outcome has been that stability and predictability has been lost in an area where stability and predictability over long time periods are of the essence. Citizens have lost trust in the ability of the state to provide for their old age—there has been considerable anxiety, and some commercial pension companies have taken advantage of the confusion to advertise their wares (Marmor *et al.*, 1990). In some cases commercial schemes have been perfectly satisfactory. In other cases there have been well-publicized examples of schemes being very poor value for money, or of schemes being sold to citizens who did not really need them, thus adding to public disquiet.

Our overall analysis would be that *there is no fundamental or universal contradiction* between innovation on the one hand and stability and continuity on the other. Indeed, there are occasions when innovation is required in order to maintain continuity—such as when back-of-office automation allows the same service to be delivered to a larger number of users without unacceptable increases in cost. This having been said, however, there are also specific contexts in which public managers do face at least a trade-off between innovation and one or more of the values of stability, continuity, predictability, trust and (as we saw in some of the above examples) egalitarianism. Such contexts confront public service managers with difficult problems of balancing divergent desiderata, and possibly disadvantaging certain sections of the community, even if an improved service is supplied to other sections of a community. Given the pervasive cost pressures and the prominence given to innovation within the reform ideology (Gore, 1997, chapters 3 and 5) it is likely that trade-off problems of this kind occur quite often. It is not our impression that the literature on management reform—either academic or professional—fully reflects this.

7.6 Make public expenditure savings/improve public sector performance

As has been glaringly apparent throughout our analysis, tighter control of public expenditure has figured as one of the most frequent and most powerful motives for public management reform—in every country we have surveyed. If translated into reduced tax burdens, this may be popular (though in practice the overall tax burden on individuals may have increased, as it did, for example under the UK Conservative administrations of 1979–97). If translated into cuts in popular welfare state services such as pensions, health care or education, however, then 'savings' tend to be unpopular, as was noted in chapter 6. Since these 'social protections' commonly take up the major share of the state budget it is usually impossible to make large-scale savings without touching them (see Appendix A for details). Thus there appears, prima facie, to be a contradiction between the commitment to holding down public spending and the commitment to improve public services.

As a first step in exploring this tension, we may note that it reflects a background discontinuity in the stream of ideas which have been taken up and used by the reformers. As explained in chapter 2, politicians and mandarins drew on various different bodies of thought to guide their actions. One important source, especially in the Anglo-Saxon countries, was micro-economics. Indeed, one commentator goes so far as to label the entire wave of contemporary public management reform 'Ricardian' (Lane, 1997). A quite different—but equally influential—source was the work of management and organization theorists, including 'gurus' such as Peter Drucker, Tom Peters, Robert Waterman and

Edward Deming. The two currents of thought have different emphases. Micro-economics is focused on the achievement of allocative and technical efficiency. Management thinking is also concerned with efficiency, but pursues a broader agenda including adaptation to new environments, cultural change and the impor-tance of measuring, meeting and (some would say) manipulating customer expect-ations.

It is not that there is a direct contradiction between the two sets of ideas (though they do tend to use fundamentally different models of individuals) but rather that there is the difference of emphasis indicated above. One might say that micro-economic thinking would tend to prioritize efficiency and savings while manage-ment thinking would focus more on improving performance in a broad sense, embracing higher quality, more flexible and 'customer-friendly' service. Management theorists also seem to embrace a slightly more optimistic, or at any rate varied, model of individual motivation, in that they allow for factors such as loyalty and cultural change, whereas micro-economists are stuck with their elegant but thin utility maximizers.

A second point is to note that it is possible to sidestep the apparent contradic-tion—at least on the level of rhetoric. In the field of social security in the UK, for example, much effort has been concentrated on improving the *process* of claim-ing—training counter staff to be more friendly, smartening up premises, speeding up processing activities and so on. Not unreasonably, this is often referred to as 'quality improvement'. Meanwhile, however, the actual benefit levels have been tightly controlled, and, in the cases of a number of benefits, eligibility categories have been narrowed. Thus is the paradox resolved—expenditure (substance) is reined in but 'quality' (process) is improved.

A third step is to see that the apparent contradiction actually has a paradox folded within it. This 'nested' paradox is that the contradiction is more likely to hold in those jurisdictions *which are most efficient and effective in service delivery*. This is because the ability to make savings and at the same time improve service seems to be closely connected with the amount of spare capacity in the system (Murray, 1998) and the most efficient jurisdictions are those which are carrying the least spare capacity. In jurisdictions which are already super-efficient there is no 'fat' left to cut, and enforced economies are bound to carve into the bone of real services.

A fourth step is to acknowledge that technological advance will sometimes be able to 'solve' the apparent contradiction. A technological leap forward may enable managers of a public service simultaneously to save money and to push up quality and productivity. There is an empirical question as to how often such technologi-cal breakthroughs occur, and there is a further empirical question about how well new technologies are implemented (Hudson, 1998; Margetts, 1998). Nevertheless, technological progress will sometimes be able to resolve the contradiction, which is no doubt one reason why it is such a universal favourite as an ingredient of the rhetoric of public management reform.

We are left, then, with a context-dependent comment on the apparent contra-diction between improved performance and expenditure savings. In contexts where a system is already fairly efficient, and where there is no technological break-through to hand, the contradiction may be real. In less efficient systems, the contradiction can be circumnavigated by drawing upon spare capacity. In systems where technological change is rapid, the contradiction may be solved by techno-logical innovation, assuming it is competently implemented.

7.7 'Responsibilize' government/privatize

These two strands in the rhetoric of reform seem to sit uneasily together. How can governments become more responsible and responsive to public wishes if at the same time they are relinquishing control of huge public enterprises—that is, apparently reducing their ability to steer the economy and ensure the delivery of specific services and utilities? The UK Conservative governments of 1979 to 1997 'returned' roughly half the public sector—and approximately 650,000 employ-ees—to private ownership. The nationalized industries shrank from 9 per cent to less than 5 per cent of GDP. In New Zealand privatizations were, proportionately, even larger (Halligan, 1997, p. 23). In other countries privatization has been a smaller component of reform, but significant sales of public assets have occurred in countries as diverse as Australia, Finland, France and the Netherlands (see Appendix A).

There is also the argument that privatization makes the state appear more and more parasitic. It no longer has a hand in producing anything that can be sold at a profit. It becomes just a taxing and redistributing authority. At the same time it loses direct touch with the world of industrial or commercial service production, and has to seek information about that world from the outside, without the benefit of any direct experience itself (in the language of economics, there is increasing information asymmetry).

Of course, *if* privatization was what the public wanted, then it would be a straightforward matter to claim that 'responsive' and 'responsible' governments should vigorously pursue such a policy. In some cases privatization seems to have been popular (the UK case of British Telecom is the one usually quoted). In others, however, individual privatization measures have clearly run directly *against* public opinion—as with the privatization of water and of British Railways in the UK. Yet initial unpopularity need not be conclusive in itself. Governments can (and do) argue that responsible privatization, accompanied by the creation of a strong regulatory regime, can safeguard the public interest in the activities concerned, while simultaneously releasing the economic benefits that flow from the efficiency-inducing pressures of the commercial marketplace.

There is also a 'your government knows better' argument to support privatiza-tion. In the UK, at least, ministers and mandarins knew how often nationalized industries had been informally 'interfered with' by ministers (e.g., to postpone needed price rises until after the next election). Privatization could be conceived of as a kind of political self-denying ordinance: 'we politicians know we are not to be trusted as managers of industrial corporations and large service operations and therefore the best thing is for us to shift them to a format where we *cannot* mess around with them'. This is 'responsible', in the same sense as an alchoholic who keeps no alchohol in the house is behaving responsibly.

Our conclusion is therefore that there is no fundamental, logical contradiction between the claim to be developing more responsive and responsible government and a vigorous programme of privatizing public assets. There is, however, a series of practical challenges which can, in specific cases, generate tension or divergence between the public interest and privatization. Governments can sell the assets too cheaply (Waugh, 1998), or can fail to put in place effective regulatory machinery, or can simply insist, for doctrinaire reasons, on privatizing activities which a majority of the public strongly wish to retain in public ownership. In these types of case the principle of privatization is not at fault, but rather the way in which it is executed.

7.8 Motivate staff and promote cultural change/weaken tenure and downsize

A whole chapter of the NPR booklet *Businesslike government* is given over to 'Creative license: unleashing the creative power of government employees' (Gore, 1997, p. 25). In many countries—particularly those where the civil service was most harshly criticized during the 1980s—the mid-1990s have seen attempts to 're-vision' and 're-motivate' public servants. 'The Public Service of Canada requires a transformation in its people, its culture and its leadership' and 'The Public Service of Canada needs champions and leaders' (Bourgon, 1998, pp. 21, 23). 'We must restore faith in the public service ethos, and convey the message that we can only deliver better government if we harness and use the talents of the civil service and other public servants' (Clark—the minister with civil service resonsibilities in the new Blair government in the UK—1997, p. 3). And so on. The contradiction here is with the threat to public service jobs, security and pay posed by expenditure cutbacks and management reforms. To tell public servants that they are highly valued at the same time that many of them are being 'let go' may strike at least part of the audience as ironic, or worse. Even the most sympathetic official statements often contain a sting in the tail: 'Absolute job security is not something that any employee . . . can expect in the competitive modern world. But we do want to look at ways of reducing insecurity, so as to minimize distractions from policy goals' (Clark, 1997, p. 20).

Can this apparent contradiction be resolved? We find it hard to see how it could be. Indeed, there have been obvious instances where the contradiction has been seen only too clearly by the staff concerned (e.g., in New Zealand—Boston *et al.*, 1996, pp. 211–24; in the USA with respect to the NPR's downsizing targets—Kettl, 1994, pp. 13–21; or during the public service strikes in France in the mid 1990s). Phrases such as 'expecting the turkeys to vote for Christmas' (UK) and 'from rowing to steering to abandoning ship' (USA) came our way from public servants as we researched this topic.

That said, the contradiction may be lived with—even blunted somewhat. Certain factors promise to assist in this. To begin with, there is the brutal fact that the public servants who matter most will be the ones who survive downsizing. It is possible to envisage a smaller, less bureaucratic, more highly skilled, perhaps even better-remunerated public service within which morale could be restored and a new performance-oriented culture solidly entrenched. Those who lose their jobs frequently also lose their voices—they are now 'outsiders', at best an embarrassment to the survivors. Note, however, that this vision depends on the perception that a new phase of relative stability has been attained. Continuing, repeated downsizings (like those which have taken place in Europe and the USA in industries such as coalmining or shipbuilding) destroy any basis for confidence and commitment. They replace the proposition of 'pain today, jam tomorrow' with the unattractive 'pain today, more tomorrow'. They also destroy institutional memory, reduce the chances of survival for any 'public service ethic' and lead to a 'hollowed out' and ultimately less competent form of government. Here the basic contradiction is left naked for all to see, and the consequences in terms of morale and trust must be expected swiftly to follow.

7.9 Reduce burden of internal scrutiny and associated paperwork/sharpen managerial accountability

The evidence seems to indicate that this particular tension is more a question of balance than of outright contradiction—although in practice it is easy for the balance to be lost. The tension between the two arises because to sharpen managerial accountability so often involves operational managers having to make new returns to the top of the organization, to provide data for new performance indicators systems, quality improvement schemes or performance audit scrutinies. Although what is being asked of operational managers is (in principle at least) a different *kind* of information—output and outcome oriented rather than input data—it can still become an onerous burden, perhaps even exceeding in volume and complexity what was required under the *status quo ante*.

Radin (1998) shows how easy it is for a series of individually well-intentioned reform measures to produce a heavy weight of requirements upon public managers. In the USA the Paperwork Reduction Act of 1995 was aimed at eliminating unnecessary paperwork and reducing the burden on form-filling for citizens and firms. Introducing the bill, President Clinton spoke of the need to 'conquer the mountain of paperwork'. This in itself appeared an unexceptional objective, although, as Radin points out, it also placed limits on the collection of the kind of performance data that would be required to fulfill the aspirations of the 1993 Government Performance and Results Act. Meanwhile, however, federal managers groaned under a series of new measures, including:

- The Federal Managers' Financial Integrity Act, 1982—which required annual assurance of the adequacy of controls.
- The Chief Financial Officers' Act, 1990—which required annual accountability reports.

- The Government Management Reform Act, 1994—which required annual financial statements to the Office of Management and Budget.
- The Information Technology Management Reform Act, 1996—which also requires annual reports, this time showing how information technology is being used to help programmes achieve their objectives.
- The Federal Financial Management Improvement Act, 1996—which requires reports on financial systems compliance by agency heads, inspectors general and the head of OMB.
- REGO 111 of the National Performance Review, 1996—which requires annual reports from agencies on how they are responding to the principles of the NPR.

The above is by no means a complete listing of all the *new* information demands, let alone the on-going ones.

This is not just a tale of some particularly American exuberance or excess. Parallels can be found in a number of other countries where reform has been given a high profile. After documenting an 'audit explosion' closely linked to new styles of management Power (1987, p. 142) comments that: 'it is clear that in the UK and elsewhere during the 1980s and the early 1990s auditing acquired an institutional momentum which insulated it from systemic enquiry'. New processes of audit or quasi-audit were devised and applied in almost every main branch of the UK public sector. In universities on-going squabbles took place over the validity and reliability of new 'audits of teaching quality', which imposed huge documentation requirements upon each and every institution, and spawned a substantial cohort of new internal committees, working to prepare their departments or universities to put the best possible face towards its next external review. In schools headteachers complained regularly of the weight of inspections by the new regulatory body, Ofsted. In the NHS elaborate systems of performance indicators and quality assurance were devised and put in place. In fieldwork during the mid-1990s one of us found the director of quality at a medium-sized hospital frustrated by the fact that the hospital was required to respond to four or five different types of quality reviews simultaneously, each with its own forms and processes (Pollitt, Birchall and Putman, 1998, p. 91).

We said at the beginning of this section that we considered the tension between reduced paperwork and increased performance monitoring to be a question of balance rather than of inherent contradiction. The above examples indicate that balance is not automatically guaranteed—it has to be constructed and then actively maintained. The paperwork burden on middle management *can* be reduced, if the performance monitoring regime is carefully designed, focused and regularly reviewed so as to prune 'excess growth'. This is the optimistic view. A slightly less sanguine perspective would be to see the whole process as a cyclic one in which monitoring and auditing systems possessed in-built tendencies to 'put on weight', but these were, from time to time, corrected by bursts of 'dieting' (reforms). This would perhaps explain why, in several countries, clear-outs of regulations and paperwork requirements seem to be hardy perennials rather than 'one-off' reforms. It would also allow for the fact that there is some evidence of performance indicator systems cycling between a smaller number of key indicators and a larger number of detailed indicators (Pollitt, 1990). What one is seeing here is therefore a trade-off rather than a contradiction: the trade is between, on the one hand, simple, light monitoring controls which permit subtleties and complexities and 'gaming' to squeeze round or through them and, on the other, detailed, heavy systems which capture more of the complexities and ploys, but which are burdensome and expensive to operate. Over time the grass on the other side of the trade-off often looks greener, hence the cycle.

7.10 Create more single-purpose agencies/improve horizontal co-ordination

The difficulty with this pair of proposals is that, *ceteris paribus*, specialization (into single-purpose agencies) *increases* the difficulty of co-ordination. As Rhodes (1997, p. 53) puts it of the Next Steps reforms in Whitehall: 'the most obvious result of the new system is institutional fragmentation'. There is some evidence that 'agentification' has exacerbated co-ordination problems in at least New Zealand (Boston *et al.*, 1996, p. 88) and the Netherlands (Roberts, 1997, pp. 106–11). In Sweden, where a system of strong, independent agencies has been in existence for a long time, there has also been a recurring concern that ministries lack the capacity and expertise effectively to manage 'their' agencies (see, e.g., OECD, 1998, p. 4 of executive summary). In fieldwork research that one of us undertook in the mid-1990s it appeared that, for hospitals, schools and providers of social housing, greater autonomy for individual service delivery organizations had indeed lessened co-ordination, at least at the level of individual cities or regions (Pollitt, Birchall and Putman, 1998).

None of this is to say that agentification does not also carry benefits. There is evidence, in several countries and many different sectors, of greater autonomy leading to improvements in economy, productivity or user responsiveness. Such benefits are, of course, not automatic: there is always the danger that poor management will fail to grasp the opportunities that are presented to them. But the existence of benefits is not the point here: the point is that there is a tension between the taking of these benefits and the simultaneous arrival of certain penalties in the form of loss of co-ordination at a higher level. (To be even-handed between both sides of the equation, it must also be acknowledged that the *potential* for co-ordination that existed under more centralized systems was by no means always taken advantage of.) Advocates of NPM-type reforms tend to deny or minimize the existence of loss of co-ordination, and, because 'co-ordination' is such a difficult concept to operationalize, it is hard absolutely to prove them wrong. According to this view, a framework which provides clear performance targets and lines of accountability should obviate fragmentation, and allow the central authorities to continue to 'steer' flotillas of agencies in some strategically sensible direction. To which we would respond that actual frameworks are often much less integrated than that (Talbot, 1996), and that, in a number of countries, perceptions of fragmentation among practitioners seems to be quite widespread. What we suspect, therefore, is that there probably *is* trade-off (not a contradiction) here, and that in practice significantly increased levels of institutional autonomy (and the benefits that brings) are usually purchased by some loss of policy or programme co-ordination. It is for politicians and public to say whether any given trade-off is acceptable, but so long as the rhetoriticians of reform insist that nothing is lost the trade-off issue cannot be properly investigated, weighed and debated.

7.11 Decentralize management authority/improve programme co-ordination

The potential problems here are similar to those discussed in the previous section. Pushing authority down and out tends to increase co-ordination difficulties. Agentification is just one case of the larger category of decentralization. A good example here is probably the EU's structural funds programmes: the management of these is highly decentralized—and highly variable. The EU Commission gives out the money, but its attempts to evaluate and steer what is going on cannot be considered to be very impressive (Barbier and Simonin, 1997; Toulemonde, 1997).

Our conclusion is therefore the same as that for agentification—that is, that in many cases there will be a trade-off, but probably not such a steep-sided choice as to justify the title of a 'contradiction'. Sensitive implementation may minimize and even succeed in concealing the trade-off, but on the bottom line shifting authority to the periphery means just that, and carries the implication that the co-ordinating authority of the centre is diminished. Of course, this consequence can be avoided in cases (not unknown) of pseudo-decentralization—those instances where the central authority claims to have 'empowered the front line' but in fact retains a full battery of controls which are reimposed the moment anything not to its liking occurs.

7.12 Increase effectiveness/sharpen management accountability

It may not be immediately apparent why there should be any tension between these two objectives. Are they not both perfectly sensible and compatible? If we consider the observations of the Canadian Auditor General, reporting on performance management reforms, we can see that this is not necessarily so:

Outputs are results that managers can control, while the outcomes managers are trying to accomplish are influenced by factors outside their programs (Auditor General of Canada, 1997, p. 5–8).

A glance back at Figure 1.1 (p. 13) will show that effectiveness is a question of securing the hoped-for *outcomes*, while efficiency is a matter of optimizing the input/*output* ratio. A good deal of evidence, spread over many years and from a number of countries, indicates two, alternating difficulties:

a) When managers are enjoined to concentrate on concrete outputs (licences issued, grants given, training courses completed) they tend to lose sight of outcomes and, therefore, to stress efficiency rather than effectiveness (East, 1997);

b) when, alternatively, managers are asked to concentrate on outcomes and effectiveness, it is hard to hold them responsible and accountable, for several reasons. This is because the attribution of outcomes to the actions of individual units or organizations is frequently obscure or doubtful, and also because, for many public programmes, measurable outcomes manifest themselves over such extended time periods that they cannot provide a sensible basis for annual accountability exercises anyway (Pollitt, 1995).

There appears to be a dilemma, or at least a trade-off, here. Go for outputs and you are likely to lose sight of effectiveness; go for effectiveness and you lose the chance of clear accountability for individual managers and their units. The easy answer is to say 'go for both simultaneously'. Unfortunately that is more easily said than done. Accountability systems are likely to slide towards outputs, as more quickly measurable, more easily attributable and much less costly to monitor. At a recent conference for senior New Zealand public managers the then minister for the civil service made 'output fixation' and the neglect of outcomes one of his chief themes (East, 1997).

There is an even more controversial aspect to the effectiveness/accountability relationship. This is pungently expressed by Wright (1997, p. 11):

A great deal of public policy is about rationing, about the distribution of scarce resources, about zero-sum games and opportunity costs. For rationing to work over any length of time it must either be ignored, obfuscated or it must be legitimised. It is an intrinsically difficult exercise to undertake by a democratic society in peacetime and in periods of stagnation or depression . . .

However, some of the current reforms, driven by good intentions, seem designed to undermine those three essential props: ignorance is being replaced by defined rights and obfuscation by transparency. Even more significant is the *delegitimation* of the process, decisions about rationing are being removed from politicians and self-regulating professions like teachers and doctors and they are being transferred to *managers* and to entrepreneurs, who quite simply lack the essential legitimacy to spread the essential misery [original emphasis].

In the light of these considerations, what can be said about the relationship between the drive for greater effectiveness and the drive for sharper management accountability? First, we are definitely *not* arguing that this is a sharp contradiction, with a steep-sided collapse of an effectiveness-orientation the moment the authorities begin to try to build management accountability, or vice versa. Second, there does, however, seem to be a tension between a focus on outputs and a focus on outcomes, with most of the cards (measurability, timeliness, attributability, cost) being stacked in favour of outputs. This is not so much a trade-off as a balance which it is difficult to hold against the slide towards 'output fixation'. Third, Wright opens up a deeper and more obviously political dilemma: that, for services which are rationed, the process of clarifying accountability and shifting it more to managers and away from public service professionals, may result in a loss of legitimacy and an increase in litigation and dispute.

7.13 Improve quality/cut costs

Quality is free was the title of a widely referenced book by one of the private sector quality gurus of the 1980s (Crosby, 1979). The happy claim was that improving quality was effectively free—that ultimately it always paid for itself. Whether or not this may have been true for commercial organizations operating in competitive markets, it certainly does not hold as an invariable proposition in the public sector. There are many public services where spending on quality improvements is unlikely to increase either the volume of customers, or the budget appropriation, or the income (if any) received from charges. The incentives for quality improvement are accordingly diminished. One of the reasons for the recent epidemic of standard-setting and guideline formulation is a recognition within the public sector that normal commercial reasons for improving service often do not apply, and that additional controls are therefore necessary. Imposing standards, a cynic might say, is cheaper than increasing the budget, and, in the Anglophone world, 'standard' has a reassuring professional ring.

The cost/quality equation is an echo—at the level of specific services—of the systemic issue of the relationship between saving money and improving performance (Section 7.6 above). It partakes of the same difference of emphasis between micro-economic thought and management theory. It also suggests two rather contrasting bases for the legitimation of management actions—one rationale founded on competitiveness and the other on organizational improvement and transformation. Clarke and Newman (1997, p. 67) describe this in the following terms:

The competitive order is characterised by its primary orientation to the market, its modelling of organisations as businesses and by the dominance of discourses of entrepreneurialism and competitive success. The transformational order is characterised by the modelling of organisation as dynamic, progressive and customer-oriented, and by the pre-eminence of the discourses of culture, HRM, quality and values.

Both orders are substantially different from traditional public administration, whether in its 'pure' bureaucratic form (as in a central ministry) or in its bureau-professional form (as in health care and education services). In many situations the two new orders may point in the same direction, at least as far as the choice of a practical line of action is concerned. In some situations, however, divisions can appear. Quality improvement schemes may be held back or under-resourced, because they are not seen as contributing directly enough or substantially enough to competitive success. Hitting this year's financial targets to the letter may be regarded as more important to a manager's reputation than achieving quality improvement or cultural change. These tensions are far from being purely theoretical: as one NHS hospital chief executive put it in the mid-1990s: 'In the real world we only get judged on narrow and short-term criteria . . . there is clearly a tension between competition and planning' (quoted in Pollitt *et al.*, 1998, p. 101).

Overall, one may hazard that the nature of the cost/quality relationship at a micro-level does indeed resemble the savings/better performance relationship at meso- and macro-levels. That is to say, the issue of trade-offs and contradictions depends on specific features of the particular context. Where an organization goes into a savings programme with plenty of 'fat' or spare capacity, then quality improvement and cost-cutting can co-exist. Where managers in a particular context can call upon technological advances (including new ways of organizing the staff) to boost productivity and enhance communications with service users, then, again, quality can be increased at the same time as costs are reduced. However, where no technological breakthrough is available, the reorganization of staff practices is severely circumscribed by professional and 'tribal' rules and conventions, *and* previous cost-cutting has already removed most of the fat, then the relationship between quality improvement and further savings becomes a trade-off, or even a contradiction. Such circumstances had, for example, become visible in some parts of the UK National Health Service by the mid-1990s—where tribalism remained extensive and many hospitals had already undergone a decade or so of 'cost improvements' (annual cost-cutting exercises). Some circumstantial evidence of a tension between costs and quality comes from a comparative study of the implementation of a range of TQM projects in NHS settings and in two commercial companies. Joss and Kogan (1995, p. 140) commented that: 'It is also clear that the funding of TQM at the NHS sites, while not inconsiderable, was more than an order of magnitude lower than in the two commercial companies.'

7.14 Reflections: balances, limits, dilemmas and paradoxes

Looking across the various 'candidate contradictions' reviewed above one can allow that not all are insurmountable. Some can be avoided—they are implementation dangers rather than fundamental logical contradictions. Others are more apparent than real (paradoxes), and in other cases still, there may be a deep-lying tension but the edge can be taken off it by skilled leadership and implementation. A considerable residue, however, remains. The various components of what has become (at least in the Anglo-Saxon countries, and in 'PUMA-speak') the vision of a modernized public sector do not add up to an integrated and harmonious whole:

Tensions such as the conflict between 'career service' and 'spot hiring' approaches to organising top public servants, legalist and managerial visions of organisational process, competition-centred and oversight-centred approaches to control over public services, are not likely to disappear through some ultimate 'modern' resolution (Hood, 1998, p. 221).

The scope of our investigation has in some ways been narrower than Hood's—he seems to be attempting to establish a set of timeless and universal trade-offs, pictured in a group/grid matrix of administrative cultures in which both his four 'pure' administrative philosophies and attempts at hybrid combinations are fundamentally unstable. We have focused more specifically upon selected elements from the package of the measures which have been proselytized in the 'radical reform' countries and in international fora such as PUMA, the World Bank and the IMF. We are more interested in the extent to which these elements can be reconciled in logic and also confirmed as mutually compatible by empirical observations. Our focus is therefore less on an exploration of the explanatory value of any one overarching taxonomy. Thus, while we entirely concur with Hood's proposition that certain tensions cannot be 'disappeared' by contemporary models of management reform, we also want to discriminate between the more- and the less-'do-able'. In the preceeding sections we have therefore reached towards a set of conclusions concerning our ten 'candidate contradictions'. We conclude the chapter by briefly recapitulating these tentative 'findings'.

7.15 The candidate contradictions revisited

1. Increase political control of the bureaucracy/free managers to manage/empower service consumers: in a perfect world these could just about be compatible. In the real world there is frequently a trade-off between one or more of the three corners of this triangle. In some contexts the trade-off becomes so sharp as to merit the title of a contradiction.

2. Promote flexibility and innovation/increase citizen trust and therefore governmental legitimacy: there is no fundamental contradiction here. However, there are specific contexts in which politicians and/or managers are obliged to trade off between, on the one hand, innovation and, on the other, values such as stability, predictability, continuity and trust. Not infrequently management innovations can relatively disadvantage certain sections of the community.

3. Give priority to making savings/give priority to improving the performance of the public sector: there is no general contradiction; much depends on the specific circumstances, especially whether the organization(s) in question has/have spare capacity, and/or whether technological advances offer the possibility of productivity gains.

4. 'Responsibilize' government/reduce the range of tasks government is involved with: again, there is no necessary or general contradiction here. On the other hand the actual implementation of privatization projects is replete with possibilities for governments to depart from the public interest. But these are implementation risks, not inevitable degradations of responsibility.

5. Motivate staff and promote cultural change/weaken tenure and downsize: this appears to be the most obvious and inescapable contradiction. Of course, it can be rhetorically papered over, but it is not clear that many public service staff are persuaded. There is a price to pay for the contradiction in terms of loss of morale, loyalty, the attractiveness of a public service career and possibly, therefore, effectiveness.

6. Reduce burden of internal scrutiny and associated paperwork/sharpen managerial accountability: this seems to be principally a question of balance. However, while it may not be a contradiction, intelligent and determined implementation is required if the balance is to be first constructed and then, subsequently, maintained.

7. Create more single-purpose agencies/improve policy and programme co-ordination: we suggest that there is an underlying trade-off here. It may be sharp or gentle, depending on context. The evidence for this is persuasive but not yet conclusive.

8. Decentralize management authority/improve programme co-ordination: a more general formulation of the previous candidate contradiction (7). Again, we argue that there is some evidence of a trade-off between these two desiderata.

9. Increase effectiveness/sharpen managerial accountability: whilst this does not appear to be a contradiction, there does seem to be some tension between these two objectives, and there is evidence that the balance is hard to hold. There may also be an underlying dilemma—for rationed services—between transparency and legitimacy.

10. Improve quality/cut costs: as with the third candidate contradiction (see above) this is a relationship which depends heavily on the context and, in particular, whether cost cuts can be achieved through the exploitation of spare capacity and/or technological advances. Where neither of these is possible, then cost-cutting exercises may well trade off directly against quality improvement. Quality is 'free' only under certain circumstances, not always.

8

Reflections: Management and Governance

'The art of government is in procrastination and in silence and delay;
  blazing bonfires left to burn will soon consume themselves away.
Of evils choose the least: great foes will tumble down in time, or wither, one
  by one.
He that rules must hear and see what's openly or darkly done.
All that is not enough: there comes a moment when to rule is to be swift and bold;
  know at last the time to strike—it may be when the iron is cold!'
(Sir Robert Cecil to Queen Elizabeth I from Benjamin Britten's opera
Gloriana. Libretto by William Plomer)

8.1 Introduction

This final chapter expresses some general views on the nature of public manage-ment reform. As we move through these reflections, the reader may care to specu-late on how far the concept of governance attributed to Sir Robert Cecil (above) should also be applied to public management.

The chapter is organized in four main sections—two pairs of contrasting perspectives. The first pair concern the overall nature of public management reform—or, at least, that almost twenty-year slice of it upon which this book has been focused. Here the contrast is between a perspective on reform as a distinct *strategy* and one of reform as a much more hit-and-miss process of muddling through particular crises and pressures as they arise (*incrementalism*). The second pair of perspectives also concern the nature of reform, but in a different sense. In this pair we ask about the extent to which useful knowledge of reform is being systematized, accumulated and applied. This time the contrast is between a first perspective which sees the reform process as a possible basis for developing a 'science' or 'craft' of public management, and another which is considerably more sceptical as to 'what has been learned', and, indeed, what is likely to be learned in the foreseeable future.

We take no final position ourselves with regard to either pair of perspectives. Indeed, part of the experience of writing this book has been an authorly oscillation, manic-depressive style, between more 'optimistic' and more 'pessimistic' views of our subject matter. Readers can find their own points of equilibrium, comfortable or otherwise.

8.2 Public management reform as strategic decision making

Let us assume a simple world in which three systems interact—a political system, a market economic system and a system of law and administration. Each of the three is set within the larger context of civil society, and the citizens of that society both participate in and form judgements as to the legitimacy of each of these systems (Figure 8.1).

Of course, such a model is too simple for some purposes. For example, in the real world executive politicians (ministers) are enmeshed in the administrative systems (typically as heads of departments of state) and some top public servants—such as, say, the President of the European Commission—may have heavily 'political' roles (as noted in chapters 3 and 6). However, we are using the model for a particular pedagogic purpose—to explore possible alternative settings for different systems of relationships within society, where each set of relationships (politics, administration, the market economy) is characterized by a significantly different set of motivations, incentives and penalties. For this purpose it is not essential that the separation depicted in Figure 8.1 and succeeding figures can be confirmed in great empirical detail, and certainly not that each and every individual can be confidently assigned to one system and one system only.

The three systems are distinguished from each other by a whole range of norms, rules and cultural assumptions—that is, they are 'high group' in terms of group/grid cultural theory (Dunleavy and Hood, 1994; Douglas, 1982; Hood, 1998). Let us further assume that the political system faces two particularly large and pressing problems. The first is a *fiscal* problem. It is widely believed (widely enough for it to count, whether or not the belief is in some empirical sense 'true') that the political system has to reduce the amount of resources consumed by the administrative and legal system, or, at least, moderate its rate of growth. Otherwise, it is said, the economic system will suffer, and the electorate will become more and more discontented. The second problem is a problem of the *legitimacy* of the political system in the eyes of the citizenry. Evidence accumulates

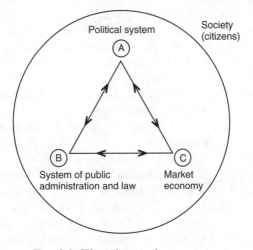

FIG. 8.1. Three interactive systems

that the 'legitimacy rating' of the political system is falling (see chapter 6). This causes various difficulties: the authority of politicians is eroded; the electoral loyalty and stability of voters is steadily reduced; public trust in political processes as efficacious ways of solving social problems declines; defiance and evasion of the law may begin to increase. (Here we refer not simply to criminal and public order laws but also to tax laws, social security laws, planning laws, and so on).

These two problems call for a strategic response from the leaders of the political system. Somehow they need to begin to save money (or give the impression that they are doing so) and simultaneously to increase their own legitimacy. How can this be done? In strategic terms there are various possibilities. They can change their own behaviour, rebuilding trust through moderate, consistent and transparent policy making. At the same time they can act explicitly and directly to restrain public expenditure. Alternatively they can search for some way of enhancing economic performance that is 'internal' to the market economy—for example through some technological breakthrough. Or they can pursue closer and more mutually supportive links between the political and the economic systems (which some, for example, would say is what the EU is mainly about). Or, third, they can take a course which, as we have seen, has proved popular in several countries at different periods—distance themselves as politicians from the system of administration and law and then blame that system for either the expenditure problem and/or the legitimacy problem. These are only three of a larger set of possible strategies, and to some extent they can and have been pursued in combination rather than isolation.

Let us dwell, for a moment, on the third strategy. The NPM is, as many commentators have noted, a bundle of disparate elements, but one of those elements has certainly been a process of distancing and blaming by political leaders. Government is the problem said President Reagan, as though it were some alien entity with which he had only a distant and basically hostile relationship. Other politicians, less rhetorically anti-government than Ronald Reagan, have also linked management reform with increased legitimacy: 'How can people trust government to do big things if we can't do little things like answer the telephone promptly and politely?' (Vice President Gore, in National Performance Review, 1997a, p. ix.) This sentence seems to imply that trust in the nation's political leaders will only return if the telephones are fixed first. If this is what it means, then Vice President Gore, or his text-writers, attribute astonishingly low powers of discrimination to the American citizenry. Such a proposition flies in the face of evidence that citizens are perfectly capable of holding one attitude towards the 'big things' and a different one towards the specifics of particular services (chapter 6). Be this as it may, the legitimacy question has been given repeated prominence in North American discussions of management reform. The invitations for a US-sponsored 'global' conference on 'Strategies for 21st century government', held in Washington, DC early in 1999, boldly declared that the proceedings would 'provide participants with a better understanding of how governments in the information age can build public trust and confidence' (Harvard University, 1998).

The strategy of *distancing and blaming* is represented in Figure 8.2. It has, as we have remarked earlier in the book, been used far more in some regimes than others—more in Australasia, North America and the UK than in Germany, France or the Nordic states. Even in such ideological settings—sympathetically attuned to suspicions of governmental competence and motivation—the blaming strategy has certain obvious limitations. First, politicians will not necessarily be believed. They may say that the problem is 'over there' in the bureaucracy, and that proper managers should be brought in, given greater flexibility and made more publicly accountable. However, the public may not believe that the problem *is* 'over there'. They may be quite able to distinguish between the political system and the administrative system, and believe that more problems lie with the former than the latter. Some, though not all, of the survey evidence referred to in chapter 6 appeared to point in this direction. Even if the public *does* focus considerable discontent on the administrative system—the 'bureaucracy'—it may nevertheless continue to hold ministers, not managers, responsible for even quite detailed occurrences and events. Politicians therefore have to be very careful when they attack the state machine, especially if they are trying to portray doctors, nurses and teachers and other popular cadres within the public services as parts of 'the problem'. Second, even if politicians are believed, they will not be believed for ever. After a few years of 'bureaucrat bashing' the public will begin to enquire when things are actually going to change—when will services improve and begin to live up to the 'visions' held out in citizens charters, political speeches and statements of service standards? In other words, distancing and blaming at best only buys a little time.

All of which brings us to the further, more profound issue raised by the distancing-and-blaming strategy. It is the question of what to do next—once political

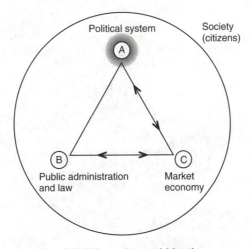

FIG. 8.2. Distancing and blaming

leaders have taken up their Olympian positions, pointing down at the failings of the bureaucratic state, what can they do to reform it? Here there appear to be a number of options. Political leaders can:

Tighten up traditional controls, restrict expenditures, freeze new hirings, run campaigns against waste and corruption and generally 'squeeze' the system of administration and law (see Figure 8.3). We may call this strategy 'MAINTAIN'.

Modernize the administrative system, bringing in faster, more flexible ways of budgeting, managing, accounting and delivering services to their users. Some of these new ways of doing things are likely to be borrowed from the market sector (hence the C > B arrow in Figure 8.4). However, such changes are also likely to require some corresponding adjustments to the political system (hence the B > A arrow in Figure 8.4). We call this approach 'MODERNIZE'. As was discussed in chapter 4, Section 9, it comes in at least two sub-varieties. While not automatically opposed to each other, each of these possesses a different 'spirit'. The first emphasizes the need for deregulation, on the assumption that public servants are often full of initiative and will improve their own operations once they are freed from heavy bureaucratic regulation from further up the traditional hierarchies. The second, by contrast, stresses that the best route to modernization is to engage citizens and service-users in a variety of participatory processes. It puts its faith in more 'bottom up', whereas the first variant is more concerned to reduce the amount of 'top down'.

Marketize the system, by instituting as many market-type mechanisms (MTMs) as possible within the system of administration and law. Public sector organizations are made to compete with each other, in order to increase efficiency and user-responsiveness. This represents a penetration of the administrative system by the

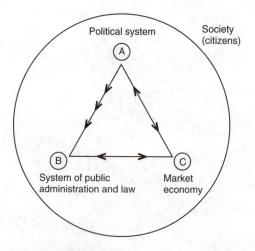

FIG. 8.3. Tightening traditional controls

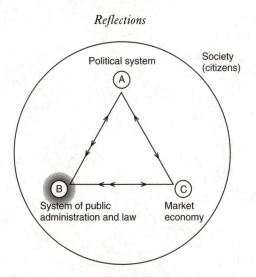

Fig. 8.4. Modernize the administrative system

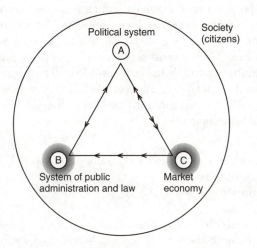

Fig. 8.5. Marketize the administrative system

culture and values and practices of the market sector—a lowering of 'group' in this respect (see Figure 8.5). 'MARKETIZE' is the label we give to this approach. Both the MODERNIZE and the MARKETIZE strategies claim to increase flexibility, and the horrible word 'flexibilize' has begun to appear in management reform document-ation.

Minimize the administrative system, handing over as many tasks as possible to the market sector (through privatization and contracting out). This is the case of what some writers have called the 'hollowing out' of the state machine. It carries a

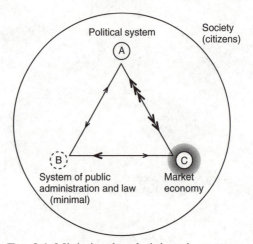

FIG. 8.6. Minimize the administrative system

number of implications, including an intensification of direct contacts between the political system and the market economy, unmediated by bureaucratic structures (see Figure 8.6). It represents a scenario in which, for example, social security payments, prisons and even security services are run by private companies, and the public administrative system dwindles to a shadow of its former self, now acting mainly as a kind of small holding company. We term this vision 'MINIMIZE'.

In this analysis, therefore, there are four basic strategies for dealing with the pressures on the state apparatus:

MAINTAIN (Figure 8.3);
MODERNIZE (with deregulatory and participatory variants—Figure 8.4);
MARKETIZE (Figure 8.5);
MINIMIZE (Figure 8.6).

As we have seen, different regimes at different times appear to have leaned towards one or other of these strategies. The '4 Ms' do not have to be taken in a particular order, but neither can they all be convincingly pursued simultaneously. Some countries have gone through the phase of distancing and blaming (8.2) first, but many have not. The Nordic countries tended to by-pass that and aim for modernizing, with some modest marketizing (8.4 with a flavour of 8.5). They also tended to try to mix deregulatory and participatory elements of the MODERNIZE approach (e.g., in Finland, where during the 1980s and early 1990s there was much emphasis on reducing and simplifying regulations, and then, in the late 1990s the stress was placed on more participation—*High quality services, good governance and a responsible civic society*, 1998a and b). The Germans have also largely avoided the blaming strategy and have moved directly to a mixture of maintaining and modernizing (8.3 and 8.4). The British, under Mrs Thatcher, certainly blamed

(8.2). In the early years (1979–82) this was combined with a mixture of tightening traditional controls (MAINTAIN) and, increasingly, MODERNIZE-style efficiency drives. Later, from the mid-1980s, the Conservative government moved much further towards a mixture of MARKETIZE and MINIMIZE (8.5 and 8.6). Later, Mr Blair moved back towards MODERNIZE, indeed, this term became one of the mantras of his adminisration, and suffused the 1999 white paper *Modernizing government* (Prime Minister and the Minister for the Cabinet Office, 1999). France has gone mainly for MODERNIZE, though there has clearly been a tension within this strategy as between more participatory and more top-down versions of reform. The Dutch, too, have preferred to MODERNIZE, although perhaps with a greater readiness to privatize than the French. Neither the Dutch nor the Nordics have indulged in much of the exaggerated political rhetoric that has been common in the Anglo-Saxon countries. Their preference for a more modest, consensus-oriented style of debate is well captured by the words of a senior Dutch public servant, responding to questions from a New Zealand public management expert 'You Anglo-Saxons, you should learn that pulling grass up doesn't make it grow any faster' (reported conversation, 1998).

Finally, we see the EU Commission as an organization which, for most of the period under consideration, has adopted a MAINTAIN strategy. Since the launch of SEM 2000 in 1995 there seems to have been a shift to a MODERNIZE strategy, though very much one of the decentralize and deregulate type (as, for example, in the MAP 2000 attempt to decentralize elements of personnel management) and not the participatory type. However, it is still too soon to say whether SEM 2000 and MAP 2000 really do amount to a fundamental modernization or not. The Commission has a large capacity to absorb and exhaust change initiatives without achieving any basic shift in internal structures or cultures.

Turning away from Europe, after 1996 the Australian government under John Howard opted for a combination of MARKETIZE and MINIMIZE (8.5 and 8.6), though with a fair amount of blaming (8.2) thrown in for good measure. 'Put another civil servant on the barbie, mate,' was one jokey characterization of their general attitude. The emphasis on privatization (MINIMIZE) and the introduction of competitive pressures into the public sector (MARKETIZE) came earlier in New Zealand which, by the mid-1990s, appeared to be entering a period of consolidation and relative calm, after a decade of hectic reform. It is worth reiterating that the concept of a 'strategy' can probably be applied more convincingly to New Zealand than to any other country in our set of ten. For New Zealand there is evidence that strategic principles were adopted, thought through and applied in a more systematic way than elsewhere (Boston, 1995). As for the North American countries, in the USA under Reagan there was much sounding-off of the MINIMIZE rhetoric, but this was never more than very selectively followed through, at least on the federal level. Instead, in practice, most of the measures actually implemented seem to fall within the MARKETIZE and MODERNIZE categories. The federal level was perhaps more securely embedded in the Canadian political culture (despite a growing challenge from the Provincial authorities), so, with the exception of some early

Mulroney rhetoric, most of the specific measures seem to be concerned with modernization, occasionally spiced with some marketization (8.4 flavoured with 8.5).

The important thing to note in all these examples is that each strategy has implications not only for the administrative corner of the triangle, but for the other two corners as well. Partly because of this, each strategy also has somewhat different impacts on the original problems of expenditure restraint and government legitimacy. If we take them one by one, MAINTAIN is the strategy that least 'rocks the boat'. Its weakness is that, as some countries have discovered, it may not yield sufficient change materially to affect either the fiscal problem or the legitimacy problem. MODERNIZE (8.4) represents a more fundamental shift, and appears to have enjoyed considerable success in, for example, Finland, the Netherlands and Sweden. Both Finland and Sweden have managed to make considerable reductions in public spending. Whether the legitimacy problem has been eased is hard to say, but the issue of 'starting lines' is again relevant here—these were both countries where the legitimacy of government had in any case held up better than in, say, the USA. Within a modernization strategy, leaders can still appeal to traditional public service values, such as career service, probity, equity, equality and so on. In value terms the basic thrust of this approach is that something valuable and worthwhile is being updated and improved—whereas MARKETIZE and, even more, MINIMIZE entail the substitution of a substantially different set of values and, by implication, a blaming and discarding of the older set (Hood, 1991; Kernaghan, 1997).

MARKETIZE (8.5) thus has somewhat different implications for the fiscal and legitimacy problems. On the one hand it may be a powerful strategy for addressing fiscal difficulties—sharp MTMs can oblige public sector agencies and departments to cut costs and search intensively for efficiencies. On the other hand, the legitimacy of some parts of the public service may actually fall further, if the public begins to perceive that fiscal priorities predominate over a service ethic, or that public agencies are more concerned with beating off 'competition' or improving their quasi-market image than with the 'bread and butter' of stable and predictable service for the average client. Something of this may be seen in the UK university sector, where huge efforts have gone into public relations, institutional performance indicators and quality control proceduralism, while the actual class contact and individual attention that most students can expect to receive has in many instances fallen considerably. The extreme consequences of an express shift to new modes of learning—and new types of student—all done on a shrinking resource base, can be seen in the much-reported 1998 resignation of the Vice Chancellor of Thames Valley University, following a highly critical report from the higher education Quality Assurance Agency (Baty and Thomson, 1998). These dangers are especially present where the service concerned is non-standardized, 'intangible'and generates outcomes which are hard to define and identify. Strong resentments can also arise as a result of increasing differentiation within the public service—for example if rank-and-file staff see their own pay being held back while their chief executive earns a private sector-comparable salary, with substantial performance bonuses.

The MARKETIZE strategy also tends to lead to the creation of flotillas of new, 'hybrid' organizations and public-private partnerships—to a blurring of the line between the martket sector and the system of public administration. Whilst these innovations may yield new flexibilities and efficiencies, they also pose new problems for accountability and legitimacy The literature addressing these issues is only now beginning to emerge.

Finally, the MINIMIZE strategy (8.6) results in a residual public sector which should certainly equate to lower direct consumption of goods and service by the state. Whether this solves the fiscal problem remains to be seen, since strong minimization or marketization strategies tend to go hand-in-hand with efforts at tax reduction, so a balance still has to be struck, even if at a considerably lower level. More fundamentally, the marketized services (health, education, etc.) still have to be paid for, so unless the political system can tolerate extensive exclusion of certain citizens because of their inadequate incomes, state subsidies will be necessary in one form or another. The legitimacy problem is transformed—and possibly clarified—because now the public's expectations are focused directly on the political leadership itself. 'Bureaucracy' and 'big government' are no longer available as whipping boys or scapegoats. Public discontents about the adequacy or quality of the (former) public services are directed towards the market economy, since that is what now provides these necessities, and towards the political leadership who remain responsible (in the public's eyes) for regulating market excesses and externalities. One can perhaps see a mild preview of what this might be like in countries which have already carried through major privatization programmes, such as New Zealand or the UK. In the UK, for example, public discontent at what are perceived as the high prices, high salaries and poor services of some of the privatized water companies has been considerable. It would be hard to claim that the legitimacy of this particular part of the market economy was very impressive.

Both marketization and minimization strategies tend to reduce the distinctiveness of the public sector. As Pierre (1998, p. 3) puts it:

The overall pattern [of public service reform, internationally] suggests that in several important respects the public service has lost much of its organisational and normative specificity; political institutions are developing new points of contact with the surrounding society and encourages new channels for citizen input on political and administrative matters.

This discussion has necessarily been a very simplified one, but in one respect the simplification has been so great that we must now acknowledge and correct it. Our oversimplification, thus far, has been to write as though management reform is always initiated, shaped and led by politicians. However, as has been clear from the very first chapter of this book, in the real world this is by no means always the case. Senior public servants are almost always heavily involved in reform attempts, and sometimes provide more of the dynamism than do the politicians. In Finland,

France, the Netherlands and Sweden, for example, public servants have themselves played leading roles in establishing reform agendas and proposing specific types of solutions. '[M]uch of what has emerged in Sweden so far ... has been driven by a small number of civil servants and, frequently, without explicit, senior political support' (Pierre, 1998, p. 6). Such 'mandarins' are powerful figures in their own right, aware of the pressures emanating from the external environment and willing, in some instances, to take pre-emptive action to preserve or enhance the role of the system of administration and law (or, at least, of their own part of that system). It may be significant that, at the time of writing, PUMA/OECD was conducting a project entitled *Strategic Review and Reform*, which aimed to identify and analyse issues with regard to strategic review and reform of the roles and functions of government, strategic decisions relating to public management reform and managing change. A seminar for 'highest level public servants' was planned for early 1999.

This additional source of dynamism therefore requires a reconsideration of Figures 8.2 to 8.5. The system of administration and law is not simply passive, being acted upon by forces from the political and market systems. It can also be pro-active, in the sense that its leadership may seek the support of leading politicians and/or business elites for particular modes of reform. Strategies may emerge *from* the bureaucracy rather than being imposed upon it. This has long been recognized by a number of theorists from a range of theoretical traditions. Working within a rational choice frame Dunleavy, for example, has developed a theory of 'bureau-shaping' in which senior public servants use the reform process to distance themselves from routine management tasks and from responsibility for substantive programmes which can so easily go wrong or appear to fail (Dunleavy, 1991). Instead they carve out for themselves roles as strategists and policy advisers, redesigning, evaluating and monitoring the 'operational' organizations 'below' them, but neatly avoiding the 'firing line' themselves. The popularity—in a number of countries—of creating corporatized bodies or executive agencies and of market-testing and contracting out can readily be fitted in to this theoretical framework. The testimony of seasoned practitioners also supports such an interpretation: consider Allen Schick's recent essay on the changing role of central budget offices:

In the typical case the budget office has divested most (or all) *ex ante* control of running costs and now leads the effort for management improvement. It has a major role in devising new institutional arrangements, integrating budgeting and other management processes, prodding departments and other public entities to measure performance and evaluate results, developing new guidelines and methods for holding managers accountable, and installing new information and reporting systems (OECD, 1997b, p. 4).

Theorists of quite different persuasions from rational choice recognize many of the same phenomena. Power (1997, p. 11) describes the explosion of audit and audit-like processes in contemporary societies, and comments that: 'As the state has become increasingly and explicitly committed to an indirect supervisory role, audit and accounting practices have assumed a decisive function. The state cannot play this indirect role without assuming the efficacy of these practices . . .' Similarly, Clarke and Newman observe that recent changes have: 'installed management as a new command system which features business managers, chief executives, quality coordinators and internal audit staff. They have also installed *managerialism* in the sense of new regimes of power structured through the domination of decision making, agenda setting and normative power' (Clarke and Newman, 1997, p. 82).

Each of these perspectives, although differing profoundly one from another in a variety of ways, holds up a picture of a dynamic strategy which is being pursued by the top tiers of the public service hierarchy. This involves taking control of the *process* of management reform and carving a new role out of the activity of orchestrating continuous change. Restructuring organizations, making strategic plans, launching quality improvement initiatives, measuring, auditing and evaluating the performance of others—these are the components of a kind of 'meta management', the practitioners of which are able themselves to avoid the hurly-burly of 'operations'. They set the targets, others have to achieve them. They redesign the organizations, others then have to manage them. This is a strategy which can be carried out in response to the demands of politicians for lower costs and higher legitimacy, or it can be launched independently by the new mandarinate, requiring nothing more from the political leadership than sympathetic acquiescence. The substantive content of the strategy is likely to be either modernization (Figure 8.4) or marketization (8.5) or some mixture of the two. Distancing (Figure 8.2) is not an easy tactic for leading public servants themselves (though they may nonetheless draw sharp contrasts between the 'bad old bureaucratic ways' and the bright new managerialism—Clarke and Newman, 1997, p. 65). Tightening up traditional controls (MAINTAIN—Figure 8.3) is widely regarded as insufficient. MINIMIZE (8.6) is unattractive because it radically diminishes the 'empire' over which the new managerial leaders can exercise their suzerainty. The new mandarinate, therefore, is most likely to go for the 'middle ways' of MODERNIZE and MARKETIZE.

8.3 Management reforms as 'muddling through'

The perspective which locates management reforms as part of a process of strategic decision making by political leaders and/or top public servants can be criticized as too neat and formulaic. Choosing between the '4 Ms' may make a good lecture or textbook, or even a piece of high-level consultancy, but are these the terms in which many of the participants actually experience reform? It is possible to explain much of what has been described in our book more in terms of 'muddling through' (Lindblom, 1959, 1979) than as an exercise in conscious strategy. On this view, the twin problems of fiscal restraint and legitimacy are real enough, but governmental responses to them have usually been *ad hoc* and partial rather than strategic.

Lindblom's original (1959) article on incrementalism was tremendously influential. In it he described a decision-making process in which policies typically emerged from a process of mutual adjustment between organized interests, with limited analysis of alternatives and frequent mixing of means and ends. The articulation of clear and well-ordered goals was the exception rather than the rule (Harrison *et al.*, 1990, pp. 8–10). Lindblom was concerned to offer what he saw as a more realistic model of most public policy making than his contemporary 'rational-comprehensive' theorists. His focus was mainly on decision making itself rather than outputs or outcomes (this has sometimes been misunderstood by commentators). At any event, twenty years later the debate between the various schools of thought was still running so strongly that Lindblom was prevailed upon to write an update of his first article. In this he distinguished between three elements:

incremental politics: the process of changing outputs and outcomes cautiously, in small steps;
incremental analysis: the process of analysing policy problems one at a time, in an *ad hoc* manner, rather than attempting grandiose, synoptic or comprehensive reviews;
partisan mutual adjustment (PMA): a process of political decision making which is fragmented and/or decentralized, and the resultant 'policies' are the amalgam of attempts at mutual persuasion by the main stakeholders, rather than the decision of a single, unitary body.

The strength of the incrementalist model can be felt the closer one approaches most of the specific reforms described in this book. In particular, incremental analysis and partisan mutual adjustment seem to have been very frequent features of public management reform, even if more-than-incremental changes in output were frequently hoped for. For example, it is easy to exaggerate both the comprehensiveness and the strategic forethought that went into the UK reform programme of the Thatcher years. It is now documented that the eventual scale of the privatization programme was simply not envisaged when the Conservatives came to power; that the *Next Steps* report (which led to the creation of many executive agencies) was the subject of fierce controversy and mutual adjustment within Whitehall (Thain and Wright, 1995) and that it was in any case a reaction to the perceived failures of the previous reform effort, the Financial Management Initiative (Zifcak, 1994). Even the radical MTMs introduced to the National Health Service through the enormously controversial 1989 White Paper, *Working for patients*, were constantly being adjusted and trimmed by successive Conservative Secretaries of State for Health, until the incoming Labour government declared that it was 'abolishing the destructive, bureaucratic competition of the internal market' altogether (Chancellor of the Exchequer, 1998, p. 46).

These examples could easily be multiplied—similar tales of how radical-sounding reforms, when viewed close-up, begin to appear less startling and more 'bargained', can be told for many countries. The boldness and clarity of vision which marked the New Zealand experiment remains the exception rather than the rule (though even there a good deal of *ad hoc* compromising took place—see

Boston *et al.*, 1996, pp. 81–2). Furthermore, the incrementalist will note, New Zealand was a small country, with an unusually compact elite and an equally unusual absence of checks and balances to force a reforming cabinet into the paths of partisan mutual adjustment. Contrast this case with that of the NPR and GPRA in the USA, where tremendous 'hype' undoubtedly led to particular improvements, and to energetic participation in some of the 'reinvention labs', but, at the same time, a highly pluralistic system of government led to several major departures from the original vision (Kettl, 1994; Radin, 1998; General Accounting Office, 1998).

From an incrementalist perspective, therefore, the nature of public management reform is 'bitty', *ad hoc* and specific, not strategic, comprehensive and driven by generic models. Models may sometimes still play a headline role, but from this perspective, they are being used as a 'selling angle' for something much more modest, or as a post hoc rationalization for the same. Their use, in short, is more as a rhetorical device than as a practical template for action. Our original scheme of reform (Figure 2.1), combined with the analysis of regime differences contained in chapter 3, explains why this should (usually) be so. To launch, sustain and implement a comprehensive strategy for reform requires certain conditions, and these are seldom all satisfied in the real world of public management reform. It requires, first, either a single authority or a set of key players who can establish a high degree of consensus over what needs to be done, and who can sustain this consensus over the kind of five-year plus timescales necessary to put in place fundamental, broad-scope reform. Second, it requires informed leadership, both from executive politicians and from a sufficient proportion of top public servants (mandarins). If either of these elite groups are opposed or uninterested then opportunities for delay, dilution and diversion will multiply and will be taken advantage of by the forces of resistance and recalcitrance which are almost bound to exist in the context of reform. Sustaining a strategy also requires a considerable organizational capacity, to plan and carry out the operational detail of the reforms, to respond to unforeseens and to ensure that suitable new knowledge and skills are brought into the public sector workforce. A degree of public acceptance, or at least acquiescence, is a further *sine qua non*, at least for reforms which affect the frontline.

Taken together, this is a formidable list of requirements. Occasionally it may be more or less met—in New Zealand between 1984 and 1990, for example, or for the 1994 Program Review exercise in Canada (Aucoin and Savoie, 1998) or in the gradual introduction of results-oriented budgeting—over a period of nearly a decade—in consensualist Finland (Pollitt *et al.*, 1997). Often, however, one or more important requirements cannot be satisfied. It was argued in chapter 3 that the probability of a stable platform for a well-focused reform strategy varies with regime type. Yet even in the most favourable circumstances (unified, centralized state, strong executive, long period in power) conditions may change. Eventually an election intervenes and a new party comes to power. Or political leadership loses interest as other issues press for attention (e.g., Pollitt, 1984, pp. 96–106; Savoie,

1994, on Prime Minister Mulroney). Or the implementation capacity is insufficient, and well-meant reforms get bogged down. Thus talk of 'strategy' is usually an idealization, or post hoc rationalization of a set of processes which tend to be partial, reactive and of unstable priority.

8.4 Management reform as a science?

It is part of the job of an academic enquiry to ask what scientific knowledge may be extracted from the many experiences of public management reform. Is there the actuality—or possibility—of cumulative knowledge, so that future reformers in country X will be able to build on the sure foundations established by the reforms implemented in country Y? There have been quite a few academic and practitioner attempts to 'take stock' and draw 'lessons' (e.g. Aucoin and Savoie, 1998; Department of Finance and Administration, 1998b; Development Team, 1998; OECD, 1996, 1997; Gore, 1997; Olsen and Peters, 1996a; Peters, 1998a). What have they yielded?

Peters (1998a) reviews some of the main 'principles' of public sector management reform and arrives at the conclusion that these should not be applied sweepingly, as though they were universals, but need rather to be tailored to specific organizational contexts. However, he is not optimistic about the availability of the necessary theory of contexts:

The problem with a highly differentiated approach to organisational reform is that organisation theory in the public sector is not yet sufficiently advanced to provide adequate guidance for would-be reformers . . . Our classification of government organisations tends to be on the basis of what they do—health, defence and so on—rather than on structural or managerial grounds that would provide more of a basis for reform recommendations. While we can think of a number of potentially important criteria, such as size, professionalisation, client involvement, there is not yet sufficient evidence to make good predictive statements to aid reformers (Peters, 1998a, p. 96).

Although some other researchers have gone a little further than this in specifying the criteria which are important in particular contexts, few would disagree with Peters's final point about insufficient evidence (Pollitt *et al.*, 1998, final chapter; Stewart, 1992). Social scientists have long written about the need to come up with a robust theory of contexts, but have yet to offer a satisfactory answer to their own call. Group/grid cultural theory, as borrowed from anthropologists by public administrationists, does provide a map of sorts but appears to lead to the dismal conclusion that administrative systems tend to drift towards their own particular form of pathology and extremism, with little to choose between four basic forms of distortion and decay (Dunleavy and Hood, 1994; Hood, 1998). This approach therefore has a number of limitations, especially from a practitioner point of view (as Hood explicitly acknowledges—Hood, 1998, chapter 10). It is, as its title suggests, a *cultural* theory, and does not say much about factors such as the specific service characteristics or dominant technologies, which others have found influential in determining appropriate organizational structures and procedures (e.g.,

Stewart, 1992). Furthermore, the finding that: 'Because . . . each way of [adminis-
trative] life has its built-in blind spots and weaknesses, along with its corresponding strengths . . . surprise and disappointment is inevitable and perpetual' (Hood,
1998, p. 191) is not a conclusion likely to be found to be particularly inspiring by
reform practitioners.

In chapters 2 and 3 we developed a model of influences on public management
reform which stressed constitutional, political and 'administrative system' factors.
Such a model takes one a certain way in understanding why certain reforms 'fit' in
one country but would be very difficult to implement in another, yet it is still
pitched at a fairly high level of generalization, and may therefore be of limited use
to those who are confronting specific reform needs in specific institutions. Perhaps
a slightly more detailed theory of contexts can be found in the work of 'realist'
evaluators of public policy, who at least provide some detailed methodologies for
ascertaining 'what might work for whom in what circumstances' (Pawson and
Tilley, 1997). However, this has yet to be taken up by the main schools of academic
thought on public management reform, and certainly cannot yet be crystallized
into the kind of recommendatory checklist beloved of practitioners.

The absence of an adequate theory of contexts leaves many academic writers
(including ourselves) very wary of coming out with specific recommendations.
True, there are a few well-worn general admonitions, such as: find a 'champion',
ensure attention by linking management reforms to processes of resource allocation, go for some inspiring 'early wins' as well as longer-term changes, stay in power
long enough to complete what you start, and so on. Unfortunately, taken together,
these could hardly be regarded as amounting to a 'science of improvement'. Most
academic commentators from the public administration community simply avoid
the issue. Peters and Savoie speak for many of their colleagues when they write that:

We soon realized that when we take stock of administrative reforms we are invariably
confronted with a confusing and contradictory picture of change. On the one hand, we
discover that a large number of changes have been adopted and implemented, and appear to
have produced some benefits for people inside and outside government . . . On the other
hand, we also discover that few, if any, of these reforms have been able to live up to the
claims of their advocates (Peters and Savoie, 1998, pp. 6–7).

Of course, not all academic disciplines are so reticent. Economists, in particular, have been much more ready to offer prescriptions. This may be part of the
explanation of why micro-economic ideas have been so influential in public sector
reforms in a several countries (see the Appendix, especially the country files on
Australia and New Zealand). Principal and agent theory and the new 'institutional
economics' have left their marks, and some, at least, of their advocates would claim
that they were definitely 'scientific'. Certainly they offer politicians and senior
public servants a clearer and more specific set of guidelines for reform than most
of the analyses provided by academics with backgrounds in public administration
and public management.

Practitioner manuals are very different from the corpus of academic work.

Generally speaking, such manuals just set out what is supposed to be done, with limited or no attention to context. Some—especially those associated with high-profile political programmes such as the US NPR or the UK *Citizen's Charter*—exude an air of confidence which admits little or no anxiety over the paucity of any scientific basis for the 'knowledge' which they are (implicitly or explicitly) claiming to convey (e.g. Gore, 1997; European Foundation for Quality Management, 1996). Others are more sober in rhetorical terms, but may still be prone to 'one-best-way-ism' and to inadequate acknowledgement of the variety of contexts which most public sectors display. 'Most what-to-do arguments in public management rely on circumstantial evidence and rhetorical power' (Hood, 1998, p. 13). Despite these common limitations, there does seem to be a good deal of practical knowledge around about how to do certain things and what problems to watch for—for example, in designing performance indicator sets (Likierman, 1995) or introducing performance management (Department of Finance and Administration, 1998a) or integrating results-based performance management and budgeting (Mayne, 1996) or evaluating EU expenditure programmes (European Commission, 1997a). This is mainly 'craft knowledge' rather than being scientifically based—though it may be none the worse for that. Craft knowledge can be tremendously useful, always assuming it is applied by craftspersons—those who already have an experienced 'feel' for what allowances to make for local taste and context, the strength or other-wise of the materials being worked with, and so on. It is, perhaps, routinely under-estimated and understudied by academics. However, craft knowledge is more likely to come unstuck when applied by newcomers or experts who are just 'passing through' on a limited term or limited focus assignment. It also has obvious limita-tions when applied to problems or in contexts which are genuinely novel.

We are therefore left with a rich, but only half-cooked mixture of two or three kinds of ingredient. There are academic theories which point in a general way to certain key issues or variables, but seldom develop these into specific recomenda-tions or practical 'tips'. There are—especially in the Anglophone countries—'up-beat' proclamations of what should be done to modernize the public service, but these frequently float in a rhetorical stratosphere, lacking any critical or analytical edge. Finally there is the 'grey literature' of guides and manuals, produced by public servants for public servants. These are sometimes mines of useful craft-based expe-rience, but tend to be weak on allowance for contextual factors and—unsurpris-ingly—to lack theoretical or systematic empirical underpinnings (and therefore scientific authority). In the final section (below) we offer a contrasting perspective on the state of the art of public management reform. Instead of looking at what we know it places more emphasis on how we *talk and write* about reform.

8.5 More rhetoric than rigour? Concluding impressions of public management reform

Reform-watching in public management can be a sobering pastime. The gaps between rhetorics and actions, and between the view from the top and the experience at the grassroots are frequently so wide as to provoke scepticism or—according to taste—cynicism. The pace of underlying, embedded achievement tends to be so much slower than the helter-skelter cascade of new announcements and initiatives, each with its own, ephemerally fashionable, abbreviation (to name but a few, PPBS, RCB, PAR, ZBO, TQM, BPR, NPR, PS 2000, SEM 2000). The apparent ability of leaders to forget the lessons and limitations of previous administrative reforms is impressive—perhaps *administrative* history, at least, really is dead. One becomes accustomed to hearing large claims touted and to discovering, subsequently, that these are founded on precious little in the way of systematic, relevant and attributable evidence. It is very common for the researcher to read in an official document that accruals accounting or efficiency planning or some other new process has started on a particular date, and then, when visiting the organizations concerned, to find that nothing much has happened beyond the circulation of a few policy papers, or that many people in the organization haven't even heard of the innovation in question. One's spirits fall when visionary futures are unfurled in terms that are carefully chosen to sound good whilst carrying no specific and testable content. It is hard to avoid a hardening of the heart against a certain kind of hyperbole:

The Government will deliver a world class education service, offering opportunity for all to reach their full potential . . . (Chancellor of the Exchequer, 1998, p. 42),

or:

that was the challenge that President Clinton handed down four years ago when he asked me to reinvent the federal government—to put the wheels back on. We agreed right then that we needed to bring a revolution to the federal government. We call it reinventing government (Gore, 1997, p. 1).

How, one wonders, do these leaders intend to rebuild trust in government—one of their avowed intentions—when they continue to resort to such implausibly exaggerated and over-sure language? Who do they think will believe such claims?

It is comparatively easy to identify the rhetorical excesses of some reform leaders. There is, however, another and much more subtle gap between rhetoric and practice. As we have noted, one difference between the current wave of public management reform and earlier phases is that this one has taken on an explicitly international dimension. An international vocabulary (an English one) has developed, actively fostered by organizations such as PUMA, SIGMA, the World Bank, and the IMF, as well as through national governments and academic and professional associations. Terms such as 'privatization', 'agentification', 'contractualization', 'continuous quality improvement', 'efficiency gains', 'activity costing' and 'performance management' are part of this international lexicon. Their repeated use seems to confirm that everyone is involved in basically the same enterprise, a global shift in the direction of modern management. Yet this is by no means necessarily the case. This special vocabulary may serve to conceal and constrain the nature of beneficial change as well as aid it. The problems are at least twofold.

First, use of these terms often generates an exaggerated impression of the uniformity of what is going on. This is because the same term may be used to refer to very different sorts of change in different places, changes which carry different meanings in different contexts. Every consultant or academic who has worked outside their mother country or mother tongue has experienced something of this—or, at least, every one we have spoken to. Anecdotes concerning the phenomenon are commonplace. One of the authors of this book once spent an entire day discussing the meaning of 'efficiency' in a Franco/German/Italian/English expert team, each member of which, at the outset, had mistakenly thought that s/he was perfectly clear as to its conceptual content, and that the day would be spent sorting out the practical details of the consultancy upon which we were supposed to be working. On another occasion a comparative researcher looking at management reforms in the Netherlands and the UK was obliged to go back and revise his report when he realized that the terms 'privatization' and 'agency' were being used to denote quite different processes/institutions by the civil servants he spoke to in the two countries. These potential confusions are not helped by the fact that many of the most influential and active propagaters of the debate are the members of central policy or management units, nationally or internationally, such as the UK Office of Public Service, the Swedish *Statskontoret*, the French *grands corps* or PUMA itself. By and large these are individuals who, whatever their many other talents may be, will not have had much experience of 'normal' operational management. Rather they tend to be high-flyers, policy advisers, intellectual synthesizers and academic entrepreneurs. So their own ability to relate the terms and ideas they use to the realities of day-to-day administration and management is limited. Thus the danger that the language of reform can take on a life of its own is further reinforced.

Second, the international vocabulary of management reform carries a definite normative 'charge'. Within the relevant community of discourse the assumption has grown that these things—performance management, activity costing and so on—*are* progress. To be progressive one has to be seen to be doing things to which these particular labels can be stuck. They constitute the *menu du jour*. Yet this is also a limiting process, in so far as items *not* on the current list are seldom discussed, and are easily rejected if and when they do appear. Suggesting, for example, that an existing or new activity would be better placed within an enlarged central ministry or as a direct, state-provided service, becomes an uphill struggle— it is 'beyond the pale', not the done thing. 'To borrow a phrase, going public is out. Going private is in' (Rockman, 1998a, p. 20). Likewise the proposition that working in partnership with a range of private and 'third sector' bodies to deliver a service may be simply time-consuming, wasteful and a threat to clear public accountability: uttering such a sacreligious thought can be instantly to brand oneself as a 'reactionary'. Within this managerialist thought-world there is only limited consciousness of the flimsiness of many of the current 'principles' of good public management. A more historically-informed awareness would show how such 'principles' or 'proverbs' come and go over time, and are often arranged in opposing and mutually-contradictory pairs (Hood, 1998; Hood and Jackson, 1991; Peters, 1998a; Simon, 1946).

And yet there is another side to public management reform, which has a more solid and sensible persona. The pressure, the rhetoric, the loosening of the old ways—all these have combined to give many public servants the opportunity to make changes which make local sense *to them*. Such 'improvements' may occasionally be self-serving, but often they are substantially other-directed, and result in gains in productivity, service quality, transparency, fairness, or some other important value. If close-up scrutiny of many 'great operations' tends to reveal incremental rather than strategic decision-processes (section 8.3 above), it also reveals endless examples of beneficial opportunism and pragmatic reform by public servants at all levels. Some of these innovations may win awards, chartermarks and the like (Borins, 1995; Löffler, 1995) but many do not. To end this book on an appropriate note of self-criticism, one of the major limitations of our approach—and the approaches of many others who have concentrated on big reforms and big ideas—is that we capture very little of this micro-improvement. As some of the most successful reform leaders in several countries have recognized, a crucial ingredient of a successful reform strategy is that it should create and sustain conditions in which 'small improvements'—many of them unforeseen and unforeseeable—can flourish.

Appendix: Country Files

A.1 The scope and purpose of this appendix

This is quite a long appendix, and more important, perhaps, than most. In it are provided some basic facts about the ten countries covered in the main text. Unlike many other multi-country studies, this book is *not* organized into single country chapters. It is deliberately and, we hope, advantageously, organized by model and theme—thus permitting a more integrated, less sequential form of inter-country comparison. However, one price that is paid for this type of integration is that the reader is not offered neat little summaries of each country's recent history and arrangements. Left thus, readers who were not already familiar with the relevant aspects of a particular country's constitution, policies, and so on, would be at a considerable disadvantage. To offset this possible handicap, this Appendix has been prepared so as to offer this type of information in a conveniently packaged form. The contents of the package are closely patterned on the model of public management reform introduced in chapter 2 (see especially Figure 2.1, p. 26). The sequence of the Appendix is therefore as follows:

- some information on major economic indicators for each country (i.e., data which help to 'fill in' the larger box 'A' in Figure 2.1);
- some information on key socio-demographic indicators for each country (i.e., data which help fill in box 'C' in Figure 2.1);
- a set of 'country files' which give snapshots of each country, organized in exactly the same categories as chapter 2 and including, *inter alia*, details of the major management reforms since 1980;
- a chronological table listing the key reforms by country, date and type.

A.2 Major economic indicators

Table A.1 lists some key economic indicators for each of the ten countries. It may help to go through the measures one by one, and to indicate their possible significance for the factors that influence public management reform. Two major limitations to these data should, however, be acknowledged at the outset. First, it is seldom, if ever, possible to read off conclusions about a country's economic health from a single indicator. Second, many of these indicators are 'snapshots'—indicators of the state of a variable at a particular point in time or, at best, over a three or five year average. These two limitations indicate that caution is necessary in interpretation. If we take the variable 'general government expenditure', for example, the table tells us what share of GDP this represented in each country in 1996, but nothing about whether the trend over time was up or down within any given country (some information of that kind *is* given in Table A.2 and also in Table 4.2 in chapter 4).

Nevertheless, despite these important qualifications, the variables listed in Table A.1 do carry significance—if often indirect—for the structure and management of the public sector in each country. They constitute some important elements of the *context* in which public management reforms unfurled. Some brief remarks to indicate the nature of the linkages are offered in the following paragraphs.

First there is size—not a factor that usually changes overnight. By and large big populations tend to be more diverse, with a greater variety of social cleavages which are likely to

TABLE A.1. *Selected key economic variables*

Variable	Australia	Canada	Finland	France	Germany	Netherlands	New Zealand	Sweden	UK	USA
Population (millions)	18.3	30.0	5.1	58.4	81.9	15.5	3.6	8.9	58.8	265.6
Per capita GDP (current exchange rates)	21.812	19.330	24.420	26.323	28.738	25.511	18.093	28.283	19.621	27.821
Per capita GDP (current PPP)	20.376	21.529	18.871	20.533	21.200	20.905	17.473	19.258	18.636	27.821
Average annual gross fixed capital growth over 5 years	5.6	2.2	-4.1	-1.5	0.2	2.2	9.6	-2.6	1.3	6.9
General government expenditure on goods and services as % of GDP	17.0	18.7	21.9	19.4	19.8	14.0	14.4	26.2	21.1	15.6
Average annual wage increase, previous 5 years	1.7	2.4	3.8	2.6	4.2	2.4	1.5	4.8	4.9	2.7
Average annual consumer price increase, previous 5 years	2.4	1.4	1.5	2.0	3.1	2.5	2.0	2.7	2.7	2.9
Export of goods as % of GDP	15.1	34.9	32.4	18.8	22.1	51.5	21.7	33.7	22.5	8.5
Average annual % export increase, previous 5 years	7.5	9.7	12.1	6.3	5.4	8.9	8.2	9.0	7.0	8.2
Import of goods as % of GDP	15.4	29.5	24.7	17.7	19.4	46.6	22.3	26.5	24.9	10.8
Average annual % import increase, previous 5 years	9.7	7.7	7.3	3.9	3.3	7.8	11.8	6.0	6.5	10.3

Notes: All figures are for 1996, unless otherwise stated. All money figures are in $US. PPP = purchasing power parities
Source: OECD

be reflected in a greater complexity of political arrangements. One might argue that the huge and diverse population of the USA—or even the ethnically, regionally and socially quite diverse 60 million people living in the UK—are inherently less straightforward to govern than the relatively homogenous five million Finns or nine million Swedes.

Second, there is the per capita wealth of a country. By global standards all ten countries studied in this volume are rich. However, there are considerable differences within this rich countries' club. All other things being equal (which is a big assumption) a super-rich country such as the USA or Germany will have more room for manoeuvre, in both public and private spheres, than a significantly less rich country such as New Zealand or the UK.

Third, Table A.1 shows diversity in terms of trends in capital growth. Both Finland and Sweden had experienced very adverse economic circumstances during the period 1991–96, and show negative rates of fixed capital formation. For a period, at least, they were evidently 'living off their capital' (albeit as rich countries with plenty of capital from which to draw). By contrast New Zealand had an average annual rate of capital formation of 9.6 per cent, the USA scored 6.9 per cent and Australia 5.6 per cent.

Fourth, the figures for general government expenditure confirm the broad comparative picture developed earlier in the book. There are relatively generous Nordic countries (Finland, 21.9 per cent; Sweden, 26.2 per cent) and relatively parsimonious Anglo-Saxon countries (Australia, 17 per cent; New Zealand, 14.4 per cent; USA, 15.6 per cent). Somewhere in between come the big continental European states (France, 19.4 per cent Germany, 19.8 per cent) and the UK (21.1 per cent).

Fifth, the figures for wage increases and price increases over five years also show considerable variation. Apparently Finns, Germans, Swedes and the British paid themselves high wage increases, in sharpest contrast to the Australians and New Zealanders. Meanwhile the highest consumer price increases were experienced by Australians, Germans, the Dutch, the Swedes, the British and the Americans. The Canadians and the Finns enjoyed the lowest price increases. Ultimately the balance between wage and price increases affect the international competitiveness of an economy as well as the purchasing power of its citizens. These factors, in turn, strongly influence the pressures on governments to spend and/or save. To take just one, obvious, example, falling international competitiveness (perhaps due to higher-than-average price increases) will lead to increasing unemployment and therefore to higher expenditure on unemployment benefits. Equally, virtuously small price increases (aided by low wage increases) will increase employment, increase the government's tax revenues, and reduce spending on unemployment benefits.

The size of exports and imports as a proportion of the total GDP provides a very rough indicator of the 'openness' of an economy to changes in global trade patterns. Here we may note that exports *and* imports are a higher proportion of the Canadian, Finnish, Dutch and Swedish economies than of the Australian, French or American economies. Germany, New Zealand and the UK come somewhere in between these two groups. This pattern illustrates the complexity of factors affecting public management reform. In the abstract one might have hypothesized countries with large import/export sectors would have been more open to the influences of economic 'globalization'—in particular increasing intensity of competition—and therefore would have been obliged to act most vigorously with respect to public management reform. In practice, however, any such hypothesis is falsified by the data in Table A.1. The 'high reformers' are New Zealand and the UK (in the 'middling' category for import/export shares) while cautious reformers such as the Netherlands and the Canadians fall in the 'high' category for import/export shares. This supports the point developed in chapter 2, to the effect that reforms cannot be 'read off' from macro-economic indicators—the influence of the latter may be profound, but it is often indirect, lagged and diffuse.

A.3 Key socio-demographic indicators

The need to constrain public expenditure (and thereby hold down rates of taxation) has been a prominent theme throughout the book. Most of the largest elements of expenditure within the ten public sectors under examination are strongly influenced by socio-demo-graphic factors. Typically pensions, health care and education are the largest spending programmes. Unemployment benefits tend to be smaller in volume, but have attracted a great deal of public attention, especially as the nature of both employment and unemployment has been changing during the 1980s and 1990s as compared with the 1950s and 1960s. Part-time employment has grown almost everywhere (although at different rates in different countries) and there has been a shift in employment away from younger people and from older men (OECD, 1996, pp. 28–9).

Among our ten countries welfare states vary hugely, not simply in terms of the shares of expenditure they absorb but also in terms of their basic structures and procedures. However, all, to a significant degree, have both fiscal and social problems to face. Expert studies sometimes classify welfare states into a Scandinavian model, an American model and a continental European model. The Scandinavian model is relatively generous, and places emphasis on the provision of social services as well as on cash payments. The American model is relatively parsimonious, leaving a wider range of service provision to the private sector than is the case in its Scandinavian counterpart. There is also a willingness to tolerate more extreme inequalities in income distribution and therefore, in both the US and the UK cases, the continuing existence of substantial pockets of deep poverty. The continental model is more 'generous' than the American, but less service-oriented (and therefore less employment-intensive) than the Scandinavian model. The emphasis is on cash transfers. The different models are also financed in different ways. All use some combination of general taxes, payroll taxes and mandatory insurance, the exact balance between these different forms varying a good deal. As a basis for welfare expenditure payroll taxes are particularly vulnerable in a globalized economy because they add directly to the cost of labour and, when employment falls, revenue shrinks more rapidly than it would from, say, a tax on consumption or even a general tax on incomes. Summing up an expert analysis of these differences one recent commentator suggested that:

The implication seems clear enough: in order to increase their sustainability, each of these three types of welfare state must primarily attend to its specific problems. The Scandinavian model must reduce its dependence on very high levels of taxation; the American model must find ways of alleviating the distress of the working poor; and the continental model must find ways to increase levels of employment without running into the problems of the other two models (OECD, 1997c, p. 218).

Returning to the socio-demographic particulars, pensions are obviously affected by the age structure of the population. *Ceteris paribus*, the higher the proportion of the population which is retired, the higher will have to be public pension expenditure, and the smaller will be the proportion of the population which is in work and therefore capable of making some contribution to this expenditure through current taxation. In practice matters are rather more complicated than this, for a variety of reasons. For example, in different countries different proportions of the retired population are covered by private pension schemes, and the adequacy of these schemes also varies. Also, many older people may still be active participants in the labour market, and variations in the extent to which this takes place can also influence the 'need' for state pensions. Further, it is the case that pensionable age varies from country to country (and since the mid 1980s there has been a trend towards shifting the age of entitlement *upwards*, so as to moderate demands on public expenditure). All these variations are important, but underneath them net changes in the elderly population remain a significant 'driver'. Within the European Union the age/dependence ratio has been calculated to increase by 50 per cent within the coming twenty years (OECD, 1997c, p. 70). In all ten countries the percentage of elderly persons in the population as a whole has been increasing, but at different rates and over slightly different time periods. Figure A.1 gives some information about this.

From Figure A.1 it can be seen, for example, that in 1990 Sweden and the UK had the highest percentages of over-65s. In both countries the increase had been considerable since 1960. For all ten countries, further increases are yet to come. However, looking forward to 2030, the coming increases in, say, Germany and the Netherlands are likely to be significantly greater than the increases in Sweden or the UK. In terms of pressures on expenditure one might say that, for Sweden and the UK, 'the worst is past', whereas for Germany and the Netherlands 'the biggest shocks are yet to come'.

The relative size of the elderly population is also very important for health care spending. For example, in the UK it was calculated that, in 1990, the average gross per capita expenditure for hospital and community health services for 16–44 year olds was £115 pounds. The equivalent annual expenditure per 85 plus capita was £1,875 pounds. Between 1971 and 1990 the population of people aged 85 and over had risen from 485,000 to 866,000 (Harrison and Pollitt, 1994, pp. 19–21). Figure A.2 gives some comparative figures for the growth of this most elderly group. As with Figure A.1 one can see growth everywhere, but

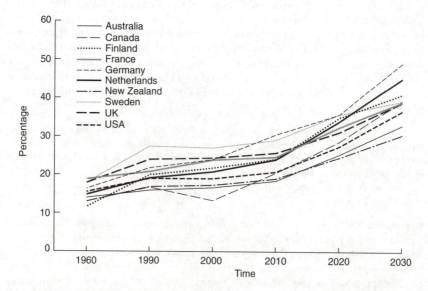

FIG. A.1. Population aged 65 and over as a percentage of the population aged 15–64

from different starting points and at different rates. Thus Sweden has an unusually large population of the very old throughout the period 1980 to 2010, whereas, in this respect at least, New Zealand appears to be a considerably 'younger' society.

Of course, there is no assumption that each country is equally generous in its social expenditures, or that there is some uniform balance between expenditures on different social groups. Some countries seem to emphasize the needs of the elderly, others the needs of, say, the young, or the unemployed (OECD, 1997c, pp. 63–80). Table A.2 offers a series of interesting contrasts between the ten countries. To begin with (first two columns) one can readily see that the proportion of the national wealth which states devote to social expenditures as a whole (social security, health, welfare, education) varies considerably. Finland, Sweden and the Netherlands are high spenders (with corresponding implications for both the generosity of their services and the levels of their tax rates) while, at the other end of the scale, the USA and Australia appear to be low. France and Germany (the 'continental model') lie in the middle, much higher than the USA but not as high as the Nordic states.

As one breaks down this pattern of aggregate spending further interesting features emerge. The middle column of Table A.2 shows the percentage of total social expenditure which goes in transfers, as opposed to the direct provision of goods and services. In very general terms countries which have a low percentage of transfers are likely to have large public service-providing operations—a fact of some importance in the context of public management reform. Canada, Sweden and the UK appear to fall within this category. Other countries may *spend* at quite high rates but display a greater propensity to transfer the money to private or charitable bodies which provide the actual services, or to transfer directly to individuals' pockets, leaving it to them to choose how and where to spend their benefits (the 'continental model' again).

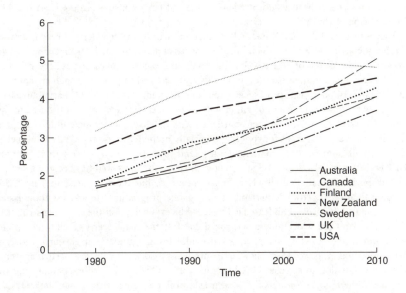

FIG. A.2. Percentage of people aged 80 and over in the whole population

Appendix: Country Files

TABLE A.2. *Age distribution of social expenditure*

	Social expenditure (% of GDP)		Spending on services as a % of transfer	Transfers to elderly/transfers to non-elderly	
	1980	1993	1993	1980	1993
Australia	11.7	16.5	15	1.3	0.7
Canada	13.3	20.1	34	1.2	1.2
Finland	18.9	35.3	16	1.1	0.8
France	25.3	28.7	7	1.5	1.6
West Germany	25.0	24.7	8	1.9	1.7
Netherlands	28.8	36.4	10	0.7	0.7
New Zealand *	18.2	23.3	2	1.8	0.8
Sweden	30.4	38.3	34	1.0	0.9
UK	18.3	23.4	19	1.6	1.0
USA	12.7	15.3	10	2.3	2.5

[*1992 instead of 1993]

Source: OECD, 1997c, p. 65

Moving on to the two right-hand columns, further levels of difference appear. Thus, in 1993, the USA and Germany seem to devote considerably larger shares of their social transfer expenditures to the elderly than Australia or the Netherlands. However, some quite startling changes took place in these ratios over the comparatively short period between 1980 and 1993. In the UK the ratio in favour of the elderly fell, as it did in Australia and New Zealand. In Canada, France and Sweden it remained fairly constant. In the USA the relative favouring of the elderly increased.

Figures A.1 and A.2 and Table A.1 are focused mainly on the elderly. There is a range of other social developments which can affect social expenditure, apart from changes in the proportion of over-65s or over-85s. For example, studies in several countries have indicated that the creation of single-parent households tends to lead to problems such as increased rates of poverty, poor health and social exclusion. Both increased rates of marital break-up and a growth in the proportion of children born outside marriage have contributed to this trend. The struggling 'lone mother', burdened with debts and unending childcare responsibilities, has become a focus for concern, especially in the USA and the UK, and also elsewhere. 'In all countries lone mother families tend to be poorer than two parent families' (OECD, 1997c, p. 84). Table A.3 shows how this type of household has become a significant proportion of all households in most countries, but more so in some (the USA, Sweden) than others (the Netherlands). New public programmes to address these issues (e.g., through subsidizing childcare facilities) can be expensive. Yet the changing structures of society—and the wider public and social costs of the *consequences* of allowing single-parent households to sink into poverty—provide strong arguments in favour of governments adopting measures to ameliorate the problems associated with this particular trend. As the introduction to a recent OECD report puts it: 'Maintaining lone parents and the long-term unemployed on benefits is seen as a problem rather than a solution' (OECD, 1997c, p. 13).

TABLE A.3. *Proportion of children living in one-parent households in the mid-1980s*

USA	24
Sweden	17
Canada	15
UK	14
France/Germany	13
Netherlands	10–12

Source: OECD, 1997c, chapter 3

A.4 Public management reform: the 'country files'

Having given some background information on the economic and socio-demographic features of the ten countries we now turn to the political and administrative specifics of each state. In the following pages a 'file' for each country is presented, organized in exactly the same categories as those used in the model of public management reform outlined in chapter 2.

AUSTRALIA

A. Socio-economic forces: general

Australia is a very large country, with a relatively modest population (18.3M in 1996). For key economic and socio-demographic data see Sections A.2 and A.3, including Tables A.1–A.3, and Figures A.1 and A.2 (above).

B. Global economic forces

See Section A.2, especially Table A.1 (above).

C. Socio-demographic change

See Section A.3, above. Two features of the 1970s and 1980s which tended to dilute the previous assumptions of Australia as an overwhelmingly white, post-colonial society were, first, an influx of Asian immigrants and, second, an increasingly strong demand for political (including territorial) rights by the aboriginal peoples. Notice, though that the pressures of an ageing society were somewhat less than those experienced by most western European states (Figure A.2).

D. National socio-economic policies

Like New Zealand, Australia was obliged, during the 1980s, to move away from previous protectionist policies which had involved a high degree of state regulation and intervention in the economy. 'Increasingly both countries turned to the private sector and the use of market principles within the public sector, which have been linked to broader programmes of economic reform' (Halligan, 1997, p. 17). Also like New Zealand, one component in the shift of economic strategy was a recognition that a higher proportion of both imports and exports were now coming from Asia, rather than from Europe (Castles *et al.*, 1996, pp. 24–6).

From 1983 to 1985 the Australian economy recovered somewhat from its previous crisis. The Hawke Labor government increased public spending as a percentage of GDP. However, the terms of trade deteriorated sharply in 1985/86 and the second half of the 1980s witnessed an intensified effort at expenditure reduction. This, in turn, focused efforts to increase public sector efficiency and streamline government. By the mid-1990s the Australian economy was performing better, but over the 1980–95 period as a whole the key indicators showed less favourable results than the OECD average.

In general it might be said that the transition to new macro-economic and micro-economic policies was both sharper and more painful in New Zealand than Australia. During the 1985–92 period Australia enjoyed much better economic growth and employment growth than New Zealand (Castles *et al.*, 1996). Micro-economic reforms were mediated through corporatist negotiations with the Australian trade unions, whereas the NZ reforms had a more 'imposed' quality.

E. The political system

Australia is a federal state, in which the federal level is strong and, indeed, served as a 'laboratory' for some of the public management reforms which were subsequently introduced at state level (Halligan and Power, 1992).

At the Commonwealth (central) level Australia has a bicameral legislature, with the upper house being directly elected and quite well endowed with legislative powers (Australia is an example of 'strong bicameralism' in Lijphart's scheme—Lijphart, 1984).

The electoral system is majoritarian, being based on an alternative vote procedure where voters are asked to indicate their first, second, third (etc.) preferences among candidates, and the preferences of those who voted for the candidate with the lowest number of first preferences are redistributed until one candidate emerges with an absolute majority of first preferences. Governments are usually dominated by a single party, either the Australian Labor Party (ALP), as between 1983 and 1992, or Liberal-National coalitions (as for the whole of the period from 1950 to 1972). The dominant style of politics is adversarial (Australia is mildly famous for the boisterousness of its political exchanges).

F. New management ideas

Australia was exposed to the same tide of 'Ricardian' or rational choice micro-economic thinking as other Western states, but does not seem to have been as directly and powerfully influenced by this as was New Zealand (Castles *et al.*, 1996)—or, at least, not until the Howard-led National government of the late 1990s. Australia was also within the global reach of the parallel wave of generic managerialist ideas such as TQM, benchmarking, re-engineering, and so on. In this case the concept of a distinctive *public* service seems to have been strong enough to dilute and delay the impact of such genericist concepts and their associated techniques somewhat more than in either New Zealand or the UK. Nevertheless, both rational choice and generic managerialism certainly exerted an influence, during the late 1970s and 1980s— as in the UK and the USA right-wing think tanks began to play prominent roles in debates about government and public affairs (Zifcak, 1994, p. 19). However, their ultimate impacts on the central government machine were less than sweeping (Halligan and Power, 1992, chapter 5). By the late 1990s, however, the Howard government was strongly advocating a familiar mix of downsizing and outsourcing in order to concentrate on 'core activities', more flexible and decentralized labour relations within the public service, stronger and more entrepreneurial public service leadership, and continuous benchmarking for performance improvement.

G. Party political ideas

By the time Labor came to power in 1983 there was a growing consensus that the public service elite had become too much of a 'law unto themselves', and there was an appetite (sharpened by the elite's long association with previous Liberal-National party govern-ments) for a reassertion of political direction. This generalized sense that the public service required reform was clearly illustrated in the incoming government's white paper on the public service (Commonwealth, 1983) and the 1984 Public Service Reform Act.

When, after a narrow victory in 1993, Labor's run of office came to an end in 1996, their National Party successors brought with them an at least equal suspicion of self-interested behaviour by the public service, combined with a stronger enthusiasm for privatization and the institution of market-type mechanisms within the public sector. As a minister in the Howard administration put it in 1997: 'It is important that the APS [Australian Public Service] takes what practices and experiences it usefully can from the private sector. We have often lagged behind private sector efficiencies, largely because we have lacked the edge of competition and the reality of meaningful performance targets' (Hawke, 1997, pp. 40–1).

H. Pressure from citizens

As with most other countries, there is no evidence of popular opinion demanding some specific and particular programme of management reform. Like elsewhere, however, some effect was probably felt from the public's unwillingness to continue putting up with poor service or bureaucratic obstructions. The Howard government (1996–) sometimes played on negative images of the public service to support its neo-conservative policies.

I. Elite perceptions of what management reforms were desirable

From 1983 onwards there was a consistent desire by the Labor governments (1983–96) and their National successor to assert full political control over the Australian public service. During the 1980s 'Managerialism offered both a new approach for directing the public service and a rationalisation for exerting greater political control' (Halligan, 1996b, p. 77). On the other hand, while the Labor politicians knew the direction in which they wanted to travel, they were not devotees of one particular model of reform: 'Australia has followed a more pragmatic mixture of principles and practice in contrast to the theory-driven reform in New Zealand' (Halligan, 1996b, p. 79). The Howard government, from 1996, was perhaps slightly more 'pure' in its doctrines, and vigorously espoused the neo-conservative ideas of downsizing, contracting out and privatizing.

J. Elite perceptions of what management reforms were feasible

The long period in office after 1983 meant that Labor politicians were able to build up confidence and knowledge in their reform efforts. Thus, for example, important new reforms were launched in 1987, after ministers had had some opportunity to observe what worked and what didn't in Canberra.

K. Chance events

None of great significance for public management reform.

L. The administrative system

At the beginning of our period (1980) the Australian Public Service remained in the classic 'Westminster' mode—separate political and mandarin careers, a strictly party-politically neutral, permanent career service, a near monopoly of policy advice to ministers, strongly hierarchical, high levels of unionization. As indicated in the following subsection (M), this 'Westminster model' has been extensively changed during the two following decades. Tenure is now less secure; the presence of partisan advisors within the system is much more extensive; levels of unionization—and the role of the unions—have been reduced; user-charging, quasi or actual contracts and outsourcing have extensively replaced administrative hierarchies.

M. Contents of the reform package

In 1983 the first priority of the new Labor government was 'to re-establish ministerial control and greater responsiveness to government policies and priorities' (Halligan, 1997, p. 31). This meant reform of the Australian public service so as to shift the balance of power between bureaucrats and politicians more in favour of the latter. Actions included a number of components which were designed to reduce the permanency of public servants, diversify sources of policy advice to ministers and increase both managerial competence and the responsiveness of public servants to the government's political priorities. A central vehicle for this was the creation of a Senior Executive Service (SES) as part of the 1984 Public Service Reform Act. The effects of this were not particularly radical to begin with, but when combined with the 1987 restructuring (see below) led to much more mobility and diversity in the upper reaches of the service.

Other key developments during the long Labor term of office from 1983 to 1996 included the following:

* 1983: launch of the Financial Management Improvement Program (FMIP), including strong elements of corporate management and programme budgeting, plus mandatory evaluation to 'close the loop' for a new system of results-oriented management (see Zifcak, 1994).
* 1984: Public Service Reform Act—creation of a Senior Executive Service. One aim was to make recruitment to senior public service appointments more open and competitive.
* 1987: Major restructuring of central departments. Twenty-eight portfolio ministries were

merged to produce sixteen large departments. In particular, 'mega' departments emerged with responsibility for Foreign Affairs and Trade, Education, Employment and Training and Transport and Communications. These changes forced a considerable reshuffling of senior posts. A Department of Administrative Services (DAS) was formed, which subsequently became associated with a strong drive to increase competition. Greater emphasis was also placed on creating a tighter regime for the Government Business Enterprises (GBEs)—the growing number of public sector units and activities which had been 'corporatized'. (Subsequently many of these were privatized—see below.)

* Late 1980s: beginnings of a sequence of significant sales of public sector assets, for example, Defence Service Homes Corporation (1988–90), Quantas airline (1992–95) and Common-wealth Bank (1994) (for more detail, see Halligan, 1996b, p. 34).
* 1993: Publication of the Hilmer Report, *National Competition Policy*, recommendations from which were subsequently embodied in an inter-governmental agreement to seek competitive neutrality (a 'level playing field') as between public and private sectors.
* 1997 Public Service Act, significantly 'deprivileging' the senior public service.
* Financial Management and Accountability Act, and launch of accruals budgeting project (moving accounting basis from cash to accruals by 2000).

N. The implementation process

Compared with countries such as the Netherlands or even the United States, the implementation of public management reforms in Australia looks to have been a fairly centralized process. Prime Ministers and the Department of Administrative Services have generally been able to get their way—although all such observations need to be taken in a context where the focus is principally on the Commonwealth government and not on the (independent) State level. Sometimes the style of implemenation has been gradual and incremental (as with much of FMIP), sometimes rapid and sweeping (as with the 1987 restructuring of departments). Most recently (since the advent of the Howard/National government in 1996) the implementation process has sometimes appeared so sudden and drastic as to be harsh. This, in turn, has generated unusually virulent opposition.

O. Reforms actually achieved

As indicated above, Australian governments not only carried through a series of significant public management reforms, they also committed themselves to a more extensive application of evaluation than did most of the other countries covered in this book. Thus, for example, the FMIP was subject to a series of evaluations, both internal and independent (Halligan, 1996b; Zifcak, 1994, pp. 96–9) and in 1992 the whole sweep of reforms was reviewed in an expensive and large-scale study (Task Force on Management Improvement, 1992).

The picture revealed by these and other studies is a mixed one. Real change has undoubtedly been achieved: the 'culture' of the public service has shifted; substantial state assets have been privatized; certain techniques such as user-charging, outsourcing and benchmarking have been widely applied; cost-consciousness and financial management skills have been considerably sharpened. The total size of the public service fell from 180,893 in 1986 (the peak year) to 143,305 in 1996, and is still falling (Halligan, 1997, p. 39).

On the other hand progress has often been significantly slower than had been envisaged by the progenitors of reform, and the costs of change have been high. For example, central finance divisions within departments were often reluctant to permit the degree of internal delegation of financial authority implied by the spirit of the FMIP. Or 'corporate planning floundered as a technique designed to enhance political and departmental strategy' (Zifcak, 1994, p. 110). The big 1992 evaluation by the Task Force on Management Improvement found that enthusiasm for many aspects of the reforms was much more pronounced at senior levels in the hierarchy than lower down, where considerable scepticism appears to have existed. By the late 1990s the downsizings and perceived anti-public service attitudes of the Howard government seemed to be generating disruption and severe morale problems.

AUSTRALIA

Country File Events: Australia

	General	Organization	Personnel	Finance
1981–1985	– Fraser: PM (Lib.) (1980) – Hawke: PM (Lab.) (1983) – 'Reforming the Australian Public Service' (APS) (1983) – Amendment of Public Service Act (1983)		– Access and Equity Programme (1985) – Merit Protection and Review Agency (MPRA) (1985)	– 'Budget Reform' (1984) – Financial Management Improvement Programme (FMIP) (1984)
1986–1990	– 'APS2000' (1989) – Hawke: PM (Lab.) (1990)	– From 28 to 16 Dpts (1987) – Efficiency Scrutiny Unit (1987) – Government Business Enterprises: reform (1987) – Management Advisory Board (MAB) (1987) – Management Improvement Advisory Committee (MIAC) (1989)	– Public Service Board abolished (1987) – Public Service Commission PSC (1987) – Devolve to Dpts (1987) – Guidelines on Official Conduct of Commonwealth Public Servants (1987) – Wage agreement based on Structural Efficiency Principle (1988) – Equal Employment Opportunity: Further Steps Forward Strategy (1989) – Access and Equity Strategy (1989) – Performance Appraisal Programme for Senior Executive Service (1989) – Joint APS Training Council (1990) – Guidelines for appraisal of performance of SEO (1990)	– 2nd Review FMIP (1988) – Programme Management and Budgeting (1988) – Regulations on Purchasing: revised (1989) – 3rd Review FMIP (Not Dollars Alone) (1990) – Purchasing Development Centre (1990)

Country File Events: Australia (*cont.*):

	General	Organization	Personnel	Finance
1991–1995	– Keating: PM (Lab.) (1991) – MAB/MIAC publications series (1991) – Code for handling conflict of interests (1991) – Unions–Government Framework Agreement (1992) – Keating: PM (Lab.) (1993) – 'Ongoing reform in the APS' (1994) – Principles and Guidelines for National Standard Setting and Regulatory Action (Council of Australian Governments) (1994) – National Competition Agreement (1994) – 'Review of the Public Service Act Report' (1995)	– MAB: launch 'Evaluation of Management Improvement' (1992) – Industry Commission: Benchmarking of Performance (1992) – PSC and MPRA merge into PSMPC (1994) – Privatization of Qantas and Aero Space Technologies (1995) – Reshuffling of Dpts (1995)	– Access and Equity Strategy: evaluated (1991) – Middle Management Development Programme (1991) – Framework for HRM (1992) – Strategic Plan for Equal Employment Opportunities (PSC) (1992) – Improving Productivity, Jobs and Pay in the APS 1992–94 (agency workplace bargaining) (1992) – Central Redeployment Unit (1993) – Guidelines on Official Conduct of Commonwealth Public Servants (1993) – Public Service Act: amended (choice: tenure or fixed-term appointment) (1994) – Guidelines on Official Conduct of Public Servants: revised (1995)	– Announcement of accrual accounting (1992) – Revised requirements for departmental annual reporting (1993) – Develop generic performance measures (1993) – Audit Act (1994): Financial Management and Accountability Bill; Commonwealth Authorities and Companies Bill; Auditor-General Bill – New Fraud Control Arrangements (1994) – Present Commonwealth budget in May rather than August (1994) – Efficiency dividend arrangements (1%) after signing Property Resource Agreement (1994)

| 1996–1998 | – Howard: PM (Lib.) (1996)
– Several MAB/MIAC projects on costs, risk, ethics, benchmarking (1996) | – Small Business Deregulation Task Force (1996)
– Competitive Tendering and Contracting (CTC) (1997) | – Workplace Relations Act (1996)
– Public Service Bill (1997): Apolitical public service; new legal employment framework; rights and obligations | – Finance Information on Resource Management (FIRM) (1996)
– Charter of Budget Honesty (1997)
– Financial Management and Accountability Act (FMA) (1997–98):
– The Commonwealth Authorities and Companies Act (CAC) (1997–98)
– Auditor General Act (1997–98)
– Accrual Budgeting Project (1997–2000): from cash to accrual; extension of performance measurement system
– Accrual Information Management System (AIMS) (1998) |

CANADA

A. Socio-economic forces: general

See Section A.2 and Table A.1 (above).

B. Global economic forces

Again, see references to Canada in Section A.2 and Table A.1.

C. Socio-demographic issues

For general picture, see Section A.3 and Figures A.1 and A.2, and Tables A.2 and A.3. Canada is rapidly becoming multi-ethnic and multi-cultural—partly through immigration. By 1991 the number of Canadians whose first language was neither French nor English reached 4.1M (out of a population of 29.2M). 626,000 defined themselves as belonging to one of the three recognized aboriginal groups. Canada, like other advanced industrial economies, is also getting older. Between 1961 and 1991 the number of citizens aged 65 and over increased 128 per cent, to 3.2M. Canada also has a relatively high divorce rate (2.8 per 1,000 population in 1992) and 60 per cent of female-headed single-parent families fell below the official low income cut-off (Statistics Canada, 1995).

D. National socio-economic policies

Relative to OECD averages, Canada suffered a disappointing economic performance during the 1980s. Control of public spending was a particular weakness. During the Mulroney administration (1984–93) public spending targets were repeatedly set and then missed. Between 1984 and 1993 the net public debt increased from $C168 billion to $C508 billion (Harder and Lindquist, 1997, pp. 80–1). However, the Chrétien administration (1993-?) largely met its expenditure reduction targets, and promised that the balanced budget of 1997/98 (the first for thirty years) would be maintained for at least a further two years.

E. The political system

Canada, like Australia, is a federal state with a 'Westminster' system (i.e., a first past the post electoral system, disciplined parties and strong, majoritarian governments). However, a simple picture of single-minded centralism would be quite inaccurate:

In a country consisting of two 'founding' linguistic groups, four or five distinct regions, and the usual cleavages between classes and other divisions characteristic of all modern societies, a governing party must try to accommodate a representation of as many interests as possible. Aboriginals, historically marginalised in the political process, are also becoming contenders in the system . . . (Mallory, 1997, p. 16).

During the nineteenth and early twentieth century central government appeared to dominate most of the significant governmental functions, but the growth of the welfare state shifted the balance in favour of provinicial and local governments. Agreements between federal and provincial governments became more and more essential for policy progress on many items, but during the 1980s the political conditions for stable multi-level agreements of this kind became less readily available.

Although in many ways a more 'state-centred' and even 'state-trusting' society than its US neighbour, there is also a widespread popular suspicion of the Ottawa political elite. The underpinnings of federal authority have been eroded from several directions:

the whole system of government in Canada is beset by a number of forces which tend to undermine it. These include a pervasive anti-elitism and populism which undermines the authority of government and thus its will to deal with issues, a pervasive and exaggerated fear of mounting public debt and public bankruptcy, and a threat to the survival of the system by the danger of Quebec separation accompanied by serious regional discontent which could of itself lead to the dissolution of the union. All these threats to survival have occurred in the past, and have been successfully surmounted. This time they seem to have all come together. But one should not underestimate the enormous inertia of the system, as well as its flexibility, which may well ensure its survival and its capacity to adjust (Mallory, 1997, p. 23)

F. New management ideas

It is clear that Canadian ministers and senior officials were well aware of the currents of new management thinking which were flowing through the Anglophone world from the late 1970s onwards. Mulroney's administration (1984–93) made extensive use of business people and also 'borrowed'—at least in part—a number of public management reform ideas from the USA and the UK. Mulroney's own rhetoric mirrored the anti-bureaucratic, pro-private-sector tone of Thatcher and Reagan (Savoie, 1994).

Just three examples will have to suffice. First, the Nielsen task force set up in 1984 took about half its members from the business community, and Nielsen himself was conscious of borrowing from Raynerism (UK) and the Grace Commission (USA) (Savoie, 1994, pp. 127–30). Second, the creation of politically-sympathetic chiefs of staff in each department drew something from the US 'spoils system', and more specifically from President Reagan's expansion of that system during the the the early 1980s. The basic idea was to give ministers greater assistance in the task of getting the permanent bureaucracy to do their bidding. Third, the Special Operating Agency programme, which was announced in 1989, obviously gained something from the UK Next Steps programme which had been widely publicized in the previous year (although the Canadian agencies were given significantly less freedom than their UK equivalents).

Under the Liberal administration from 1993 the public service regained some of its self-confidence, and by 1998 the Clerk to the Privy Council (the most senior civil servant) felt able to proclaim a 'Canadian model' of public management reform. This included a rejection of the proposal that minimizing government was always a good thing and an embracing of experiment and diversity in organizational forms (Bourgon, 1998).

G. Party political ideas

The decisive shift towards public management reform came (as in the UK and the USA) when a right-wing government was elected in place of a somewhat 'worn out' centre-left government (in the Canadian case, Trudeau's Liberal government). Mulroney's Progressive Conservative administration was imbued with anti-bureaucratic rhetoric and carried with it a general suspicion of the established bureaucracy and its seemingly close previous relationships with long-standing Liberal governments. However, although the incoming administration had plenty of generalized prejudices against bureaucracy and in favour of private sector dynamism, there is no evidence that it had any well-worked-out scheme for public management reform, or any coherent set of operationalized ideas on which to base such a plan.

The popularity of private sector management concepts faded somewhat during the long life of the Mulroney government, and were certainly less to the fore during the succeeding, more 'state-friendly' Liberal government. It is not clear that Chrétien's regime had any distinct plan of conception for management reform *per se*, but it was determined to bring expenditure under control and to try to link that to a more positive agenda of modernization and developing alternative modes of public service delivery. Most of the specific ideas, however, seem to have come from the senior bureaucrats themselves.

H. Pressure from citizens

As elsewhere, citizens in Canada did not rush forward with specific proposals for management reform. However, a perceived dissatisfaction with government, and alleged citizen demands for greater accountability, were certainly a factor mentioned by executive politicians and senior officials as one reason for public management reform (e.g. Foreword to President of the Treasury Board, 1997).

It is important to disentangle the various strands and dimensions of citizen opinion, for example, by distinguishing the satisfaction levels of service users with a particular service from more general citizen views of the competence or trustworthiness of government at large (Canadian Centre for Management Development, 1998a). Much of the expressed distrust of government in general appears to have been focused on politicians and on government in general, with public servants being regarded with greater confidence. Furthermore, when due allowance for differences were made, user satisfaction levels with many public services were not systematically worse than with private sector services (Canadian Centre for Management Development, 1998b).

I. Elite perceptions of what management reforms are desirable

See Section G, above. The Mulroney administration developed a series of specific initiatives on the basis of some generalized attitudes and prejudices, but there does not seem to have been any coherent overall plan. Even the specific initiatives that were launched frequently encountered implementation difficulties (see Sections M and N below).

After the fall of the Progressive Conservative administration in 1993 there was a shift in ministerial preferences. More emphasis was now placed on finding creative forms of 'Alternative Service Delivery', on partnership operations with the provinces, on shrewd use of advanced information technology and on more transparent accounting to Parliament for results (Aucoin and Savoie, 1998; President of the Treasury Board, 1997).

J. Elite perceptions of what management reforms are feasible

Here Canadian ministers and officials had to temper their enthusiasm for particular directions of reform with a recognition of the complex, multi-level, sectoralized nature of the political and administrative systems. They did not enjoy the powers of (say) New Zealand or UK prime ministers to drive through major reforms even against significant opposition. The picture of the 'Canadian model' drawn by the Secretary to the Privy Council (Bourgon, 1998) is essentially incremental and anti-doctrinal. It speaks of reform being carried out 'calmly, competently, without much fanfare' (ibid., p. 1). Considerable stress is laid on sharing and co-operation with the provinces.

K. Chance events

Several chance events appear to have had some influence over the trajectory of management reform. One was the dropping of Erik Nielsen from the Mulroney cabinet in mid-1986—for reasons unconnected with his leadership of the programme review task force. This cannot have helped the implementation of the still-new report, which afterwards largely faded away. A second coincidence, of rather larger impact, was the Mexican currency crisis of late 1994, which by all accounts helped significantly strengthen the determination of the Chrétien cabinet to push ahead with the downsizings and programme adjustments of the Program Review exercise, in case Canada became the next state to suffer currency 'meltdown' (Aucoin and Savoie, 1998).

L. The administrative system

In February 1997 there were 24 departments, 37 crown corporations and at least 48 other service organizations responsible to federal ministers. Total employment was 370,000 FTEs. A strong form of ministerial responsibility prevails (ministers responsible for all the actions of their 'portfolio' of departments, crown corporations, service agencies, tribunals, etc., no 'accounting officers' along UK lines).

Within this ensemble the central agencies have remained relatively large and influential. The main ones are the Privy Council Office (approximately 300 staff), the Treasury Board Secretariat (800), the Department of Finance (700), the Prime Minister's Office (80) and the Public Service Commission (2,000) (Savoie, 1997). Management reforms tend to be led by the Privy Council Office and the Treasury Board Secretariat.

The public service itself is non-partisan, and Deputy Ministers (the chief officials in the departments) usually remain in place when the government changes. Nearly all Deputy Ministers are career civil servants. There is quite a strong 'mandarin culture', with considerable horizontal communication between senior civil servants in different departments (Bourgault and Carroll, 1997, p. 97)

M. Contents of the reform package

From a bird's-eye view the recent history of management reforms in the Canadian federal administration appears as a bewildering series of over-lapping and only loosely co-ordinated intiatives, many of which seem to fade away or lose momentum after a relatively short time. Several commentators confirm that—certainly under the Mulroney administrations of 1984–93—the political leadership lacked any 'grand design' and gave management issues only intermittent attention (documented in Savoie, 1994).

Mulroney came to power following a campaign which had been sharply critical of 'big government' in Ottawa, and which had promised greater 'frugality' and radical changes in the the bureaucracy. He was re-elected in 1988 and finally lost office in 1993. During his period in power he launched a number of initiatives, including:

• A 1984 review, under Deputy Prime Minister Erik Nielsen, of existing government programmes, to make them 'simple, more understandable and more accessible to their clientele', as

well as to decentralize them and cut out programmes for which there was not a demonstrable need.
- The creation, in each ministry, of a politically appointed chief-of-staff position at assistant deputy minister level (i.e. the second highest civil service grade).
- A target of a 15,000 downsizing of the civil service within six years.
- The 1985 Increased Ministerial Authority and Accountability initiative (IMAA). This was designed to give individual ministers and departmental managers greater flexibility in allocating and reallocating resources within their departments (partly by reducing the detailed control of central agencies). One part of this was the creation of Treasury Board Memoranda of Understanding (MOUs) which were supposed to provide greater freedoms to departments which negotiated them with the Treasury Board.
- From 1986, a 'make or buy' policy to encourage competitive tendering for public services.
- Also from 1986, the establishment of a privatization office.
- The 1988 establishment of the Canadian Centre for Management Development (CCMD), to strengthen management training for the Canadian public service.
- It was decided that Deputy Ministers (the most senior civil servants) could henceforth be called before Parliamentary committees for questioning (Bourgault and Carroll, 1997, p. 3).
- The effective scrapping of the previous Policy and Expenditure Management System (PEMS) and its replacement, from 1989, with a new system of cabinet committees, centred upon an Expenditure Review Committee (ERC).
- A high-profile, broad-scope exercise entitled Public Service 2000 (PS 2000), which was to empower civil servants, cut red tape and improve service to the public. PS 2000 was announced in December 1989. In 1990 a white paper *The renewal of the public service in Canada* was published.
- The creation of a new type of decentralized agency, the Special Operating Agency (SOA), which was to enjoy greater managerial flexibility, whilst remaining within the framework of ministerial departments. The first five SOAs were announced in December 1989.
- The idea of Shared Management Agendas (SMAs), which evolved alongside PS 2000. These were agreements between the Treasury Board and Deputy Ministers in departments to identify the top management priorities for the forthcoming twelve months.

Further reforms followed the fall of the Mulroney administration in March 1993. Some of the more significant were:

1993: Service Standards Initiative, to encourage departments and agencies to develop and publish service standards. By 1995 two-thirds of departments were said to be well advanced in this exercise.

June 1993: a radical restructuring of the machinery of central government by Mulroney's Progressive Conservative successor, Kim Campbell. The size of the Cabinet was reduced from 35 to 23 and a number of departments were merged or eliminated.

Campbell's government was short-lived. In October 1993 the Liberals, under Jean Chrétien, returned to power.

February 1994: a process of Program Review was launched. Unlike some previous expenditure reduction exercises this one was able to mobilize considerable collective support within Cabinet, and was carried through to implementation in the 1995 and subsequent budgets. It went beyond simple cost-cutting and entailed a broad reconsideration and prioritization of the role of the federal government in Canadian society (Aucoin and Savoie, 1998)

February 1995: a new Expenditure Management System (EMS) was introduced which considerably tightened the previous approach to the use of budgetary reserves. Under EMS it is assumed that all new programmes and programme increases will have to be financed by reallocations within departments' budgetary envelopes. The government also committed itself to the introduction of full accruals accounting.

June 1995: a Quality Services Initiative approved by Cabinet. Aimed at increasing measured client satisfaction.

1996: introduction of Improved Reporting to Parliament system (IRPP) with the aim of enhancing the accountability of ministers and departments to Parliament.

1996: Secretary to the Privy Council launched an initiative named *La Relève* designed to tackle what was said to be a 'quiet crisis' in the Canadian public service. 'This was the result of years of downsizing and pay freezes, criticism, insufficient recruitment, and the premature departure of experienced public servants' (Bourgon, 1998, p. 18). Initiatives were invited from departments to revitalize the public service.

1997: Publication of *Accounting for results* (President of the Treasury Board, 1997) which for the first time brought together results statements for all departments.

N. The implementation process

The implementation process in Canada appears to have been a somewhat uncertain one, at least in the sense that a number of the initiatives petered out after a relatively short period, leaving only traces rather than the significant achievements that had been predicted at the time of their initiations. Even the Canadian government's own account, as published in a recent OECD text, concedes that 'use of performance measures has been uneven, with departments and agencies having considerable discretion over their development and use' (OECD, 1997a, p. 39).

Examples of such disappointments include:

- 'Notwithstanding its early support, the Mulroney government did not follow through on the great majority of the Nielsen recommendations . . . Indeed, the great majority of programs reviewed are still in place and virtually intact' (Savoie, 1994, p. 130).
- The 'make-or-buy' policy of 1986 did not make much progress beyond the pilot project phase, and was abandoned in 1990.
- Despite the early development of a privatization plan, substantive progress on this policy had dwindled to rather little by 1987. The Department of Finance insisted that revenues from privatization sales should go into the Consolidated Revenue Fund, and departmental ministers became increasingly resistant to 'losing' 'their' crown corporations or subsidiaries.
- The success of IMAA was limited. Six years after its introduction only about one third of departments had agreed to sign an MOU with the Treasury Board, and those that did sometimes complained of a mass of paperwork for only limited real autonomy.
- 'Even its most ardent supporter admits that PS 2000 is not living up to expectations' (Savoie, 1994, p. 241). The expectation that central agencies would be cut back was not fulfilled. There was a widespread perception that PS 2000 remained a top-down exercise which produced more reports than action.
- Mulroney's programme for downsizing the civil service produced a reduction of only 15,000 and about half these positions were actually transferred to provincial governments or other parts of the public sector (Savoie, 1994, pp. 266–7).
- 'Although the experiences with SOAs have been positive, it is not clear whether they are sufficiently different from traditional departments to support flexible and innovative service delivery' (OECD, 1997, p. 44).
- During the 1980s 'governments became increasingly pre-occupied with the deficit and the debt, but were unable to come to grips with it. The period was characterized by unachievable

deficit reduction targets and regular across-the-board cuts, primarily targeted at operations' (Harder and Lindquist, 1997, p. 80). Net public debt increased from $168 billion in 1984 to $508 billion in 1993.

After 1994 conditions for implementation improved somewhat. The Canadian economy began to improve, and a very experienced Prime Minister (Chrétien) was able to establish a relatively disciplined Cabinet. The 1994 Program Review exercise and the 1995 budget were generally regarded as successful exercises. It remains to be seen how long this new stability can be maintained. There also remains a doubt about the connections between the higher levels of the federal government—especially the central agencies—and 'middle management' in the operational agencies and the departments. Reforms may achieve agreement at the top, but to what extent is implementation 'owned' by those outside Ottawa?

O. Reforms actually achieved

There has been no systematic evaluation of public management reform in Canada during this period, although there have been a number of specific reviews or assessments of particular initiatives. Notable among these have been the sometimes sharply critical reports of the Auditor General (e.g., Auditor General of Canada, 1993, 1997).

As indicated above (N), it appears that Canada suffers (or, at least, suffered) from a significant 'implementation gap', with many initiatives failing to meet anything like their full expectations. The 1994 Program Review exercise, thanks to a favourable set of political circumstances surrounding its launch, appears to be an important exception to this, but it would be optimistic to expect such circumstances to continue indefinitely (Aucoin and Savoie, 1998).

CANADA

Country File Events: Canada

	General	Organization	Personnel	Finance
1981–1985	– Trudeau: PM (Lib.) (1980) – Turner: PM (Lib.) (1984) – Mulroney: PM (Progr. Cons.) (1984) – Focus on reducing public expenditure (1984) – Increased Ministerial Authority and Accountability (IMAA) (1986)	– Office of Privatization and Regulatory Affairs (OPRA) (1986)	– Creation of a 'Management Category' (1981)	– Policy and Expenditure Management System (PEMS): Multi-Year Revenue Expenditure Plan, Multi-Year Operational Plan (MYOP) (programmes with activities) (1981)
1986–1990	– 'Public Service 2000'-initiative (1989) – 'Enterprising Management' (on IMAA) (1989) – Public Service 2000 White Paper (1990) – Service standards and client surveys (1990)	– Canadian Centre for Management Development (CCMD) (1988) – Treasury Board Senior Advisory Committee: re-established (1989) – Special Operating Agencies (SOA) (1989)	– Personnel Management Manual: streamlined (1989) – Administrative Policy Manual: consolidated (1989) – Human Resources Development Council (HRDC) (1990) – Management Trainee Programme (1990)	– Memoranda of Understanding (MOU) (3 Year: Performance Indicators, targets, expectations, accountability) (1988)
1991–1995	– Budgetary measures (1991) – Government's Economic Statement: cuts and freezes (1992) – Public Service 2000: Progress Report (1992) – Co-location of related federal government services (1992) – Review of regulatory regimes (1992)	– OPRA functions to DoF and Treasury Board Secretariat (TBS) (1991) – Dpts: from 32 to 24 (1993) – Cabinet Members: from 35 to 23 (1993) – Cabinet Committees from 11 to 4 (1993) – Blueprint for Renewing Government Services Using Information Technology	– Public Service Reform Act: amended (1992): Public Service Employment Act; Public Service Staff Relations Act	– Shared Management Agenda (SMA) (deputy ministers, TBS, Comptroller General) (1991) – 12 operating budgets (1991) – Public Service Reform Act: amended (1992): Financial Administration Act; Surplus Crown Assets Act – Expenditure Management System (EMS) (1994): Improved Reporting to Parliament

Country File Events: Canada (*cont.*)

General	Organization	Personnel	Finance
– Campbell: PM (Progr. Cons.) (1993) – Chrétien: PM (lib.) (1993) – Budget cuts (1994) – 2nd Annual Report on the Public Service (1994) – Efficiency of the Federation Initiative (1994) – Declaration of Service Quality (1994) – Deputy Ministers Task Forces (1995):Future of Public Service; Service Delivery Models; Federal Presence; Overhead Services; Value Ethics; Policy Planning and Horizontal Issues – 3rd Report (1995) – Quality Service Initiative (1995)	– (1994) – Intergovernmental and interdepartmental co-operation: Canada Business Service Centres (1994) – Alternative Service Delivery (ASD) (1995)		Project (IRPP): Performance Reports and Reports on Plans and Priorities – Business Plans replace MYOP – Government Wide Performance Reporting – Reviews (1994): Program Review; Agency Review; Review of major sectors and horizontal activities; Internal Audits – Annual Strategic Planning Cycle (1994) – Service standards for major business lines required (1995)

| 1996–1998 | – Policy Research Committee established: interdep. Group of Ass. Deputy Ministers (1996)
– 'Getting Government Right' (1996, 1997)
– Policy Research Secretariat established (1997): co-ordinate interdep. research networks
– First balanced budget since 1969 (1997–98)
– Fifth Annual Report to the PM on the Public Service of Canada (1998) | – Canadian Food Inspection Agency (1997) | – 'La Relève: A Commitment to Action' (1997)
– Replace 'La Relève Task Force' by 'The Leadership Network' (1998) | – Continuation of EMS (1996)
– President of Treasury Board's Second Annual Report on Review (1996)
– All federal Dpts and agencies: Performance Reports (1997)
– President of Treasury Board's Third Annual Report: Accounting for Results (1997)
– Financial Information Strategy (FIS): accrual accounting, upgrading financial management (1997)
– Planning Reporting Accountability Structure (PRAS): Dpts with business lines (1997)
– 80 federal Dpts and agencies: Reports on Plans and Priorities (1998) |

FINLAND

A. Socio-economic forces: general

See Table A.1 and discussion in Section A.2 (above).

B. Global economic forces

See Table A.1 and discussion in Section A.2 (above). Note that the Table refers to 1996, and that the previous five years were, for Finland, an unusually adverse period economically (see Section D, below)

C. Socio-demographic issues

See Tables A.2 and A.3 and Figures A.1 and A.2 above. Finland shares most of the problems of an ageing population that are present in the rest of Western Europe. Generally speaking Finnish society is relatively homogenous and peaceful. There is a different ethnic group (the *Saami* people) in the far north (Lapland) but their numbers are small, and their significance for a study of the reform of central government limited.

D. National socio-economic policies

Finland enjoyed a good growth rate and relatively low unemployment through most of the 1980s. From 1991, however, the sudden collapse of trade with its neighbour, the Soviet Union, together with the more general recession in the West, sparked a severe economic crisis. Trade fell, banks got into great difficulties, unemployment soared to unprecedented heights (18.4 per cent in 1994). Between 1990 and 1993 GDP volume fell by 12 per cent. Faced with these problems, central government launched a strong programme of budgetary reform and restraint. By 1997 growth had returned, budgetary discipline was maintained and Finland was able fully to satisfy the Maastricht 'convergence criteria' for EU monetary union. Unfortunately, unemployment never returned to its 1980s levels at the end of the 1990s.

E. The political system

Finland is a unitary state, though with a strong tradition of relatively autonomous municipal government, protected by the constitution (like Sweden). The basic pieces of legislation are the Constitution Act (1919) and the Parliament Act (1928). There is a multi-party political system and governments are usually coalitions. The Cabinet acts collegially, with the Prime Minister having less personal prominence than in the 'Westminster' systems of the UK and New Zealand. Formally the power of execution lies with a Council of State, consisting of government ministers and the Chancellor of Justice. There is a President, who is elected every six years, retains some responsibility for foreign policy and is commander-in-chief of the armed forces. In general it might be said that the Finnish President, while considerably more active and politically powerful than his/her German counterpart, is also nothing like as dominant as the French President.

The legislature (*Eduskunta*) is unicameral, with 200 seats. Eighty per cent of MPs tend also to be municipal politicians—so the interests of the municipalities are strongly represented at the centre. The three big parties in recent years have been the Social Democrats, the National Coalition (conservatives) and the Centre Party (originally an agrarian party). The reforming coalitions since the late 1980s have been led by the National Coalition (Holkeri, 1987–91), the Centre Party (Aho, 1991–95) and the the Social Democrats (Lipponen's 'Rainbow Coalition', 1995–99). The Communist Party was a significant political force during the 1960s and 1970s, but has since lost most of its strength.

F. New management ideas

Finland has been an active member of many international organizations, both governmental and academic (e.g., PUMA, European Group for Public Administration). In that sense it has been open to and acquainted with the full range of contemporary management concepts and techniques as applied to the public sector. However, it has not slavishly followed fashions but rather carefully selected and piloted those ideas considered suitable for Finnish needs. To take two examples, TQM and ISO 9000 approaches to service quality improvement were widely adopted in Finnish local government (Association of Finnish Local Authorities, 1995a, b) and, in central government, accruals accounting practices in other countries were closely studied but then only partly adopted. What has been notable, however, is that Finnish central government has not made intensive use of consultants or other 'outsiders' to implement reform (in the way that occurred in, say, the UK). Consultants have been used to gather information, but actual implementation has remained, for the most part, firmly in the hands of career civil servants.

G. Party political ideas

Party political ideas *per se* have not had a big influence on public management reform in Finland. On the contrary, reforms have been mainly the work of a fairly small elite of senior civil servants and a few politicians. Media interest in the reforms has not been particularly strong either (Ministry of Finance, 1997, pp. 73 and 81). Finland did not experience strongly ideological governments with strong views about changing the role of the state in the way that the USA did under President Reagan or the UK under Prime Minister Thatcher.

H. Pressure from citizens

We are not aware of any evidence pointing to sustained pressure for specific reforms from the Finnish public—or, indeed, for reversal of any of the changes which have been implemented (see Section G, above). During the 1980s and 1990s public attitudes towards the state appear to have been mixed. On the one hand, 'Finns are a people very loyal to the state, who see change as a governmental process rather than a grass root level reform of the society' (Centre for Finnish Business and Policy Studies, 1996, p. 2). The radically anti-state attitudes which are common in the USA are rare in the Nordic countries. On the other hand there have been a limited number of instances where popular discontent has been manifested over specific aspects of the changes—for example, over the closure of some small rural post offices and the substitution of postal counters in local shops. Senior officials are aware of the dangers of loss of legitimacy (Ministry of Finance, 1997, p. 82) and some of them believe that administrative modernization, including improvements in the quality of services, openness to greater citizen participation and visible efficiency will help contribute to sustaining political stability and trust (*High quality services, good governance and a responsible civic society*, 1998a, b).

I. Elite perceptions of what management reforms were desirable

The process by which Finnish reforms came into being was quite long drawn-out and cautious. It was not a matter of a few individuals passionately advocating specific 'solutions' (which would be unusual anyway within the Finnish politico-administrative culture), but rather the gradual, consensual formation of a set of proposals for streamlining the state apparatus and, after 1991, for restraining expenditures in response to the sudden economic downturn. Within this process some central themes were the lightening of the bureaucratic 'weight' of central government (especially by reforming the national-level agencies); a shift from input budgeting to a stronger focus on results; a parallel shift to frame (block) budgeting for central transfers to municipalities; a commitment to service quality improvement and some measure of decentralization. Thus, for example, 'the goal is to create a single-level central government; in the central administration only the ministries will in general exercise administrative authority vis a vis lower levels' (*General principles and special instructions on payments by results within the state system*, 1994, p. 5).

In the late 1990s there was some thinking by senior civil servants about the possibility of a fairly comprehensive restructuring of central government into different relational categories (e.g., organizations where the government was principally exercising the interests of an owner, organizations where the government's interest was as a direct service provider, and so on). However, although schemes were produced for internal discussion, the policy guidelines which were eventually adopted were considerably less ambitious than this, and were in some ways quite vague (*High quality services, good governance and a responsible civil society*, 1998a).

J. Elite perceptions of what management reforms were feasible

Desirability and feasibility perhaps seem closer together in Finland than some other countries, in the sense that habits of thought of most reformers are so pervasively imbued with a sensitivity to the consensual process, and to coalition government, that not a lot of time is wasted dreaming of sweeping initiatives of a highly sectional or doctrinaire nature. The main themes were as indicated in the previous section (I), and implementation of reforms along these lines was considered perfectly feasible. The Ministries of Finance and the Interior were well equipped to implement the ideas that had been worked out, and technical and other problems were often explored through the device of pilot projects that were run before a reform was rolled out to the whole of government.

It should be noted, however, that the independence and political strength of the municipalities meant that it was not feasible for Finnish central government to intervene in the reform of local government to the same extent as occurred in the UK.

K. Chance events

One might argue that the collapse of the Soviet Union had a significant, if indirect influence on public management reform. By triggering economic crisis it strengthened the hand of reformers, particularly with respect to budgetary reform (e.g., the rapid implementation of frame budgeting was seen as a vital part of regaining control of public spending). But most of the reforms (e.g., results-oriented budgeting) were already firmly on the agenda, before the economic downturn.

L. The administrative system

For many years Finland, like Sweden, had an administrative system consisting of ministries, national-level agencies with considerable powers of rule-making and detailed intervention, and a municipal level. However, in the mid-1990s the agency level was subject to fairly fundamental reform, shrinking its size and numbers and reorienting its role away from detailed regulation (Ministry of Finance, 1995, pp. 1–2—see also Section M below). It should be noted that, although this account is focused principally on the central state, local (municipal) government employs roughly three quarters of the public sector workforce.

The population of central ministries has been fairly stable over the past two decades. In the 1990s there were twelve ministries and the Prime Minister's Office, which itself has the status of a ministry (Prime Minister's Office and Ministries, 1995). The Ministries of Finance and the Interior are the two with the most important responsibilities for administrative reform.

Traditionally each ministry has independent responsibility for implementation and control of laws and policies within their own sphere so, although the Ministry of Finance may be, in some general sense, the most 'powerful' ministry, it usually cannot impose its own programmes on other ministries to the degree that has occasionally been possible in more centralized systems such as that in France, New Zealand or the UK.

There is a career civil service, and political and 'mandarin' careers are usually separate. However, some of the top three levels of civil service appointment go to known sympathizers with particular political parties, according to a kind of informal 'quota' system (Tiihonen, 1996, p. 40). In the past senior Finnish civil servants were mainly lawyers, but this balance has shifted somewhat over the past generation, with more people with a training in economics or the social sciences being recruited into senior posts. Public management reform has been mainly an 'insider' process, with senior civil servants playing a crucial role. External consultants, although used for certain purposes, have not been as influential as in, say, the UK or the USA (Ministry of Finance, 1997, p. 74).

M. The contents of the reform package

There was much internal discussion of reform during the early and mid-1980s, but the first major initiatives came with the arrival in office of the Holkeri government in 1987. The subsequent decade was then a busy one, with several main lines of reform unfolding simultaneously or in sequence. The two changes of government (1991 and 1995) did not appear to make any dramatic difference to the general thrust of the reforms, although possibly it could be said that the level of political interest in management reform (never overwhelmingly high among the majority of politicians) declined somewhat after 1994.

The main lines of reform were as follows (See the pamphlet *Government decision in principle on reforms in central and regional government*, 1993):

- Results-oriented budgeting was piloted from 1987 and rolled out to the whole government from 1994. This required a number of potentially important changes including the definition of results indicators for agencies (to enable their performance to be assessed more explicitly by their 'parent' ministries) and the creation of unified running costs budgets for ministries and agencies. The pilot projects appeared to show that significant running cost savings could be achieved, but that some ministries were slow to take up the challenge of using indicators as an active form of performance management (Summa, 1995).

* An Administrative Development Agency (later retitled the Finnish Institute of Public Management) was set up in 1987 to provide training and consultancy to support reform. The Agency/Institute has been obliged to operate along increasingly commercial/self-financing lines.
* The transformation of a number of agencies with commercial functions into, first, State Enterprises (twelve were created 1989–97) and then, subsequently and in some cases, State-Owned Companies. The law enabling the creation of State Enterprises was passed in 1988. The further transformation to state-owned joint stock companies included Post and Telecommunications and Railways.
* The introduction from 1993 of a framework budgeting system to control central government aid to municipalities. This was partly a decentralization measure, aimed at reducing the amount of detailed central intervention in municipal decision making, but it was also a way of gaining firm control of the *totals* of municipal spending at a time of great budgetary pressure, and of delegating painful decisions about spending priorities down to municipal leaders. The total aid going to a given municipality was henceforth calculated as a lump sum based on the values taken by certain indicators, such as the number and age structure of the population. At the time of writing this system was being further developed into a strategic management system: 'Framework management will be developed into a central procedure steering the preparation of the State budget by the government' (*High quality services, good governance and a responsible civic society*, 1998a, p. 10).
* A restructuring of the central agencies. This was also a decentralization measure. The agencies with commercial functions were turned into State Enterprises (see above). Others were merged or downsized, and their role was changed from that of regulation to one of providing research and development and evaluation to the ministries. Their internal governance structures were also changed—usually away from collegial forms towards more managerial and/or monocratic arrangements.
* Government data collection streamlined and barriers to data transfer between different parts of the state reduced.
* Regional state administration unified and lightened. Combining the offices of different ministries at regional level
* Human Resource Management Reforms, including provision for performance-related pay and for more decentralized management of staff. The main decisions and announcements here were made during the Aho administration (1991–95) but subsequent implementation has been quite slow.
* In 1998 it was announced that 'The quality as well as the citizen- and customer-orientation of the services will be developed by means of a new type of Service Charters to be given to the customers' [*sic*] (*High quality services, good governance and a responsible civic society*, 1998a, p. 15).

Thus the balance of the reforms leant towards decentralization, simplification and tighter control of spending (Ministry of Finance, 1993; Puoskari, 1996). There was no great enthusiasm for widespread privatization, although the Finnish governments were quite prepared to privatize selectively, when it seemed to make sense on its own terms (e.g., the government printing company).

N. The implementation process

Overall, the implementation process has been gradual and deliberate, with pilot projects and extensive training programmes to ensure the smoothest possible implementation. One does not get the sense of the hectic pace and urgency which undoubtedly prevailed during, say, 1986–92 in New Zealand or 1987–92 in the UK.

At the highest level the co-ordination of the reform programme was ensured by the creation of a ministerial committee on which all the main political parties in government were represented (Ministry of Finance, 1997, p. 69). Stability was also enhanced by the long-term participation of a small number of senior civil servants from the Ministry of Finance and the Ministry of the Interior. One Finnish commentator went so far as to term the Finnish approach 'technocratic' (Puoskari, 1996, p. 105).

O. Reforms actually achieved

The reforms mentioned above (Section M) were all 'achieved', in the sense that relevant legislation was passed and new procedures were put in place. What is harder to determine is how vigorously the originally announced aims of the reforms were pursued, and how far they were eventually achieved. In some cases (e.g., corporatization of former agencies into enterprises and then state-owned companies) change has been undeniable and quite rapid. In others (e.g., the introduction of a new personnel regime into the public service) legislation has been passed, but the implementation seems to have been fairly slow. For example, a new system of job classification and payment by results was first introduced in the mid-1980s, but by 1997 covered only about 5 per cent of state employees (Ministry of Finance, 1997, p. 78).

The number of personnel financed directly through the state budget fell by about 40 per cent (from 213,000 to 130,000) between 1989 and 1995 (thanks partly to the creation of off-budget state enterprises and companies, which accounted for about 54,000 of the 78,000 'losses').

The Finnish government has supported a programme of evaluations of its reforms (Holkeri and Summa, 1996). It is not clear that these evaluations (for an example, see Pollitt *et al.*, 1997 and Ministry of Finance, 1997) have had any clear and direct effect on subsequent decisions, but the evaluation function has now been firmly established in Finland as an on-going component of modern public management.

Finally, an interesting reflection on the reforms of the 1987–97 period appears in the 1998 Government Resolution *High quality services, good governance and a responsible civic society* (1998a):

earlier administrative reforms have been experienced to have increased the bureaucracy of administration. The Government wants to ensure the democratic development of the policy of governance . . . On all administrative levels, the real possibilities of the citizen to influence matters as well as openness and transparency of administration will be increased (p. 8).

FINLAND

Country File Events: Finland

	General	Organization	Personnel	Finance
1981–1985	– Koivisto (Soc., Centre) (1979) – Sorsa (Soc., Centre) (1983)			
1986–1990	– Holkeri (Cons., Soc.) (1987) – First programme for reforms (1988) – 'Service Declaration': general principles (1988) – Government guidelines on decentralized decision making (1988) – Decree on use of information technology (1988) – Second programme for reforms (1989) – MoF: measurement of productivity project (1989) – Min. of Communication: national information and services network (1989) – White Paper on information mgt in central government and role of IT in administrative reform (1989) – Government decision: leaving 10% of open positions unfilled (1990)	– Permanent Ministerial Committee for Public Management Reform (1987) – Administrative Development Agency (ADA) (1987) – General legislation on public enterprises (1988) – New types of public enterprises (1989) – Proposal to reorganize national boards of central agencies (1989) – Free Municipal Experiment in 56 municipalities (1989) – Simplify procedures for permits and licences (1989) – Railways and Post and Telecom: new types of public enterprise (1990) – Act requiring agencies to renew ordinances and regulations by end 1990 (1990)	– Proposals for productivity based bonus system, individualized pay system, decentralized classification of posts (1989) – Personnel Committee: proposals to reform personnel policy (1990)	– MoF: new instructions to reform State budget implementation procedure (1989) – Frame budgeting (1990) – 3 agencies: results oriented budget (frame budgeting, performance oriented budgeting) (1990)

1991–1995				
	– Aho (Centre, Cons.) (1991) – 'Rationalization' project launched (1991) – Legislation proposed to reform State aid to municipalities (1991) – Public Sector Mgt Reform decision: MTM, financial mgt, personnel mgt (1992) – Budget cuts (1992) – Comprehensive citizen's guide (1992) – Project : general strategy for information mgt (1992) – Regional Development Act: transfer of competencies to joint municipal boards (1994) – Comprehensive reform of Municipalities Act (1994) – Lipponen (Soc., Cons.) (1995) – Regional Administration 2000 project (1995) – Ministerial Working Group on Public Mgt Reform (1995) – Evaluation Programme of Public Mgt Reforms (1995) – Programme for improving regulatory mgt (1995) – Membership of the EU (1995)	– All agencies: keep a register of regulations (1991) – 'Rationalization' project report: focus on decentralization and reorganization (1992) – Proposals to reform regional administration (1992) – Joint stock companies for four bodies (1992): computing, printing, restaurants, mint – Broaden ownership of six industrial companies (1994) – Public enterprise: Forest Administration (1994) – Joint Stock Company: Post and Telecom, Map Centre (1994) – Separation of Immigration and Naturalization Service from Interiors (1995) – Joint Stock Company (1995): Railway, Purchasing Centre, Uniforms Factory, public building service, part of State Granary – Status (1995): 12 public enterprises, 15 public companies – Administrative Development Agency replaced by Finnish Institute of Public Management (1995)	– Task Force: develop a uniform uniform employment category and collective bargaining system (1991) – Pension committee: harmonize with private sector (1991) – Special top mgt training programme (1991) – Leaving 15% of open positions unfilled in 1992–5 (1991) – New State Civil Servants Act (1994) – Budgetary ceilings and personnel numbers and costs (1993)	– 12 agencies: result oriented budget (1991) – Schedule and test accrual-based accounting system for agencies (1992) – Management by Results (1993): performance contracts, annual reports, audit by Audit Office, performance measurement systems set up, receive lump sum for operational expenses (1991) – Statutory annual reports for all ministries and agencies (1993) – Reform of the State Grant system (1993) – Generalize Performance Budgeting: all agencies (1995)

Country File Events: Finland (*cont.*):

	General	Organization	Personnel	Finance
1996–1998	– Governance Project (1997) – Evaluation Report (FINREF) 1997): – Portfolio for Government Wide Planning (1998) – Reform provincial administration: from 11 to 5 provinces – Quality Strategy for public services: Service Charters (1998) – 'High Quality Services, Good Governance and a Responsible Civic Society' (1998) – Gvt Resolution on electronic transactions, development services and reduction of data gathering (1998)	– 110 one-stop shops (1996) – Establishment of Regional Employment and Business Development Centres (1997) – Joint Stock company (1996–98): Car Inspection Services, State Occupational Health Services, Technical Inspection Centre – Privatize: Map Centre, Finnish Telecom (into Sonera Ltd.)	– Government decision on the principles in recruiting senior civil servants; accountability (1997) – Performance Related Pay-schemes in some ministries and agencies (1997) – Evaluation of the State personnel policy (1998)	– Budget reform principles (1996): bring budget structure in line with (accrual) accounting reforms – MoF (1996): project to improve system of monitoring perform-ance and the quality and coverage of information – Reform State Grant System (1997) – Implement Accrual Accounting (1998) – Statutory Annual Reports for Ministries (1998)

FRANCE

A. Socio-economic forces: general

For general background, see Section A.2 and Table A.1 (above). France is a large country (population 58.4M in 1996) in a central position in the most economically advanced part of Europe.

B. Global economic forces

Again, see Section A.2 and Table A.1 for background. Economic globalization brought increasing pressure upon the previous system of state-directed 'sectoral corporatism' (Jobert and Muller, 1987). In consequence there has been 'a more general loss of centrality of the state in social mediation and public policy' (Clark, 1998, p. 101). Successive governments have been seen to have little success in solving the problem of high unemployment (well over 10 per cent for most of the 1990s).

C. Socio-demographic change

See Section A.3, including Figure A.1 and Tables A.2 and A.3.

D. National socio-economic policies

Traditionally France has sought a somewhat greater degree of state control over its economy than either Germany or the UK. This stance has come under increasing strain as the forces of economic globalization appear to have favoured more open, competitive economies (see Jobert and Muller, 1987, and Section B, above).

E. The political system

The French political system is distinctive, belonging fully neither to the 'majoritarian' camp with the UK and Australasia nor to the consensual systems which prevail in the Netherlands and the Nordic countries (see chapter 3). Elections are according to plurality and cabinets are usually one-party or a minimal coalition, but these majoritarian features are offset by the existence of a multi-party system and a strong, directly elected presidency.

During the period since 1980 there has been a fairly frequent alternation of the parties in office, with these sometimes matching the party identification of the President but sometimes not (the periods of *cohabitation*, as with the Chirac government under President Mitterand, 1986–88, the Baladur government, also under Mitterand, 1993–95 and the Jospin government under President Chirac, 1997-?). Obviously, all things being equal, a President is stronger when his own party also forms the government.

F. New management ideas

France is usually regarded as a country that has been quite resistant to the NPM ideas which have emerged from the UK and Australasia since the early 1980s. France has developed its own, distinctive thinking and rhetoric about administrative reform, centred on the themes of modernization and decentralization. However, during the 1980s there was a shift towards neo-liberal ideas within the elite at the Ministry of Finance, albeit in the form of favouring the modernization of the public sector through private sector methods, rather than maximum privatization or the 'hollowing out' of the state (Clark, 1998, p. 103). The contractualization of public services, stressed as a key component of Prime Minister Juppé's 1995 circular *Réforme de l'État et des services publics*, was reflection of this tendency.

G. Party political ideas

In France neo-liberalism has been embraced by the right (especially when Chirac was Prime Minister, 1986–88) but has been interpreted in a managerial rather than a doctrinaire, anti-state fashion. This has meant that the 'modernization' theme was also acceptable (with some changes in the 'filling') by governments of the left. The public service 'renewal' programme of 1989–93 was negotiated with and broadly supported by the public service unions. However, left and right parted company over the desirability of reforms to social security and central personnel regulation, where the right's attempts to push through changes sparked major public service strikes during 1995 (Howard, 1998).

H. Pressure from citizens

Most political scientists have regarded France as traditionally a state-centred system, where the intensity and variety of pressure group activity has tended to be moderate in comparison with, say, the USA or the UK. The system has tended to sectoral corporatism rather than active pluralism—that is, governments have done deals with a smaller number of peak associations (big employers, big unions) rather than being particularly permeable to a wider range of interest or issue groups. Such deals have been facilitated by the frequency with which members of the *grands corps* move between government and business positions. Certainly, in respect of public management reform, the pressures from the citizenry in general appears to have been limited. Nevertheless, there has been a general decline in public confidence in the French system, and some popular critiques of the rigidity of some public services and of the corruption and remoteness of some of the state elite. This general loss of perceived legitimacy has been a factor in encouraging the elite to launch such initiatives as the public service charter (Ministère de la Function Publique et des Réformes Administratives, 1992) and the *L'année de l'accueil dans les service publics* (Ministère de la Fonction Publique, 1994).

I. Elite perceptions of what management reforms are desirable

The limited move towards neo-liberal ideas as a basis for modernization has been mentioned above (section G). There has been a widely shared desire to rehabilitate the reputation of the state apparatus, but some differences as to how this might best be done. One line of tension is between the central politico-administrative elite (*Inspections des Finances, Cour des Comptes, Conseil d'État*) and the growing autonomy of the field services of ministries and the regional and local authorities.

J. Elite perceptions of what management reforms are feasible

The division of opinion here is perhaps between those who still believe that technocratic reforms, imposed by the centre, can ultimately succeed, and those who argue for a new and more inclusive form of political action. One view is that: 'The strikes of 1995 made clear what should have been evident: France cannot be reformed by decree. Technocratic solutions, however well conceived, are not possible in modern, individualist democracies' (Howard, 1998, p. 216)

K. Chance events

On one view, the emergence of various cases of corruption could be viewed as chance events which have contributed to a crisis of confidence in 'an elite that had discredited itself' (Howard, 1998, p. 201). From another perspective, however, these cases are not so much one-off, chance events as 'business as usual' within a system in which certain forms of corruption and 'cronyism' had become endemic.

L. Administrative system

France has possessed a strong administrative tradition since at least Napoleonic times. Five main features of the system as it existed in the late 1970s may be noted (Clark, 1998, pp. 98–100):

- A tradition of state direction of the economy and society (*dirigisme*).
- Centralized direction of the state apparatus by two sets of *grands corps*. The first set are administrative and comprise the *Inspection des Finances* (a kind of financial inspectorate), the *Conseil d'État* (the Council of State—a supreme administrative court) and the *Cour des Comptes* (the national audit office). This group recruit their members (*Énarques*) from the prestigious *École Nationale d'Administration* (ENA). The second set are technical (e.g., *Ponts et Chausées*) and recruit from the *École Polytechnique* via various *Grandes Écoles*. Members of the *Grands Corps* enjoy highly mobile careers and frequently take up top executive positions in the private sector or, indeed, in politics. For example, up to 1993, eight of the previous eleven Prime Ministers had been civil servants.
- A strong central state presence subnationally through the person of a *préfet* (prefect) in each *département* and region. The prefect co-ordinates central government services and, until 1982, held a supervisory authority (*tutelle*) over many decisions taken by local authorities.
- Division of the civil service into a large number of *corps* (1,800 at the end of the 1980s) each with its own educational entry requirements and its own set of hierarchically arranged posts, defined by a general civil service law. This feature of the French administrative system has proved a source of considerable rigidity and resistance in the context of management reform.
- The importance of a special body of administrative law in regulating administrative procedures and appointments. The French system 'is a "legal model" in the sense that it is regulated by legal rules which conceive the state administration as inhabiting an autonomous domain apart from civil society' (Clark, 1998, p. 100).

Each of these five features has come under strain during the last twenty years, but the modernization process thus far has probably made greater impact on the first and third than the other three.

M. Contents of the reform package

There was no one, single package that lasted for very long, but rather a series of separate initiatives by different governments which could, at best, be said to be grouped around certain broad themes. The two most prominent were, first, decentralization and deconcentration and, second, modernization. The strategic shift towards decentralization came in the mid-1980s, when the socialist government under President Mitterand removed the prefects' *tutelle* and created local collectivities as autonomous authorities. Direct elections were established for regional councils and legislation during 1982 gave local collectivities significant new taxing and budget-making powers. The ripples spreading out from this deep change have continued through to the present (de Montricher, 1996), and have been amplified by the effects of EU regional policies. The 'deconcentration charter' of 1992 marked a further step in shifting authority from the centre to the periphery. In the French context: 'decentralisation means transfer of authority from the central state to regional and local governments. Deconcentration means devolution of competence and managerial authority to the local administrative units of central government . . . as well as the agencies' (OECD, 1997a, p. 67).

The second theme—modernization—came to prominence under Prime Minister Rocard in 1989, although earlier discussions and initiatives had occurred throughout the 1980s. In February 1989 Rocard issued an important circular entitled *Renouveau du service public* which contained a series of initiatives: the creation of responsibility centres (*centres de responsabilité*—CDRs) within ministries, personnel reforms, greater emphasis on decentralized management of field services and responsiveness to public service users, and the institutionalization of policy evaluation across many sectors of government. Renewal—or modernization—continued under the succeeding Cresson and Bérégovoy governments (1992-93). In 1995 Prime Minister Juppé issued a circular, *Réforme de l'État et des services publics*, which proposed the reorganization of certain field services and an experiment in contractualizing the relationship between central ministries and their field services. Thus 'the successive phases of "administrative modernization" have been characterized by a broad continuity of policy, rather than by partisan differences between governments of the Left and the Right' (Clark, 1998, pp. 106–7)

A third theme—one characterized by much greater divergence between the parties which held power—was that of privatization. During the period of the socialist government of 1981–86 extensive nationalizations were carried through (exactly the opposite of the trend which was beginning to develop in the UK). However, the neo-liberal government of Chirac (1986–88) reversed this, listing sixty-five companies that were to be sold off. During a relatively short period in office nearly 300,000 industrial workers and 100,000 bank staff were 'privatized' (Wright, 1989, p. 105). This flurry came to an end with the return of left governments in 1988, but when the right regained power in 1993 significant privatization resumed (e.g., steel in 1995). Overall the period since 1980 has seen a significant fall in the public sector's share of the French labour force.

N. Implementation process

The French reforms have been implemented in a fairly piecemeal way, with different initiatives coming from different ministries at different times, and a good deal of successive 'repackaging' of some basically similar ideas (e.g., about being more responsive to citizen-users). For example, CDRs have been pushed much further in some ministries than in others (Trosa, 1995). However, the *Grands Corps* appear to have remained in control of most of the changes, and their central roles have not been seriously undermined (Rouban, 1996, pp. 154–5).

Prime Ministers have often played a leading role in reforms, especially Chirac, Rocard and Juppé. The procedural device of the circular has been much resorted to. The ministries most heavily involved have been the Ministry of Public Service (which has undergone several slight changes of name), the Ministry of Finance and the Ministry of the Interior (patron ministry for the prefects, and heavily involved in decentralization and deconcentration reforms). Naturally, the *Grands Corps* have been major players.

An officially stated feature of implementation has been that it should be a judicious mixture of 'top-down' and 'bottom-up': 'Performance management programmes are initiated from the central level through legal instruments but they are usually not very prescriptive. The actual content of the reforms is therefore to a large extent determined at the level of local agencies and services' (OECD, 1997a, p. 68). In practice it seems that reform implementation has moved more smoothly and quickly in technical ministries and field services than elsewhere.

O. Reforms actually achieved

Despite the construction, from 1989, of an elaborate network of evaluation institutions (Duran, Monnier and Smith, 1995) there seems to have been no across-the-board systematic evaluation of French management reforms. There have, however, been some assessments of particular aspects, for example, the 1996 *Cour des Comptes* report on CDRs. Less formal assessments have been made by some academics (e.g., Clark, 1998; de Montricher, 1996; Flynn and Strehl, 1996; Rouban, 1995) and by some officials (Trosa, 1995, 1996). In general it might be said that outcome data are hard to come by, but that, thematically, French governments have held more closely to the values of a strong administrative state committed to some form of strategic planning than did Australia, New Zealand or the UK. Significant modernization has taken place, and the decentralization reforms of 1982 seem to have been a genuine political and managerial watershed. However, much of the machinery of a centralized civil service remains fundamentally unaltered. In particular centralized control of personnel still survives, and reforms aimed at bringing budgeting, accounting and performance measurement within a single, compatible framework have only recently been given much momentum. Partly because of these constraints, the experiments with organizational diversity and user-responsiveness, though certainly substantial, have been somewhat less pervasive than in Australasia or the UK.

FRANCE

Country File Events: France

	General	Organization	Personnel	Finance
1981–1985	– Mitterand: President (Soc.) (1981) – Mauroy: PM (Soc.) (1981) – Decentralization Acts (1982) – Fabius: PM (Soc.) (1984)		– Economic restructuring: salary constraints and staff reduction (1982)	
1986–1990	– Chirac: PM (Cons.) (1986) – Mitterand: President (Soc.) (1988) – Rocard: PM (Soc.) (1988) – Reform of Administrative Courts (1988) – 'Renewal of the Public Service': Prime Minister (1989) – Economic and Social Council: report on modernization (1989) – Committee on government effectiveness: preparation of Tenth Plan (1989) – First government seminar led by PM (1989) – Second government seminar (1990) – Diagnosis of deconcentrated central administration (by each prefect) (1990) – Interministerial Committee on Evaluation (1990)	– Each ministry: modernization including IT Master Plan (1989) – 200 service projects (redefine responsibilities) (1990) – 60 centres of responsibility (1990) – Innovation Network by DG for Administration and the Public Service (1990) – 101 decentralization and regulatory simplification measures identified (1990) – Reform of Post and Telecom starts (1990)	– Pay agreements with five of seven public servant trade unions (1988) – Two Decrees on broader promotion opportunities (1988) – Framework Agreement with five unions: continuing training (1989) – Protocol of Agreement with five public servant trade unions (qualifications and salary scales) (1990) – 29 regional colloquia on renewal (1990)	

1990–1995			
– Cresson: PM (Soc.) (1991) – Third government seminar (1991) – Committee for Renewal of Public Service chaired by Minister of Public Service (unions, administration, experts) (1991) – Interministerial Committee on Evaluation: five policy areas for evaluation (1991) – Interministerial Committee for Territorial Administration (CIATER) (1991): relocate 5% of employees outside Ile-de-France within 3 years – Bérégovoy: PM (Soc.) (1992) – New Act on regional administration (1992): redefine roles and forms of co-operation – Decree (containing the Deconcentration Charter) (1992) – Circular on reform of State structures (implementation of subsidiarity principle) (1992) – Balladur: PM (Cons.) (1993) – Report (Picq) on measures to improve the efficiency of the State (1993)	– 470 'service projects' – 85 'centres of responsibility' (1991) – PTT transformed into two independent public establishments linked to the State by a planning contract (1991) – Implementation of deconcentration measures for regulatory procedures (1991) – Deconcentration Charter (1992) – Implementation of policy for cities with development of local partnerships (1992) – 127 centres of responsibility (contract on objectives and resources with parent department) (1992) – 315 deconcentration measures: CIATER (1993) – New Committee for the Reorganization and Deconcentration of the State Administration (1993) – 4-year ministerial plan for reorganization and deconcentration (1993)	– Salary agreement with four public servant trade unions (1991) – Deconcentration of interministerial training appropriations to regional prefects (1991) – Law: opening public employment to EC citizens (1991) – Renewal of Framework Agreement on continuing training with six unions (1992) – Ethics Committee to supervise the departure of civil servants (1993) – Act: conditions for appointments of civil servants and supervising departures (1994) – Act on the organization of work time, recruitment, transfers: make it possible for motivated public servants to be posted to urban areas suffering from severe social problems and high social insecurity (1994) – Circular: mgt of State employees to deconcentrated	– Simplify budgetary and accounting procedures (consolidation of operating appropriation) (1991) – Circular on the control of financial management (1994) – Pilot experiment: deconcentration of financial control of deconcentrated spending (1995)

Country File Events: France (*cont.*):

	General	Organization	Personnel	Finance
	– Joint declaration: central government, local authorities, public establishments, welfare agencies: quality of customer services (1994) – 11 interregional platforms on quality (1994) – Adjustment to judicial boundaries (1994) – Chirac: President (Cons.) (1995) – Juppé: PM (Cons.) (1995) – National 'synthesis' forum chaired by PM on customer services – Government seminar on State Reform (1995) – Circular: PM customer service improvements (1995) – Circular: PM on implementation of the reform (1995)	– Interministerial Committee for Rural Planning and Development (CIDAR) (1994): special centres to ensure equal access to high quality services – New Interministerial Committee for State Reform and State Reform Commission (1995) – Committee for the Simplification of Administrative Formalities (COSIFORM) (1995)	services (1994) – All decisions concerning reorganization or abolition must be preceded by an impact study on the opportunites of distance working (1995)	
1996–1998	– Cour des Comptes: report on responsibility centres (1996) – Jospin: PM (Soc.) (1997)	– All prefectures become responsibility centres (1996) – Balladur launches TQM (1997) – Deconcentration of some administrative competencies of ministries to prefectures (1997)	– 3rd 3-Year Framework Agreement on continuing training (1996)	– Extension of the reform of financial control of deconcentrated spending (1996)

THE FEDERAL REPUBLIC OF GERMANY

A. Socio-economic forces: general

See Section A.2 and Table A.1 (above). It is important to remember that Germany is by far the biggest and most populous, as well as one of the richest, of the six European states in this book.

B. Global economic forces

Again, see Section A.2

C. Socio-demographic forces

Although there were some pressures (e.g., the integration with the former German Democratic Republic) which affected all three levels of German administration, there are other problems which only local authorities have to face.

These include high rates of unemployment with more people depending on social welfare benefits, which are provided by local authorities. Local authorities, not state or federal administrative bodies, have to deal directly with the problems of citizens. Citizens have also become more demanding and more self-confident in their relationship with public services, many of which are provided by local authorities. Local government is therefore under much greater pressure to introduce improved services for citizens. Furthermore, due to increasing competition for production facilities, local authorities are involved in conducting policies of regional economic development, and have to provide new models of services for business communities (Röber, 1996, p. 175).

D. National socio-economic policies

Compared to the EU norm Germany still has a large manufacturing sector. This results in significant competition with the USA and the former Asian 'tigers'. The German currency, the DM, has been one of the strongest in the world and the related monetary policy is directed by the *Bundesbank* which develops its policy independently from the political executive.

E. The political system

The German system is a Chancellor model (*Kanzlerdemokratie*), which means that the Chancellor is above other ministers and is more than the *primus inter pares*. The President has a primarily symbolic function, unlike the French or even (to a lesser extent) the Finnish President.

At the federal level there are two major parties, the Christian Democratic Union of Germany CDU/Christian Social Union CSU, of the former Chancellor Helmut Kohl and the Social Democratic Party (SPD), which won the 1998 election and at the time of writing this book is led by Helmut Schröder. Except for the big coalition between CDU/CSU and the SPD from 1966 till 1969, federal politics were dominated by coalitions of CDU/CSU with the small free liberal party (FDP) from 1946 until 1966 and again from 1982 till 1998.

There was also a coalition of the SPD with the FDP from 1969 until 1982. At the *Länder* level the SPD and the Greens have formed coalition governments. The political leverage of the CDU/CSU has been constantly declining, partly to the benefit of the socialists.

The smaller parties are :

* The FDP (Free Democratic Party) which never went beyond 10 per cent of the national vote but has always been important as a coalition partner for either the CDU or the SPD. Since the unification of Germany its relative share of votes has also decreased, because of a lack of programme and leadership.
* The Greens started as a movement and turned into a political party. As a consequence they still have two major tendencies, 'fundamentalists' and 'realists'. The more it becomes feasible to join governments, the more influence the *'realos'* seem to have. The Greens are part of some *Länder* and the post-1998 Federal governments.
* The former communists, the Party of Democratic Socialism PDS (former SED) has gained momentum, especially in former Eastern Germany.

To get into the federal Parliament (*Bundestag*) political parties have to have a minimum of 5 per cent of the votes. This eliminates the smaller parties and sometimes posed problems for the FDP and the Greens. The voting system is mixed. The first vote (*Erststimme*) is majoritarian, and the second vote (*Zweitstimmme*) is proportional.

F. New management ideas

The German changes could be characterized more by administrative tightening up and modernization (MAINTAIN and MODERNIZE in terms of chapter 8) than by marketization or minimization (Derlien, 1998). The German trajectory has also been marked more by incrementalism ('permanent flexibility of institutional frameworks') than by fundamental change (Benz and Götz, 1996, p. 5), and more by improvement of the existing system rather than an import of other systems (König, 1997).

At the local level, where most management reforms have taken place (see H), new management ideas were promoted by the Local Management Co-op or the 'Joint Local Government Agency for the Simplification of Administrative Procedures' (*Kommunale Gemeinschaftstelle für Verwaltungsvereinfachung*, KGSt). The KGSt is an independent consultancy agency organized by a voluntary membership of municipalities, counties and local authorities with more than 10,000 inhabitants.

Following the Tilburg model from the Netherlands, the KGSt propagated a modern system of local government, which is labelled the 'New Steering Model' (*Das Neues Steuerungsmodell*). Main characteristics of this model are 'clear-cut responsibilities between politics and administration, a system of contract management, integrated departmental structures and an emphasis on output control' (Röber, 1996, p. 176; see also Klages and Löffler, 1996, p. 135). Elements of this 'New Steering Model' have been applied in a growing number of big cities and counties, city-states and *Länder* (e.g., Berlin, Baden-Württemberg and Schleswig-Holstein). At the time of writing, however, the reform enthusiasm is over and there is more and more acknowledgement of 'reform fatigue' (Röber and Löffler, 1999; Hill and Klages, 1993, 1995; Löffler, 1995).

Modernization has also been a major focus of the Bertelsmann Foundation through its research initiatives and publications, its international network for better local government (since 1995), and, since 1993, its Carl Bertelsmann Prize 'Democracy and Efficiency in Local Government'.

G. Party political ideas

There is no serious challenge to the *Rechtsstaat* and the basic functioning of the system. The concept of modernization does not really include radical downsizing and is the product of agreements made between management and the trade unions (Röber and Löffler, 1999).

In 1992 the then candidate chancellor Engholm (SPD) released a managerialist public sector reform paper. In 1993 there was a similar party paper by the ruling Christian Democrats. In general, specifically party political 'lines' on administration seem to be absent. Party political ideas are not developed at the federal level but basically at the state and local levels since the electoral process is focused at these levels. This results in sometimes diverging visions and practices according to specific situations, which are then not translated in a common federal party line. *Landtage* became interested in the New Steering Model, especially in 'Global budgets' which are more flexible. The *Landtag* of Rheinland-Pfalz organized a symposium on these issues in 1997 and in 1998 a hearing (public consultation) took place at the *Landtag* of Nordrhein-Westfalen.

H. Pressure from citizens

The focus on democracy and citizen participation was always very present in Germany and was labelled as *Ausserparlamentarische Opposition* (APO), which is citizen opposition outside parliament. The fact that the CDU/CSU was in power for almost twenty years encouraged leftist intellectuals to organize themselves to fight government policies and to protect democracy outside the legislative. Since the SPD joined government, first as part of the Big Coalition, then as the ruling party in the 1970s, APO was weakened. In the 1970s the pressure from citizens resulted in Citizen Initiatives (*Bürgerinitiativen*) where citizens gathered and tried (unlike the APO, which opposed those in power) to approach positively political parties, administrations and institutions. Thousands of Initiatives were taken in the fields of public infrastructures, environmental matters, housing, transport, or education. In the 1970s, there was also the concept of 'democratic, participatory public administration'.

I. Elite perceptions of what management reforms are desirable

Administrative reforms seem to have been supported by a strong elite consensus and could be summarized in five stages (see Table A.4).

J. Elite perceptions of what management reforms are feasible

At present, the perspective of the state as a provider of services is predominant in Germany. However, the Federal plan for the elderly of 1993 is a first indication that the German state will increasingly act as facilitator rather than as a direct provider.

The legal status of the civil service has always been a political issue of administrative reforms. The constitutionally guaranteed status of civil servants remains untouched and is unlikely to change fundamentally because so many German MPs are civil servants.

Finally, '[T]he question whether to impose a national administrative reform program from above or whether to leave freedom for local and actoral initiatives is only a theoretical one in the Federal Republic of Germany where federal structure and tradition by nature forbid a centralized approach to administrative reforms' (Klages and Löffler, 1996, p. 143).

TABLE A.4. *Stages of German administrative reform*

Stage	Decade	Reform or reform objective	Main content
1	1950s	Deregulation	New legal system and denazification
2	1950s and 1960s	Territorial reform	*Länder* and municipal gerrymandering
3	1960s	Reform of functions	Recentralization and decentralization
4	1970s and 1980s	Citizen-oriented adminstrative simplification	Debureaucratization, increased transparency, improved participation
5	1990s	Modernize administration '*Neues Steuerungsmodell*'	Administration as performance-oriented service delivery to citizens

Source: Naschold *et al.*, 1994

K. Chance events

At the end of the 1970s the Baader-Meinhof Group (Red Army Faction) developed terrorist activities against representatives of the political, industrial and administrative establishment. This resulted in a discussion on the presence and the removal of 'extremists' in the public service (*Berufsverbot*). This was in line with a concern to neutralize civil servants who had been Nazis, then communists, and finally sympathizers with the terrorist RAF.

German unification caused serious pressure at all levels and aspects of society. Financially, there was the political decision to equal an eastern to a western *Deutsch Mark*. Economically the '*Treuhandanstalt*' organized the privatization of most of the East Germany economy and the resulting unemployment had to be absorbed by the social security system. At the universities, academic posts were reconsidered. The former DDR administrative system was reformed according to the BRD system, and even the location of the capital changed from Bonn to Berlin. The transformation of local government in East Germany was 'between imposed and innovative institutionalization' (Wollmann, 1997).

L. The administrative system

The 'legal state' or *Rechtsstaat* is a key element in the German system.

While the *Rechtsstaat* and federal principles constitute the essential formal parameters for policy making and public-sector change, the market economy and the welfare state establish substantial norms which delineate functions and responsibilities of the state . . . These complex arrangements between state and market economy, based on neo-corporatist linkages and intermediary organizations, allow the co-existence of market ideals such as free enterprise, individualism and subsidiarity, with a positive evaluation of the welfare state (Benz and Götz, 1996, p. 17).

Within this setting, the Federal Republic of Germany has 16 *Länder*, of which three are city states (Berlin, Bremen and Hamburg), and local governments. The size of the *Länder* varies from 17.7 million inhabitants (N. Rhine-Westphalia) to 700,000 (Bremen), or from 70,000 km^2 (Bavaria) to 400 km^2 (Bremen). Local government consists of 329 counties (*Kreise*), 115 non-county municipalities (*Kreisefreie Städte*), and 14,915 municipalities (*Gemeinde*) which are governed according to different models.

The administrative structure in the Federal Republic of Germany is moulded by three principles. The first principle is the principle of 'separation of powers' which distibutes legislative, executive and judicial powers among separate institutions. A second principle is Federalism, which defines *Länder* as 'members of the Federation yet retaining a sovereign state power of their own' (Röber, 1996, p. 170). Local government is the last founding principle. Local government in Germany mainly operates on two levels, that of the local authorities and of the counties (Röber, 1996, p. 170). Local self-government has a long tradition in Germany. The Basic Law and all *Land* constitutions guarantee the right of every community to govern local affairs under its own responsibility (OECD country profiles, 1992, p. 126; OECD, 1997d).

The development of public management in Germany has not been uniform because German administration is extremely varied and complex. Central government only plays a modest part in the direct administration of public services. Many public duties, such as education and police, are administered by the states (*Länder*) which have considerable political and administrative power, whilst other public duties (e.g. social services) are administered by local authorities. As a consequence the impact of public management and public managers varies throughout Germany and at different levels of public administration (Röber, 1996, p. 169–70).

The role of federal administration is mainly limited to law-making and is not concerned with service delivery as such, which therefore reduces the need for administrative reform at that level. The concept of *Rechtsstaat* and the principle of legality are embedded in a negotiating and contracting state (Sommerman, 1998).

The German system of public administration is characterized by the classical bureaucratic model with strong emphasis on legality and proper fulfilment of regulatory functions (*Ordnungsaufgaben*). This model is based on the Weberian ideal type of bureaucracy with a tall hierarchy of positions, functional specialization, strict rules, impersonal relationships, and a high degree of formalization (Röber, 1996, p. 170).

The upper levels of the federal civil service are extensively politicized. It is common for many such senior officials to change jobs or take study leave when the political colour of the government changes (Götz, 1997).

M. Contents of the reform package

The modernization of public administration in Germany has to be understood in 'terms of a "bottom-up" revolution: there are essentially no reform initiatives at the federal level, at least some German Länder show up as modernization pioneers, but the truly new entrepeneurs in the field of modernization are the local governments' (Klages and Löffler, 1996, p. 134).

The elements of the 'New Steering Model' that local governments and some *Länder* have put into practice are the following:

result-oriented budgeting;
cost calculation of administrative products;
introduction of commercial bookkeeping;
decentralized resource accountability;

definition of indicators for quality standards;
customer orientation;
outsourcing, contracting-out and privatization;
openness to 'competition'.

Klages and Löffler (1996, p. 137–41) assert that there was an east–west division in the modernization approach of local government, due to the specific problems facing public administration in East Germany. The restructuring of the East German public sector was so dramatic that it is accurate to refer to it as a transformation with its own distinctive problems and solutions. The transformation encompassed changes in governmental competencies (from holistic planning authority to a balancing function, typical for a market economy), civil service (from political cadre administration to a civil service based on professional qualifications), organization (from unity of powers to horizontal and vertical separation of powers), and procedures (from the guidance principle of the Party to legalistic administrative behaviour). Territorial restructuring of local authorities was necessary in the face of the enormous financial problems the local authorities faced. As to the characteristics of the local public sector in the eastern part of Germany, the Weberian model was put in place, while in the western part there were experiments with NPM.

N. The implementation process

The initiation and implementation of changes in Germany is through pilot projects rather than by a comprehensive approach. This creates problems of dual structures and jeopardizes islands of reforms. Lower levels of governments are experimenting rather than higher levels. This is well summarized in a title of a research project of Naschold *et al.*, 'The country needs new cities' (Naschold *et al.*, 1994). The modernization pressure comes from the lower levels of government and is pushing through the *Länder* to the federal level. However, the merger with East Germany and the related modernization was definitely a top-down process.

O. Reforms actually achieved

There is no evaluation of the outcomes of reform at the various levels of government. There are surveys of the German Association of Cities (and the KGSt) on the degree of implementation of the New Steering Model (see also, Grömig and Thielen, 1996; Grömig and Gruner, 1998). Reform processes and initiatives have been described by Hill and Klages (1995, 1996a, 1996b) referring to the general implementation of the New Steering Model in local governments (Duisburg, Bad Oldesloe, Saarbrücken, Rheine, Pforzheim, Soest, Heidelberg, München, and Nürnberg), or to more specific dimensions of the modernization such as controlling (Offenbach, Ludwigshafen, Heidelberg, Leipzig, Soest, and Detmold), teambuilding (Aachen), cost reduction (Kronach), decentralized service centres (Ludwigsburg), performance related organizing (Main-Kinzig, Meissen), holding structure (Oberhavel), benchmarking (Osnabrück), contracting out (Pinneberg), and budgeting (Waldshut).

The 'Cities for tomorrow' initiative of the Bertelsmann Foundation includes the HRM-case of the City of Duisburg.

Systematic evidence at the level of *Länder* and definitely at the federal level is not available.

THE FEDERAL REPUBLIC OF GERMANY

Country File Events: Germany

	General	Organization	Personnel	Finance
1981–1985	– Schmidt: Chancellor (Soc.) (1980) – Kohl: Chancellor (CD) (1982) – Government resolution to promote de-bureaucratization (1983) – Independent Federal Commission to Simplify Law and Administration (Interiors) (1983) – Major cut-back budgets and curbing legal rights of citizens to receive benefits (1983) – Study Act to Repeal Unnecessary Regulations and Consolidate Existing Law (1983)	– comprehensive attempt to reform ministerial bureaucracy in Baden-Württemberg (1985) – Co-operation with private industry (1985) – De-bureaucratization in all *Länder*, and sunset administrative regulations (1980–89)		– Amendment to Federal Budget Code: uniform accounting system in three steps involving organizational simplification and better use of IT (1986)
1986–1990	– Kohl: Chancellor (CD) (1983) – Bertelsmann Foundation sponsors research on public mgt (1987) – Kohl: Chancellor (CD) (1987) – First stage of Trade Union ÖTV Programme (Public Service, Transport and Traffic): Future of Public Services (ZÖD) (1988)	– Ministry of environmental affairs (1986) – First steps to privatize federal mail and telecom (1987) – Start of privatization of East Germany (1990)	– Law amending provisions for working conditions (part time, unpaid leave, etc.) (1989) – Speyer Federal Academy of PA: in-service training programme for *Länder* (1990)	– New controlling systems in various cities (1987) – Transfer of budget law to East Germany (1990)

Country File Events: Germany (*cont.*):

	General	Organization	Personnel	Finance
	– Federal: guidelines for the use of IT (1988) – Federal: strategy for improving federal legislation (1989) – Unification Treaty (1990) – Construction of *Länder* gvts in East Germany (1990) – Major local gvt constitution reform in East Germany (1990) – Debate about necessity of regional authorities in new *Länder* (1990)			
1991–1995	– Kohl: Chancellor (CD) (1991) – Move capital from Bonn to Berlin (1991) – Major cut-back budgets (1992) – Basic Law: *Länder* more power to influence decision-making on matters of the EU (1992) – *Ad hoc* group on 'simplification of the administration and reduction of government tasks' (Conference of Federal and *Länder* Ministers of Interiors) (1993)	– Local Management Co-op (KGSt) launches the Steering Model (1991) – Ongoing implementation of the New Steering Model in *Länder* and local government; Adjust Household Laws (1991–95) – All federal ministries: divisions to examine European legislation issues, co-ordination and implementation requirements (1992) – Working group 'on expediting planning and licensing procedures' (Economic Affairs):	– Large secondments of civil servants to new *Länder* (1991) – Public Service Reform Act (1994)	– Working group on 'possibility of promoting efficiency through an improvement of accounting in the government sector of public administration (Conference of Federal and *Länder* Ministers of Interiors) (1993) – Working group 'methods of business accounting in government' (1993) – Test pilot schemes of flexible budget instruments (carry over unspent resources) (1995) – Cost-accounting in specific areas (1995)

– Joint working group on privatization (Federal MoF and Economics, *Länder*, local authorities) (1993) – Reform of revenue redistribution system between *Länder*, between *Länder* and federal gvt (1993) – Kohl: Chancellor (CD) (1994) – Interministerial working group on 'increasing efficiency/critical review of tasks' (Interiors) to report to Committee for Organizational Matters (1994) – Federal Ministry of Interiors: Lean State Advisory Council: facilitate public mgt reform process (1995)	– reduce unnecessary functions, charge third parties with tasks, simplify procedures, streamline organization of administration (1993) – Privatization of federal rail (1993) – Number of junior ministers reduced to 27 (1993)				
1996–1998	– Amendment Administrative Procedure Act (flexibility permitting procedure) (1996) – Second stage of Trade Union ÖTV Programme (Public Service, Transport and Traffic): Future of Public Services (ZÖD) (1996) – Final Report of Lean State Advisory Committee (1997) – Schröder: Chancellor (Soc.) (1998)	– *Länder* and cities continue to implement the so-called New Steering Model (1996) – Federal: improving organizational structure: reduction of number of Federal authorities (1996) – Change of the Federal Framework Household Law (1997) – Steering Committee on Administrative Organization (1997)	– Amendment of the Federal Civil Servant Law (1996) – Act to Reform the Law on the Civil Service: performance mobility, management – Reduction of staff caused by Unification (from 381,000 in 1992 to 315,000 in 1998); reduction of staff in ministries (from 21,300 in 1991 to 18,500 in 1998) – Pensions Reform Act (1998)	– Cabinet commissions Federal MoF to develop Cost and Results Accounting (CRA) (1997) – CRA introduced in more than 20 authorities or Ministries (1998) – Act on the Further Development of Budgetary Law (more flexibility) (1998) – Amendment of the Budget Act (more flexibility) (1998)

THE NETHERLANDS

A. Socio-economic forces: general

See Section A.2 and Table A.1 (above).

B. Global economic forces

Again, see Section A.2.

C. Socio-demographic issues

See Section A.3, and Figure A.1 and Tables A.2 and A.3. In 1993 the Netherlands was second only to Sweden (among the ten countries reviewed here) in respect of the high proportion of GDP devoted to social expenditure.

D. National socio-economic policies

Until the recession of the 1970s the post-war history of the Dutch public sector had been one of more or less continuous expansion. Then, between 1974 and 1982 the budget situation deteriorated from surplus to a large deficit. Unsurprisingly, the 1980s were a period of sharp cutbacks in the public sector, combined with a series of measures to develop tighter control over state expenditures. Since 1989 the Dutch economy has performed better, although it shared in the international slowdown of the early 1990s. Employment growth since 1994 has been ahead of many other EU member states. The governments of the mid- and late 1990s have enjoyed a less threatening position on public spending than their 1980s predecessors.

E. The political system

The Netherlands are a unitary, but decentralized state: 'traditionally, the Dutch state . . . has always resisted centralisation of state authority' (Kickert and In't Veld, 1995, p. 45). The political system is consociational, consensual, multi-party and corporatist (Lijphart, 1984). Elections take place according to a system of proportional representation. Recently, the main parties have been Christian Democrat (a 1980s merger of previously separate Christian parties), a Liberal Party (conservative), a Progressive Liberal party and a Social-Democrat party. The Christian parties were continuously in government from the First World War until 1994, allied to varying groupings of other parties. Through the 1970s the governing coalitions were centre left, in the 1980s centre right. Unusually, in 1994, a 'purple' (left-right) coalition was formed *without* Christian Democrat participation.

In the Netherlands almost every sector of government policy consists of a myriad of consultative and advisory councils, which are deeply intertwined with government and form an 'iron ring' around the ministerial departments . . . Deliberation, consultation, and pursuit of compromise and consensus form the deeply rooted basic traits of Dutch political culture (Kickert and In't Veld, 1995, p. 53).

F. New management ideas

The system of consultative and advisory councils (see E, above) affords many channels for both business-based and academic ideas to enter public administration: 'the Dutch ministries are relatively open organisations. They are not only populated by career civil servants, but also by many external consultants and scientists who contribute enthusiastically to policy making in general' (Kickert and In't Veld, 1995, p. 56). In this respect, therefore, the Netherlands is dissimilar to more closed, *Rechtsstaat*-type regimes such as Germany or France. Following the Second World war there was a noticable 'dejuridification' of public administration. During the 1980s specific reform ideas came from a number of other countries, especially Sweden, the UK and the USA (Roberts, 1997, p. 101).

As in many other countries, during the 1980s notions of comprehensive plannning were in rapid retreat, and business-origin management ideas increasingly penetrated the public sector. However, in the Netherlands, the drive for efficiency and savings did not carry the same anti-government ideological edge as it did, for example, in the UK under Thatcher or in the USA under Reagan.

It should also be noted that the Netherlands, relative to its size, has one of the largest community of public administration academics in western Europe. Many professors played some part in advising government on administrative reform. During the 1980s open systems approaches and network theories provided alternative perspectives to business management approaches and, during the 1990s, the Dutch academic community played an important part in developing the 'new steering model' of governance (Kickert and In't Veld, 1995, pp. 59–60).

G. Party political ideas

Whilst political parties undoubtedly developed broad notions about how Dutch government should be reformed it is necessary to remember that the significance of the ideas of any one party for practical action is likely to be less in a consensual, multi-party system than in the kind of one-party dominance which has usually characterized government in New Zealand and the UK. That having been said, one may note a number of party political themes which gained some salience.

First, it is clear that the first Lubbers government, which came to power as a centre-right coalition in 1982, was influenced by the right-wing Anglo-American neo-liberal governments of the time. It adopted a rhetoric which was pro-privatization and in favour of slimming the central state. Over time this emphasis became somewhat diluted, especially when the third Lubbers' administration (1989–94) included the Social Democrats as major partners (instead of the Liberals, as in the first and second Lubbers' governments). Simultaneously, however, the Social Democrats muted their previous ideological resistance to various forms of business-like practices being (selectively) introduced to the public sector. Additionally, the pressures to cut back public spending receded during the 1990s, so that the context for debate was less acute.

Later, during the 1990s, there was a certain disenchantment with some of the reforms. Following some critical analyses (e.g., *Algemene Rekenkamer*, 1995) of the many ZBOs (autonomous administrative bodies) created during the 1980s, the new 'purple' coalition government of the mid-1990s declared its intention of restoring the 'primacy of politics', meaning a greater measure of public accountability and transparency for non-ministerial public bodies (Roberts, 1997).

H. Pressure from citizens

Whilst there is a popular suspicion that 'the bureaucracy' is inefficient, and whilst public service seems to have become a less attractive career for young people, Dutch public opinion does not seem to support the strongly anti-government attitudes which have been quite popular in the USA and, to a lesser extent, in Australia, New Zealand and the UK. One might also mention that the Dutch have a certain cultural aversion to public figures 'showing off', and this may have meant that the potential popular appeal of politicians with bold, doctrinaire programmes (such as Thatcher, Reagan, Howard, Lange or Mulroney) is less in the Netherlands than in some other countries.

In general, 'The Dutch seem to like representative government by general local, regional or national governments. The underlying idea is that intersectoral judgements can best be made in this type of democratic body' (Kickert and In't Veld, 1995, p. 58).

I. Elite perceptions of what management reforms are desirable

Much elite attention was focused on budgetary problems. The development of performance indicators, contractualization and output budgeting were all seen as desirable.

J. Elite perceptions of what management reforms are feasible

During the 1980s and early 1990s the political elite was most interested in strategies for achieving cutbacks. Top officials, however, were more enthusiastic about the possibilities of management reforms *per se*.

K. Chance events

None of great significance.

L. The administrative system

'*Ministerial responsibility* is the cornerstone of our system' (Kickert and In't Veld, 1995, p. 46). Ministers are responsible politically, in criminal and in civil law. Collective decision making takes place in the weekly council of ministers. The Prime Minister is not as strong a co-ordinating and centralizing force as in the UK system—indeed, various attempts during the 1980s and 1990s to strengthen the PM's office have been rejected or dropped. S/he remains *primus inter pares*.

In the mid-1990s there were 14 ministries (the number has varied over time, e.g. in 1982 the new government abolished the Ministry of Public Health and Environment and transferred its functions to two new ministries). Because of the absence of a strong central power each has considerable autonomy—more so than would be the case in either New Zealand or the UK. The highest civil servant in each ministry is the Secretary General, and ministries are generally divided into directorates general. The civil service is not partisan, and civil service and political careers are separate. Ministries are fairly open organizations, at least in the sense that they frequently bring outside experts into the processes of policy deliberation (see F above).

The provincial and municipal levels are highly significant in terms of services, expenditure and personnel. There are 12 provinces and 625 municipalities. These subnational tiers are responsible for most of the expensive, labour-intensive welfare state services (municipalities account for roughly one third of public expenditure, though much of this is financed by central government). Many of the cutbacks of the 1980s were directed at these levels.

M. Contents of the reform package

The contents of the reform package developed over time, with shifts in the coalition government, and with changes in the fortunes of the Dutch economy. In general terms it might be said that the package appeared most radical in the early part of our period, especially under the 'Lubbers I' centre-right coalition of 1982–86. Privatization was a prominent theme, but the scope for returning state bodies to private ownership was less than in the UK or New Zealand, because the extent of pre-existing state ownership was more modest. Nevertheless the Postbank (10,500 staff), Posts and Telecommunications (95,000 staff), the Royal Mint and the Fishery Port Authority—the four main state companies—were either corporatized or wholly or partly sold off.

Alongside privatization, the 'Lubbers I' administration announced a series of 'great operations'. These comprised measures to trim central government spending, decentralize activities to lower levels of government and simplify legal and bureaucratic procedures.

The 1980s was also a period in which many new ZBOs were created. A survey showed that, by 1992, 18 per cent of total state expenditure passed through these semi-autonomous bodies. Some were long-established (e.g., the state universities) but more than 40 per cent dated from after 1980 (*Algemene Rekenkamer*, 1995).

In the 1990s the departmental agency, rather than the ZBO, became the fashionable format for decentralizing administrative authority. Between 1991 and 1998 more than 20 agencies were set up (Ministerie van Financiën, 1998). These included (for example) agencies for Meteorology, Immigration and Naturalization, Defence Telematics and the Government Buildings Service.

In Human Resource Management/personnel management there was a gradual shift towards the 'normalization' of the terms of public service, that is, bringing them more in line with private sector labour conditions. The Netherlands, along with most other countries in this study, experienced a tension between the desire to use HRM to build a more skilled and highly motivated workforce and the desire to shed jobs and economize (Korsten and van der Krogt, 1995).

Throughout the period there was a trend to develop and refine performance indicators for a widening range of public services. Mol (1995) provides an interesting case study of the strengths and weaknesses of this process in the National Logistic Command.

During the 1980s extensive financial management reforms were instituted in both central and local government.

A key element of this initiative consisted in the introduction of encumbrance accounting in central government, to be applied in conjunction to the cash concept of accounting already in use. Accounting for obligations may be considered a key factor in controlling central government spending, as cash disbursements will inevitably result from previously established operations (Boorsma and Mol, 1995, p. 229).

N. The implementation process

In many, perhaps most countries, the rhetoric of public managment reform outdistances the actual changes in practice. This has certainly been true for the Netherlands during the 1980–97 period. The implementation of decentralization is a good example:

the decentralisation process in the 1980s and 1990s became largely a power struggle. Spending departments often held out resolutely (and with success) against the transfer of power to provinces and municipalities. Decentralisation only began to asume any importance when spending cuts and decentralisation were brought together in a single context: municipalities were permitted to take over certain tasks if they were prepared to accept 90% funding; the 10% contraction was (without much evidence) justified as "efficiency gains" (Derksen and Korsten, 1995, p. 83).

More generally, implementation has been an incremental and selective process—much less of a series of dramatic 'waves' as in the UK or New Zealand. This is perhaps only to be expected of a politico–administrative system that prides itself on its consensual character.

O. Reforms actually achieved

The Netherlands is a country where programme and policy evaluation has been fairly widely practised (a 1991 survey recorded 300 evaluations being undertaken across 14 ministries) but relatively little of this effort seems to be been focused upon management reforms *per se*. For example, many ZBOs were created during the 1980s, but, writing in the mid-1990s, one Dutch expert considered that evidence about their performance was severely lacking (Leeuw, 1995). Certainly there does not seem to have been any overall evaluation of the reforms or even of significant sections of them, such as the 'great operations' of the Lubbers I and II administrations.

Some questioning of the reforms has come from the national court of audit (*Algemene Rekenkamer*). In particular, they published a 1995 report which was highly critical of the lack of public accountability of some ZBOs. For example, the report indicated that only 22 per cent of the ZBOs surveyed produced performance indicator data for their parent ministries. Financial control procedures were often weak and in some cases the legal basis for certain tasks was not clear (*Algemene Rekenkamer*, 1995).

More recently, the Ministry of Finance has sponsored an assessment of the programme (1991–98) of creating agencies (Ministerie van Financiën, 1998).

THE NETHERLANDS

Country File Events: Netherlands

	General	Organization	Personnel	Finance
1981–1985	– Van Agt: PM (CD, Soc.) (1981) – 'Major Operations': Deregulation, Privatization, Reconsideration (1981) – Lubbers: PM (CD, Lib.) (1982)	– Reorganization including decentralization (1982) – Transfer competencies to lower-level line managers (1984)	– Bonus-payments for special efforts (1984) – Central steering committee on personnel policy (1984)	
1986–1990	– Lubbers: PM (CD, Lib.) (1986) – Targets for job reduction (1988) – Lubbers: PM (CD, Soc.) (1989) – Management Development Advice Centre (Interiors) (1989) – Ministerial Committee 'Great Efficiency Operation' (reducing asks, improving organization, cost reduction) (1990)		– Ministry of Interiors asks universities to set up mgt training (1988) – System of pay differentials (1989) – School of Public Administration (1989) – 'Small-scale efficiency operation': increase labour productivity (1990)	– Performance Indicators (PI) in budget (estimates, efficiency, effectiveness): first stage: (input) estimates (1990)
1991–1995	– 'Core Business' operation: central tasks; reduce personnel (1991) – Minister of Justice presents report to Parliament on short-comings in legislation (1991) – 'Towards More Results-Oriented Management' report of gvt (1992)	– Civil service centres: experiment (1991) – Agreement between central and local to transfer tasks (1992) – Starr agencies: 4 (1994) – Agencies: 7 – Gvt position: semi-privatized bodies (1995)	– Significant steps to 'normalize' status of government employees (1991) – Evaluation of performance related pay schemes (1991) – Agreement by gvt and trade unions to privatize the General Pension Fund for public employees by 1996 (1992)	– Closing of 'financial accountability operation' (1986–91) – MoF: quantitative and qualitative improvement of measurement: estimates, planning and controlling systems, allocation of resources (1991) – Completion of 'financial

Country File Events: Netherlands (*cont.*):

General	Organization	Personnel	Finance
– 'Great Efficiency Operation' (Interiors): privatization and staff reduction (1992) – Committee on Constitutional Renewal (Parliament) (1992) – 'Tailor made Advice': revision of advisory bodies (1993) – 'Towards core ministries': small administration centres (1993) – 'Organization and Working Methods of the Civil Service': core tasks (1993) – Kok: PM (Soc., Lib.) (1994) – 'Choices for the Future' (1994) – Ministerial Committee for Political Reform (Interiors) (1994)	– Gvt position: autonomous public bodies (ZBO) vs ministerial responsibility (1995) – Start screening 253 ZBOs (1995)	– Increase mobility by 'temporary assignments' (1992) – 'People and management in the civil service': first annual report on personnel mgt (1994) – Senior Public Service (SPS) (PM and Interiors): Intertop database, mobility (1995)	accountability operation': each ministry responsible for accounting system, independent agencies, streamline budget process, reassess rules on financial and personnel mgt (1992) – Ministries obliged to report on policy evaluation programmes in annual budget explanation (1992) – Strengthen Accounting Law 1976: more PIs (1992) – Application of broader rules of budgetary discipline (end of year margin: 0.25%) (1993) – Policy: charges cover costs (1993) – Set up of policy evaluation programme: budget looks at current, planned, completed evaluations (1993)

	– Ministerial (PM) Committee for Market Improvement, Deregulation and Legislative Quality (1994) – Gvt policy document: 'Back to the Future': ICT and use of information (1995)			– Project: indicators for the cost of implementing regulations (1993) – Control of the integrated operating budget (personnel and equipment) (1994) – MoF: Manual PI (1994) – 'Reconsideration' Procedure replaced by 'Interdepartmental Policy Audit' (1994) – Agencies: 5 double book-keeping (1995) – End of year margin: 1% (1995) – Review procedure topic: financial reform (1995)
1996–1998	– Framework Act on Advisory System (1996) – Financial Relations Act (1996): redistribution of finances among municipalities – Evaluation of agencies (1997) – Cohen report: Market and Government (1997) – Further reduction of number of municipalities to about 550 (1998) – Kok: PM (Soc., Lib.) (1998)	– 19 agencies (1998) – Policy intention to restructure parts of the implementation social security in autonomous administrative authorities (1998)	– 36-hour week introduced in most sectors of public service (1997) – Extension of the SPS to all management positions (more than 1,500 public servants) (1998)	– Adjust Accounting Law (1995) – More stringent rules for contract and equipment mgt (1996) – Parliament: Commission of Finance audits PIs (1996) – PIs in budget: second stage: outputs (1997) – PIs in budget: third stage: link cost/expenses–outputs (efficiency) (1998) – 'Interdepartmental Management Audit ' (1998) – Budget for the 21st Century Project (1999)

NEW ZEALAND

A. Socio-economic forces: general

New Zealand is a small country (population 3.8M) in a peripheral geographical location (2,000 km from Australia). GNP per capita 90 in 1985 and 76 in 1992 (where OECD average = 100). Close economic and cultural ties to the UK, but these began to dwindle after the UK joined the European Community in 1973, and it became obvious that the favoured arrangements for NZ agricultural exports to the UK market could not survive indefinitely. Two main population groups—whites and Maoris. The latter (12 per cent of the population) have been increasingly politically active in insisting on their rights and pointing to inequalities—a process sometimes described as 'internal decolonization' (Castles *et al.*, 1996, chapter 7).

See Sections A.2 and A.3 (above) for details of New Zealand's comparative position.

B. Global economic forces

The system of protectionism which had been in place since the Second World War was close to the point of collapse by the early 1980s. In 1952 65 per cent of exports had gone to the UK and only 1.7 per cent to Asia. By 1982 the first figure had fallen to 14.7 per cent and the second had risen to 31.8 per cent (Castles *et al.*, 1996, p. 25).

When the new Labour government led by David Lange came to power in July 1984 the economy was stagnant and the national debt was large. The NZ Reserve Bank suspended trading in the NZ dollar and a 20 per cent devaluation quickly followed. The government's first priorities were tax reform, financial deregulation and privatization. The comprehensive public management reforms of 1984–90 flowed directly from this financial and economic crisis. (there continues to be controversy about the extent to which the exchange rate crisis was also the symptom of a deeper economic crisis—critics say the new government exploited the situation to push through its radical agenda.)

Restructuring the economy was undertaken at high speed, but the beneficial impacts took more than five years to show through. The interim period was very tough. In 1985 inflation reached 13 per cent. Overseas firms were prominent beneficiaries of the privatization programme, being mainly responsible for the purchase of the railways, the telephone system and (thanks to financial deregulation) most of the major banks. Between 1985 and 1992 the economy actually shrank by 1 per cent (though the 1992 measure is taken during a recession).

See also Section A.2.

C. Socio-demographic change

Prior to 1984 unemployment had usually been low (less than 5 per cent) in NZ. It rose rapidly between 1985 and the early 1990s, reaching more than 10 per cent in 1992/93. The social effects of this were widespread and harsh. This was partly because many social benefits were linked to employment status but also because from 1990 the National Government initiated the rapid dismantling of much of the previous welfare state system. Speaking of the 1980s Castles *et al.* (1996, p. 101) refer to:

a very substantial decline in real wages over the latter half of the period was accompanied by distributional effects . . . These included an increased incidence of low pay for men, a decline in the share of real gross income of wage and salary earners accruing to each of the bottom three quintiles and a marked increase in the share of the top quintile.

One might add that, as might be expected, women and ethnic minorities were particularly hard hit by the simultaneous worsening of employment conditions and slimming down of welfare provision.

See also Section A.3. New Zealand has a somewhat lower percentage of elderly people in its population than most west European countries.

D. National socio-economic policies

A very clear commitment to a comprehensive economic restructuring (see above). Tax reform (to lower the tax burdens on business); financial deregulation (to attract foreign capital); privatization (to promote efficiency and relieve pressures on public spending). The generous NZ welfare state was left largely intact at first, but major reforms aimed at reducing welfare and social security expenditure were instituted by the incoming National Party government of 1990. An Employment Equity Act introduced by the Labour Government in 1990 was soon repealed by its National successor. The Employment Contracts Act significantly deregulated the labour market.

E. The political system

The political executive is drawn exclusively from a small legislature, organized on Westminster principles. There is no upper house. There is no single written constitutional document nor any other major constraint on the government in power.

Until 1996 the electoral system was based on a single-constituency-member, 'first-past-the-post' system, which usually delivered a single party to power. Once in power: 'Public servants and their managers have long operated in a context in which the Prime Minister and cabinet could, if they wished, ride roughshod over any opposition' (Boston *et al.*, 1996, p. 68).

However, following a constitutional referendum in 1993 the electoral system has now been changed (from 1996) to one based on mixed member proportional representation (MMP). This has produced a coalition government, though the longer-term effects of the change are not yet entirely clear. The National/New Zealand First party coalition collapsed in August 1998 and was succeeded by a minority National-led government.

Unlike other small countries in our set (Finland, the Netherlands), New Zealand has traditionally been fairly centralized. There has been: 'A preference for retaining key governmental powers and responsibilties at the central government level, with only limited devolution to sub-national government, despite considerable rhetoric about devolution in the 1980s' (Boston *et al.*, 1996, p. 5).

F. New management ideas

The public management reforms in NZ were unusual both in their comprehensiveness and in the relatively high degree to which they were based on explicitly theoretical ideas about management. The then Central Financial Controller to the Treasury wrote: 'A number of literatures contributed . . . The sources included public choice theory, managerialism, transaction cost economics, public policy, public sector financial management and accounting' (Ball, 1993, p. 5).

There was a shared intellectual background within the quite small group of key ministers, senior civil servants and businessmen who drove through the reforms: 'there were a series of quite close relationships set up, from about 1982 on, by a group that encompassed the corporate business sector, the senior Labour parliamentary group' (Canadian Broadcasting Corporation, 1994, p. 3). The highly theoretical character of much of this thinking was novel:

Like their British counterparts, senior New Zealand public servants had not been known in the past for their interest in theory. The current emphasis on using theory to guide policy is, therefore, a relatively recent phenomenon, and seems to be due, at least in part, to the growing influence of economists and the particular kind of higher education which many of these economists, especially those in the Treasury, have received (Boston, 1995, p. 168).

The content of this thinking, in institutional terms, may be expressed as follows (borrowing from Boston *et al.*, 1996, pp. 81–2):

a) prefer private sector over state sector organizations wherever possible, especially for commercial functions;
b) prefer non-departmental organizations over ministerial departments, especially for policy implementation;
c) prefer small to large organizations;
d) prefer single-purpose to multi-purpose organizations;
e) allow pluriform administrative structures rather than seeking uniformity ('horses for courses');
f) separate policy from operations;
g) separate funding from purchasing and purchasing from providing;
h) separate operations from regulation;
i) separate provision from review and audit;
j) prefer multi-source to single-source supply;
k) place like with like (primarily on the basis of the purpose or the type of activity);
h) aim for short ('flat') rather than long hierarchies;
l) aim for 'straight-line' accountability/avoid 'multiple principals';
m) decentralize wherever possible.

G. Party political ideas

Until the advent of proportional representation in 1996 the main electoral competition had taken place between the Labour Party (broadly social democratic) and the National Party (broadly conservative). It is noticeable that the NZ Labour and Australian Labor governments were the only Labor/social democrat executives in the OECD to respond to the global economic pressures of the 1980s by actively embracing market-oriented reforms (Castles *et al.*, 1996, p. 2). Labour had been in power from 1935 until 1949, and during that time had established what was arguably the world's first comprehensive welfare state. After this, however, Labour enjoyed only brief periods in power (1957–60 and 1972–75) before their coming to office in 1984.

Specifically *party* political ideas do not appear to have had much influence on the NZ reforms of 1984–90. The policies which were put in place were developed rapidly and without much external consultation by the governing elite (Castles *et al.*, 1996). Unlike the Australian Labor Party the NZ party did not have particularly close links with the trade union movement, and its relatively unrestrained constitutional position allowed it to choose its policies with remarkably few major constraints.

H. Pressure from citizens

The rush of reforms from 1984 to 1990 could not be described as a response to direct pressure from citizens, in fact at first they were controversial and widely unpopular. They were a package pushed through quickly by an elite which took the opportunity for radical reform when faced with immediate and powerful external pressures (see Sections B above and I below). However, the slowing of reform in the mid-1990s may have been influenced by a distinct public 'reform fatigue'

I. Elite perceptions of what management reforms were desirable

The small, elite group of Labour Party ministers and civil servants who drove the NZ reforms from 1984 to 1990 were, in the main, enthusiasts for the new management ideas spelled out in section F above. When the National Party returned to power in 1990 there was no great change to this 'menu', other, perhaps, than a willingness to apply these concepts even more vigorously than before to the social protection system.

J. Elite perceptions of what management reforms were feasible

In the NZ case, the gap between what was desired and what it was possible to carry out was smaller than for many of the other countries in this study. This was because of the way in which the political and administrative systems permitted a determined government to operate with relatively few checks and balances (see E above).

Nevertheless, it would be mistaken to see the NZ example as the pure and undiluted application of a set of tightly knit theoretical ideas. To begin with, the ideas do not all fit together perfectly—sometimes different principles or guidelines seem to point in different directions. Furthermore, many detailed, practical compromises had to be made (Boston *et al.*, 1996, pp. 82–6). For example: 'despite the substantial privatisation programme during the late 1980s, a number of important commercial organisations remain in public ownership, and there has been little public or political support for privatisation in areas like education, health care, and scientific research' (Boston *et al.*, 1996, p. 82).

K. Chance events

It is not obvious that any chance events had a major and direct influence on the course and content of the public management reforms. However, it might be said that, towards the end of our period, the Cave Creek disaster (in which, in 1993, fourteen young people died when an observation platform collapsed in a Department of Conservation nature reserve) provided a focus for much public unease about the changes which had been implemented over the previous decade. One theme in the media treatment of the Cave Creek tragedy was the lack of individual responsibility in the decentralized public service (Gregory, 1998).

L. The administrative system

At the outset of the reforms the NZ public service was a unified, non-party political, career service. Senior public servants 'tended to take a broad service-wide perspective at least as much as a narrow departmental focus' (Boston *et al.*, 1996, p. 56). It was heavily rule-bound (especially in matters of personnel and industrial relations) and by the early 1980s was widely regarded as inefficient.

Much of this was changed by the 1988 State Sector Act (see below) and other reforms. Personnel powers were decentralized and senior civil servants were henceforth employed on performance-related contracts. Large departmental structures were broken up into a larger number of smaller agencies, each with a more closely defined set of objectives and targets (see next section).

In general terms, however, New Zealand had—and still has—quite a centralized politico-administrative system.

M. The contents of the reform package

The key management changes were embodied in four pieces of legislation:

- *The State Owned Enterprises Act, 1986.* This provided the basis for converting the old trading departments and corporations into businesses along private sector lines.
- *The State Sector Act, 1988.* Chief Executives became fully accountable for managing their departments efficiently and effectively. The role of the State Services Commissioner shifted from that of employer and manager of the public service to that of employer of the chief executives and advisor to the government on general management and personnel issues. Chief executives became the managers of their own departmental staff.
- *The Public Finance Act, 1989.* Introduced accruals accounting and insisted on a focus on outputs and outcomes rather than inputs and activities.
- *The Fiscal Responsibility Act, 1994.* Obliged the government to set out its fiscal objectives and explain how these were related to stated principles of responsible fiscal management.

N. The implementation process

The implementation process was vigorous—at times harsh—and fairly continuous for the eight years following the 1984 election. The key civil servants at the Treasury and the State Services Commission played central roles. Much use was also made of management consultants and other experts brought in from outside. The human relations climate was often poor—formally a fairly humanist model of Human Resource Management was adopted during the 1980s, but in practice there were many job losses, large restructurings, great pressures and many upheavals (Boston *et al.*, 1996, p. 213).

O. Reforms actually achieved

The NZ government achieved what was probably the most comprehensive and radical set of public management reforms of any OECD country. For example, between 1988 and 1994 employment in the public service declined from 88,000 to 37,000 (though this includes civil servants who were transferred 'off books' to Crown Entities or State Owned Enterprises).

Unlike many other countries New Zealand governments have commissioned at least two broad-scope evaluations of the reforms (Steering Group, 1991; Schick, 1996). Both came to positive conclusions, while identifying some areas of continuing concern. The Steering Group believed that: 'In the view of most people we spoke to or heard from, the framework is sound and substantial benefits are being realized' (Steering Group, 1991, p. 11). Allen Schick, the American expert, concluded that 'the reforms have lived up to most of the lofty expectations held for them' (Schick, 1996, Executive Summary). Major productivity and quality improvements have been won in the state trading sector. The range of policy advice to ministers seems to have broadened. There is much greater flexibility of employment, and operational managers wield genuinely decentralized powers. There is much more performance information in the public domain (Boston *et al.*, 1996, pp. 359–61).

Less positive results include:

- The costs of reform have not been closely estimated but seem very likely to have been high. These include extensive disruption, loss of continuity and of 'institutional memory'.
- A greater focus on outputs has been achieved, but sometimes at the expense of some loss of attention to *outcomes*.
- The accountability and monitoring arrangements for the somewhat diverse 'crown entity' category of institutions are unclear.

NEW ZEALAND

Country File Events: New Zealand

	General	Organization	Personnel	Finance
1981–1985	– Muldoon: PM (NP) (1975) – Lange: PM (Lib.) (1984) – Start departmental restructuring (1985)	– Establishment of new population based ministries (Women's Affairs, Youth Affairs, Pacific Island Affairs) (1985)	– Start equal employment initiatives (1985)	– User-pays principle introduced for many State services (1985)
1986–1990	– State Owned Enterprise Act (SOE) (1986) – Intention to reform local gvt system (1987) – State Sector Act (SSA) (1988) – SSA: autonomy, accountability, service to community, integrity, State as good employer (1988) – Palmer: PM (Lib.) (1989) – Amend SSA: include education, other State services, estructured SSC (1989) – Moore: PM (Lib.) (1990) – Bolger: PM (NP) (1990)	– SOE: separating trading activities from administrative and regulatory ones (1986) – Corporatization of trading activities in SOEs (1987) – Restructuring gvt departments: separate policy advice—operational functions (agriculture, labour, justice, social welfare) (1987) – Seperate policy advice from regulatory, review and monitoring (education, transport) (1987) – Privatization: gvt assets, trading activities (1988) – Local gvt: from 600 to 94: abolition of most special purpose authorities (1989) – Corporatization of Local Authority Trading Enterprises (LATEs) (1989)	– SSA: devolve personnel mgt to chief executive (1988) – Establishment of Senior Executive Service (SES) (1988) – Annual performance agreements between CEs and ministers (1988) – SSA: major changes in industrial relations and wage-fixing (1988) – State Services Commission (SSC): restructured to focus more ministers (1989) – SSC: 'Public Service Code of Conduct': minimum standards of integrity and conduct (1990)	– SSA: devolve financial mgt to chief executive (1988) – Announce new budget cycle, performance agreements (1988) – Public Finance Act (PFA) (1989) – PFA: output/outcome; owner/purchaser; modes of appropriation (accrual vs revolving funds) (1989) – Comprehensive Bill: reform resource mgt and allocate responsibility for implementation (1989) – All core public sector bodies: move to new financial mgt system: outputs specified and agreed, operating full accrual accounting, cash arrangement system, new financial reporting (1990)

1991–1995				
– Logan Review of State Sector Reforms (1991): accountability and collective interest; departmental performance, cost/benefit of reporting and audit requirements, quality of senior mgt – IT in tax and social welfare (1991) – Various ministerial task forces to develop more competitive mechanisms for service delivery (1992) – Referendum to move to proportional system (1993) – 'The Next Three Years' (1994) – Reinforcing the 'collective interests': Government's 'Strategic Result Areas' (SRAs) (1994) – SRA reflected in departments: Key Result Areas (KRAs) (1994) – Guidance issued on public service principles, conventions, practices (1995) – 'Investing in our future' (1995)	– PM Office and Cabinet Office: new structure: improve co-ordination and quality of advice (1989) – PM and Cabinet: adjust for policy co-ordination and PP task forces (1991) – Establishment of 10 Crown Research Institutes (1991) – Sale of shares in airports, port companies, and local utilities (1991) – Crown Research Institutes, Crown Health Enterprises, Regional Health Authorities, new (commercial) organizational forms used in social services (hospitals, housing and transport, etc.) (1992) – Establishment of 23 Crown Health Enterprises (1993) – Privatizations: Gvt Computing Services Ltd, Prime Rate Housing Corporation (1994) – New Fishery Dpt (separate policy from mgt, research in Crown entity) (1995) – Restructuring of Dpt of Justice separating policy from implementation, clarity of of organizational purpose (1995)	– Employment Contracts Act (ECA) (1991) – ECA: new legal and institutional arrangements for private and public sector industrial relations; SSC for core State sector; but delegation of bargaining authority (1991) – Review gvt pension scheme (1991) – More individual contracts than collective arrangements (1991) – Union bargaining rights contestable (1991) – SSC collaborates with chief executives to develop guidelines and codes of ethics (1992) – Public Sector Training Organization (detect needs and provide or co-ordinate training) (1995)	– Introduce capital charges to reflect cost of capital used by departments in price of outputs (1991) – Part (user) charges in health (1992) – Legislation identifies uniform accountability and financial reporting structure (1992) – Financial statements include Crown-owned and core bodies (1993) – Separate purchase from performance agreements (1993) – Fiscal Responsibility Act (FRA) (1994): responsible fiscal mgt and strengthen reporting requirements of the Crown – Estimates vs DFR (Departmental Forecast Reports) (1994) – DFR: reflect producer/capital user orientation; forward-looking versions of annual reports; 'Vote Minister's' purchase expectations vs 'Responsible Minister's' ownership interest (1994) – Estimates: responsibility of Treasury (1994)	

Country File Events: New Zealand (*cont.*):

	General	Organization	Personnel	Finance
1996–1998	– 'The spirit of Reform' (Schick Review) (1996) – Major review of mgt framework: structure, organizational capacity, managing public money, accounting for results (1996) – First election under proportional electoral system (1996) – Standing Orders for operation of House of Representatives (1996) – Local Government Act (1996) (transparency and accountability) – Shipley: PM (NP) (1997) – New SRAs (1997–2000)	– Merger of four Regional Health Authorities (RHAs) into one Health Funding Authority (1996)	– Management Development Centre: caters for needs of public sector managers (1996)	– House: changes in annual financial cycle (1996) – Compliance Cost Assessment Cost Statement; Compliance Framework: Compliance Cost Statement; Compliance Cost Assessment Report (1996)

SWEDEN

A. Socio-economic forces: general

See Section A.2 and Table A.1 (above).

B. Global economic forces

Again, see Section A.2 and Table A.1.

C. Socio-demographic issues

According to political scientists Lane and Ersson, who surveyed data on a number of social cleavages (1991, chapter 2), Sweden is among the most homogenous, least socially and/or ethnically divided countries in Western Europe. Nevertheless, it has experienced the same difficulties of an ageing population and increasing rates of family break-up as most other western European and North American states. In the late 1980s and early 1990s the growth in the elderly population was particularly fast (see Figures A.1 and A.2 and Section A.3 generally).

D. National socio-economic policies

Throughout the period under study Sweden maintained the largest (as a proportion of GDP) public sector in the western world. It built and has maintained one of the world's most generous and egalitarian welfare states (Esping-Andersen, 1990). This was already giving rise to fiscal problems in the late 1970s, and the budget deficit peaked at 13 per cent of GDP in 1982. Although the budget moved briefly into surplus in 1987, Sweden subsequently experienced a further—and spectacular—deterioration in its budget balance. Some expert commentators began to see this as a virtually insoluble problem within the existing political and administrative system (Lane, 1995). Certainly, the late 1980s and early 1990s were a particularly difficult time, as Table A.5 shows.

A Conservative government came to power in 1991, and the early and mid-1990s were dominated by the acute necessity of making cuts and efficiency savings. However, by the late 1990s, budget balance had been restored (OECD, 1998). Whether this recovery proves any more durable than the short-lived balanced budgets of 1987–90 remains to be seen.

E. The political system

Sweden is a unitary, but highly decentralized state. It has had a constitutional monarch since 1866, but the monarch's role is almost exclusively ceremonial. Executive power rests with

TABLE A.5. *Swedish economic growth, 1970–93*

	1970–77	1978–86	1987–93
Sweden	1.7	2.1	0.1
OECD Europe	2.5	2.0	2.3
All OECD	3.8	2.5	2.3

Source: adapted from Lane, 1995, p. 580, based on OECD data

the Prime Minister and the Cabinet (*Regering*). Most important decisions are made collect-ively, not by individual ministers. The legislature (*Riksdag*) is a unicameral body with 349 seats. Much of its work goes on in a relatively non-partisan spirit unlike, say, the UK House of Commons or the Australian parliament. The process of forming a government is initi-ated by the Speaker of the *Riksdag* (who plays a non-partisan role). S/he nominates a candi-date for Prime Minister, but if more than 50 per cent of the members vote against then another name must be put forward.

Elections to the *Riksdag* and to local governments take place every four years under a system of proportional representation. However, since the 1970s:

Not only has power been transferred from the *Riksdag* to the Cabinet, but public power appears to have become more diffused among several groups of actors, among which may be mentioned various bureaucracies that have grown from the exceptional expansion of the Swedish public sector, different organised interests, regional and local groups of actors (Lane and Ersson, 1991, p. 262).

Since the 1920s, the Social Democratic Party has become the 'establishment' party in Sweden. It was continuously in government (often in coalition with smaller parties) from 1932 to 1976. Lane and Ersson (1991, p. 262) write that:

The strong position of the Social Democratic Party in state and society opened the way for the participation of organised interests in policy-making, exercising influence at various stages of the policy process. The major interest organisations include: the LO (*Landsorganisationen*), the TCO (white collar workers), the SACO-SR (academics), the SAF (employers' association) and the LRF (farmers' association).

F. New management ideas

The new management ideas which were circulating so vigorously in the Anglo-Saxon world during the 1980s and 1990s (see country files for New Zealand and the UK) also reached Sweden. The Swedish system is a very 'open' one, in the sense that Swedish officials and academics play an active role in many international fora (probably disproportionately so for a country of Sweden's modest population) and most educated Swedes are comfortable as Anglophones. However, the Swedish governing elite did not embrace fashionable manage-ment ideas as enthusiastically as did their counterparts in some other countries. 'Marketization' ideas, although briefly in official favour from 1991 to 1994, never achieved the penetration which they enjoyed in Australia during the 1990s or New Zealand and the UK during the 1980s. Other new management concepts were more readily assimilated—for, example, TQM was quite widely adopted, in various forms. And performance management, based on a shift from an orientation to input and procedural controls to a system based on the achievement of measured results, became a central philosophy of the public manage-ment reforms from the late 1980s onwards.

G. Party political ideas

Premfors (1991) explains the internal political debate during the first half of the 1980s as a struggle between three camps—the decentralists, the traditionalists and the economizers. The 1985 programme favoured decentralist ideas, but, quite quickly thereafter, the minis-ter most concerned was heavily criticized on the grounds that he was more talk than action. In any case, by the late 1980s, with a fiscal crisis fully in process, decentralization and participation tended to seem less pressing than cutting expenditures. The economizers took over as the dominant group. Management by results became one of the most salient themes in administrative reform.

At the 1991 elections Sweden acquired its first Conservative Prime Minister since 1930. Neo-liberal ideas such as privatization and market testing, extensively borrowed from New Zealand and the UK, were now in favour among the political elite (Premfors, 1998, pp. 151–2). However, this was a relatively brief phase, and when the Social Democrats were voted back into power in September 1994 the 'reform talk' soon lost its high emphasis on the power of markets to solve problems. The stress on economy and efficiency continues, as budget problems are too deep to be solved overnight.

H. Pressure from citizens

According to Premfors (1998) Swedish public attitudes towards their governments have been quite fickle. For example, the public sector, together with the Social Democrat leadership, fell rapidly from favour in the late 1980s and early 1990s, but as soon as 1992 there were signs that confidence in public sector institutions was increasing, and that the electorate feared any radical dismantling of the generous Swedish welfare state. In general it might be said that, during the period under consideration, most Swedes were impatient of the more bureaucratic aspects of the large government machine, but were protective of most of their welfare provisions, and were certainly not enamoured of the kind of 'new right', pro-market doctrines that were fashionable in the UK and the USA during the 1980s.

I. Elite perceptions of what management reforms were desirable

One Swedish expert has suggested that, during the period covered by this study, there were three main schools of thought and opinion as to how the Swedish government should respond to its problems (Premfors, 1991—see section G above). Decentralizers wanted to relax the detailed grip of the central state, and push out both operational management decisions and some increasingly uncomfortable resource allocation decisions to other levels of government, and even down to individual institutions, such as schools and hospitals. Economizers were mainly concerned with the looming deficit, and the in-built tendencies for welfare expenditures to expand. They sought to weaken the 'distributional coalitions' in Swedish policy making. Traditionalists concentrated on preserving as much as they could of both the substance and the process of the Swedish state, as it had existed during its 'golden age' in the 1960s and early 1970s. From the late 1980s the economizers appeared to gain the upper hand, but Premfors (1998) suggests that, by the late 1990s, the decentralizers were once more gaining ground.

J. Elite perceptions of what management reforms were feasible

The issue of feasibility was determined partly by the strongly entrenched *process* by which government decisions are arrived at in Sweden. Typically, agencies plan with the aid of boards on which trade unions, employers associations and other interest groups are strongly represented. Thus feasibility questions are soon aired with those who will have to 'live' with any proposed reform, unlike the policy making systems in, for example, the UK and New Zealand, where some reforms were conceived and promulgated by quite small groups of politicians and senior officials.

K. Chance events

None of particular prominence.

L. The administrative system

As of 1994 only 17.3 per cent of public servants worked for central government (compared to 48.7 per cent in France and 47.7 per cent in the UK—see Table 3.2). This reflects the importance of the county and municipal levels in the Swedish administrative system. There are 23 counties and 286 municipalities. The counties are responsible for most health care and are entitled to raise an income tax. Municipalities are responsible for housing, education and social welfare. Lane and Ersson give Sweden a high score for regional and local discretion (1991, pp. 224–5, see also Table 3.3).

Even central government is unusually decentralized by international standards, and long has been. Swedish central government agencies have their operational autonomy protected by the constitution, and are responsible to the Cabinet collectively, not to individual ministers. There are over 300 of them, and in the mid-1990s they employed roughly 320,000 staff (compared to the ministries, which employed only 2,900). Thus the ministries themselves tend to be small and largely devoted to policy advice and the preparation of legislation. Doubts have frequently been expressed concerning their capacity to guide or control the agencies (OECD, 1997a, p. 94, 1998; Wilks, 1996).

The Swedish civil service is non-partisan, and minister/mandarin career paths are normally separate (see Table 3.1). However, the top three officials in ministries—the under secretary of state, the permanent secretary and the under secretary of legal affairs—are appointed by the minister.

Policy making is typically an open process, with extensive participation by experts and interested groups. Freedom of information legislation gives the public access to almost all official papers, even including most of the Prime Minister's correspondence.

M. Contents of the reform package

Following its 1976 ousting from government (for the first time in forty-four years) the Social Democratic Party analysed the reasons. One factor appeared to be the way in which many people associated it, as the 'establishment' party, with bureaucratic inertia. When the Social Democrats returned to power in 1982 they were therefore determined to change their image in this respect, and to make the state machine more responsive and accessible to the ordinary citizen. They recreated a Ministry of Public Administration as a symbol of their reforming intent. In 1985 a Government Modernization Programme laid considerable stress on decentralization from the centre to counties and municipalities (although it should be noted that decentralization was a long-standing political theme, and by no means the preserve of the Social Democrats—Premfors, 1998). Increased choice and user responsiveness were also emphasized. Deregulation and de-bureaucratization were further themes. Personnel authority was decentralized, so that agencies could now hire their own staff and set their own salary ranges, within national frameworks.

At that stage privatization was not favoured. As one senior civil servant put it in 1987: 'The Swedish government in principle rejects privatisation as a means of solving the problems of the [public] sector. The main objection is that this would lead to distributive injustices' (Gustaffson, 1987, p. 180).

In the late 1980s a second phase of reform began, overshadowed by the growing fiscal crisis. The need to make efficiency gains and savings was paramount. In 1990 an Administration Programme was announced which aimed to generate a 10 per cent reduction in the size of the public sector. This was supposed to be achieved through a combination of measures: abolishing or merging agencies, increased delegation and various productivity improvement initiatives. The focus on economy intensified with the arrival of a conservative (Bild) government in 1991. At this point there was considerable rhetoric in favour of privatization, but in practice the government soon had to compromise on its original and quite extensive privatization schemes. In any case, the Social Democrats returned to power in 1994, though by that time they had abandoned their opposition in principle to privatization, and were prepared to accept it on a selective and pragmatic basis. Between 1990 and 1996 13 agencies did become public companies (the Swedes, like the Finns, tended to prefer a combination of the corporate format with state ownership rather than outright privatization like New Zealand and the UK).

From 1988 to 1993 a series of strong financial management reforms were implemented, including results-oriented budgeting, frame appropriations and accruals accounting. Results-oriented management was officially adopted for all state organizations from 1988. The rise of this form of output- and outcome-oriented approach was accompanied by a parallel decline in the previously formidable machinery of Swedish planning (Wilks, 1996). Since 1993 each agency has been required to publish an annual report which includes performance data, an income statement, a balance sheet, an appropriation account and a financial analysis (OECD, 1997a, p. 90). In 1996 the budget process itself was reformed, with a better defined first stage to the process in which firm ceilings to overall expenditure were fixed (OECD, 1998).

Continued decentralization measures went hand in hand with the attempts to make savings. In 1993 a new system of central government grants to the municipalities strengthened the latter's autonomy (fewer detailed regulations from the centre) but also permitted central government to fix tight frame budgets and leave the local authorities to sort out how they would allocate their circumscribed allocations.

Over the whole period from the mid-1980s, a variety of service quality improvement schemes were adopted, often based on TQM or ISO 9000 principles. These were implemented at all levels of government but there was no central plan or framework equivalent to, say, the UK *Citizen's charter* (OECD, 1997a, p. 91).

N. The implementation process

Sweden has tended to avoid the sometimes strident or harsh styles of implementation favoured by Mrs Thatcher's administration in the UK, Mr Lange's in New Zealand or Mr Howard's in Australia. The traditional Swedish processes of intensive, corporatist discussions between the main interested parties prior to action has, with a few exceptions, persisted. As in Finland, extensive use was made of pilot projects to test out key innovations (e.g., results-oriented budgeting) before they were 'rolled out' to the government more generally. An example would be the 1984 'Free municipalities' experiment, in which nine municipalities and three county councils piloted a system of greater freedom from central state regulation. Strenuous efforts were also made to minimize compulsory redundancies among public servants.

O. Reforms actually achieved

There is no doubt that substantial decentralization of powers to counties and municipalities has been achieved during the 1980s and 1990s. It is also clear that budgeting systems have been extensively modernized, and that a much more output-oriented set of arrangements has been firmly put in place since the late 1980s. Productivity studies, after showing a large overall deterioration in public sector productivity during the 1970s, and a smaller one even during the 1980s, indicated a productivity gain for the early 1990s (see discussion in chapter 5).

Sweden has developed a strong interest in evaluation, and a variety of evaluation bodies. The National Audit Office (*Riksrevisionsverket*) has an extensive role in evaluation and performance auditing, and has taken an interest in a number of public management reforms (Pollitt *et al.*, 1999). There is also an Expert Group on Public Finance, which has conducted large-scale studies of public productivity, and a Swedish Agency for Administrative Development. Yet, despite the existence of these units, no overall evaluation of the main reforms appears to have been undertaken.

Against these substantial achievements must be set the continuing concern that the central ministries lack the capability to set a really well-informed yet demanding set of performance targets for the agencies (OECD, 1997a, 1998). Furthermore, it is by no means clear that the members of the *Riksdag* are overwhelmingly interested in making use of the increased flow of performance data that is now available. Finally, and most importantly, it is too soon to be confident that the underlying problem of chronic budget deficit has been definitively solved.

SWEDEN

Country File Events: Sweden

	General	Organization	Personnel	Finance
1981–1985	– Fälldin: PM (Agrar., Lib.) (1979) – MoF: Independent Expert Group on Public Finance (ESO): transfer in welfare state and productivity of agencies (1981) – Palme: PM (Soc.) (1982) – Palme: PM (Soc.) (1985)			– Experiment: 3-year budget frames (administrative expenditures) (1985)
1986–1990	– Carlsson: PM (Soc.) (1986) – Parliamentary Decision on Public Management (1987) – Government Agency Ordinance: guidelines for administrative reform (1987) – Carlsson: PM (Soc.) (1988) – Free Municipal Experiment: increasing autonomy, restructure central, regional, municipal relations (1988) – Administration: slim down by 10%: decentralization, deregulation, inter-nationalization (1990) – Expanded survey of regulatory impact (1990) – Number of laws and	– New instructions for 200 agencies: decentralization, results, long-term objectives, increased autonomy, discretionary authority for managers (1988) – Ministry of Public Administration: reorganization, re-enforcement, leader of renewal process (1988)	– More flexibility: recruitment, mobility of senior executives (1988) – Study on pay scales, remuneration (1988) – Public Employment Act modernized (1988)	– Supplementary Budget Bill: 3-year budget frames (first: 1991/92) (1988) – Results based mgt: measurement, accounting, budget cycles (request and *regleringsbrev*) (1988) – In-depth budget requests: analyses of resources, environ-ment, results (minus 2, plus 3 years)(1988) – Methodology for determining costs of regulations refined (1988) – Government Budget Ordinance on budgetary reform (goals and results) (1988) – Supplementary Budget Bill: guidelines for public sector renewal (1988)

Country File Events: Sweden (*cont.*):

	General	Organization	Personnel	Finance
	ordinances in force: lowest level: result of regulatory review and computerization (1990) – New Local Government Act: clearer powers, financial mgt reforms, more importance for accounting and auditing, freer committee structure (1990)			– On-going reorganization of budget process: specify results (1990)
1991–1995	– Bildt: PM (Cons.) (1991) – Management by results: emphasis on analysis and evaluation (1991) – Budget Bill Annex: report on progress with rule simplification (1991) – Deregulation efforts speeded up: over 1,000 agency regulations abolished (1991) – Local Authority Act: free to structure activities, promote deregulation, privatization, market orientation (1991) – Economic Policy Statement: budget deficit reduction (1992) – Criteria to determine when State Company is suitable for	– MoF: responsible for central matters of public administration (1991) – Ministry of Public Administration: regional and local authorities; rest is transferred to MoF, Agency for Administrative Development, National Audit Bureau, National Agency for Government Employers (1991) – Cabinet Office: political Co-ordination Chancery (1991) – Privatization of certain State-owned enterprises (1991) – Ordinances for all agencies:	– Comprehensive Job Security System (1991) – Job Security Foundation (1991) – Pension system similar to private sector (1991) – New classification system for civil service wage and salary statistics (1991) – Each agency responsible for training and development (1992) – 'State and Employee Organization' report: Unions should pay for help received in negotiations (1992) – Programme of training in financial mgt (1992) – New Organization for State	– Review of budget process (1992) – National Audit Bureau Commission: rating system to evaluate the capacity of agencies (1992) – Flexible budget frame periods introduced (1992) – Agencies deliver first annual financial report directly to Government (audited by National Audit Bureau): balance sheet, income statement, appropriation report, changes in financial position, performance report (1992) – New Budgeting and Accounting forms: better account of the financial situation (1993)

– privatization, transformation, closure (1992) – Decrease structural deficit (1993) – Criteria for corporatization of State activities (1993) – Management by results proceeds (1993) – Carlsson: PM (Soc.) (1994)	– clearer goal and results control (1992) – Reorganize Government Chancery, framework budget (1992) – Dissolve National Institute for Civil Service Training and Development (SIPU) (1992) – Abolish Postal Giro's monopoly of State payments (1993) – Selling 49% of shares of forest industry (1994)	– Employers controlled and financed by government agencies (1994)	– Agencies pay interest on drawings on the State budget (1993) – Agencies: borrow money for investments, risk analysis (1993) – Changes in financial control of agencies: new accrual accounting model, technique of frame appropriation, interest accounts, loan model for investments in fixed assets (1993) – Ordinance on Internal Audit of Government Agencies (1994)
1996– 1998	– Persson: PM (1996) – Riksdag resolution on implementing expenditure ceiling (1995) – VESTA: integrated, consolidated system for central gvt forecasting, budgeting, consolidated accounting, performance monitoring and payment information by 2000 (1997) – Central Government Administration in the Citizen's Service: Government Bill (1997–98)	– Further corporatization of various state activities (1996–?)		– Booster project: 10 ministries and 10 agencies (1995) – Budget year coincides with calendar year (1997) – 260 agencies: performance follow-up reports (1998)

UNITED KINGDOM

A. Socio-economic forces: general

See Section A.2 (above).

B. Global economic forces

See Section A.2 (above).

C. Socio-demographic issues

See Section A.3 (above).

D. National socio-economic policies

The advent of Mrs Thatcher's Conservative government in 1979 marked the final abandonment of Keynesian policies of macro-economic management and the beginning of an era of vigorous monetarism. The general view was that the Public Sector Borrowing Requirement (PSBR) was a key variable that a responsible government should seek to minimize. This, in turn, implied a tight fiscal policy. So did the government's continuing determination to control inflation (which had reached frighteningly high levels during the 1970s and which was still running faster than that of most of the UK's main economic competitors). Thus the Conservative governments were committed to reducing the proportion of GDP that was represented by public spending. In practice, however, they were not tremendously successful at first (see Thain and Wright, 1995 for the details). By the 1990s the public expenditure/GDP ratio had fallen (see chapter 5, Table 5.1) but this was partly an artefact of changed definitions.

The incoming 1997 Labour government inherited a fairly healthy economic situation, but committed itself to maintaining the previous government's tough spending plans for at least two years. It conducted a comprehensive spending review and then announced targeted increases for certain sectors, especially health care and education (Chancellor of the Exchequer, 1998).

E. The political system

The UK is a unitary and highly centralized state. The political system is majoritarian and adversarial, with a first-past-the-post electoral basis. There are two major parties (Conservative, Labour) and a number of minor parties, the most important of which is the Liberal-Democrat party. All governments since the Second World War have been Labour or Conservative. The Cabinet is mainly concerned with enforcing collective responsibility among ministers and with endorsing new policies. Most policies, however, are developed outside Cabinet, in departments or cabinet committees. The executive is powerful, reinforced by tight party discipline in the lower house of the legislature (the Commons). In normal times it can almost always get its legislation through. The upper house, a mixture of a heriditary aristocracy and appointed 'life peers', is, at the time of writing, scheduled for major reform (to remove the hereditary element). However, the upper house (the Lords) basically only has the power to delay, not to destroy, government legislation.

Another constitutional change which is underway as we go to press is the creation of elected assemblies for Scotland and Wales. It is not yet clear what implications this may have for public administration.

F. New management ideas

The UK has been very much part of the Anglophone, US-dominated world of managerialism, management consultants and management gurus (Pollitt, 1993, chapters 1 and 2). The Conservative governments of 1979–97 were particularly open to generic management thinking, and to ideas injected into government by the private sector. Mrs Thatcher's first efficiency adviser, Derek Rayner, was a businessman, and many other managers were subsequently brought into government in various advisory capacities (Metcalfe and Richards, 1990). The succeeding Labour administration has continued to use high-profile business people for important public roles (e.g., reviewing the *Citizen's charter* initiative).

G. Party political ideas

The decisive shift towards managerialism came in 1979, when a neo-conservative government was elected in place of a centre-left administration (see also Canada and the USA— but note that managerialist reforms in Australia and New Zealand were launched principally by centre-left parties, see Castles *et al.*, 1996). However, that is not to say that Conservative politicians necessarily had very precise ideas about management reform. Rather it was a case of certain broad beliefs and doctrines which inclined the government in a particular direction. Among these were beliefs that the private sector was inherently more efficient than the public sector, that the civil service was too privileged and complacent and that the state was too big and too interventionist (Pollitt, 1993). However, ideas evolved during the long period of office and it would be mistaken to suppose that the incoming government of 1979 had a clear plan for all the management reforms which subsequently appeared.

H. Pressure from citizens

There was no single, citizen-inspired movement for reform. Management changes came from political, business and administrative elites. Nevertheless, public opinion played a part. The popularity of early measures of privatization (selling public housing to the tenants, issuing shares for British Telecom) helped convince the government that this was a policy that could be pursued much further. The public was also receptive to the government's message that the quality of public services should be raised although, ironically, the 1991 *Citizen's charter* was launched very much as a top-down exercise, with little consultation of public opinion (Prime Minister, 1991)). The general 'decline of deference' was also a significant background influence on a number of user-oriented reforms.

I. Elite perceptions of what management reforms were desirable

The radicalness of Mrs Thatcher's Conservative government grew as its political confidence was boosted by the election victories of 1983 and 1987. By the late 1980s some members of the Cabinet, probably including Mrs Thatcher herself, perceived the possibility of a mixture of marketizing and minimizing, that is, the return of many hitherto public functions and activities to the private sector combined with the introduction of market-type mechanisms to much of the remaining, 'rump' public sector. This general orientation continued into the Major administration (1990–97), as evidenced by the further privatizations of the railways and British Coal, the selling-off of some Next Steps executive agencies and the expansion of the Private Finance Initiative. The aspirations of the incoming Labour government of 1997 were different, but not enormously so. The urge to privatize disappeared, but there was no countervailing desire to take organizations or functions back into public ownership. The Private Finance Initiative was retained. Even if the tone was more sympathetic to public sector staff, the general belief in the scope for improving public management and providing more efficient and high quality services persisted.

J. Elite perceptions of what management reforms were feasible

The unusual dominance of a single party form of executive within the British system gives governments an equally unusual ability to realize their reform desires, even when these are controversial in Parliament or unpopular in the country (e.g., the 1989 reform of the National Health Service was hugely unpopular, both among NHS staff and the wider public, but the 'provider market' was forced through all the same, see Pollitt, Birchall and Putman, 1998). It is clear that, since 1979 governments have regarded continuing and deep administrative change as perfectly feasible. In the UK the barriers to (and political costs of) this kind of reform are considerably lower than in many other countries.

K. Chance events

There are none which stand out as having an immediate, large and direct effect of management reform (unless one counts the Falklands War as a chance, with its tonic effect on the Conservative government's electoral ratings and subsequent success in the 1983 general election—though even this would have to be seen as an indirect influence).

On the other hand there have been particular events in particular organizations or sectors which have had significant local influences. Examples would include a series of tragic failures in child protection (which obliged governments to address the reform of social services departments) and the behaviour of certain left-wing local councils which provided central government (under Mrs Thatcher) with one of its pretexts for abolishing certain large, urban councils and instituting various additional controls on the remainder (Cochrane, 1993).

L. The administrative system

The permanent civil service is still the main source of advice and support for ministers, though it is probably less dominant in this role than it was thirty years ago and the use of partisan political advisers is now firmly entrenched. The civil service is neutral in party political terms, right up to the most senior level (Permanent Secretary). The culture of the upper civil service is generalist (and non-legalist). The single most important constitutional doctrine for senior civil servants remains that of 'ministerial responsibility' which means (roughly) that ministers must answer to the House of Commons for all the doings of their ministries, and that civil servants normally remain anonymous but have a prime duty to support and protect 'their' minister. Therefore civil servants are *not* held to have any higher duty towards 'the state' (not a concept much in use), the legislature or the citizenry.

Central government is organized into departments, most of which are headed by a

Cabinet minister. The majority of non-industrial civil servants now work in semi-autonomous executive agencies, which are still, constitutionally, part of their 'parent' departments (O'Toole and Jordan, 1995).

Local government is less protected from central government interventions than in most other European states. The period of Conservative government from 1979 to 1997 was one of considerable tension between the centre and local authorities. Central government both passed many new pieces of legislation restricting the discretion of local authorities (especially in relation to finance) and gave many functions to local quangos and other non-elected bodies (Cochrane, 1993; Painter *et al.*, 1996; Stoker, 1988).

M. The contents of the reform package

With the advantage of hindsight, the period of Conservative government could be said to have three broad phases of development in respect to management reform. From 1979 until 1982–83 there was a fierce drive for economies and the elimination of waste. Civil service numbers were cut, first by 14 per cent and then, subsequently, by a further 6 per cent. Rayner scrutinies (see Metcalfe and Richards, 1990) sought to find more efficient ways of undertaking tasks, and usually concluded that staffing reductions were possible.

In the early 1980s, however, the emphasis shifted to improving financial and general management, and increasing efficiency. The Financial Management Initiative was launched in 1982 and embraced the whole of central government with its philosophy of more decentralized management, more decentralized budgets, more targets and more professionalism (Zifcak, 1994). The National Audit Office and Audit Commission were brought into being (the relevant legislation being passed in 1983 and 1982, respectively), and each was given a mandate that stressed the '3Es'—economy, efficiency and effectiveness. In the National Health Service central government insisted on the introduction of general managers to every health authority (Harrison *et al.*, 1992). Performance indicator systems began to sprout for most public services, central and local (Pollitt, 1986).

During the mid-1980s the privatization programme gathered momentum, with the sales of British Telecom (1984), British Gas (1986), the British Airports Authority (1987) and water supply and sewerage (1989). Between 1979 and 1990 about 800,000 employees were transferred from the public sector to the private.

The third phase of Conservative reform was the most radical. Following their convincing victory in the 1987 election, Mrs Thatcher's administration launched a series of fundamental restructurings. Market-type mechanisms were introduced on a large scale—in healthcare, community care and education. The 'purchaser/provider split' was imposed by central government as a basic model for most locally provided services (Pollitt, Birchall and Putman, 1998). Performance measurement systems were sharpened, and the annual publication of national league tables for schools and hospitals became significant media events. Privatization continued (electricity, 1990–93; railways 1994). In central government the *Next steps* report of 1988 led to the creation, within ten years, of more than 140 executive agencies which employed in excess of 70 per cent of the non-industrial civil service (Chancellor of the Duchy of Lancaster, 1997; O'Toole and Jordan, 1995). During the mid-1990s a number of central ministries were significantly downsized, following a programme of management reviews (e.g., H. M. Treasury, 1994). In 1991 both the *Citizen's charter* (Prime Minister, 1991) and ambitious programmes of contracting out and market-testing were launched (*Competing for quality*—H. M. Treasury, 1991). These two well represented the main tendencies of the 1990s: a huge emphasis on 'customer service' (Clarke and

Newman, 1997) and an equally intense concern to keep up the pace of contracting out and marketization.

The new Labour government of 1997 reversed very little of what had gone before. Although ideologically more sympathetic to the public sector they did not reverse the privatizations or the purchaser/provider splits, although they took some steps to ameliorate the least popular consequences of the latter. If anything, they intensified the 'league table' system still further, 'rebranded' the *Citizen's Charter* programme and launched a 'Service first' initiative. Many of their proposals shared the underlying assumptions about the transformatory capacity of better, more professional public management which had been characteristic of their Conservative predecessors (e.g., the idea of a benchmarked Procurement Excellence model or the 'Best value' initiative in local government—see Chancellor of the Exchequer, 1998). In 1999 the Prime Minister issued a White Paper, *Modernizing government*, which offered a slightly curious mixture of old themes (e.g., greater responsiveness and quality) with faintly millenarial visions of the government's role in the 'Information Age' (Prime Minister and the Minister for the Cabinet Office, 1999).

N. The implementation process

In the UK reform has been continual, often intense, and sometimes harsh. Public sector employees have become accustomed to constant restructurings, downsizings and new 'initiatives'. Much of the change has been strongly driven from the top. The Treasury and the Cabinet Office (Office of Public Service) have been the main actors, though most departments have been heavily involved, especially Health (for the NHS), Environment (for local government), Education (the reform of schools, colleges and universities) and Social Security.

O. Reforms actually achieved

As noted above (Sections E, J) British central government is relatively unfettered in its ability to make administrative changes. So when it determines to carry something through, it usually can. As section M made clear, many large-scale reforms have been put in place. That is not to say that all have achieved the results forecast or claimed for them. Sometimes one can 'take a horse to water but not make him drink' (see Pollitt, Birchall and Putman, 1998, for an assessment of this factor in health care, education and housing reforms).

The Conservative governments of 1979–97 were not enthusiastic about mounting large-scale evaluations of their management reforms. Ministers tended to take the line that reform was essential, and self-evidently desirable, and that formal, public evaluation might prove a delay and distraction. Internal management reviews were more common. The Labour government since 1997 is at least rhetorically more committed to formal evaluation, but it is too soon to say how far this will be observed in practice, especially if evaluation findings indicate that high-profile reforms are not working well.

There have, however, been a number of specific evaluations of particular initiatives, and some of these were made available within the public domain. For example, there was a useful series of assessments of the Next Steps programme, which were basically positive in tone (e.g., Trosa, 1994).

Country File Events: United Kingdom

	General	Organization	Personnel	Finance
1981–1985	– Thatcher: PM (Cons.) (1979) – Thatcher: PM (Cons.) (1983) – First set of national PI for the NHS (1983) – 'Government Purchasing: Review of Government Contract and Procurement Procedures' (1984) – White Paper: 'Lifting the Burden': on deregulation (1985)	– Management and Personnel Office (MPO) created in Cabinet Office (1981) – Privatization B Aerospace (1981) – Central Unit on Purchasing created: report annually on progress in VFM targets (1984) – Privatization B Telecom (1984)	– Civil Service Dpt disbanded (1981)	– Rayner scrutinies (efficiency studies) launched (1979) – Treasury gets part of responsibilities of Civil Service Dpt (1981) – Financial Mgt Initiative (FMI): delegates financial and personnel matters to line managers (1982)
1986–1990	– White Paper: 'Building Business … Not Barriers' (1986) – Thatcher: PM (Cons.) (1987) – White Paper: 'Releasing Enterprise' on deregulation (1988) – Continued efficiency scrutinies and policy reviews (1989) – NHS White Paper 'Working for Patients': introduction for MTM in the health sector from 1991 onwards (1989) – Major: PM (Cons.) (1990) – First annual review of Next Steps (1990) – Central gvt takes power to cap local authority budgets, to set tax rate on local business (1990)	– Privatization B Gas (1986) – Privatization BAA (1987) – Next Steps initiative: Executive Agencies: CE accountable to ministers who set performance targets (1988) – Privatization Water (1989) – 34 agencies (80,000 staff) established (1990) – 29 candidates (200,000) identified (1990) – Privatization: 1990–93: Electricity Generation (1990) – Trading Fund Act: extends range of gvt business able to benefit from trading fund status (Royal Mint, Central Office of Information, Fire Service College) (1990)	– Office of the Minister of Civil Service (OMCS): reconstituted MPO; support PM Cabinet Office (1987) – Treasury: 21 flexibilities for Dpt and Agencies on personnel mgt, pay, allowances (1989) – New career arrangements for IT and Purchasing and Supply Staff: more professionalism (1989) – Flexible pay, recruitment, mgt development, training (1989) – Equal opportunity initiatives; revision of Code of Practice for employing disabled (1990) – 600 secondments between civil service and industry/commerce (1990)	– Multi-departmental Review of Budgeting: tool for resource allocation (1986) – Progess report on budgeting reforms (1988)

Country File Events: United Kingdom (*cont.*):

	General	Organization	Personnel	Finance
1991–1995	– 'Making the most of Next Steps': relation of dpts and agencies (1991) – Second and Third annual review of Next Steps (1991) – White Paper: 'Citizen's Charter' (1991) – Booklet: 'Cutting Red Tape for Business': on deregulation (1991) – White Paper: 'Competing for Quality': set and published targets for new areas of activity in market (1991) – First Citizen's Charter Report and 28 follow-up charters published (1992) – Charter Mark Award; 36 Awards by PM (1992) – Plans to market test 1.5 billion £ (1992) – Conservative election victory (small majority) (1992) – Programme of Fundamental Reviews launched (1993) – White Paper: 'Continuity and Change' (1994)	– 57 agencies established (40% of civil servants) (1991) – Privatization: 900,000 jobs transferred; State-owned sector reduced by 2/3 (1991) – Office of Public Service and Science (OPSS) in Cabinet Office: merger of OMCS, Next Steps Team, Citizen's Charter, Efficiency Unit, Market Testing Unit (1992) – Scheme to increase interchange with local authorities launched (1992) – 76 agencies (50% of civil service) and 29 identified (1992) – Gvt Office for the Region (one window for Transport, Trade and Industry, Employment, Environment) (1994) – Beginning of a series of 'fundamental reviews' of major ministerial departments leading to average downsizing of more than 20% (1994)	– Treasury: 40 flexibilities for dpts and agencies on personnel mgt, pay, allowances (1991) – Dpts and agencies: greater flexibility: pay and grading (1991) – Programme of Action for Women in Civil Service (1992) – 13 agencies: group bonus schemes linked to quality of service targets and funded from efficiency savings (1992) – Civil Service (Management Functions) Act: facilitates delegation of central mgt responsibilities (1992) – Efficiency Unit Report: Career Mgt and Succession Planning (1993) – Introduction of central funding scheme: helps dpts meet costs of early departures (1994) – All dpts: forward plans 'Investors in People' (1994) – White Paper: 'Taking Forward Continuity and Change' (1995) Public Sector MBA launched (1995)	– Audit Commission: 77 indicators for local governments to report on performance (1992) – Private Finance Initiative launched (1994) – Green Paper: resource accounting by 1998, resource budgeting by 2000 (1994) – Fundamental Review of Expenditure: leads to 25% downsizing of HM Treasury (1994) – Dpts: prepare efficiency plans each year (1995) – White Paper: 'Resource Accounting and Budgeting in Government': from cash mgt to mgt of resources against achievement of objectives (1995) – 'Burdens of Bureaucracy': efficiency scrutinies (1995) – Efficiency Scrutiny of Management Information Systems published (1995)

– 'Next Steps: Moving on' (1994)	– OPSS loses Sciences and becomes OPS (1995)	– Civil Service Code into effect (1996)	– Efficiency Plans of Agencies (1997)
– White Paper: 'Competitiveness' (1994)	– Central Information Technology Unit in OPS (1995)	– New Senior Civil Service created (1996)	
– Citizen's Charter Second Report; 98 Charter Marks; 53 reviews of Complaints Task Force; 16 Charter Quality Networks (1994)	– Remaining Treasury responsibilities for Civil Service mgt transferred to OPS (1995)	– Senior Mgt Reviews completed (1996)	
– Code of Practice on Access to Government Information (1994)	– Privatization: B Coal (1995)	– White Paper: 'Development and Training for Civil Servants' (1996)	
– Deregulation and Contracting Out Act (1994)			

1996–1998

- Evaluation of first three years of 'Competing for Quality' (1996)
- Blair: PM (Lab.) (1997)
- Benchmarking initiative for executive agencies (1996–98)
- White Paper: Better Government (1997)
- 'Service First' (Citizen Charter relaunch) (1998)
- White Paper: 'Modernizing Government' (1998)

- 127 agencies (387,000 civil servants: 72%); 37 candidates (1996)
- Privatization B Railways (1996)
- New Better Government Team (1997)

USA

A. Socio-economic forces: general

See Section A.2 above. The USA is unique among the ten countries in this study in its status as a military and economic 'superpower'. Thus it is probably in a better position than other states to influence the course of global trends.

B. Global economic forces

Again, see Section A.2.

C. Socio-demographic issues

See Section A.3. Although rich on the basis of average per capita incomes (Table A.1) the USA spends a surprisingly small amount of government money on social expenditure (Figure A.1, first two columns). By comparison with most European countries it has only a 'thin' welfare state.

D. National socio-economic policies

The 1980s was a period during which political and popular awareness of the federal deficit grew—alongside the growth of the deficit itself. Very high levels of defence spending under the Reagan administration, together with its failure to cut back on social programmes as sharply as had originally been intended, contributed to this problem (Stockman, 1986). These increases dwarfed the savings and cuts that flowed from managerial efficiency improvements (see Section M below). Under Clinton from 1992, however, more effective measures were taken to control the deficit, and at the same time the economy entered a long boom. In 1997 President Clinton and the Republican-dominated Congress agreed a five-year plan to balance the budget, and by the time President Clinton made his 1999 State of the Union address, a political debate was building up on the question of what to do with the anticipated budget surpluses.

E. The political system

The USA possesses a unique political system, with no close parallel within our set of ten countries. It is a federal state, with a constitutionally entrenched division of powers between the executive, legislature and judiciary. From its foundations, the American political elite has been much concerned with maintaining a system of 'checks and balances' to ensure that no one of the three main branches of government can become dominant (Maidment and McGrew, 1986).

There is a two-party system (Republican and Democrat) but the parties are each 'broad churches', and, by European standards, there is little party discipline within the legislature, each Congressman/woman or Senator being free to vote and act according to his/her own dictates. Individual committees within the legislature also enjoy high independence, and the chairs of the senior committees are major political figures in their own right. Specific constituency interests have a strong influence on voting patterns. There is no equivalent to the social democrat or socialist parties which are such a familiar presence in western European politics. The President is directly elected every four years and cannot serve more than two successive terms.

The legislature is bicameral and, relative to the executive, unusually powerful by European standards. The President and the Executive cannot rely on getting their way—certainly not in matters of administrative reform (Savoie, 1994, p. 213). The agencies of the executive may be partly or wholly 'captured' by interest groups represented within the legislature. Many expert commentators have remarked on the legislature's predilection for 'micro-managing' the federal bureaucracy (e.g., Kettl, 1994).

Washington politics is also characterized by a 'spoils system', in which an incoming administration hands out large numbers of senior administrative posts to political sympathizers. These (often short-term) political appointees then work alongside career civil servants (Heclo, 1977). During the 1980s the spoils system grew in size under Presidents Reagan and Bush.

Finally, it must not be forgotten that, although the main focus of this book is on national-level governments, the USA has an extensively decentralized and democratized system of governance (see Table 3.2 in chapter 3—there are more than 80,000 'governments' within the USA).

F. New management ideas

The USA is characterized by a 'business-oriented', 'free enterprise' culture. Its system of government is also very open and fragmented. These factors have meant that it has been very easy for private sector management concepts to enter the public sector. At various times the federal administration has expressed enthusiasm towards most of the contemporary management techniques and approaches, including management by objectives, downsizing, TQM, benchmarking and re-engineering.

A historical perspective indicates that there is nothing particularly new in this openness to business techniques. For example, in the 1960s the federal government famously adopted PPBS, and in the 1970s other techniques with private sector conceptual origins, such as ZBB and organizational development, were also enthusiastically embraced.

G. Party political ideas

These, too, were influenced by the general 'free enterprise' culture, and by the absence of a social democratic or socialist party of any size or salience. Thus a majority of both Republicans and Democrats have been willing to sign up to notions of more 'businesslike' government. Since the late 1970s, however, a substantial group of right-wing Republicans have taken a more radical stance. Deeply sceptical of the efficacy of federal actions, they have argued for fundamental downsizing of the civil service and a general reduction in 'government interference'. In the mid-1990s the Republicans gained control of Congress, and, at the time of writing, the anti-federal-bureaucracy theme is being propounded as vigorously as ever.

H. Pressure from citizens

Since the 1970s US public opinion has tended to become increasingly critical of both the motives and the competence of federal government (Bok, 1997; Kaufman, 1981). Most

Americans believe that the federal bureaucracy wastes huge sums of money. However, the accuracy of popular perceptions of its federal government can be questioned: for example, as mentioned earlier, a majority believe that the administrative overheads eat up more than 50 per cent of the social security programme, whereas the true figure is less than 2 per cent (Bok, 1997, p. 56). Nevertheless, US Presidents and their colleagues have to operate against a background in which the proportion of Americans who believe that public officials don't care what people think has grown from 36 per cent in 1964 to 66 per cent in 1996, and the proportion who think that quite a few people in government are crooked has risen (over the same period) from 29 per cent to 51 per cent (Orren, 1997). This set of attitudes does not so much point towards specific management reforms as it does handicap all reformers, in so far as their efforts and motives are likely to be regarded with widespread scepticism by the public.

I. Elite perceptions of what management reforms were desirable

It is less appropriate to speak of a (singular) elite perception in the USA than in some more centralized and homogenous European countries. Traditionally, in the USA, executive perceptions of what was needed tended to be somewhat at variance with the perceptions of leading groups within the legislature. Whilst it may have been relatively easy to secure consensus on the proposition that the federal government needs to be more flexible, efficient, customer-friendly and co-ordinated, it has been much more difficult to build a broad coalition of support for a package of specific and concrete measures to achieve this.

By the end of the 1980s there were signs of a real collapse of morale within the federal service (Volcker, 1989). This was in hardly anyone's interest, and provided the incoming Clinton administration with a base on which to build support for a new attempt at reform. This took the form of the National Performance Review and the Government Performance and Results Act (see Section M below).

J. Elite perceptions of what management reforms were feasible

As indicated above (Sections E, G, H) reformers had to contend with a general loss of trust in the federal machine, a tendency which was sometimes encouraged by Presidents themselves. In the US system feasibility frequently depends heavily on the mood of Congress and the current standing of the incumbent President. It is noticeable that large scale structural reforms (e.g., merging agencies, consolidating or splitting up major departments), though prominent in the earlier reform attempts of the 1930s and 1950s, have been tried rather less frequently by the Presidents of the 1980s and 1990s (and with disappointing results—both Reagan's 1986 Civil Service Simplification Act and Clinton's Personnel System Reinvention and Omnibus Civil Service Reform Acts failed). Evidently changes in technique—budgetary and accounting systems, customer service systems, performance management—have been regarded as more feasible/less politically controversial than wholesale redesign of the government machine.

K. Chance events

Some events had an impact on specific aspects or sectors of the federal administration. Two examples would be the 1986 Challenger space shuttle explosion (which had a huge impact on the National Aeronautics and Space Administration, one of the largest federal agencies) and the 1994 Oklahoma City bombing, which starkly illustrated the depths of hatred for the federal authorities felt by some groups on the radical right of the American political spectrum.

L. The administrative system

The US administrative system is quite fragmented and highly permeable to influences from outside the executive itself. Unlike many European countries, the USA never developed a unified and powerful central state apparatus. It democratized before it industrialized, and industrialized before the main era of state-building (Amenta and Skocpol, 1989). During the twentieth century a patchwork of departments and agencies grew up, which successive attempts at reform (especially the Brownlow Committee of 1936 and the Hoover Commissions of 1949 and 1955) only partly succeeded in rationalizing (Savoie, 1994).

By the mid 1990s the federal machine consisted of a wide variety of organizational forms (Peters, 1995). These included fourteen cabinet departments, a large number of independent executive organizations (e.g., the National Aeronautics and Space Administration), independent regulatory commissions (e.g. the Federal Trade Commission) and public corporations (e.g., the Tennessee Valley Authority, the Federal Deposit Insurance Corporation).

There are also organizations within the sphere of the legislature which are important players in financial and management issues—especially the Congressional Budget Office (CBO) and the General Accounting Office (GAO).

While a modest employer in terms of its proportion of the total labour force (2.4 per cent) or of the total public labour force (only 15 per cent), the federal government is still a big employer in absolute terms—3 million or so staff prior to the NPR downsizings of the mid- and late-1990s (Peters, 1995, p. 22).

M. Contents of the reform package

Of the ten countries in this study the USA is probably the one which has been home to the strongest anti-government rhetoric, and the lowest public trust of government (it is not clear which is the cart and which the horse). Each of the last four Presidents (Carter in 1976, Reagan in 1980 and Clinton and Bush in 1992) felt it politically advantageous to include criticism of the federal bureaucracy as a significant element in their electoral campaigns. In practice, however, their actions have varied from attempts at sympathetic modernization of the federal departments and agencies (Carter and Clinton) to scatter-gun attacks on bureaucratic 'waste' combined with the introduction of more and more political appointees (Reagan).

One reform which took place just before the period covered by this book, but which needs to be mentioned, was President Carter's 1978 Civil Service Reform Act (CSRA—see Ban and Ingraham, 1984). This created a Senior Executive Service (SES) of about 8,000, and introduced performance appraisal and merit pay. The SES provision had been designed partly to cater for growing public/private pay differentials (in favour of the latter) but Congress soon cut the share of SES positions that were eligible for bonuses from 50 per cent to 20 per cent. One rueful contemporary comment on the implementation of the CSRA was that Congressional support for it was 'a mile wide but an inch deep'. President Reagan was subsequently able to make good use of the 1978 Act to dominate personnel administration to a greater extent than his predecessors had been able to.

The Reagan administration introduced a welter of reforms, many of them designed to bring 'business disciplines' to the federal civil service. It was also systematic in exploiting the Presidency's huge power of patronage to appoint conservatives to key positions throughout Washington (Savoie, 1994). Some of the principal initiatives were:

- Appointing Donald Devine, an arch-conservative and virulent critic of the federal bureaucracy, to be head of the Office of Personnel Management (OPM). 'Career officials were shocked and demoralized by Devine's hostility to them' (Savoie, 1994, p. 222).
- The President's Council on Integrity and Efficiency (founded 1981). 'It questioned many practices, identified billions of savings as a result of audits, launched civil and criminal actions, and introduced many sanctions against government agencies or employees' (Savoie, 1994, p. 189).
- Reform 88 (launched in 1982). This was a broad-scope programme, somewhat lacking in focus. Actions under its umbrella included upgrading computer systems and improving financial management and accountability.
- The Council on Management and Administration (1982).
- The President's Private Sector Survey on Cost Control (PPSSCC, better known as the 'Grace Commission', 1982).
- The Council on Management Improvement (1984). This was a council of Assistant Secretaries from across federal departments and agencies, tasked to develop long-range management improvement plans and reinforce the implementation of Reform 88.
- The President's Productivity Program (from 1985). This was aimed at increasing the productivity of government agencies by 20 per cent by 1992. Measures included the widespread adoption of TQM.
- 'Although not nearly as successful as he would have liked, Reagan promoted privatisation, contracting out, and user fees at every opportunity' (Savoie, 1994, p. 215)

The Grace Commission was one of the most publicized of these initiatives, and in some ways typified the Reagan administration's approach. It involved bringing in large numbers of business people (2,000, supported by 859 companies) with a brief to identify bureaucratic 'waste'. Over a two-year period it generated forty-seven reports containing 2,478 recommendations. It claimed potential savings of $298 billion, though a General Accounting Office analysis suggested that the true figure was more like $98 billion. Some of its recommendations were partly or wholly implemented, but many were not (Pollitt, 1993, pp. 91–5). In proportion to the size of the effort (and of the fanfare—see Grace, 1984) it left only a small trace. The much less widely publicized Council on Integrity and Efficiency probably had a considerably greater impact.

President Bush (1988–92) was less overtly anti-bureaucrat than Reagan—possibly because he had a lifetime of public service behind him. He presided over a growing crisis in the morale of the federal service, but was seemingly unable to take any particularly strong action to counter it. In 1989 a task force identified serious weaknesses in the public service (including pay, performance appraisal and career development systems and morale—Volcker, 1989). In 1990 a General Accounting Office study came to broadly similar conclusions (US General Accounting Office, 1990). Yet no major reforms were undertaken. As one observer wrote at the time: 'America's flame of managerial reform seems to have died down to a glowing ember' (Hede, 1991, pp. 507–8). President Bush's main interests seem to have lain with high policy issues rather than management reform.

By contrast, the incoming Clinton administration of 1992 was keen to restore status to the federal machine, and to do so by pursuing a high-profile reform which would lead to a government that 'works better and costs less'. The centrepiece of their programme, entrusted to Vice President Gore, was the National Performance Review (NPR—see Gore,

1996, 1997; National Performance Review, 1997; and countless other publications). This package included proposals for savings (promises of $108 billion worth) and downsizing (by 252,000, subsequently raised by Congress to 272,900), as well as for 'empowerment' and 'reinvention'. Different stakeholders have stressed different aspects, and from the start it was clear that there were tensions between, for example, the 'savings and downsizing' theme and the 'empowerment and reinvention' theme. 'In practice NPR has been a messy and sometimes disorganised multi-front war against the government's performance problems' (Kettl, 1994, p. 5).

A second major management reform proceeded alongside the NPR. The 1993 Government Performance and Results Act (GPRA) mandated the development of strategic planning and performance measurement throughout the federal government (National Academy of Public Administration, 1994). Its origins went back to draft Congressional legislation from the Bush era (Radin, 1998, p. 308). Three years of pilot projects were planned before the reporting requirements were 'rolled out' to the rest of the federal government in 1997.

N. The implementation process

Implementing management reform has always been difficult for US Presidents. As noted above, the powers of Congress to intervene in organizational restructurings are as extensive as its powers to reshape budgets. Neither are the agencies themselves under such clear and unequivocal hierarchical authority as would be usual in the case of, say, a British or French agency. Many exist as one corner in an 'iron triangle', with Congress as a second corner and one or more major interest groups as a third (e.g., farmers, or the oil companies, or the defence industries). These links can give agencies the capacity to resist unwelcome changes through political channels.

Furthermore, implementation of some important reforms has been entrusted mainly to political appointees (rather than career civil servants). For example, the 'reinvention' teams established under the NPR were usually led by Clinton appointees. Sometimes this helps give impetus, but at other times it produces oscillations and discontinuities, as political appointees find their attentions are drawn away to other issues of current political salience, or, indeed, they themselves leave their posts (the turnover among political appointees can be quite brisk).

Unsurprisingly, therefore, the record of implementation of reforms has been patchy. Organizationally the key player in management changes would normally be the Office of Management and Budget (OMB). In practice, however, this has not always been a substantial force for management reform. Within OMB the emphasis on management has varied, and for considerable periods the bulk of their effort has been directed to short-term budgetary issues, with management improvement taking a poor second place (see Savoie, 1994, for an account of the changing role of OMB under Reagan). Recently, under Clinton, OMB has taken a lead role in implementing the GPRA, but, by contrast, has made only limited inputs to the NPR reinvention activities. Even with the GPRA, however, the nature of the US governmental system leads to implementation difficulties:

Although the aims of GPRA suggest that the information produced under the Act will support more rational decisionmaking, both the structure of the US government and current developments in other areas make this extremely difficult. The structure creates a disconnect between budget functions, agency organisation, and the jurisdictions of appropriations committees. The fragmented nature of decisionmaking, including budget decisionmaking, limits the ability of any institution of government in either the executive or the legislative branch to look at crosscutting issues and the government as a whole (Radin, 1998, p. 311).

O. Reforms actually achieved

Despite the existence of a flourishing evaluation culture in the US public sector, it is extremely difficult to come to any sure assessment of the impact of the reforms since 1980. At a micro-level there have clearly been many examples and cases of efficiency gains, modernization of systems and increased attention to customer responsiveness. Some of the NPR publications are spattered with up-beat examples of such performance improvements (e.g., Gore, 1997). However, broad-scope evaluations seem thin on the ground. An academic reviw of NPR reinvention laboratories identifies some successes (especially where there has been 'stubborn' leadership) but also some failures and continuing problems (Ingraham, Thompson and Sanders, 1998). Certainly most of the reforms of the Reagan administration were not subject to scientific evaluation—the mood of the times was somewhat against evaluation, as being itself a further symptom of bureaucratic empire-building and obfuscation. More recently, a major evaluation has been planned of the effects of the GPRA, but the results are not yet in. Early assessments by the GAO indicate a mixed picture with some performance plans following well short of what the act seems to require (e.g., General Accounting Office, 1998). In theory the Government-Wide Performance Plan, responsibility for preparing which has been given to the Office of Management and Budget, could in future provide a vehicle for a broad-scope assessment of government performance.

Country File Events: United States of America

	General	Organization	Personnel	Finance
1981–1985	– Reagan: President (Rep.) (1980) – Reagan: President (Rep.) (1984) – Simplification efforts include cutting 30,000 pages from Federal Acquisition Regulation (1984)	– President's Council on Integrity and Efficiency (1981) – Council on Management and Administration (1982) – President's Private Sector Survey on Cost Control (PPSSCC/the Grace Commission) (1982) – Reform '88 (1982) – Council on Management Improvement (1984)		– Replacement of central budget system by single gvt-wide financial system (1981)
1985–1990	– Extensive effort to improve quality (1986) – Bush: President (Rep.) (1988) – Increase number of contracts subject to competition from 41% in 1981 to 58% (1988) – President's Mgt Improvement Program: Reform 88 (1988) – Overview of broad issues for programme emphasis into the next century (1989) – Review of development and use of IT (1989) – MBO system to allow President and senior officials to monitor and evaluate some 50 programmes/policies (1989)	– President's Productivity Program (1985) – President's Council on Competitiveness (1989) – Review of adequacy of management controls in 65 Dpts (1989)	– Reduce number of personnel payroll systems from 132 (1983) to 53 (1988) – Studies to hire and retain skilled personnel (1989) – Federal Employees Pay Comparability Act (1990)	– Increase in number of agencies having inspector generals: audit and investigate wasteful and inefficient practices (1988) – Improvement of lending programmes – Reduce number of financial systems from 379 (1984) to 253 (1988) – Establish a formal integrated structure for financial mgt (goal setting, preparation annual statements, chief financial officer in 23 agencies) (1990) – Federal Accounting Standards Advisory Board established (1990) – Presidential Legislation on Financial Mgt (1990)

Country File Events: United States of America (*cont.*):

	General	Organization	Personnel	Finance
	– Programme evaluation: accelerates (1990) – OMB: monitor 100 high-risk areas (1989)			– New Budget Deficit Reduction Law—Budget Enforcement Act (1990) – Federal Credit Reform Act (1990)
1991–1995	– Clinton: President (Dem.) (1992) – Voucher programmes in child care and housing extended (1992) – President: moratorium on new regulations (1992) – Senate: Government Performance and Results Act (GPRA) (1992) – Vice-President Gore: National Performance Review (NPR) (1993) – NPR: 'From Red Tape to Results: Creating a Gvt that Works Better and Costs Less' (1993) – Presidential EO: Regulatory Planning Review (cut obsolete regulations, reward result, getting out of Washington, negotiate, grassroots partnerships) (1993) – Presidential EO: 'Setting Customer Service Standards' (1993)	– CFOA: establishment of Office of Federal Financial Mgt in the OMB (1991) – National Economic Council (White House): domestic issues (1993) – Abolish President's Council on Competitiveness (1993) – President's Management Council: all Chief Operating Officers of Dpts and agencies (1993) – 200 Reinvention Labs (1993) – Federal interagency–state partnerships with Oregon and Connecticut (1994)	– Postal Services: 5% employee reduction (1992) – Cut 100,000 positions, cut White House staff by 25% (1993) – National Partnership Council (NPC): Federal Mgt and Employees: collaboration, customer service, cutting costs (1993) – Federal Workforce Restructuring Act (FWRA) (1994): cut 272,000 FTE by 1999, buyout authority – Elimination of the 10,000 page Federal Personnel Manual (1994)	– Chief Financial Officers Act (CFOA) (1991): publication of guidelines and standards for financial reporting/accounting – Initial set of annual audited financial statements (several agencies and 27 corporations) (1991) – Pilot regulatory budget (covered by CAA) (1991) – Increased emphasis to measurement of programme performance (1991) – OMB asks agencies to provide cost/benefit data for all significant regulations (1991) – MBO discontinued (1991) – GPRA: all Federal agencies: 5-year strategic plan, annual performance plans, report on performance (1993) – Expand Government Mgt Reform Act (GMRA) (1994): audit of financial statements for entire operations to all 24 CFO agencies – Pilot projects in all 14 Cabinet

	– GPRA (Congress) (1993) – Federal Acquisition Streamlining Act (FASA) (1994): reform procurement – Gvt-wide electronic contracting system (1995) – Reauthorize Paperwork Reduction Act (1995)	– Information Technology Mgt Reform Act (ITMRA): Chief Information Officer in each agency, new schemes for mgt and acquisition (1996) – Educations Department's Student Financial Aid Office: first Congressionally created performance-based organization (PBO) (1998)	Dpts and 13 agencies: annual plans, performance goals, and reports on actual and planned (also in military combat and R&D) (1994) – No mandates for State, local and tribal gvts without money (1995) – Unfunded Mandates Reform Act (1995)
1996–1998	– Clinton: President (Dem.) (1996) – Budget: 1997: consolidation, devolution, privatization, termination (from 271 progrs to 27 'Performance Partnerships') (1996) – Federal Acquisition Reform Act (FARA) (1996) – 'National Performance Review' becomes 'National Partnership for Reinventing Government' (1998)		– Line Item Veto Act (LIVA) President may cancel discretionary spending, new entitlement authorization and tax provisions (1996) – All agencies submit strategic plans under GPRA (1997) – First balanced budget in 30 years (1998)

Bibliography

Ahonen, P. and Salminen, A. (1997) *Metamorphosis of the administrative state*, Frankfurt am Main, Peter Lang.

Algemene Rekenkamer (1995) *Tweede Kamer*, 1994/95, 24120, no. 3.

Amenta, E. and Skocpol, T. (1989) 'Taking exception: explaining the distinctiveness of American public policies in the last century', pp. 292–333 in F. Castles (ed.) *The comparative history of public policy*, Oxford, Polity.

Aristotle (1963) *Aristotle's Politics* (translated by B. Jowett), Oxford, Clarendon Press.

Ascher, K. (1987) *The politics of privatisation: contracting out public services*, Basingstoke, Macmillan.

Association of Finnish Local Authorities (1995a) *Total Quality Management in municipal service provision*, Helsinki, Association of Finnish Local Authorities.

—— (1995b) *Quality in the procurement of municipal services*, Helsinki, Association of Finnish Local Authorities.

Aucoin, P. (1998) *Accountability in public management: making performance count*, paper presented to the authors' roundtable, Revitalising the public service, Ottawa, Canadian Centre for Management Development, 12th–14th November.

—— and Savoie, D. (1998) *Program Review: lessons for strategic change in governance*, Ottawa, Canadian Centre for Management Development.

Auditor General of Canada (1993) 'Canada's public service reform, and lessons learned from selective jurisdictions', *Report, 1993*, chapter 6, Ottawa, Auditor General of Canada.

—— (1997) *Annual report*, Ottawa, Auditor General of Canada.

Ball, I. (1993) *New Zealand public sector management*, paper presented to the 1993 National Accountants in Government Convention, Hobart, 26–28 May.

Ban, C. and Ingraham, P. (1984) *Legislating bureaucratic change: the Civil Service reform Act of 1978*, New York, SUNY Press.

Barberis, P. (1998) 'The new public management and a new accountability', *Public Administration*, 76:3, pp. 451–70, Autumn.

Barbier, J.-C. and Simonin, B. (1997) 'European Social Programmes: can evaluation of implementation increase the appropriateness of findings?', *Evaluation*, 3:4, October, pp. 391–407.

Baty, P. and Thomson, A. (1998) 'Brought low by high ambitions', *The Times Higher*, 20th November, pp. 6–7.

Beale, V. and Pollitt, C. (1994) 'Charters at the grass roots: a first report', *Local Government Studies*, 20:2, Summer, pp. 202–25.

Bellamy, C. and Taylor, J. (1998) *Governing in the information age*, Buckingham, Open University Press.

Benz A. and Götz, K. (1996) 'The German public sector: national priorities and the international reform agenda', pp. 1–26 in A. Benz and K. Götz (eds) *A new German public sector? Reform, adaptation and stability*, Aldershot, Dartmouth.

Boje, D., Gephart, R. and Thatchenkey, T. (eds) (1996) *Postmodern management and organization theory*, London, Sage.

Bok, D. (1997) 'Measuring the performance of government', pp. 55–76 in J. Nye, P. Zelikow and D. King (eds) *Why people don't trust government*, Cambridge, Mass., Harvard University Press.

Boorsma, P. and Mol, N. (1995) 'The Dutch public financial revolution', pp. 219–32 in W. Kickert and F. van Vught (eds) *Public policy and administration sciences in the Netherlands*, London, Prentice Hall/Harvester Wheatsheaf.

Borins, S. (1995) 'Public sector innovation: the implications of new forms of organisation and work', pp. 260–87 in G. Peters and D. Savoie (eds) *Governance in a changing environment*, Montreal and Kingston, Canadian Centre for Management Development and McGill-Queen's University Press.

Boston, J. (1995) 'Lessons from the Antipodes', pp. 161–77 in B. O'Toole and G. Jordan (eds) *Next steps: improving management in government?*, Aldershot, Dartmouth.

—— Martin, J., Pallot, J. and Walsh, P. (1996) *Public management: the New Zealand model*, Auckland, Oxford University Press.

Bouckaert, G. (1994) 'The history of the productivity movement', pp. 361–97 in M. Holzer and A. Halachmi (eds) *Competent government: theory and practice: the best of Public Productivity and Management Review, 1985–1993*, Burke, Chatelaine Press.

—— (1995) 'Improving performance measurement', pp. 379–412 in A. Halachmi and G. Bouckaert (eds) *The enduring challenges of public management: surviving and excelling in a changing world*, San Francisco, Jossey-Bass.

—— (1996) 'Measurement of public sector performance: some European perspectives', pp. 223–37 in A. Halachmi and G. Bouckaert (eds) *Organisational performance and measurement in the public sector*, London, Quorum Books.

—— and Ulens, W. (1998) *Mesure de la performance dans le service public: exemples étrangers pour les pouvoirs publics Belges*, Bruxelles, Service Fédereaux des Affaires Scientifiques, Techniques et Culturelles.

—— and Van Reeth, W. (1998) 'Budget modelling for efficiency and effectiveness: the case of the Flemish Government' , pp. 43–53 in G. de Graan and F. Volmer (eds) *Performance budgeting: a perspective on modelling and strategic planning*, Delft, Eburon.

Bourgault, J. and Carroll, B. (1997) 'The Canadian senior public service: the last vestiges of the Whitehall model?', pp. 91–100 in J. Bougault, M.Demers and C. Williams (eds) *Public administration and public management in Canada*, Quebec, Les Publications du Quebec.

—— and Savoie, D. (1998) *Managing at the top*, paper for the authors' roundtable, Revitalising the public service, Ottawa, Canadian Centre for Management Development, 12th–14th November.

—— Dion, S. and Lemay, M. (1993) 'Creating corporate culture: lessons from the Canadian federal government', *Public Administration Review*, 53:1, pp. 73–80.

Bourgon, J. (1998) *Fifth annual report to the Prime Minister on the public service of Canada*, Ottawa, Privy Council Office.

Boyne, G. (1998) 'Bureaucratic theory meets reality: public choice and service contracting in US local government', *Public Administration Review*, 58:6, November/December.

Brunsson, N. (1989) *The organisation of hypocrisy: talk, decisions and actions in organisations*, Chichester, John Wiley.

Bureau of Transport and Communications (1995) *Evaluation of the Black Spot Program*, Canberra, Australia Government Publishing Service.

Burrell, G. (1997) *Pandemonium: towards a retro-organization theory*, London, Sage.

Caiden, N. (1988) 'Shaping things to come', pp. 43–58 in I. Rubin (ed.) *New directions in budget theory*, Albany, SUNY Press.

Cameron, D. and Simeon, R. (1998) *Intergovernmental relations and democratic citizenship*, paper presented to the authors' roundtable, Revitalising the public service, Ottawa, Canadian Centre for Management Development, 12th–14th November.

Camp, R. (1989) *Benchmarking: the search for industry best practices that lead to a superior performance*, Milwaukee, Quality Press.

Canadian Broadcasting Corporation (1994) *The remaking of New Zealand*, Toronto, CBC Radio Works.

Canadian Centre for Management Development (1998a) *Citizen/client surveys: dispelling myths and redrawing maps*, Ottawa, CCMD.

—— (1998b) *Government at your service: a progress report from the Citizen-Centred Service Network*, Ottawa, CCMD.

Carter, N. (1998) 'On the performance of performance indicators', pp. 177–94 in M-C. Kesler, P. Lascoumbes, M. Setbon and J.-C. Thoenig (eds) *Évaluation des politiques publiques*, Paris, L'Harmattan.

—— Klein, R. and Day, P. (1992) *How organisations measure success: the use of performance indicators in government*, London, Routledge.

Castles, F., Gerritsen, R. and Vowles, J. (eds) (1996) *The great experiment: Labour parties and public policy transformation in Australia and New Zealand*, St Leonards, NSW, Allen and Unwin.

Centre for Finnish Business and Policy Studies (1996) *Not revolution but re-evaluation: a report of political decision-making in Finland*, April, Helsinki (translated by the Public Management Department, Ministry of Finance).

Chancellor of the Duchy of Lancaster (1997) *Next steps: agencies in government: review, 1996*, Cm3579, London, The Stationery Office.

Chancellor of the Exchequer (1998) *Modern public services for Britain: investing in reform*, Cm4011, London, The Stationery Office.

Chapman, R. (1998) 'Problems of ethics in public sector management', *Public Money and Management*, 18:1, January/March, pp. 9–13.

Clark, D. (1997) *The civil service and new government*, speech by the Rt. Hon. Dr David Clark, MP, Chancellor of the Duchy of Lancaster, QE11 Centre, London, 17th June.

—— (1998) 'The modernization of the French civil service: crisis, change and continuity', *Public Administration*, 76:1, Spring, pp. 97–115.

Clarke, J. and Newman, J. (1997) *The managerial state*, London, Sage.

Cochrane, A. (1993) *Whatever happened to local government?*, Buckingham, Open University Press.

Comité pour la réorganisation et la déconcentration de l'administration (1995) *33 propositions pour rendre plus efficace l'administrat territoriale de l'État*, Rapport du Comité, Paris, April.

Commonwealth (1983) *RAPS/Reforming the Australian Public Service: a statement of the Government's intentions*, Canberra, AGPS.

Commonwealth Secretariat (1993) *Administrative and managerial reform: a Commonwealth portfolio of current good practice*, London, Management Development Programme, Commonwealth Secretariat.

Cowper, J. and Samuels, M. (1997), 'Performance benchmarking in the public sector: the United Kingdom experience', pp. 11–31 in OECD, *Benchmarking, evaluation and strategic management in the public sector*, Paris, PUMA/OECD.

Crosby, P. (1979) *Quality is free*, New York, McGraw Hill.

Dahlberg, L. and Isaksson, C. (1997) 'The implementation of benchmarking from a Swedish perspective', pp. 33–48 in PUMA *Benchmarking, evaluation and strategic management in the public sector*, Paris, PUMA/OECD.

Denham, A. and Garnett, M. (1998) *British think-tanks and the climate of opinion*, London, UCL Press.

Department of Finance (1996) *Measuring up: a primer for benchmarking in the Australian Public Service*, Discussion Paper No. 4, Canberra, Resource Management Improvement Branch.

—— (1998a) *The performance improvement cycle: guidance for managers*, Canberra, Department of Finance and Administration.

—— (1998b) *Lessons learned from others: international experience on the identification and monitoring of outputs and outcomes*, Discussion Paper 2, Canberra, Department of Administration and Finance.

Derksen, W. and Kortsen, A. (1995) 'Local government: a survey', pp. 63–86 in W. Kickert and F. van Vught (eds) *Public policy and administration sciences in the Netherlands*, London, Prentice Hall/Harvester Wheatsheaf.

Derlien, H.-U. (1998) *From administrative reform to administrative modernization*, Bamberg, Verwaltungswissenschaftliche Beitrage 33.

Development Team (1998) *International experience on the identification and monitoring of outputs and outcomes*, Canberra, Department of Finance and Administration, March.

Douglas, M. (1982) *In the active voice*, Routledge, London.

Dryzek, J. (1996) 'The informal logic of institutional design', pp. 103–25 in R. Goodin (ed.) *The theory of institutional design*, Cambridge, Cambridge University Press.

Duhamel, R. (1996) *Evaluation report: Improved Reporting to Parliament Project on Performance Indicators*, a report of the Parliamentary Working Group, Ottawa, December.

Dunleavy, P. (1991) *Democracy, bureaucracy and public choice: economic explanations in political science*, Hemel Hempstead, Harvester Wheatsheaf.

—— (1994) 'The globalisation of public service production: can government be the "best in the world"?', *Public Policy and Administration*, 9:2, Summer, pp. 36–65.

—— and Hood, C. (1994) 'From old public administration to new public management', *Public Money and Management*, 14:3, July/September, pp. 9–16.

Dunn, W. (1993) 'Policy reforms as arguments', pp. 254–90 in F. Fischer and J. Forester (eds) *The argumentative turn in policy analysis and planning*, London, UCL Press.

Dunsire, A. (1973) *Administration: the word and the science*, London, Martin Robertson.

—— (1993) 'Modes of governance', pp. 21–34 in J. Kooiman (ed.) *Modern governance: new government-society interactions*, London, Sage.

Duran, P., Monnier, E. and Smith, A. (1995) 'Evaluation *à la française*', *Evaluation*, 1:1, July, pp. 45–63.

East, P. (1997) *Opening address to Public Service Senior Management Conference*, Wellington, NZ, 9th October.

Efficiency Unit (1988) *Improving management in government: the next steps*, London, HMSO.

Employment Service (1994) *Employment Service: an evaluation of the effects of agency status, 1990–1993*, London, Employment Department Group.

Esping-Andersen, G. (1990) *The three worlds of welfare capitalism*, Cambridge, Polity.

European Commission (1995) *Eurobarometer: trends, 1974–94*, Brussels, European Commission.

—— (1997a) *Evaluating EU expenditure programmes: a guide*, (1st edition), Brussels, DGXIX/02, European Commission.

—— (1997b) *MAP 2000: modernisation of administration and personnel policy for the year 2000* (draft memorandum from Mr Liikanen in agreement with the President: doc.IX/486/97), Brussels, DGIX.

—— (1998) *SEM 2000: implementation by the services: information note from the President, Mrs Gradin and Mr Liikanen*, SEC(98)760 final, Brussels, Secretariat General, 14th May.

European Foundation for Quality Management (1996) *Self-assessment, 1997: guidelines for public sector*, Brussels, EFQM.

Evers, A., Haverinen, R., Leichsenring, K. and Wistow, G. (1997) *Developing quality in personal social services: concepts, cases and comments*, Aldershot, Ashgate.

Executive Office of the President of the United States (1995) *Budget of the United States Government, Fiscal Year 1995*, Washington DC.

Farnham, D., Horton, S., Barlow, J. and Hondeghem, A. (eds) (1996) *New public managers in Europe: public servants in transition*, Basingstoke, Macmillan.

Fischer, F. and Forester, J. (eds) (1993) *The argumentative turn in policy analysis and planning*, London, UCL Press.

Flösser, G. and Otto, H.-U. (1998) *Towards more democracy in social services: models of culture and welfare*, Berlin, de Gruyter.

Flynn, N. and Strehl, F. (eds) (1996) *Public sector management in Europe*, London, Prentice Hall/Harvester Wheatsheaf.

Foster, C. (1992) *Privatization, public ownership and the regulation of natural monopolies*, Oxford, Blackwell.

Foster, C. and Plowden, F. (1996) *The state under stress*, Buckingham, Open University Press.

Gaertner, K. and Gaertner, G. (1985) 'Performance-contingent pay for federal managers', *Administration and Society*, 17:1, pp. 7–20.

Geertz, C. (1973) *The interpretation of culture*, London, Hutchinson.

General Accounting Office (1990) *Why and how the GAO is reviewing federal college recruiting*, Washington, DC, US House of Representatives.

—— (1994) *Deficit reduction: experiences of other nations*, Washington DC, GAO/AIMD–95–30, December.

—— (1995) *Managing for results: experiences abroad suggest insights for federal management reforms*, Washington, DC, GAO/GGD-95-120.

—— (1997) *Performance budgeting: past initiatives offer insight for GPRA implementation*, Washington, DC, GAO/AIMD-97-46, March.

—— (1998) *The Results Act: observations on the Department of State's Fiscal Year 1999 Annual Performance Plan*, Washington, DC, GAO/NSIAD-98-210R, June.

General principles and special instructions on payments by results within the State system (1994) Helsinki, Ministry of Finance (pamphlet).

Giddens, A. (1990) *The consequences of modernity*, Cambridge, Polity Press.

Gillibrand, A. and Hilton, B. (1998) 'Resource accounting and budgeting: principles, concepts and practice', *Public Money and Management*, 18:2, April/June, pp. 21–8.

Götz, K. (1997) 'Acquiring political craft: training grounds for top officials in the German core executive', *Public Administration*, 75:4, Winter, pp. 753–75.

Goodin, R. (1996) *The theory of institutional design*, Cambridge, Cambridge University Press.

Gore, A. (1996) *The best-kept secrets in government: a report to President Bill Clinton*, Washington, DC, US Government Printing Office, National Performance Review.

—— (1997) *Businesslike government: lessons learned from America's best companies*, Washington, DC, National Performance Review.

Government decision in principle on reforms in central and regional government (1993) Helsinki, Council of State.

Grace, P. (1984) *Burning money: the waste of your tax dollars*, New York, Macmillan.

Gregory, R. (1998) 'Political responsibility for bureaucratic incompetence: tragedy at Cave Creek', *Public Administration*, 76:3, pp. 519–38, Autumn.

Greve, C., Flinders, M. and van Thiel, S. (1999) 'Quangos—what's in a name: defining quangos from a comparative perspective', *Governance*, 12:1 (in press).

Grömig, E. and Gruner, K. (1998) 'Reform in den Rathäusern. Neueste umfrage des Deutschen Städtetages zum them Verwaltungsmodernisierung', *Der Städtetag*, 8, pp. 581–7.

—— and Thielen, H. (1996) 'Städte auf dem reformweg: zum stand der Verwaltungsmodernisierung', *Der Städtetag*, 9, pp. 596–600.

Gunn, L. (1987) 'Perspectives on public management', pp. 33–46 in J. Kooiman and K. Eliassen (eds), *Managing public organizations: lessons from European experience*, London, Sage.

Gustafsson, L. (1987) 'Renewal of the public sector in Sweden', *Public Administration*, 65:2, pp. 179–92.

Habermas, J. (1976) *Legitimation crisis*, London, Heinemann.

Halachmi, A. and Bouckaert, G. (1995) *The enduring challenges of public management*, San Francisco, Jossey-Bass.

Halligan, J. (1996a) 'The diffusion of civil service reform', pp. 288–317 in H. Bekke, J. Perry and T. Toonen (eds) *Civil service systems in comparative perspective*, Bloomington and Indiana, Indiana University Press.

—— (1996b) 'Australia: balancing principles and pragmatism', pp. 71–112 in J. Olsen and B. Peters (eds) *Lessons from experience: experiential learning in administrative reforms in eight democracies*, Oslo, Scandinavian University Press.

—— (1997) 'New public sector models: reform in Australia and New Zealand', pp. 17–46 in J.-E. Lane (ed.) *Public sector reform: rationale, trends and problems*, London, Sage.

—— and Power, J. (1992) *Political management in the 1990s*, Melbourne, Oxford University Press.

Hammer, M. and Champy, J. (1995) *Reengineering the corporation: a manifesto for a business revolution* (revised edition), London, Nicholas Brealey.

Handy, C. (1993) *Understanding organisations*, Harmondsworth, Penguin.

Harden, I. (1992) *The contracting state*, Buckingham, Open University Press.

Harder, P. and Lindquist, E. (1997) 'Expenditure management and reporting in the government of Canada: recent development and backgrounds', pp. 71–89 in J. Bougault, M. Demers and C. Williams (eds) *Public administration and public management: experiences in Canada*, Québec, Les Publications de Québec.

Harrison, S. and Pollitt, C. (1994) *Controlling health professionals: the future of work and organisation in the NHS*, Buckingham, Open University Press.

—— Hunter, D. J. and Pollitt, C. (1990) *The dynamics of British health policy*, London, Unwin Hyman.

—— —— Marnoch, G. and Pollitt, C. (1992) *Just managing: power and culture in the National Health Service*, Basingstoke, Macmillan.

Hartley, J. (1983) 'Ideology and organizational behaviour', *International Studies of Management and Organization*, 13:3.

Harvard University (1998) Invitation letter to a conference in Washington DC, *Strategies for 21st Century government: a global forum on re-inventing government*, Cambridge, Mass., John F. Kennedy School of Government, 18th November.

Heclo, H. (1977) *A government of strangers*, Washington, DC, Brookings Institution.

Hede, A. (1991) 'Trends in the civil services of Anglo-American systems', *Governance*, 4:4, October, pp. 489–510.

Held, D. (1987) *Models of democracy*, Cambridge, Polity.

Heintzman, R. (1997) 'Canada and public administration', pp. 1–12 in J. Bourgault, M. Demers and C. Williams (eds) *Public administration and public management: experiences in Canada*, Québec, Les Publications du Québec.

Hencke, D. (1998) 'Jobcentres fiddled the figures', *Guardian*, 8th January, p. 2.

Heseltine, M. (1980) 'Ministers and management in Whitehall', *Management Services in Government*, 35.

High quality services, good governance and a responsible civic society (1998a) The Government Resolution, Helsinki, Oy Edita Ab.

—— (1998b) Background Material, Helsinki, Oy Edita Ab.

Hill, H. and Klages, H. (1995) 'Verbindung mit dem Deutschen Landkreistag' in H. Hill and H. Klages (eds) *Kreisverwaltung der zukunft. Vergleichende untersuchung aktueller modernisierungsansätze in ausgewählten Kreisverwaltungen*, Düsseldorf, Raabe Fachverlag.

—— —— (eds) (1993) *Qualitäts- und erfolgsorientiertes verwaltungsmanagement. Aktuelle tendenzen und entwurfe*, Berlin, Duncker and Humblot.

—— —— (eds) (1996a) *Wege in die neue Steurung*, Düsseldorf, Raabe Fachverlag.

—— —— (eds) (1996b) *Controlling im neuen Steurungsmodell. Werkstattberichte zur Einführung von Controlling*, Düsseldorf, Raabe Fachverlag.

Hjerppe, R. and Luoma, K. (1997) *Finnish experiences in measuring and promoting productivity in the public sector*, Helsinki, VATT Discussion Papers, No. 150.

H. M. Treasury (1991) *Competing for quality*, Cm1730, London, HMSO, November.

—— (1994) *Fundamental review of H. M. Treasury's running costs* (the 'Southgate report'), London, H. M. Treasury.

—— (1998) *Whole of government accounts*, July, London, H. M. Treasury.

Hojnacki, W. (1996) 'Politicization as a civil service dilemma', pp. 137–64 in H. Bekke, J. Perry and T. Toonen (eds) *Civil service systems in comparative perspective*, Bloomington and Indiana, Indiana University Press.

Holkeri, K. and Summa, H. (1996) *Contemporary developments in performance management: evaluation of public management reforms in Finland: from ad hoc studies to a programmatic approach*, paper presented to PUMA/OECD, 4th–5th November, Paris.

Holmes, M. and Shand, D. (1995) 'Management reform: some practitioner perspectives on the past ten years', *Governance*, 8:4, October, pp. 551–78.

Hood, C. (1976) *The limits of administration*, London, Wiley.

—— (1991) 'A public management for all seasons', *Public Administration*, 69:1, Spring, pp. 3–19.

—— (1995) 'Contemporary public management: a new global paradigm?', *Public Policy and Administration*, 10:2, Summer, pp. 104–17.

—— (1996) 'Exploring variations in public management reform of the 1980s', pp. 268–317 in H. Bekke, J. Perry and T. Toonen (eds) *Civil service systems in comparative perspective*, Bloomington and Indianapolis, Indiana University Press.

—— (1998) *The art of the state: culture, rhetoric and public management*, Oxford, Oxford University Press.

—— and Jackson, M. (1991) *Administrative argument*, Aldershot, Dartmouth.

—— James, O., Jones, G., Scott, C. and Travers, T. (1998) 'Regulation inside government: where New Public Management meets the audit explosion', *Public Money and Management*, 18:2, April/June, pp. 61–8.

Howard, D. (1998) 'The French strikes of 1995 and their political aftermath', *Government and Opposition*, 33:2, Spring, pp. 199–220.

Hudson, J. (1999) *Informatization and the delivery of government services: a political science perspective*, Ph.D. thesis, Department of Government, Brunel University.

Hughes O. (1998) *Public management and administration: an introduction* (2nd edition), Basingstoke, Macmillan.

ICM (1993) *Citizen's Charter customer survey* (conducted for the Citizen's Charter Unit), London, ICM Research.

Immergut, E. (1992) *Health politics: interests and institutions in Western Europe*, Cambridge, Cambridge University Press.

Ingraham, P. (1996) 'The reform agenda for national civil service systems: external stress and internal strains', pp. 247–67 in H.Bekke, J.Perry and T. Toonen (eds) *Civil service systems in comparative perspective*, Bloomington and Indiana, Indiana University Press.

—— (1997) 'Play it again Sam; it's still not right: searching for the right notes in administrative reform', *Public Administration Review*, 57:4, July/August, pp. 325–31.

—— Peters, G. and Moynihan, D. (1998) *Public employment and the future of the public service*, paper presented to the authors' roundtable, Revitalising the public service, Ottawa, Canadian Centre for Management Development, 12th–14th November.

—— Thompson, J. and Sanders, P., (eds) (1998) *Transforming government: lessons from the reinvention laboratorories*, San Francisco, Josey-Boss.

Jauvin, N. (1997) 'Government, ministers, macro-organisation chart and networks', pp. 45–58 in J. Bourgault, M. Demers and C. Williams (eds) *Public administration and public management: experiences in Canada*, Quebec, Les Publications du Québec.

Jobert, B. and Muller, P. (1987) *L'État en action*, Paris, Presses Universitaires de France.

Johnson, J. (1998) 'Strategy, planning, leadership and the Financial Management Improvement Plan: the Australian Public Service 1983 to 1996', *Public Productivity and Management Review*, 21:4, June, pp. 352–68.

Joss, R. and Kogan, M. (1995) *Advancing quality: total quality management in the National Health Service*, Buckingham, Open University Press.

Kaufman, H. (1981) 'Fear of bureaucracy: a raging pandemic', *Public Administration Review*, 41:1, January/February, pp. 1–9.

Kaufmann, F., Majone, G. and Ostrom, V. (eds) (1986) *Guidance, control and evaluation in the public sector*, Berlin, de Gruyter.

Keeling, D. (1972) *Management in government*, London, Allen and Unwin.

Kernaghan, K. (1997) 'Values, ethics and public service', pp. 101–11 in J. Bourgault, M. Demers and C. Williams (eds) *Public administration and public management: experiences in Canada*, Québec, Les Publications du Québec.

Kettl, D. (1994) *Reinventing government? Appraising the National Performance Review*, Washington, DC, The Brookings Institution.

—— Ingraham, P., Sanders, R. and Horner, C. (1996) *Civil service reform: building a government that works*, Washington, DC, The Brookings Institution.

Kickert, W. (ed.) (1997) *Public management and administrative reform in Western Europe*, Cheltenham, Edward Elgar.

—— and In't Veld, R. (1995) 'National government, governance and administration', pp. 45–62 in W. Kickert and F. van Vught (eds) *Public policy and administration sciences in the Netherlands*, London, Prentice Hall/Harvester Wheatsheaf.

—— Klijn, E.-H. and Koppenjan, J. (eds) (1997) *Managing complex networks: strategies for the public sector*, London, Sage.

King, G., Keohane, R. and Verber, S. (1994) *Designing social enquiry: scientific inference in qualitative research*, New Jersey, Princeton University Press.

Klages, H. and Löffler, E. (1996) 'Public sector modernisation in Germany: recent trends and emerging strategies', pp. 132–45 in N. Flynn and F. Strehl (eds) *Public sector management in Europe*, London, Prentice Hall/Harvester Wheatsheaf. *

—— —— (1998) 'New public management in Germany: the implementation process of the New Steering Model', *International Review of Administrative Sciences*, 64, pp. 41–54.

König, K. (1996) *On the critique of New Public Management*, Speyer, 155, Speyerer Forschungsberichte.

—— (1997) 'Entrepreneurial management or executive administration: the perspective of classical administration', pp. 217–36 in W. Kickert (ed.) *Public management and administrative reform in Western Europe*, Cheltenham, Edward Elgar.

Korsten, A. and van der Krogt, T. (1995) 'Human Resources Management', pp. 233–48 in W. Kickert and F. van Vught (eds) *Public policy and administration sciences in the Netherlands*, London, Prentice Hall/Harvester Wheatsheaf.

Lane, J.-E. (1995) 'The decline of the Swedish model', *Governance*, 8:4, pp. 579–90.

—— (ed.) (1997) *Public sector reform: rationale, trends and problems*, London, Sage.

—— and Ersson, S. (1991) *Politics and society in Western Europe* (2nd edition) London, Sage.

Laurance, J. (1997) 'New national checks after breast cancer screening "disgrace" ', *The Independent*, 4th November, p. 5.

Lawrence, R. (1997) 'Is it really the Economy, Stupid?', pp. 11–132 in J. Nye, P. Zelikow and D. King (eds) *Why people don't trust government*, Cambridge, Mass., Harvard University Press.

Leeuw, F. (1995) *The Dutch perspective: trends in performance measurement*, paper presented at the International Evaluation Conference, Vancouver, 1st–5th November.

Leftwich, A. (ed.) (1984) *What is politics? The activity and its study*, Oxford, Blackwell.

Le Grand, J. and Bartlett, W. (1993) *Quasi markets and social policy*, Basingstoke, Macmillan.

Lehtoranta, O. and Niemi, M. (1997) *Measuring public sector productivity in Finland: progress report*, paper presented to OECD/UNECE/EUROSTAT Meeting of National Accounts Experts, Paris, June.

Le Loup, L. (1988) 'From micro-budgeting to macro-budgeting', pp. 19–42 in I. Rubin (ed.) *New directions in budget theory*, Albany, SUNY Press.

Leon, L. de (1997) 'Administrative reform and democratic accountability', pp. 237–54 in W. Kickert (ed.) *Public management and administrative reform in Western Europe*, Cheltenham, Edward Elgar.

Light, P. (1995) *Thickening government: federal hierarchy and the diffusion of accountability*, Washington, DC, Brookings Institution.

Lijphart, A. (1984) *Democracies: patterns of majoritarian and consensus government in twenty-one countries*, London, Yale University Press.

Likierman, A. (1995) 'Performance indicators: twenty lessons from early managerial use', pp. 57–66 in P. Jackson (ed.) *Measures for success in the public sector*, London, Public Finance Foundation/Chartered Institute of Public Finance and Accountancy.

—— (1998a) 'Resource accounting and budgeting: where are we now?', *Public Money and Management*, 18:2, April/June, pp. 17–20.

—— (1998b) 'Report: recent developments in Resource Accounting and Budgeting (RAB)', *Public Money and Management*, 18:4, October/December, pp. 62–4.

Lindblom, C. (1959) 'The science of muddling through' *Public Administration Review*, 19:3, pp. 79–88.

—— (1979) 'Still muddling, not yet through', *Public Administration Review*, 39:6, pp. 517–26.

Listhaug, O. and Wiberg, M. (1995) 'Confidence in public and private institutions', pp.

298–322 in H.-D. Klingemann and D. Fuchs (eds) *Citizens and the state: beliefs in government*, vol.1, Oxford, Oxford University Press.

Löffler, E. (1995) *The modernisation of the public sector in an international perspective: concepts and methods of awarding and assessing quality in the public sector in OECD countries*, Speyer Forschungsberichte 151, Speyer, Forschungsinstitut für Öffentliche Verwaltung.

Lomas, K. (1991) *Contemporary Finnish poetry*, Newcastle-upon-Tyne, Bloodaxe Books.

Lowndes, V. (1996) 'Varieties of new institutionalism: a critical appraisal', *Public Administration*, 74:2, Summer, pp. 181–97.

—— and Skelcher, C. (1998) 'The dynamics of multi-organisational partnerships: an analysis of changing modes of governance', *Public Administration*, 76:2, Summer, pp. 313–33.

McGrew, A. (ed.) (1997) *The transformation of democracy? Globalization and territorial democracy*, Cambridge (Polity) and Buckingham (Open University Press).

Maidment, R. and McGrew, A. (1986) *The American political process*, London, Sage.

Majone, G. (1996) *Regulating Europe*, London, Routledge.

Mallory, J. (1997) 'Particularities and systems of government', pp. 15–23 in J.Bourgault, M. Demers and C. Williams (eds) *Public administration and public management: experiences in Canada*, Québec, Les Publications du Québec.

Management Advisory Board (1993a) *Accountability in the Commonwealth public sector*, Canberra, MAB/MIAC, No. 11, June.

—— (1993b) *Building a better public service*, Canberra, MAB/MIAC No.12, June.

—— (1994) *On-going reform in the Australian public service: an occasional paper to the Prime Minister*, Canberra, MAB/MIAC No. 15, October.

March, J. and Olsen, J. (1995) *Democratic governance* New York, Free Press.

Margetts, H. (1998) *Information technology in government: Britain and America*, London, Routledge.

Marmor, T., Mashaw, J. and Harvey, P. (1990) *America's misunderstood welfare state*, New York, Basic Books.

Matheson, A., Scanlan, G. and Tanner, R. (1997) *Strategic management in government: extending the reform model in New Zealand*, pp. 81–99 in OECD, *Benchmarking, evaluation and strategic management in the public sector*, Paris, PUMA/OECD.

Mayne, J. (1996) *Implementing results-based management and performance-based budgeting: lessons from the literature*, Discussion Paper No. 73, Ottawa, Office of the Auditor General of Canada.

Mazel, V. (1998) 'Supporting managerial growth of top Dutch civil servants', *Public Management Forum*, IV:6, pp. 4–5, November/December.

Metcalfe, L. (1993) 'Public management: from imitation to innovation', pp. 173–89 in J. Kooiman (ed.) *Modern governance: new government-society interactions*, London, Sage.

—— (1996) 'The European Commission as a network organisation', *The Journal of Federalism*, 26:4, Fall, pp. 43–62.

—— and Richards, S. (1987) 'Evolving public management cultures', pp. 65–86 in J. Kooiman and K. Eliassen (eds) *Managing public organizations*, London, Sage.

—— —— (1990) *Improving public management* (enlarged edition), London, Sage/European Institute of Public Administration.

Meyer, J. and Gupta, V. (1994) 'The performance paradox', *Research in Organizational Behavior*, 16, pp. 309–69.

—— and Rowan, B. (1991) 'Institutionalised organisations: formal structure as myth and ceremony' in W. Powell and P. DiMaggio (eds) *The new institutionalism in organisational analysis*, Chicago, University of Chicago Press.

Middlemas, K. (1995) *Orchestrating Europe: the informal politics of European Union, 1973–1995*, London, Fontana.

Ministère de la Fonction Publique et des Réformes Administratives (1992) *La charte des services publiques*, Paris, Ministère de la Fonction Publique.

—— (1994a) *L'accueil dans les services publiques*, Paris, Ministère de la Fonction Publique.

—— (1994b) *Circulaire sur la création de points publics en milieu rural*, Paris, Ministère de l'Intérieur et de l'Aménagement du Territoire, 8th August.

Ministerie van Financiën (1998) *Verder met resultaat: het agentschapsmodel 1991–1997*, Den Haag, Dutch Ministry of Finance.

Ministry of Finance (1993) *Government decision in principle on reforms in central and regional government*, Helsinki, Ministry of Finance.

—— (1995) *The public sector in Finland*, Helsinki (document prepared for a meeting of EU Directors General).

—— (1997) *Public management reforms: five country studies*, Helsinki, Ministry of Finance.

Mol, N. (1995) 'Quality improvement in the Dutch Department of Defence', pp. 103–28 in C. Pollitt and G. Bouckaert (eds) *Quality improvement in European public services: concepts, cases and commentary*, London, Sage.

Montricher, N. de (1996) 'France: in search of relevant changes', pp. 243–71 in Olsen, J. and Peters, B. (eds) *Lessons from experience: experiential learning in administrative reforms in eight democracies*, Oslo, Scandinavian University Press.

—— (1998) 'Public sector values and administrative reforms', pp. 108–36 in B. G. Peters and D. Savoie (eds) *Taking stock: assessing public sector reforms*, Montreal and Kingston, McGill-Queen's University Press and Canadian Centre for Management Development.

Moore-Wilson, M. (1997) 'Challenges facing the Australian Public Service', *Canberra Bulletin of Public Administration*, No. 85, pp. 38–47, August.

Murray, R. (1998) *Productivity as a tool for evaluation of public management reform*, paper presented to the European Evaluation Society Conference, Rome, 29th–31st October.

Naschold, F. and von Otter, C. (1996) *Public sector transformation: rethinking markets and hierarchies in government*, Amsterdam, John Benjamins Publishing Company.

—— Oppen, M., Tondorf, K. and Wegener, A. (1994) *Neue Städte braucht das Land*, Berlin, Wissenschaftszentrum Berlin für Sozialforschung.

National Academy of Public Administration (1994) *Towards useful performance measurement: lessons learned from initial pilot performance plans prepared under the Government Performance and Results Act*, November, Washington, DC, National Academy of Public Administration.

National Audit Office (1995) *The Meterological Office: evaluation of performance*, HC693, 25th August, London, HMSO.

—— (1996) *State audit in the European Union*, London, National Audit Office.

—— (1997) *Annual report, 1997*, London, National Audit Office.

National Performance Review (1997a) *Blair House papers*, Washington DC, January, National Performance Review (see also NPR website, http://www.npr.gov).

—— (1997b) *Serving the American publics: best practices in customer-driven strategic planning*, Federal Benchmarking Consortium Study Report, Washington, DC, National Performance Review.

Next Steps Team (1998) *Towards best practice: an evaluation of the first two years of the Public Sector Benchmarking Project, 1996–98*, London, Efficiency and Effectiveness Group, Cabinet Office.

Niemi, M. (1998) *Measuring public sector productivity: productivity change between years 1995 and 1996 in central government*, Helsinki, Statistics Finland (unpublished paper).

Nivette, N. (1996) *The decline of deference*, Peterborough, Broadview Press.

Nye, J. Jnr., Zelikow, P. and King, D. (eds) (1997) *Why people don't trust government*, Cambridge, Mass., Harvard University Press.

OECD (1992) *OECD country profiles*, Paris, OECD.

—— (1993a) *Managing with market-type mechanisms*, Paris, PUMA/OECD.

—— (1993b) *Private pay for public work: performance-related pay for public service managers*, Paris, PUMA/OECD.

—— (1994) *Public management developments: survey 1993*, Paris, PUMA/OECD.

—— (1995) *Governance in transition: public management reforms in OECD countries*, Paris, PUMA/OECD.

—— (1996) *Responsive government: service quality initiatives*, Paris, PUMA/OECD.

—— (1997a) *In search of results: performance management practices*, Paris, PUMA/OECD.

—— (1997b) *The changing role of the central budget office*, OCDE/GD(97)109, Paris, PUMA/OECD.

—— (1997c) *Family, market and community: equity and efficiency in social policy*, Social Policy Studies No. 21, Paris, OECD.

—— (1997d) *OECD country profiles*, Paris, OECD.

—— (1998) *Budgeting in Sweden*, Paris, PUMA/OECD.

Office of the US President (1993) *Budget baselines, historical data and alternatives for the future*, Washington, DC, January.

Olsen, J. and Peters, B. (eds) (1996) *Lessons from experience: experiential learning in administrative reforms in eight democracies*, Oslo, Scandinavian University Press.

Osborne, D. and Gaebler, T. (1992) *Reinventing government: how the entrepreneurial spirit is transforming the public sector*, Reading, Mass., Adison Wesley.

O'Toole, B. and Jordan, G. (eds) (1995) *Next steps: improving management in government*, Dartmouth, Aldershot.

Packwood, T., Pollitt, C. and Roberts, S. (1998) 'Good medicine? A case study of business re-engineering in a hospital', *Policy and Politics*, 26:4, pp. 401–15.

Page, E. (1997) *People who run Europe*, Oxford, Clarendon Press.

Painter, C., Rouse, J., Isaac-Henry, K. and Munk, L. (1996) *Changing local governance: local authorities and non-elected agencies*, Luton, Local Government Management Board.

Pawson, R. and Tilley, N. (1997) *Realistic evaluation*, London, Sage.

Perrow, C. (1972) *Complex organisations*, Glenview, Scott Foreman.

Perry, J. and Kraemer, K. (eds) (1983) *Public management: public and private perspectives*, California, Mayfield.

Perry, J. and Pearce, J. (1985) 'Civil service reform and the politics of performance appraisal', pp. 140–60 in D. Rosenbloom (ed.) *Public personnel policy: the politics of civil service*, London, Associated Faculty Press.

Peters, G. (1995) 'Bureaucracy in a divided regime: the United States', pp. 18–38 in J. Pierre (ed.) *Bureaucracy in the modern state: an introduction to comparative public administration*, Aldershot, Edward Elgar.

—— (1996a) 'Theory and methodology', pp. 13–41 in H. Bekke, J. Perry and T. Toonen (eds) *Civil service systems in comparative perspective*, Bloomington and Indiana, Indiana University Press.

—— (1996b) *The future of governing: four emerging models*, Kansas, Univesity Press of Kansas.

—— (1997) 'A North American perspective on administrative modernisation in Europe', pp. 255–70 in W. Kickert (ed.) *Public management and administrative reform in Western Europe*, Cheltenham, Edward Elgar.

—— (1998a) 'What works? The antiphons of administrative reform', pp. 78–107 in B. G. Peters and D. Savoie (eds) *Taking stock: assessing public sector reforms*, Montreal and Kingston, Canadian Centre for Management Development and McGill-Queen's University Press.

—— (1998b) 'Managing horizontal government: the politics of co-ordination', *Public Administration*, 76:2, Summer, pp. 295–311.

—— and Savoie, D. (1998) 'Introduction', pp. 3–19 in B. G. Peters and D. Savoie (eds) *Taking stock: assessing public sector reforms*, Montreal and Kingston, Canadian Centre for Management Development and McGill-Queen's University Press.

Peters, T. (1987) *Thriving on chaos: handbook for a management revolution*, London, Pan.

Pew Research Centre (1998) *Deconstructing distrust: how Americans view government*, hhtp://www.people-press.org/trustrpt.htm.

Pierre, J. (1998) *Externalities and relationships: rethinking the boundaries of the public service*, paper for the authors' roundtable, Revitalising the Public Service, Ottawa, Candian Centre for Management Development, 12th–14th November.

—— (ed.) (1995) *Bureaucracy in the modern state: an introduction to comparative public administration*, Aldershot, Edward Elgar.

Pollitt, C. (1984) *Manipulating the machine: changing the pattern of ministerial departments, 1960–83*, London, Allen and Unwin.

—— (1986) 'Beyond the managerial model: the case for broadening performance assessment in government and the public services', *Financial Accountability and Management*, 2:3, Autumn, pp. 155–70.

—— (1990) 'Performance indicators: root and branch', pp. 167–78 in M. Cave, M. Kogan and R. Smith (eds) *Output and performance measurement in government: the state of the art*, London, Jessica Kingsley.

—— (1993) *Managerialism and the public services* (2nd edition), Oxford, Blackwell.

—— (1995) 'Justification by works or by faith? Evaluating the New Public Management', *Evaluation*, 1:2, October, pp. 133–54.

—— (1996a) 'Anti-statist reforms and new administrative directions: public administration in the United Kingdom', *Public Administration Review*, 56:1, January/February, pp. 81–7.

—— (1996b) 'Public administration', pp. 699–701 in A. Kuper and J. Kuper (eds) *The social science encyclopaedia* (2nd edition), London, Routledge.

—— (1998a) 'Managerialism revisited', pp. 45–77 in B. G. Peters and D. Savoie (eds) *Taking stock: assessing public sector reforms*, Montreal and Kingston, McGill-Queen's University Press and Canadian Centre for Management Development

—— (1998b) *Integrating financial and performance management: a concept paper* PUMA/RD(98)6, Paris, PUMA/OECD, 28th October.

—— (1998c) 'Evaluation and the New Public management: an international perspective', *Evaluation Journal of Australasia*, 9: 1 and 2, pp. 7–15.

—— and Bouckaert, G. (eds) (1995) *Quality improvement in European public services: concepts, cases and commentary*, London, Sage.

—— and Summa, H. (1997a) 'Trajectories of reform: management change in four countries', *Public Money and Management*, 17:1, January/March, pp. 7–18.

—— —— (1997b) 'Reflexive watchdogs? How Supreme Audit Institutions account for themselves', *Public Administration*, 75:2, Summer, pp. 313–36.

Pollitt, C., Birchall, J. and Putman, K. (1998) *Decentralising public service management: the British experience*, Basingstoke, Macmillan.

—— Cave, M. and Joss, R. (1994) 'International benchmarking as a tool to improve public sector performance; a critical overview', pp. 7–22 in PUMA Public Management Occasional Papers 1994, No. 4, *Performance measurement in government: issues and illustrations*, Paris, OECD.

—— Girre, X., Lonsdale, J., Mul, R., Summa, H. and Waerness, M. (1999) *Performance or compliance? Performance audit and public management in five countries*, Oxford, Clarendon Press.

—— Hanney, S., Packwood, T., Rothwell, S. and Roberts, S. (1997) *Trajectories and options: an international perspective on the implementation, of Finnish public management reforms*, Helsinki, Ministry of Finance.

Power, M. (1997) *The audit society: rituals of verification*, Oxford, Oxford University Press.

Premfors, R. (1991) 'The "Swedish model" and public sector reform', *Western European Politics*, 14:3, July.

—— (1998) 'Reshaping the democratic state: Swedish experiences in a comparative perspective', *Public Administration*, 76:1, Spring, pp. 141–59.

President of the Treasury Board (1997) *Accounting for results, 1997*, Ottawa, Treasury Board Secretariat.

Pressman, J. and Wildavsky, A. (1973) *Implementation*, Berkeley, University of California Press.

Prime Minister (1988) *Civil service management reform: the next steps*, Cm.542, London, HMSO.

—— (1991) *The citizen's charter: raising the standard*, Cm.1599, London, HMSO.

—— Chancellor of the Exchequer and Chancellor of the Duchy of Lancaster (1994) *The civil service: continuity and change*, Cm.2627, London, HMSO.

Prime Minister and the Minister for the Cabinet Office (1999) *Modernising government*, Cm.413, London, The Stationery Office.

Prime Minister's Office and Ministries (1995) Helsinki, Prime Minister's Office (a short description and organization chart).

Puoskari, P. (1996) *Transformation of the public sector*, Helsinki, Ministry of Finance.

Radin, B. (1998) 'The Government Performance and Results Act (GPRA): hydra-headed monster or flexible management tool?', *Public Administration Review*, 58:4, July/August, pp. 307–16.

Rainey, H. and Steinbauer, P. (1999) 'Galloping elephants: developing elements of a theory of effective government oganizations', *Journal of Public Administration Research and Theory*, J. Part, 9:1, pp. 1-32.

Rhodes, R. (1997) 'Re-inventing Whitehall, 1979–1995', pp. 43–60 in W. Kickert (ed.) *Public management and administrative reform in Western Europe*, Cheltenham, Edward Elgar.

Ridley, F. (1996) 'The New Public Management in Europe: comparative perspectives', *Public Policy and Administration*, 11:1, Spring, pp. 16–29.

Röber, M. (1996) 'Germany', pp. 169–94 in D. Farnham, S. Horton, J. Barlow and A. Hondeghem, *New public managers in Europe*, Macmillan, Basingstoke.

—— and Löffler, E. (1999) 'Flexibilities in the German civil service', in S. Horton and D. Farnham (eds) *Human resource flexibilities in the public services: international comparisons*, Basingstoke, Macmillan.

Roberts, S. (1997) 'The implementation of Dutch public management reforms 1980–1996', pp. 91–130 in Ministry of Finance *Public management reforms: five country studies*, Helsinki, Ministry of Finance.

Rockman, B. (1998) 'The changing role of the state', pp. 20–44 in B. G. Peters and D. Savoie (eds) *Taking stock: assessing public sector reforms*, Montreal and Kingston, Canadian Centre for Management Development and McGill-Queen's University Press.

Rouban, L. (1995) 'The civil service culture and administrative reform', pp. 23–54 in B. G. Peters and D. Savoie (eds) *Governance in a changing environment*, Montreal and Kingston, Canadian Centre for Management Development and McGill-Queen's University Press.

—— (1997) 'The administrative modernisation policy in France', pp. 143–58 in W. Kickert (ed.) *Public management and administrative reform in Western Europe*, Cheltenham, Edward Elgar.

Rubin, I. (1992) 'Budgeting: theory, concepts, methods and issues', pp. 3–22 in J. Rabin (ed.) *Handbook of public budgeting*, New York, Marcel Dekker.

Savoie, D. (1994) *Thatcher, Reagan, Mulroney: in search of a new bureaucracy*, Toronto, University of Toronto Press.

—— (1997) 'Central agencies: a government of Canada perspective', pp. 59–69 in J. Bourgault, M. Demers and C. Williams (eds) *Public administration and public management: experiences in Canada*, Quebec, Les Publications du Québec.

Schick, A. (1996) *The spirit of reform: managing the New Zealand state sector in a time of change*, Wellington, State Services Commission.

Schröter, E. and Wollmann, H. (1997) 'Public sector reforms in Germany: whence and where? A case of ambivalence', *Administrative Studies/Hallinnon Tutkimus*, 3, pp. 184–200.

Shergold, P. (1997) 'A new Public Service Act: the end of the Westminster tradition?', edited text of an address, *Canberra Bulletin of Public Administration*, no. 85, August, pp. 32–7.

Simon, H. (1946) 'The proverbs of administration', *Public Administration Review*, 6, pp. 53–67.

Sommerman, K.-P. (1998) 'Autorité et contrat dans l'administration moderne en Allemagne', *Annuaire Européen d'Administration Publique*, XX, Aix-Marseilles.

Sorber, B. (1996) 'Experiences with performance measurement in the central government: the case of the Netherlands', pp. 309–18 in A. Halachmi and G. Bouckaert (eds) *Organisational performance and measurement in the public sector: towards service, effort and accomplishment reporting*, Westport, Conn., Quorum Books.

Spierenberg, D. (1979) *Proposals for reform of the Commission of the European Communities and its services*, Brussels, Commission of the European Communities.

Statistics Canada (1995) *Canada: a portrait*, Ottawa, Minister of Industry.

Steering Group (1991) *Review of state sector reforms*, Auckland, State Service Commission.

Steunenberg, B. and Mol, N. (1997) 'Fiscal and financial decentralization: a comparative analysis of six West European countries', pp. 235–56 in J.-E. Lane (ed.) *Public sector reform: rationale, trends and problems*, London, Sage.

Stewart, J. (1992) *Managing difference: the analysis of service characteristics*, Birmingham, Institute of Local Government Studies.

—— (1994) 'The rebuilding of public accountability', pp. 75–9 in N. Flynn (ed.) *Reader: change in the civil service*, London, Public Finance Foundations.

Stockman, D. (1986) *The triumph of politics*, London, Bodley Head.

Stoker, G. (1988) *The politics of local government*, Basingstoke, Macmillan.

Stone, B. (1995) 'Administrative accountability in the "Westminster" democracies: towards a new conceptual framework', *Governance*, 8:4, pp. 505–26.

Stone, D. (1996) *Capturing the political imagination: think tanks and the policy process*, London, Frank Cass.

Straw, J. (1998) 'Resource accounting and NHS trusts', *Public Money and Management*, 18:2, April/June, pp. 35–8.

Summa, H. (1995) 'Old and new techniques for productivity promotion: from cheese-slicing to a quest for quality', pp. 155–65 in A. Halachmi and G. Bouckaert (eds) *Public productivity through quality and strategic management*, Amsterdam, IOS Press.

Swedish Ministry of Finance (1997) *Public sector productivity in Sweden*, Stockholm, Budget Department/Swedish Ministry of Finance.

Talbot, C. (1994) *Re-inventing public management: a survey of public sector managers' reactions to change*, Northants, Institute of Management.

—— (1996) *Ministers and agencies: control, performance and accountability*, London, CIPFA.

—— (1997) *Public performance: towards a public service excellence model*, Discussion Paper No. 1, Monmouthshire, Public Futures.

Task Force on Management Improvement (1992) *The Australian Public Service reformed: an evaluation of a decade of management reform*, Canberra, Management Advisory Board, AGPS.

Thain, C. and Wright, M. (1995) *The Treasury and Whitehall: the planning and control of public expenditure, 1976–1993*, Oxford, Clarendon Press.

Thompson, G., Frances, J., Levacic, R. and Mitchell, J. (eds) (1991) *Markets, hierarchies and networks: the co-ordination of social life*, London, Sage.

Tiihonen, S. (1996) *The administration of the summit in Finland*, unpublished conference paper.

Toulemonde, J. (1997) 'Europe and the member states: cooperating and competing on evaluation grounds', pp. 117–32 in O. Rieper and J. Toulemonde (eds) *Politics and practices of intergovernmental evaluation*, London, Transaction.

Treasury Board of Canada (1996) *Getting government right: improving results measurement and accountability*, Ottawa, Ministry of Public Works and Government Services.

Trosa, S. (1994) *Moving on: Next Steps*, London, Efficiency Unit, Cabinet Office.

—— (1995) *Moderniser l'administration: comment font les autres?*, Paris, Les Éditions d'Organisation.

—— (1996) 'Quality strategies in three countries: France, the United Kingdom and Australia', pp. 265–97 in OECD, *Responsive government: service quality initiatives*, Paris, PUMA/OECD.

—— (1997) 'Chairman's summary', pp. 5–9 in OECD, *Benchmarking, evaluation and strategic management in the public sector*, Paris, PUMA/OECD.

Vallemont, S. (1998) 'France moves from a rating system to a performance appraisal system', *Public Management Forum*, IV:6, pp. 8, 16, November/December.

Volcker, P. (1989) *Leadership for America: rebuilding the public service*, task force report to the National Commission on the Public Service, Washington, DC, National Commission on the Public Service.

Vowles, J., Aimer, P., Catt, H., Lamarre, J. and Miller, R. (1995) *Towards consensus: the 1993 election in New Zealand and the transition to proportional representation*, Auckland, Auckland University Press.

Waugh, P. (1998) 'State sell-off errors "cost UK billions" ', *Independent*, 3rd September, p. 4.

Weber, M. (1947) *The theory of social and economic organisation* (translated by A. M. Henderson and Talcott Parsons), Glencoe, Ill., The Free Press.

Weiss, C. (1992) *Organisations for policy analysis: helping government think*, London, Sage.

Wilks, S. (1996) 'Sweden', pp. 23–49 in N. Flynn and F. Strehl (eds) *Public sector management in Europe*, London, Prentice Hall/Harvester Wheatsheaf.

Williamson, O. (1975) *Markets and hierarchies: analysis and anti-trust implications*, New York, Free Press.

Wise, C. (1990) 'Public service configurations and public organizations: public organizational design in the post-privatization era', *Public Administration Review*, 50:2, pp. 141–55.

Wollmann, H. (1997) 'Modernization of the public sector and public administration in the Federal Republic of Germany: (mostly) a story of fragmented incrementalism', pp. 79–103 in M. Muramatsu and F. Naschold (eds) *State and administration in Japan and Germany: a comparative perspective on continuity and change*, Berlin, de Gruyter.

Wright, V. (1989) *The government and politics of France* (3rd edition), London, Unwin Hyman.

—— (1997) 'The paradoxes of administrative reform', pp. 7–13 in W. Kickert (ed.) *Public management and administrative reform in Western Europe*, Cheltenham, Edward Elgar.

Yin, R. (1994) *Case study research: design and methods* (2nd edition), London, Sage.

Zifcak, S. (1994) *New managerialism: administrative reform in Whitehall and Canberra*, Buckingham, Open University Press.

Index